THE FIRE AND
THE CLOUD

THE FIRE AND THE CLOUD

An Anthology
of
Catholic Spirituality

edited by

REV. DAVID A. FLEMING, S.M.

PAULIST PRESS
New York/Toronto/Ramsey

Library of Congress
Catalog Card Number: 77-83582

ISBN: 0-8091-2065-8

Published by Paulist Press
Editorial Office: 1865 Broadway, New York, N.Y. 10023
Business Office: 545 Island Road, Ramsey, N.J. 07446

Printed and bound in the
United States of America

ACKNOWLEDGMENTS

Thomas Merton, THE WISDOM OF THE DESERT. Copyright © 1960 by The Abbey of Gethsemani, Inc. Reprinted by permission of New Directions Publishing Corporation, New York, New York.

St. John Climacus, THE LADDER OF DIVINE ASCENT, translated by Archimandrite Lazarus Moore. Reprinted by permission of Faber and Faber, Ltd., London.

Gregory of Nyssa, LIFE OF MOSES. Reprinted by permission of Charles Scribner's Sons from FROM GLORY TO GLORY, selected and edited by J. Daniélou, S.J., translated by H. Musurillo, S.J. Copyright © 1961 Charles Scribner's Sons, New York, New York.

Bernard of Clairvaux, ON LOVING GOD, translated by Robert Walton, O.S.B., in BERNARD OF CLAIRVAUX: TREATISES II (Cistercian Father Series, Nbr. 13), Washington, Cistercian Publications/Consortium Press, 1974; distributed by Cistercian Publications, Kalamazoo, Michigan, 49008.

Richard of St. Victor, BENJAMIN MAJOR. Reprinted by permission of Faber and Faber, Ltd., from RICHARD OF ST. VICTOR: SELECTED WRITINGS ON CONTEMPLATION, translated by Clare Kirchberger.

Gregory of Sinai, INSTRUCTIONS TO HESYCHASTS. Reprinted by permission of Faber and Faber, Ltd., from WRITINGS FROM THE PHILOKALIA ON PRAYER OF THE HEART, translated by E. Kadloubovsky and G. E. H. Palmer.

St. Francis of Assisi: ENGLISH OMNIBUS OF SOURCES—WRITINGS AND EARLY BIOGRAPHIES, ed. by Marion A. Habig, O.F.M. Chicago, Franciscan Herald Press, 1973. Reprinted with permission of the publisher.

From THE CLOUD OF UNKNOWING and the BOOK OF PRIVY COUNSELING, edited, with an introduction, by William Johnston. Copyright © 1973 by William Johnston. Reprinted by permission of Doubleday & Company, Inc.

Julian of Norwich, REVELATIONS OF DIVINE LOVE, translated by Clifton Wolters (Penguin Classics, 1966). Copyright © Clifton Wolters, 1966. Reprinted with permission.

From MEISTER ECKHART: A MODERN TRANSLATION by Raymond Bernard Blakney. Sermon 23, "Distinctions Are Lost In God," and Sermon 28, "Blessed Are The Poor." Copyright 1941 by Harper & Row, Publishers, Inc. Reprinted with permission.

Blessed Henry Suso, THE EXEMPLAR, translated by Sister M. Ann Edward. Reprinted with the permission of The Priory Press, River Forest, Illinois.

THE COLLECTED WORKS OF ST. JOHN OF THE CROSS, translated by Kieran Kavanaugh and Otilio Rodriguez. Washington, ICS Publications, 1973. Reprinted with permission.

STORY OF A SOUL: THE AUTOBIOGRAPHY OF ST. THÉRÈSE OF LISIEUX, translated by John Clarke. Washington, ICS Publications, 1975. Reprinted with permission.

THE WAY OF A PILGRIM AND THE PILGRIM CONTINUES HIS WAY by R. M. French. Reprinted by permission of The Society for Promoting Christian Knowledge, London, and The Seabury Press, Inc., New York, New York.

THE DIVINE MILIEU by Pierre Teilhard de Chardin, translated by Bernard Wall. Originally published in French as LE MILIEU DIVIN. Copyright 1957 by Editions du Seuil. English translation copyright © 1960 by Wm. Collins Sons & Co., London and Harper & Row, Publishers, Inc., New York, New York. Reprinted by permission of Harper & Row, Publishers, Inc.

HYMN OF THE UNIVERSE by Pierre Teilhard de Chardin, translated by Simon Bartholomew. Copyright © 1961 by Editions du Seuil. Copyright © 1965 in the English translation by William Collins Sons & Co., Ltd., London, and Harper & Row, Publishers, Inc., New York, New York. Reprinted by permission of Harper & Row, Publishers, Inc.

Contents

PART V—EXTRA-MONASTIC MOVEMENTS IN MEDIEVAL SPIRITUALITY

PART VI—COUNTER-REFORMATION SPIRITUALITY

Introduction

Only a few years ago, study of the history of spirituality was relegated to out-of-the-way and rather boring lectures given perhaps once a week in a few novitiates and seminaries. Recent years, however, have witnessed a reawakening of interest in the classic spiritual writers of the Christian tradition. Since 1970, publications on these authors have multiplied at a pace surprising even to specialists in the history of spirituality. In a time when human beings are beginning to recognize the limits and the pitfalls of technological and economic expansion, they are increasingly fascinated by records of inner spiritual experience coming from all traditions. The reawakening of interest in Christian spirituality is simply part of a worldwide revival in spirituality within all religious traditions.

The aim of this anthology is to provide materials for readers who wish to begin the study of Christian spirituality in a historical context. The present collection of classic texts is designed to serve both individual readers and teachers of spirituality by offering a sampling of primary sources that illustrate the major currents from the early Church until the present.

In choosing items for this anthology, I have attempted to concentrate on key figures and movements that have come to take on great historical significance and that, to one degree or another, are looked upon today as guideposts for Christian life. Although this collection is principally aimed at Roman Catholics and attains a degree of breadth and depth only within the Roman Catholic tradition, a few representatives of Eastern Orthodoxy have been included because of their intrinsic richness, because of the many points of contact between them and Western spiritual traditions, and because of the pervasive influence of Orthodox spirituality in the contemporary reawakening of interest. Figures representative of other Christian traditions, especially the great Protestant authors of spirituality, have not been included because they are better known and more easily available in other collections that can give them a more complete coverage.

As much as possible, selections are given here without evaluative comment. Editorial commentary is limited to brief historical notes that situate author and text, and that help the reader understand the context. Individual readers and teachers are thus invited to make their own interpretations on the basis of the primary sources.

The present collection is published in the hope that it will help many readers delve into the wealth of Christian spirituality as it has taken on varied forms throughout the ages, and that it will open up avenues of exploration into the vast amount of material now becoming available for further study.

"And the Lord went before them by day in a
pillar of a cloud, to lead them the way;
and by night in a pillar of fire, to give
them light" (Exodus 13:21).

"O lámparas de fuego,
En cuyos resplandores
Las profundas cavernas del sentido,
Que estaba oscuro y ciego,
Con extraños primores
Calor y luz dan junto a su Querido!"
— St. John of the Cross, *The Living Flame of Love*

Part I

First Witnesses of Christian Spirituality

Let each of you enter into this choir: then, in the harmony of concord, you will take, by your very unity, the keynote of God, and you will all sing with one single voice, through the mouth of Jesus Christ, the praises of the Father who will hear you and, by your good works, will recognize you as the members of His Son. It is therefore to your advantage to keep yourself in irreproachable unity; it is thereby that you will enjoy a constant union with God Himself.

St. Ignatius of Antioch (c. 35-108 A.D.)

1

ST. IGNATIUS OF ANTIOCH

To the Romans

Head of the Christian community at Antioch, St. Ignatius was apprehended by Roman authorities and condemned to martyrdom about A.D. 108. The following letter, written during his voyage to the capital where he was to be executed, illustrates a fervent attitude toward total sacrifice and a spirituality centered in the imitation of Christ. References to the Eucharist indicate the importance of that sacrament at a very early date. The centrality of martyrdom as a paradigm of all subsequent Christian attempts at radical spirituality is established by this document more than by any other.

Ignatius, who is also called Theophorus, to her who has obtained mercy in the greatness of the Most High Father, and of Jesus Christ his only Son; to the Church beloved and enlightened by the will of him who has willed all things which are, according to the love of Jesus Christ, our God, which also has the presidency in the country of the land of the Romans, worthy of God, worthy of honour, worthy of blessing, worthy of praise, worthy of success, worthy in its holiness, and preeminent in love, named after Christ, named after the Father, which also I greet in the name of Jesus Christ, the Son of the Father; to those who are united in flesh and spirit in every one of his commandments, filled with the grace of God without wavering, and filtered clear from every foreign stain, abundant greeting in Jesus Christ, our God, in blamelessness.

Forasmuch as I have gained my prayer to God to see your godly faces, so that I have obtained more than I asked—for in bondage in Christ Jesus I hope to greet you if it be his will that I be found worthy to the end. For the beginning has been well ordered, if I may obtain grace to come unhindered to my lot. For I am afraid of your love, lest even that do me wrong. For it is easy for you to do what you will, but it is difficult for me to attain to God, if you do not spare me.

For I would not have you "men-pleasers" but "God-pleasers," even as you do indeed please him. For neither shall I ever have

such an opportunity of attaining to God, nor can you, if you be but
silent, have any better deed ascribed to you. For if you are silent
concerning me, I am a word of God; but if you love my flesh, I shall
again be only a cry. Grant me nothing more than that I be poured
out to God, while an altar is still ready, that forming yourselves
into a chorus of love, you may sing to the Father in Christ Jesus,
that God has vouchsafed that the bishop of Syria shall be found at
the setting of the sun, having fetched him from the sun's rising. It
is good to set to the world towards God, that I may rise to him.

You never have envied anyone, you taught others. But I desire
that those things may stand fast which you enjoin in your instructions. Only pray for me for strength, both inward and outward, that
I may not merely speak, but also have the will, that I may not only
be called a Christian, but may also be found to be one. For if I be
found to be one, I can also be called one, and then be deemed
faithful when I no longer am visible in the world. Nothing visible is
good, for our God, Jesus Christ, being now in the Father, is the
more plainly visible. Christianity is not the work of persuasive-
ness, but of greatness, when it is hated by the world.

I am writing to all the Churches, and I give injunctions to all
men, that I am dying willingly for God's sake, if you do not hinder
it. I beseech you, be not "an unseasonable kindness" to me. Suffer
me to be eaten by the beasts, through whom I can attain to God. I
am God's wheat, and I am ground by the teeth of wild beasts that I
may be found pure bread of Christ. Rather entice the wild beasts
that they may become my tomb, and leave no trace of my body, that
when I fall asleep I be not burdensome to any. Then shall I be truly
a disciple of Jesus Christ, when the world shall not even see my
body. Beseech Christ on my behalf, that I may be found a sacrifice
through these instruments. I do not order you as did Peter and
Paul; they were Apostles, I am a convict; they were free, I am even
until now a slave. But if I suffer I shall be Jesus Christ's freedman,
and in him I shall rise free. Now I am learning in my bonds to give
up all desires.

From Syria to Rome I am fighting with wild beasts, by land
and sea, by night and day, bound to ten "leopards" (that is, a
company of soldiers), and they become worse for kind treatment.
Now I become the more a disciple for their ill deeds, "but not by this
am I justified." I long for the beasts that are prepared for me; and I
pray that they may be found prompt for me; I will even entice them
to devour me promptly; not as has happened to some whom they
have not touched from fear; even if they be unwilling of them-

selves, I will force them to it. Grant me this favour. I know what is expedient for me; now I am beginning to be a disciple. May nothing of things seen or unseen envy me my attaining to Jesus Christ. Let there come on me fire, and cross, and struggles with wild beasts, cutting, and tearing asunder, rackings of bones, mangling of limbs, crushing of my whole body, cruel tortures of the devil, may I but attain to Jesus Christ!

The ends of the earth and the kingdoms of this world shall profit me nothing. It is better for me to die in Christ Jesus than to be king over the ends of the earth. I seek Him who died for our sake. I desire Him who rose for us. The pains of birth are upon me. Suffer me, my brethren; hinder me not from living, do not wish me to die. Do not give to the world one who desires to belong to God, nor deceive him with material things. Suffer me to receive the pure light; when I have come thither I shall become a man. Suffer me to follow the example of the Passion of my God. If any man have him within himself, let him understand what I wish, and let him sympathize with me, knowing the things which constrain me.

The Prince of this world wishes to tear me in pieces, and to corrupt my mind towards God. Let none of you who are present help him. Be rather on my side, that is on God's. Do not speak of Jesus Christ, and yet desire the world. Let no envy dwell among you. Even though when I come I beseech you myself, do not be persuaded by me, but rather obey this, which I write to you: for in the midst of life I write to you desiring death. My lust has been crucified, and there is in me no fire of love for material things; but only water living and speaking in me, and saying to me from within, "Come to the Father." I have no pleasure in the food of corruption or in the delights of this life. I desire the "bread of God," which is the flesh of Jesus Christ, who was "of the seed of David," and for drink I desire his blood, which is incorruptible love.

I no longer desire to live after the manner of men, and this shall be, if you desire it. Desire it, in order that you also may be desired. I beg you by this short letter; believe me. And Jesus Christ shall make this plain to you, that I am speaking the truth. He is the mouth which cannot lie, by which the Father has spoken truly. Pray for me that I may attain. I write to you not according to the flesh, but according to the mind of God. If I suffer, it was your favour: if I be rejected, it was your hatred.

Remember in your prayers the Church in Syria which has God for its Shepherd in my room. Its bishop shall be Jesus Christ alone—and your love. But for myself I am ashamed to be called one of them, for I am not worthy; for I am the least of them, and "born out of time"; but I have obtained mercy to be someone, if I may attain to God. My spirit greets you, and the love of the Churches which have received me in the Name of Jesus Christ, not as a mere passer by, for even those which did not lie on my road according to the flesh went before me from city to city.

Now I am writing these things to you from Smyrna by the blessed Ephesians, and Crocus, a name very dear to me, is also with me, and many others. Concerning those who have preceded me from Syria to Rome to the glory of God, I believe that you have received information; tell them that I am close at hand; for they are all worthy of God and of you, and it is right for you to refresh them in every way. I write this to you on the 24th of August. Farewell unto the end, in the endurance of Jesus Christ.

SECOND EPISTLE OF CLEMENT

The Second Epistle *of Clement is a homily written, perhaps at Corinth, near the middle of the second century and attributed falsely to Pope Clement I. It is a general exhortation to the practice of Christian life and was highly venerated in the early Church.*

It is, then, brothers, in doing the will of God our Father that we belong to the first Church, the spiritual Church, which was created before the sun and the moon . . . the Church of life. . . . The Church is not of the present age, but from on high. She existed, in fact, spiritually, like our Jesus, and she has been manifested at the end of time to save us.

THE DIDACHE OF THE APOSTLES

The following passage, taken from an anonymous document of the early second century, summarizes Christian spirituality as a way of simplicity in contrast to the way of duplicity current among

*evil men. A variant form of the same passage appears in another
early Christian document, the* Epistle of Barnabas. *The source of
both of these passages may well be a Jewish document adapted by
Christians as an adequate expression of their spiritual outlook. Its
emphasis on moral uprightness and on simplicity of intention
helped to establish the basics of Christian moral life and of all forms
of spirituality.*

There are two Ways, one of Life and one of Death, and there is
a great difference between the two Ways.

The Way of Life is this: "First, thou shalt love the God who
made thee, secondly, thy neighbour as thyself; and whatsoever
thou wouldst not have done to thyself, do not thou to another."

Now, the teaching of these words is this: "Bless those that
curse you, and pray for your enemies, and fast for those that
persecute you. For what credit is it to you if you love those that love
you? Do not even the heathen do the same?" But, for your part,
"love those that hate you," and you will have no enemy. "Abstain
from carnal" and bodily "lusts." "If any man smite thee on the right
cheek, turn to him the other cheek also," and thou wilt be perfect.
"If any man impress thee to go with him one mile, go with him two.
If any man take thy coat, give him thy shirt also. If any man will
take from thee what is thine, refuse it not"—not even if thou canst.
Give to everyone that asks thee, and do not refuse, for the Father's
will is that we give to all from the gifts we have received. Blessed is
he that gives according to the mandate; for he is innocent. Woe to
him who receives; for if any man receive alms under pressure of
need he is innocent; but he who receives it without need shall be
tried as to why he took and for what, and being in prison he shall be
examined as to his deeds, and "he shall not come out thence until
he pay the last farthing." But concerning this it was also said, "Let
thine alms sweat into thine hands until thou knowest to whom
thou art giving."

But the second commandment of the teaching is this; "Thou
shalt do no murder; thou shalt not commit adultery"; thou shalt not
commit sodomy; thou shalt not commit fornication; thou shalt not
steal; thou shalt not use magic; thou shalt not use philtres; thou
shalt not procure abortion, nor commit infanticide; "thou shalt not
covet thy neighbour's goods"; thou shalt not commit perjury, "thou
shalt not bear false witness"; thou shalt not speak evil; thou shalt
not bear malice. Thou shalt not be double-minded nor double-

tongued, for to be double-tongued is the snare of death. Thy speech shall not be false nor vain, but completed in action. Thou shalt not be covetous nor extortionate, nor a hypocrite, nor malignant, nor proud, thou shalt make no evil plan against thy neighbour. Thou shalt hate no man; but some thou shalt reprove, and for some shalt thou pray, and some thou shalt love more than thine own life.

My child, flee from every evil man and from all like him. Be not proud, for pride leads to murder, nor jealous, nor contentious, nor passionate, for from all these murders are engendered. My child, be not lustful, for lust leads to fornication, nor a speaker of base words, nor a lifter up of the eyes, for from all these is adultery engendered. My child, regard not omens, for this leads to idolatry; neither be an enchanter, nor an astrologer, nor a magician, neither wish to see these things, for from them all is idolatry engendered. My child, be not a liar, for lying leads to theft, nor a lover of money, nor vain-glorious, for from all these things are thefts engendered. My child, be not a grumbler, for this leads to blasphemy, nor stubborn, nor a thinker of evil, for from all these are blasphemies engendered, but be thou "meek, for the meek shall inherit the earth"; be thou long-suffering, and merciful and guileless, and quiet, and good, and ever fearing the words which thou hast heard. Thou shalt not exalt thyself, nor let thy soul be presumptuous. Thy soul shall not consort with the lofty, but thou shalt walk with righteous and humble men. Receive the accidents that befall to thee as good, knowing that nothing happens without God.

My child, thou shalt remember, day and night, him who speaks the word of God to thee, and thou shalt honour him as the Lord, for where the Lord's nature is spoken of, there is he present. And thou shalt seek daily the presence of the saints, that thou mayest find rest in their words. Thou shalt not desire a schism, but shalt reconcile those that strive. Thou shalt give righteous judgment; thou shalt favour no man's person in reproving transgression. Thou shalt not be of two minds whether it shall be or not.

Be not one who stretches out his hands to receive, but shuts them when it comes to giving. Of whatsoever thou hast gained by thy hands thou shalt give a ransom for thy sins. Thou shalt not hesitate to give, nor shalt thou grumble when thou givest, for thou shalt know who is the good Paymaster of the reward. Thou shalt not turn away the needy, but shalt share everything with thy brother, and shalt not say that it is thine own, for if you are sharers in the imperishable, how much more in the things which perish?

Thou shalt not withhold thine hand from thy son or from thy

daughter, but thou shalt teach them the fear of God from their youth up. Thou shalt not command in thy bitterness thy slave or thine handmaid, who hope in the same God, lest they cease to fear the God who is over you both; for he comes not to call men with respect of persons, but those whom the Spirit has prepared. But do you who are slaves be subject to your master, as to God's representative, in reverence and fear.

Thou shalt hate all hypocrisy, and everything that is not pleasing to the Lord. Thou shalt not forsake the commandments of the Lord, but thou shalt keep what thou didst receive, "adding nothing to it and taking nothing away." In the congregation thou shalt confess thy transgressions, and thou shalt not betake thyself to prayer with an evil conscience. This is the way of life.

But the Way of Death is this: First of all, it is wicked and full of cursing, murders, adulteries, lusts, fornications, thefts, idolatries, witchcrafts, charms, robberies, false witness, hypocrisies, a double heart, fraud, pride, malice, stubbornness, covetousness, foul speech, jealousy, impudence, haughtiness, boastfulness. Persecutors of the good, haters of truth, lovers of lies, knowing not the reward of righteousness, not cleaving to the good nor to righteous judgment, spending wakeful nights not for good but for wickedness, from whom meekness and patience is far, lovers of vanity, following after reward, unmerciful to the poor, not working for him who is oppressed with toil, without knowledge of him who made them, murderers of children, corrupters of God's creatures, turning away the needy, oppressing the distressed, advocates of the rich, unjust judges of the poor, altogether sinful; may ye be delivered, my children, from all these.

See "that no one make thee to err" from this Way of the teaching, for he teaches thee without God. For if thou canst bear the whole yoke of the Lord, thou wilt be perfect, but if thou canst not, do what thou canst.

CLEMENT OF ALEXANDRIA

VI Stromata

Father of the Church and representative with Origen of the great theological school of Alexandria, Clement was a convert to

Christianity. A cultured Greek philosopher and scholar, he was one of the first minds to probe the relationships between Christianity and Greek thought, faith and philosophy, true Christian knowledge and pseudo-Christian gnosticism. His Stromata (Carpets) *constitutes an anthology of his most important reflections on Christian life.*

Love is no longer a tendency of him who loves; it is a loving intimacy, which establishes the spiritual man in the unity of faith, without his having any further need of time nor of space. Already established by love in the good things that he will possess, having anticipated hope by spiritual knowledge, he no longer tends toward anything, having everything that he could tend toward. He remains, then, in the one unchanging attitude, loving in a spiritual fashion, and he does not have to desire to be made like beauty, for he possesses beauty by love.

Part II

THE BEGINNINGS OF MONASTICISM

Blessed is the monk who regards every man as a god after
  God.
Blessed is the monk who looks on the salvation and progress
  of all as though they were his own.
Blessed is the monk who considers himself as the dregs of all
  men.
A monk is he who, withdrawing from all men, is united with
  all men.
A monk is he who regards himself as existing with all men
  and sees himself in each man.

St. Nilus of Sinai (c. 360-450)

ST. ATHANASIUS

The Life of Antony

Christian monasticism as a well-defined movement first appeared in the Egyptian desert during the latter part of the third century. Its spirit was deeply influenced by two earlier forms of Christian radicalism: martyrdom and consecrated ascetic life in the family home. The attraction of the new desert monasticism lay in the radicality of the commitment it demanded, in the example of ascetics of many religions in the late Roman Empire, and in the liberation it promised from the weakening of fervor that seemed to be creeping inevitably into the Christian Church.

The first and greatest popularizer of Egyptian desert monasticism was St. Athanasius (c. 296–373), Patriarch of Alexandria. Exiled from Egypt during long periods of his life because of the bitter hostility of his Arian opponents, he authored, about 365, his Life of Antony, *a biography of the founder of monasticism and a propaganda piece for the ascetic movement. Christians in all parts of the Roman Empire found in this work an inspiration to begin monastic life on their own, in imitation of Antony. Few texts in religious history have exerted so powerful a historical and institutional impact. The beginning of this work, here reproduced, gives us a glimpse of the origins of the monastic movement.*

The life and conversation of our holy Father, Antony: written and sent to the monks in foreign parts by our Father among the Saints, Athanasius, Bishop of Alexandria.

Athanasius the bishop to the brethren in foreign parts.

You have entered upon a noble rivalry with the monks of Egypt by your determination either to equal or surpass them in your training in the way of virtue. For by this time there are monasteries among you, and the name of monk receives public recognition. With reason, therefore, all men will approve this determination, and in answer to your prayers God will give its fulfilment. Now since you asked me to give you an account of the blessed Antony's way of life, and are wishful to learn how he began

13

the discipline, who and what manner of man he was previous to this, how he closed his life, and whether the things told of him are true, that you also may bring yourselves to imitate him, I very readily accepted your behest, for to me also the bare recollection of Antony is a great accession of help. And I know that you, when you have heard, apart from your admiration of the man, will be wishful to emulate his determination; seeing that for monks the life of Antony is a sufficient pattern of discipline. Wherefore do not refuse credence to what you have heard from those who brought tidings of him; but think rather that they have told you only a few things, for at all events they scarcely can have given circumstances of so great import in any detail. And because I at your request have called to mind a few circumstances about him, and shall send as much as I can tell in a letter, do not neglect to question those who sail from here: for possibly when all have told their tale, the account will hardly be in proportion to his merits. On account of this I was desirous, when I received your letter, to send for certain of the monks, those especially who were wont to be more frequently with him, that if I could learn any fresh details I might send them to you. But since the season for sailing was coming to an end and the letter-carrier urgent, I hastened to write to your piety what I myself know, having seen him many times, and what I was able to learn from him, for I was his attendant for a long time, and poured water on his hands; in all points being mindful of the truth, that no one should disbelieve through hearing too much, nor on the other hand by hearing too little should despise the man.

1. Antony you must know was by descent an Egyptian: his parents were of good family and possessed considerable wealth, and as they were Christians he also was reared in the same Faith. In infancy he was brought up with his parents, knowing nought else but them and his home. But when he was grown and arrived at boyhood, and was advancing in years, he could not endure to learn letters, not caring to associate with other boys; but all his desire was, as it is written of Jacob, to live a plain man at home.[1] With his parents he used to attend the Lord's House, and neither as a child was he idle nor when older did he despise them; but was both obedient to his father and mother and attentive to what was read, keeping in his heart what was profitable in what he heard. And though as a child brought up in moderate affluence, he did not trouble his parents for varied or luxurious fare, nor was this a source of pleasure to him; but was content simply with what he found nor sought anything further.

2. After the death of his father and mother he was left alone with one little sister: his age was about eighteen or twenty, and on him the care both of home and sister rested. Now it was not six months after the death of his parents, and going according to custom into the Lord's House, he communed with himself and reflected as he walked how the Apostles[2] left all and followed the Saviour; and how they in the Acts[3] sold their possessions and brought and laid them at the Apostles' feet for distribution to the needy, and what and how great a hope was laid up for them in heaven. Pondering over these things he entered the church, and it happened the Gospel was being read, and he heard the Lord saying to the rich[4] 'If thou wouldest be perfect, go and sell what thou hast and give to the poor; and come follow Me and thou shalt have treasure in heaven.' Antony, as though God had put him in mind of the Saints, and the passage had been read on his account, went out immediately from the church, and gave the possessions of his forefathers to the villagers—they were three hundred acres, productive and very fair—that they should be no more a clog upon himself and his sister. And all the rest that was movable he sold, and having got together much money he gave it to the poor, reserving a little however for his sister's sake.

3. And again as he went into the church, hearing the Lord say in the Gospel[5] 'be not anxious for the morrow,' he could stay no longer, but went out and gave those things also to the poor. Having committed his sister to known and faithful virgins, and put her into a convent to be brought up, he henceforth devoted himself outside his house to discipline, taking heed to himself and training himself with patience. For there were not yet so many monasteries in Egypt, and no monk at all knew of the distant desert; but all who wished to give heed to themselves practised the discipline in solitude near their own village. Now there was then in the next village an old man who had lived the life of a hermit from his youth up. Antony, after he had seen this man, imitated him in piety. And at first he began to abide in places outside the village: then if he heard of a good man anywhere, like the prudent bee, he went forth and sought him, nor turned back to his own place until he had seen him; and he returned, having got from the good man as it were supplies for his journey in the way of virtue. So dwelling there at first, he confirmed his purpose not to return to the abode of his fathers nor to the remembrance of his kinsfolk; but to keep all his desire and energy for perfecting his discipline. He worked, however, with his hands, having heard, 'he who is idle let him not eat,[6]

and part he spent on bread and part he gave to the needy. And he was constant in prayer, knowing that a man ought to pray in secret unceasingly.[7] For he had given such heed to what was read that none of the things that were written fell from him to the ground, but he remembered all, and afterwards his memory served him for books.

4. Thus conducting himself, Antony was beloved by all. He subjected himself in sincerity to the good men whom he visited, and learned thoroughly where each surpassed him in zeal and discipline. He observed the graciousness of one; the unceasing prayer of another; he took knowledge of another's freedom from anger and another's loving-kindness; he gave heed to one as he watched, to another as he studied; one he admired for his endurance, another for his fasting and sleeping on the ground; the meekness of one and the long-suffering of another he watched with care, while he took note of the piety towards Christ and the mutual love which animated all. Thus filled, he returned to his own place of discipline, and henceforth would strive to unite the qualities of each, and was eager to show in himself the virtues of all. With others of the same age he had no rivalry; save this only, that he should not be second to them in higher things. And this he did so as to hurt the feelings of nobody, but made them rejoice over him. So all they of that village and the good men in whose intimacy he was, when they saw that he was a man of this sort, used to call him God-beloved. And some welcomed him as a son, others as a brother.

5. But the devil, who hates and envies what is good, could not endure to see such a resolution in a youth, but endeavoured to carry out against him what he had been wont to effect against others. First of all he tried to lead him away from the discipline, whispering to him the remembrance of his wealth, care for his sister, claims of kindred, love of money, love of glory, the various pleasures of the table and the other relaxations of life, and at last the difficulty of virtue and the labour of it; he suggested also the infirmity of the body and the length of the time. In a word he raised in his mind a great dust of debate, wishing to debar him from his settled purpose. But when the enemy saw himself to be too weak for Antony's determination, and that he rather was conquered by the other's firmness, overthrown by his great faith and falling through his constant prayers, then at length putting his trust in the weapons which are 'in the navel of his belly' and boasting in them—for they are his first snare for the young—he attacked the young man, disturbing him by night and harassing him by day, so

that even the onlookers saw the struggle which was going on
between them. The one would suggest foul thoughts and the other
counter them with prayers: the one fire him with lust, the other, as
one who seemed to blush, fortify his body with faith, prayers, and
fasting. And the devil, unhappy wight, one night even took upon
him the shape of a woman and imitated all her acts simply to
beguile Antony. But he, his mind filled with Christ and the nobility
inspired by Him, and considering the spirituality of the soul,
quenched the coal of the other's deceit. Again the enemy suggested
the ease of pleasure. But he like a man filled with rage and grief
turned his thoughts to the threatened fire and the gnawing worm,
and setting these in array against his adversary, passed through
the temptation unscathed. All this was a source of shame to his foe.
For he, deeming himself like God, was now mocked by a young
man; and he who boasted himself against flesh and blood was being
put to flight by a man in the flesh. For the Lord was working with
Antony—the Lord who for our sake took flesh and gave the body
victory over the devil, so that all who truly fight can say, 'not I but
the grace of God which was with me.'[8]

6. At last when the dragon could not even thus overthrow
Antony, but saw himself thrust out of his heart, gnashing his teeth
as it is written, and as it were beside himself, he appeared to
Antony like a black boy, taking a visible shape in accordance with
the colour of his mind. And cringing to him, as it were, he plied him
with thoughts no longer, for guileful as he was, he had been
worsted, but at last spoke in human voice and said, 'Many I deceived, many I cast down; but now attacking thee and thy labours
as I had many others, I proved weak.' When Antony asked, Who art
thou who speakest thus with me? he answered with a lamentable
voice, 'I am the friend of whoredom, and have taken upon me
incitements which lead to it against the young. I am called the
spirit of lust. How many have I deceived who wished to live soberly,
how many are the chaste whom by my incitements I have over-
persuaded? I am he on account of whom also the prophet reproves
those who have fallen, saying, "Ye have been caused to err by the
spirit of whoredom."[9] For by me they have been tripped up. I am he
who have so often troubled thee and have so often been overthrown
by thee.' But Antony having given thanks to the Lord, with good
courage said to him, 'Thou art very despicable then, for thou art
black-hearted and weak as a child. Henceforth I shall have no
trouble from thee, "for the Lord is my helper, and I shall look down
on mine enemies."'[10] Having heard this, the black one straight-

way fled, shuddering at the words and dreading any longer even to come near the man.

7. This was Antony's first struggle against the devil, or rather this victory was the Saviour's work in Antony, 'Who condemned sin in the flesh that the ordinance of the law might be fulfilled in us who walk not after the flesh but after the spirit.'[11] But neither did Antony, although the evil one had fallen, henceforth relax his care and despise him; nor did the enemy as though conquered cease to lay snares for him. For again he went round as a lion seeking some occasion against him. But Antony having learned from the Scriptures that the devices[12] of the devil are many, zealously continued the discipline, reckoning that though the devil had not been able to deceive his heart by bodily pleasure, he would endeavour to ensnare him by other means. For the demon loves sin. Wherefore more and more he repressed the body and kept it in subjection[13] lest haply having conquered on one side, he should be dragged down on the other. He therefore planned to accustom himself to a severer mode of life. And many marvelled, but he himself used to bear the labour easily; for the eagerness of soul, through the length of time it had abode in him, had wrought a good habit in him, so that taking but little initiation from others he shewed great zeal in this matter. He kept vigil to such an extent that he often continued the whole night without sleep; and this not once but often, to the marvel of others. He ate once a day, after sunset, sometimes once in two days, and often even in four. His food was bread and salt, his drink, water only. Of flesh and wine it is superfluous even to speak, since no such thing was found with the other earnest men. A rush mat served him to sleep upon, but for the most part he lay upon the bare ground. He would not anoint himself with oil, saying it behoved young men to be earnest in training and not to seek what would enervate the body; but they must accustom it to labour, mindful of the Apostle's words, 'when I am weak, then am I strong.'[14] 'For,' said he, 'the fibre of the soul is then sound when the pleasures of the body are diminished.' And he had come to this truly wonderful conclusion, 'that progress in virtue, and retirement from the world for the sake of it, ought not to be measured by time, but by desire and fixity of purpose. He at least gave no thought to the past, but day by day, as if he were at the beginning of his discipline, applied greater pains for advancement, often repeating to himself the saying of Paul: 'Forgetting the things which are behind and stretching forward to the things which are before.'[15] He was also mindful of the words spoken by the prophet Elias, 'the

Lord liveth before whose presence I stand to-day.'[16] For he observed that in saying 'to-day' the prophet did not compute the time that had gone by: but daily as though ever commencing he eagerly endeavoured to make himself fit to appear before God, being pure in heart and ever ready to submit to His counsel, and to Him alone. And he used to say to himself that from the life of the great Elias the hermit ought to see his own as in a mirror.

8. Thus tightening his hold upon himself, Antony departed to the tombs, which happened to be at a distance from the village; and having bid one of his acquaintances to bring him bread at intervals of many days, he entered one of the tombs, and the other having shut the door on him, he remained within alone. And when the enemy could not endure it, but was even fearful that in a short time Antony would fill the desert with the discipline, coming one night with a multitude of demons, he so cut him with stripes that he lay on the ground speechless from the excessive pain. For he affirmed that the torture had been so excessive that no blows inflicted by man could ever have caused him such torment. But by the Providence of God—for the Lord never overlooks them that hope in Him—the next day his acquaintance came bringing him the loaves. And having opened the door and seeing him lying on the ground as though dead, he lifted him up and carried him to the church in the village, and laid him upon the ground. And many of his kinsfolk and the villagers sat around Antony as round a corpse. But about midnight he came to himself and arose, and when he saw them all asleep and his comrade alone watching, he motioned with his head for him to approach, and asked him to carry him again to the tombs without waking anybody.

9. He was carried therefore by the man, and as he was wont, when the door was shut he was within alone. And he could not stand up on account of the blows, but he prayed as he lay. And after he had prayed, he said with a shout, Here am I, Antony; I flee not from your stripes, for even if you inflict more nothing shall separate me from the love of Christ.[17] And then he sang, 'though a camp be set against me, my heart shall not be afraid.'[18] These were the thoughts and words of this ascetic. But the enemy, who hates good, marvelling that after the blows he dared to return, called together his hounds and burst forth, 'Ye see,' said he, 'that neither by the spirit of lust nor by blows did we stay the man, but that he braves us, let us attack him in another fashion.' But changes of form for evil are easy for the devil, so in the night they made such a din that the whole of that place seemed to be shaken by an earthquake, and

the demons as if breaking the four walls of the dwelling seemed to enter through them, coming in the likeness of beasts and creeping things. And the place was on a sudden filled with the forms of lions, bears, leopards, bulls, serpents, asps, scorpions, and wolves, and each of them was moving according to his nature. The lion was roaring, wishing to attack, the bull seeming to toss with its horns, the serpent writhing but unable to approach, and the wolf as it rushed on was restrained; altogether the noises of the apparitions, with their angry ragings, were dreadful. But Antony, stricken and goaded by them, felt bodily pains severer still. He lay watching, however, with unshaken soul, groaning from bodily anguish; but his mind was clear, and as in mockery he said, 'If there had been any power in you, it would have sufficed had one of you come, but since the Lord hath made you weak you attempt to terrify me by numbers: and a proof of your weakness is that you take the shapes of brute beasts.' And again with boldness he said, 'If you are able, and have received power against me, delay not to attack; but if you are unable, why trouble me in vain? For faith in our Lord is a seal and a wall of safety to us.' So after many attempts they gnashed their teeth upon him, because they were mocking themselves rather than him.

10. Nor was the Lord then forgetful of Antony's wrestling, but was at hand to help him. So looking up he saw the roof as it were opened, and a ray of light descending to him. The demons suddenly vanished, the pain of his body straightway ceased, and the building was again whole. But Antony feeling the help, and getting his breath again, and being freed from pain, besought the vision which had appeared to him, saying, 'Where wert thou? Why didst thou not appear at the beginning to make my pains to cease?' And a voice came to him, 'Antony, I was here, but I waited to see thy fight; wherefore since thou hast endured, and hast not been worsted, I will ever be a succour to thee, and will make thy name known everywhere.' Having heard this, Antony arose and prayed, and received such strength that he perceived that he had more power in his body than formerly. And he was then about thirty-five years old.

11. And on the day following he went forth still more eagerly bent on the service of God, and having fallen in with the old man he had met previously, he asked him to dwell with him in the desert. But when the other declined on account of his great age, and because as yet there was no such custom, Antony himself set off forthwith to the mountain. And yet again the enemy seeing his

zeal and wishing to hinder it, cast in his way what seemed to be a great silver dish. But Antony, seeing the guile of the Evil One, stood, and having looked on the dish, he put the devil in it to shame, saying, 'Whence comes a dish in the desert? This road is not well-worn, nor is there here a trace of any wayfarer; it could not have fallen without being missed on account of its size; and he who had lost it having turned back to seek it, would have found it, for it is a desert place. This is some wile of the devil. O thou Evil One, not with this shalt thou hinder my purpose; let it go with thee to destruction.' And when Antony had said this it vanished like smoke from the face of fire.

12. Then again as he went on he saw what was this time not visionary, but real gold scattered in the way. But whether the devil showed it, or some better power to try the athlete and show the Evil One that Antony truly cared nought for money, neither he told nor do we know. But it is certain that that which appeared was gold. And Antony marvelled at the quantity, but passed it by as though he were going over fire; so he did not even turn, but hurried on at a run to lose sight of the place. More and more confirmed in his purpose, he hurried to the mountain, and having found a fort, so long deserted that it was full of creeping things, on the other side of the river; he crossed over to it and dwelt there. The reptiles, as though some one were chasing them, immediately left the place. But he built up the entrance completely, having stored up loaves for six months—this is a custom of the Thebans, and the loaves often remain fresh a whole year—and as he found water within, he descended as into a shrine, and abode within by himself, never going forth nor looking at any one who came. Thus he employed a long time training himself, and received loaves, let down from above, twice in the year.

13. But those of his acquaintances who came, since he did not permit them to enter, often used to spend days and nights outside, and heard as it were crowds within clamouring, dinning, sending forth piteous voices and crying, 'Go from what is ours. What dost thou even in the desert? Thou canst not abide our attack.' So at first those outside thought there were some men fighting with him, and that they had entered by ladders; but when stooping down they saw through a hole there was nobody, they were afraid, accounting them to be demons, and they called on Antony. Them he quickly heard, though he had not given a thought to the demons, and coming to the door he besought them to depart and not to be afraid, 'for thus,' said he, 'the demons make their seeming onslaughts

against those who are cowardly. Sign yourselves therefore with the cross and depart boldly, and let these make sport for themselves.' So they departed fortified with the sign of the Cross. But he remained in no wise harmed by the evil spirits, nor was he wearied with the contest, for there came to his aid visions from above, and the weakness of the foe relieved him of much trouble and armed him with greater zeal. For his acquaintances used often to come expecting to find him dead, and would hear him singing, 'Let God arise and let His enemies be scattered, let them also that hate Him flee before His face. As smoke vanisheth, let them vanish; as wax melteth before the face of fire, so let the sinners perish from the face of God;'[19] and again, 'All nations compassed me about, and in the name of the Lord I requited them.'[20]

14. And so for nearly twenty years he continued training himself in solitude, never going forth, and but seldom seen by any. After this, when many were eager and wishful to imitate his discipline, and his acquaintances came and began to cast down and wrench off the door by force, Antony, as from a shrine, came forth initiated in the mysteries and filled with the Spirit of God. Then for the first time he was seen outside the fort by those who came to see him. And they, when they saw him, wondered at the sight, for he had the same habit of body as before, and was neither fat, like a man without exercise, nor lean from fasting and striving with the demons, but he was just the same as they had known him before his retirement. And again his soul was free from blemish, for it was neither contracted as if by grief, nor relaxed by pleasure, nor possessed by laughter or dejection, for he was not troubled when he beheld the crowd, nor overjoyed at being saluted by so many. But he was altogether even as being guided by reason, and abiding in a natural state. Through him the Lord healed the bodily ailments of many present, and cleansed others from evil spirits. And He gave grace to Antony in speaking, so that he consoled many that were sorrowful, and set those at variance at one, exhorting all to prefer the love of Christ before all that is in the world. And while he exhorted and advised them to remember the good things to come, and the loving-kindness of God towards us, 'Who spared not His own Son, but delivered Him up for us all,[21] he persuaded many to embrace the solitary life. And thus it happened in the end that cells arose even in the mountains, and the desert was colonised by monks, who came forth from their own people, and enrolled themselves for the citizenship in the heavens.

EVAGRIUS PONTICUS

Educated for life as a cleric and courtier of the Byzantine Empire, Evagrius fled from Constantinople and wandered first to Jerusalem and finally to Egypt in search of a life of perfection. His many works on asceticism popularized the teaching of the Desert Fathers throughout the Roman Empire.

In every man self-opinion prevents self-knowledge.
Do you wish to know God? Learn first to know yourself.
                                        (c. 350-399)

WISDOM OF THE DESERT

Many of the first Egyptian monks, like Antony, were hermits leading a solitary life focused entirely on God. As time went on, however, more and more of these monks entered into communitarian forms of existence in order to provide for sound formation in spirituality and continuous spiritual direction.

During the fourth and fifth centuries, Egyptian monasticism attracted many adherents, developed institutionalized forms (such as those of Pachomius of Tabbenisi), and spread abroad to Syria, Asia Minor, Italy, Ireland and Gaul.

Something of the simple spirit of the "Fathers of the Desert" is preserved in collections of their sayings (Apophthegmata Patrum, Verba Seniorum) *that circulated widely throughout the Middle Ages. A few selections of these sayings are presented here in a modern translation made by Thomas Merton.*

Once some brethren went out of the monastery to visit the hermits who lived in the desert. They came to one who received them with joy and seeing that they were tired, invited them to eat before the accustomed time and placed before them all the food he had available. But that night when they were all supposed to be sleeping the hermit heard the cenobites talking among themselves and saying: These hermits eat more than we do in the monastery. Now at dawn the guests set out to see another hermit, and as they were starting out their host said: Greet him from me, and give him this message: Be careful not to water the vegetables. When they reached the other hermitage they delivered this message. And the second hermit understood what was meant by the words. So he made the visitors sit down and weave baskets, and sitting with them he worked without interruption. And in the evening when the time came for lighting the lamp, he added a few extra psalms to the usual number, after which he said to them: We do not usually eat every day out here, but because you have come along it is fitting to have a little supper today, for a change. Then he gave them some dry bread and salt, then added: Here's a special treat for you. Upon which he mixed them a little sauce of vinegar, salt and oil, and gave it to them. After supper they got up again and started in on the psalms and kept on praying almost until dawn, at which the hermit said: Well, we can't finish all our usual prayers, for you are tired from your journey. You had better take a little rest. And so when the first hour of the day came, they all wanted to leave this hermit, but he would not let them go. He kept saying: Stay with me a while. I cannot let you go so soon, charity demands that I keep you for two or three days. But they, hearing this, waited until dark and then under cover of night they made off.

An elder said: Do not judge a fornicator if you are chaste, for if you do, you too are violating the law as much as he is. For He who said thou shalt not fornicate also said thou shalt not judge.

One of the Fathers told a story of a certain elder who was in his cell busily at work and wearing a hairshirt when Abbot Ammonas came to him. When Abbot Ammonas saw him wearing a hairshirt he said: That thing won't do you a bit of good. The elder said: Three thoughts are troubling me. The first impels me to withdraw somewhere into the wilderness. The second, to seek a foreign land where no one knows me. The third, to wall myself into this cell and see no one and eat only every second day. Abbot Ammonas said to him: None of these three will do you a bit of good. But rather sit in your cell, and eat a little every day, and have always in your heart the words which are read in the Gospel and were said by the Publican,[1] and thus you can be saved.

One of the elders used to say: In the beginning when we got together we used to talk about something that was good for our souls, and we went up and up and ascended even to heaven. But now we get together and spend our time in criticizing everything, and we drag one another down into the abyss.

Yet another elder said: If you see a young monk by his own will climbing up into heaven, take him by the foot and throw him to the ground, because what he is doing is not good for him.

Abbot Bessarion, dying, said: The monk should be all eye, like the cherubim and seraphim.

Abbot Pastor said: Get away from any man who always argues every time he talks.

A certain elder said: Apply yourself to silence, have no vain thoughts, and be intent in your meditation, whether you sit at prayer, or whether you rise up to work in the fear of God. If you do these things, you will not have to fear the attacks of the evil ones.

Abbot Lot came to Abbot Joseph and said: Father, according as I am able, I keep my little rule, and my little fast, my prayer, meditation and contemplative silence; and according as I am able I strive to cleanse my heart of thoughts: now what more should I do? The elder rose up in reply and stretched out his hands to heaven, and his fingers became like ten lamps of fire. He said: Why not be totally changed into fire?

Abbot Pastor said: Any trial whatever that comes to you can be conquered by silence.

Once there was an elder in the lower parts of Egypt, and he was a very famous hermit, living all alone in a desert place. Satan brought it about that a woman of easy virtue said to some young men: What will you give me, and I will go out and knock down that hermit of yours? So they agreed on a certain sum they would give her. And going out one evening she came to his cell pretending to have lost her way. She knocked at his door and he came out. Seeing her he was disturbed and said: How did you get out here? She pretended to weep, and said: I have lost my way. So, being moved to pity, he let her in to the front room of his cell, and for his part he went on to the inner room and locked the door. But the unfortunate woman cried out: Father, the wild animals will eat me out here. Once again the elder was disturbed and thought of the Judgment of God, and said: How did this dreadful thing ever happen to me? But, opening his door, he let her in. And the devil began to shoot flaming arrows into his heart. But he said within himself: The ways of the enemy are darkness, and the Son of God is light. So he lit a lantern. But the temptation continued and he said to himself: Well, let's see whether you will be able to bear the flames of hell. And he put a finger into the flame. But though the flame burned him he did not feel it, so strong was the fire of lust in him. And he went on like that until morning, burning all his fingers. The unfortunate woman, watching what he was doing, was so struck with terror that she almost turned into stone. In the morning the two young men came to the hermit and said: Did a woman come here last night? Yes, said the hermit, she is over there asleep. But they said: Father, she is dead! Then he, throwing back the cloak he had on, showed them his hands and said: Look what she did to me, that child of hell! she has cost me all my fingers. And having told them all that had taken place he ended with: It is written thou shalt not render evil for evil. So he said a prayer and she revived. She was converted, and lived chastely for the rest of her life.

———————

Abbess Syncletica of holy memory said: There is labour and great struggle for the impious who are converted to God, but after that comes inexpressible joy. A man who wants to light a fire first is plagued by smoke, and the smoke drives him to tears, yet finally he gets the fire that he wants. So also it is written: Our God is a consuming fire. Hence we ought to light the divine fire in ourselves with labour and with tears.

Abbot Pastor said that Abbot John the Dwarf had prayed to the Lord and the Lord had taken away all his passions, so that he became impassible. And in this condition he went to one of the elders and said: You see before you a man who is completely at rest and has no more temptations. The elder said: Go and pray to the Lord to command some struggle to be stirred up in you, for the soul is matured only in battles. And when the temptations started up again he did not pray that the struggle be taken away from him, but only said: Lord, give me strength to get through the fight.

Once some robbers came into the monastery and said to one of the elders: We have come to take away everything that is in your cell. And he said: My sons, take all you want. So they took everything they could find in the cell and started off. But they left behind a little bag that was hidden in the cell. The elder picked it up and followed after them, crying out: My sons, take this, you forgot it in the cell! Amazed at the patience of the elder, they brought everything back into his cell and did penance, saying: This one really is a man of God!

There was an elder who had a well-tried novice living with him, and once, when he was annoyed, he drove the novice out of the cell. But the novice sat down outside and waited for the elder. The elder, opening the door, found him there, and did penance before him, saying: You are my Father, because your patience and humility have overcome the weakness of my soul. Come back in; you can be the elder and the Father, I will be the youth and the novice: for by your good work you have surpassed my old age.

ST. MAXIMUS THE CONFESSOR

First Century on Charity

Byzantine courtier, theologian, and monk, Maximus the Confessor (c. 580-662) expressed in a powerful way the final synthesis of the first centuries of monasticism in the East. His Centuries on Charity *are collections of brief thoughts on the spiritual life designed for the meditative reading of monks.*

Blessed is the man who can love all men equally.
Blessed is the man who is attached to nothing
    subject to corruption and time.
Blessed is the mind which, passing by all creatures,
    constantly rejoices in God's Beauty.

JOHN CASSIAN

Conference X On Prayer

In his youth John Cassian (c. 360–433) experienced the monastic life in Palestine and Egypt. After years spent in Constantinople and Rome, he moved on to Gaul and began founding monasteries near Marseilles about the year 415. In order to educate his new Gallic monks, Cassian gave them series of conferences, many of which have been preserved, in which he summarized the teachings of the Eastern monks whom he had come to know and admire. The collection of his conferences provides us with a thoroughgoing synthesis of the first century of Christian monastic experience. The conferences became normative for the monastic life of the entire Middle Ages and were read daily in most monasteries for a thousand years and more. The following Conference *provides us with a sampling of Cassian's writings on purity of heart and prayer and illustrates his subtle psychological insights into human attempts at leading a life of deep spirituality.*

Mindset of early Church = concern about heresy because. philosophical influence of Greeks — necessary to establish doctrine of Church — Today mindset = more aware of distinction between rational knowledge & intuitive knowledge — which is a relationship I + Thou ?

JOHN CASSIAN 29

1. I have tried, however unskilfully, to describe with God's help the sublime customs of the hermits. The order of my discourse now forces me to insert a passage which may seem like a pimple on a lovely body. Yet I have no doubt that less educated readers will learn much from it about the image of Almighty God which Genesis describes. So I insert it with a view to a better understanding of a great doctrine which cannot be misapprehended without blasphemy and heresy.

2. The clergy of Egypt observe the feast of Epiphany as the time of our Lord's birth as well as the time of his baptism, and, unlike the western Church with its two separate festivals, keep both commemorations upon the same day. They keep a custom of immemorial antiquity that after Epiphany the Bishop of Alexandria sends a letter to every church and monastery in Egypt declaring the dates for the beginning of Lent and Easter Day.

A few days after the first conference with Abba Isaac, arrived the customary festal letter from Bishop Theophilus of Alexandria.[1] Besides declaring the date of Easter, he included in the letter a long refutation of the absurd heresy of the Anthropomorphites. Nearly all the monks in Egypt, being uneducated and therefore holding wrong ideas, received this with bitterness and hostility: and a large majority of elders from all the ascetic brotherhood decreed that the bishop was guilty of a grave and hateful heresy, because (by denying that Almighty God was formed in the fashion of a man, when Scripture bears clear witness that Adam was created in his image) he seemed to be attacking the text of Holy Scripture. Even the hermits in the desert of Scete, who were more educated and more spiritually advanced than any other Egyptian monks, rejected the letter of Theophilus. The priests who were presiding over three of the four churches in Scete would not allow the letter to be read at their meetings: and the only exception was Abba Paphnutius, who was the priest of my own congregation.

which is the paradigm — God a man.

Concern with heresy.

3. Among those caught by the error was a monk named Sarapion, who had for many years lived a life of strict discipline and had achieved the leading of a truly good life. Almost first among monks in merit and in years in the desert, equally he was almost first in his ignorant prejudice against orthodox believers. The saintly priest, Paphnutius, used many exhortations to bring him back to the true belief, but unsuccessfully. To Sarapion the view seemed a novelty, not found in tradition.

It chanced that a deacon of great learning, named Photinus, arrived from Cappadocia with the object of visiting the brothers in

Scete. Paphnutius gave him a warm welcome. And to support the doctrine contained in the letter of Bishop Theophilus, he led Photinus into the middle of the congregation, and in the presence of all the brothers, asked how the Catholic Churches of the East understood the text in Genesis: "Let us make man after our image and likeness."[2] Photinus explained how all the leaders of the churches understood the text spiritually, not literally nor crudely, and made a long speech adducing numerous proofs from Scripture. "That unmeasurable, incomprehensible, invisible majesty cannot be limited by a human frame or likeness. His nature is incorporeal, uncompounded, simple, and cannot be seen by human eyes nor conceived adequately by a human mind."

At last old Sarapion was moved by the numerous and convincing assertions of this learned man, and consented to the traditional faith of Catholics. Abba Paphnutius and the rest of us felt great joy at his assent; joy that the Lord had not allowed a man of such age and goodness, who had erred in simple ignorance, to end his days unorthodox in the faith.

When we stood up to give thanks to the Lord in prayer, the old man felt mentally bewildered at having to pray, because he could no longer sense in his heart the anthropomorphic image of God which he had always before his mind's eye when praying. Suddenly he broke into bitter weeping and sobbing, and throwing himself prostrate on the ground with groans, cried: "Woe is me! They have taken my God away from me, and I have none to grasp, and I know not whom to adore or to address."

Germanus and I were deeply moved by this scene. And with the effect of the last Conference still in our hearts, we returned to Abba Isaac. When we reached his presence we addressed him thus:

4. "Your last Conference on prayer stirred our desire to put aside all else and return to you. But this new incident has strengthened the desire still further. Abba Sarapion, misled by skilful demons as we believe, fell into grave error. And this has cast us down into a state of hopelessness. We are thinking how for fifty years he has so admirably lived as a great ascetic in this desert, and yet through ignorance not only lost the merit of that life but incurred a risk of eternal death. So, first, we want to know how and why this grave error crept upon him.

Secondly, we ask you to teach us how we can reach the state of prayer of which earlier you taught us at length, and so finely. Your earlier conference made us admire that state, but did not show us how to achieve or secure it."

5. Isaac: "It is not surprising that a very simple man who had never received any instruction on the being and nature of God could be caught and deceived, even until now, by an error which he mis-learnt a long time ago. This error is not, as you suppose, a modern illusion of demons, but an inheritance from the ignorance of the old heathen. They used customarily and erroneously to worship demons fashioned in the likeness of men, and even now they think to worship God in his majesty—the incomprehensible and indescribable—in the limited form of some statue. And they suppose they have nothing to worship unless they have in front of them a statue, which they can continually address in their devotions, can mentally conceive, and can keep in front of their eyes. Against this error is directed the text: 'And they changed the glory of the incorruptible God into the likeness of the image of corruptible man.' And Jeremiah says: 'My people have changed their glory for an idol.'[3]

This is the way in which this error has been implanted in some men. Nevertheless, in people whose souls have never been polluted by heathenism, the error is contracted by ignorance, under cover of this text: 'Let us make man in our image and likeness.' Hence the so-called Anthropomorphite heresy has risen out of the detestable interpretation of this text, a heresy which maintains obstinately and perversely that the limitless and simple nature of God is fashioned in human form and features. Anyone well-instructed in Catholic doctrine will detest the idea as heathen blasphemy: and in detesting it he will come to that pure state of prayer where the person will allow (I need not say) no effigy of God to be mingled in his prayers, and will not even admit the recollection of a saying or an action, or the outline of a character.

6. I said in my first Conference that every soul attains the kind of prayer proportionate to its purity: for it can abandon the contemplation of the earthy and material only in proportion as its state of purity carries it upwards to see Jesus in the mind's eye—Jesus still in the humility of his incarnate life, or Jesus glorified and coming in majesty. Jesus coming in his kingdom shall not be seen by men who are restrained by a weakness like that of the Jews and therefore cannot say with St Paul: 'And if we have known Christ after the flesh, yet now we know him so no more.'[4] Only those of purest sight look upon his divinity, men who have climbed up from earthly acts and thoughts and have gone apart with him into a high and lonely mountain. Jesus, untroubled by any earthly thought and passion and sin, exalted in the purity of his

faith and goodness, discloses the brightness of his face and likeness to men who can look upon him because their souls are pure.

Inhabitants of cities and villages and hamlets, men engaged in the ordinary and virtuous pursuits of life, sometimes see Jesus; but they cannot see him with the distinctness possible to those who can climb up with him upon the mount of saintliness, as did Peter, James and John. So in the wilderness he appeared to Moses, and spoke with Elijah. He wanted to teach us this and leave us an example of perfect purity. As the source of holiness, a source unpolluted like a spring of fresh water, he did not need to go apart in the wilderness to attain that perfect purity. No dirt, no stain from the crowds of human society could lessen the fulness of his purity of heart, for he it is who cleanses and purges all pollution.

Yet he went apart alone to the mountain to pray. He gave an example of withdrawal, to teach us that if we want to address God with a heart of integrity we should go apart from all crowd and tumult that disturbs our peace; and there, though still mortal men, we may in part succeed in attaining at least the shadow of the bliss promised to the saints in the future, and God may be to us all in all.[5]

7. Then our Saviour's prayer, wherein he prayed the Father for his disciples, will be truly fulfilled in us: 'that the love wherein thou lovedst me may be in them, and they in us': and 'that they all may be one, as thou, Father, art in me and I in thee, that they also may be one in us.' This unity will be when that perfect love of God, wherewith 'he first loved us'[6] has passed into the affections of our own hearts. So his prayer will be fulfilled, and we believe that that prayer cannot fail of its effect.

Then God shall be all our love, all we desire and seek and follow, all we think, all our life and speech and breath. The unity which now is between Father and Son shall be poured into our feelings and our minds: and as he loves us with a pure, sincere, unbreakable charity we on our side shall be linked to him by a lasting affection that nothing can spoil. In that union, whatever we breathe or think or speak is God. So the end of his prayer is attained in us—'that they all may be one as we are one: I in them, and thou in me, that they also may be made perfect in one': and 'Father, those whom thou hast given me, I will that where I am, they may also be with me.'

This should be the aim and purpose of the solitary: to seek to possess in some measure, even while mortal man, the first bridal gifts from the heavenly country and its glory. I repeat: this is the end of all true goodness, that the mind may every day be lifted beyond the material sphere to the realm of spirit, until the whole life and every little stirring of the heart becomes one continuous prayer."

8. Germanus: "We were bewildered by the first conference and returned to you for further explanation. But now our bewilderment has grown. Certainly this doctrine stirs us to long for the bliss of heaven; but the more we yearn, the more we despair. For we still do not know how to achieve the sort of disciplined life which can enable us to reach this lofty goal. I beg you to be patient and allow me to explain (perhaps at some length) what we had begun to consider during our daily meditations in our cell. I know that you are unused to being troubled by the silly questions of weak brothers like ourselves. Yet it is worth bringing these silly questions into the open, so that the absurdity in them may be corrected.

We think that every art or science must begin with rudiments easy and suitable for the uninitiated. A man must be trained, so to speak, on the milk of the intellect, and thereby may grow, step by step, from ignorance to education. First he acquires the more obvious principles, passes the gateway to his subject, and thereby can climb without difficulty to the pinnacles of knowledge. A boy cannot frame sentences until he has learnt the alphabet properly. He cannot become a quick reader unless he can first read short and simple nouns. The man ignorant of grammar will never be able to write elegant prose or to become a sound philosopher.

This higher discipline in which we learn to cleave to God continually, must doubtless have first principles, foundations on which a man may build to raise the lofty tower. I think, though hesitantly, that its first principles consist in learning by what meditations God may be grasped and conceived; and then, how to preserve this thought, whatever it is, uninterruptedly: and I am sure that this uninterrupted preservation is the true perfection of the discipline.

We want you to show us material for this recollectedness by which God is conceived in the mind and the conception is retained permanently. Thereby we may keep it in front of us; and, when we feel we have fallen away, may at once be able to return, without any delay or ignorant meandering of the thoughts.

Sometimes, when my mind has wandered away from contemplating God, I wake up as if from a sleep as sound as death; I look round like a drowsy man just out of bed, for the subject-matter to recreate recollectedness. The process of finding the material distracts and delays me: before I find the vision again, my purpose of heart is beginning to fade. I am sure it happens because I do not keep before my eyes some special intention in the way of a formula to which the wandering mind could be recalled from its travels—so to say, a quiet harbour after a long and stormy voyage. Thus the mind, constantly hampered by this ignorance, teeters to and fro like a drunkard and does not even grasp the spiritual thought which comes to it, unasked and unsought. As it goes on receiving one sensation after another, it is unconscious of their arrival, their origin, or their departure."

9. Isaac: "Your question is intricate: and the fact that you have asked it proves you to have made headway towards purity of mind. To ask questions, still more to use a delicate introspection in this matter, is only possible to a person who by mental zeal and alertness has reached a stage where he can understand the complications of the problem; to a person whose constant attempts at a disciplined life have given him the experience whereby he may knock at the gates of mental purity. I see that you are no longer standing at the outer gate of true prayer, but are knocking at its inner door, and have already pushed it half open. A visitor who has reached the main hall of a house can easily be shown its inner rooms: and with God's guidance I think it will be easy to bring you to the heart of true prayer. I believe you will allow no obstacle to hinder your self-examination. The man who knows what questions to ask is on the verge of understanding: the man who is beginning to understand what he does not know is not far from knowledge.

So I am not afraid of the charge of speaking irreverently or betraying secrets if I now disclose what I omitted from my earlier Conference. I think that by God's grace your own study would have taught you the way even if you had no words of mine to help you.

10. You made an admirable comparison between spiritual discipline and the education of children. A child cannot recognize or make letters before he has become used to seeing them every day in wax copies. I must give you the formula for contemplation. If you carefully keep this formula in front of you, and learn to recollect it all the time, you can use it to mount to the contemplation of high truth. Every monk who looks for continual recollection of God uses this formula for meditation, and with the object of driving every other sort of thought from his heart. You cannot keep the formula before you unless you are free from all bodily care.

The formula was given us by a few of the oldest fathers who

[handwritten margin note top: use of techniques goes back to early spirituality of the Ch — but difference from today's use of techniques is the motivation (purity of heart) to be united with God total giving of oneself to God — rather than modern search for fulfillment]

remained. They did not communicate it except to a very few who
were athirst for the true way. To maintain an unceasing recollection of God it is to be ever set before you.

The formula is: 'O God, make speed to save me: O Lord, make
haste to help me.'[7]

This verse has rightly been selected from the whole Bible for
this purpose. It fits every mood and temper of human nature, every
temptation, every circumstance. It contains an invocation of God, a
humble confession of faith, a reverent watchfulness, a meditation
upon our frailty, a confidence in God's answer, an assurance of his
ever-present support. The man who continually invokes God as his
guardian, is aware that he is always at hand. The formula contains
a fervent charity, a fearful contemplation of the devil's power, a
regard for the defender's succour which alone can relieve the be-
leaguered soul from the devil's siege by day and night. The verse is
an impregnable battlement, a shield and coat of mail which no
spear can pierce. Souls sunk in accidie or worry or melancholy
thoughts of any kind find the cure of despair in this verse, which
shows them God's watch over their struggles and their prayers.
Souls happy in their spiritual progress, it warns against a bubble-
like complacency, assuring them that only with God's protection
can they keep what they have won; teaching them not merely to
ask his help, but to ask it speedily.

[handwritten margin note: centering prayer]

I repeat; each of us, whatever his condition of spiritual life,
needs to use this verse. The man who wants to be helped in all
circumstances and at all times, shows that he needs God to help
him in prosperity and happiness as much as in suffering and
sorrow. He needs to be delivered from the one, and maintained in
the other. For he knows that frail human nature cannot remain
unimpaired in either state without God's help.

Suppose I feel gluttonous; I look around for food unknown
among hermits; in the middle of the desert I scent the cooking of a
dish fit for kings, and against my better will I cannot help hunger-
ing for it. Then I must say immediately: 'O God, make speed to save
me, O Lord, make haste to help me.' Or I am tempted to eat supper
too early, or am struggling to eat no more than the right and
customary quantity, I must cry out: 'O God, make speed to save me;
O Lord, make haste to help me.' I need severe fasts to quench lust,
yet I dare not undertake them through the delicacy or dryness of
my stomach. And so to quieten the lust without severe fasting, I
must pray: 'O God, make speed to save me: O Lord, make haste to
help me.' I go to supper at the correct time and shudder at the food

and cannot eat what I must eat to live, then I must sigh: 'O God, make speed to save me: O Lord, make haste to help me.'

Perhaps I want to keep my heart stable by forcing myself to read the Bible. But a headache stops me, by nine o'clock in the morning I have fallen asleep with my head on the page—and I am driven to go to bed before the appointed hour, and so fail to say the full office and the proper series of psalms—again I must say: 'O God, make speed to save me: O Lord, make haste to help me.' Perhaps night after night I suffer some devilish insomnia and am exhausted from lack of sleep, gain no refreshment from my night's rest. I must breathe: 'O God, make speed to save me: O Lord, make haste to help me.'

Perhaps, if I have not yet tamed the flesh, some sudden temptation against chastity comes upon me softly at night: and I must prevent this invading fire from burning up the fragrant flowers of chastity. So I must call: 'O God, make speed to save me: O Lord, make haste to help me.' Perhaps I feel the heat of passion to have cooled. Then this virtue—nay, this grace, for it is a gift of God—I must keep within me by saying carefully: 'O God, make speed to save me: O Lord, make haste to help me.'

Perhaps temptations to anger, or avarice, or melancholy afflict me and force me to disturb my calm state, so pleasant to me. I must prevent myself being bitter by crying aloud: 'O God, make speed to save me: O Lord, make haste to help me.' Perhaps some temptation to accidie, or vanity, or pride, or to despise the half-heartedness of other monks, creeps upon the mind. To stop this devilish suggestion, I must pray with deep contrition: 'O God, make speed to save me: O Lord, make haste to help me.'

Perhaps I have repented long and so have pricked the bubble of pride and gained the grace of humility and simplicity. So that 'the foot of pride' may not again 'come against me,' and 'the hand of the sinner disturb me'[8] and that satisfaction at my success may not cause still worse moral damage, I must call with my whole heart: 'O God, make speed to save me: O Lord, make haste to help me.'

Perhaps wandering thoughts career about the soul like boiling water, and I cannot contest them, nor can I offer prayer without silly mental images interrupting it; I feel so dry that I seem incapable of spiritual feeling, and many sighs and groans cannot save me from dreariness—I must needs say: 'O God, make speed to save me: O Lord, make haste to help me.'

Perhaps by some joyous rapture I feel that the Holy Spirit has visited me, and I have gained a re-directed purpose, a concentration of mind, a liveliness of heart. And through these overflowing sensations I discern a sudden disclosure by the Lord of sacred truths hidden from me till now. To dwell upon these truths for more than a moment, I must be careful to keep praying: 'O God, make speed to save me: O Lord, make haste to help me.'

Perhaps in the night I am encompassed by appearances of unclean spirits and in my turn am thrown into a despair even of life and salvation. I shall find in the whole-hearted praying of that verse a safe fortress for the fugitive: 'O God, make speed to save me: O Lord, make haste to help me.' Then the Lord restores and consoles me, and I feel that he is garrisoning me with his countless hosts of angels, and suddenly I can dare to go out to face the enemy and provoke them to fight, when a moment before I was trembling with fear of death and shuddering in mind and body at their touch or proximity. To abide by God's grace in this strength and courage, I must say with my whole heart: 'O God, make speed to save me: O Lord, make haste to help me.'

Continuously and ceaselessly, in adversity that we may be delivered, in prosperity that we may be preserved but not puffed up, we ought to send up this prayer. Meditate on it, never stop turning it over within your breast. Whatever work or ministry or journey you are undertaking, go on praying it. While you are going to sleep, or eating, or in the last necessities of nature, think on it. It will be a saving formula in your heart, will guard you from the attacks of demons, will cleanse you from the stains of earthly life, lead you to contemplate the unseen things of heaven, and carry you up to the ineffable glow of prayer which very few have experienced. Sleep ought to catch you thinking about this verse, until you are so moulded by its use that you pray it when asleep. When you wake it should be your first thought, it should force you from your bed to your knees, and thence send you out to your daily work, there to be always with you. You should think on it, in Moses' words,[9] at home or on a journey, going to bed or rising from bed. You should write it on the doors of your lips, the walls of your house, the sanctuary of your breast. Whether you kneel down to pray or whether you rise up from praying and turn to the needs of your daily life, this should be your prayer.

11. This formula the mind should go on grasping until it can cast away the wealth and multiplicity of other thoughts, and restrict itself to the poverty of this single verse. So you will attain with ease that Gospel beatitude which holds first place among the other beatitudes: 'Blessed are the poor in spirit: for theirs is the

kingdom of heaven.' This noble poverty will fulfil the prophet's saying: 'The poor and needy shall praise the name of the Lord.'[10] Truly, what higher or holier poverty can there be than this, that a man knowing he is defenceless of his own, asks help for daily life from another's generosity, and realizes his life and being to depend every moment on God's help. Such a one truly confesses himself 'the beggar of the Lord,' like the Psalmist who said: 'I am a beggar and a poor man: and God helps me.'[11]

So by God's light he mounts to the manifold knowledge of God and thereafter to feed on mysteries loftier and more sacred: the prophet said: 'The high hills are a refuge for the stags, and the rocks for the hedgehogs.'[12] I think this meaning of the text is appropriate for this reason. A man who perseveres in simplicity and innocence, is aggressive to none and content to defend himself from being spoiled by his enemies; like the hedgehog hiding under a rock, he is protected, by his continual recollection of the Lord's passion and meditation upon this verse of the psalms. With the same spiritual intention the book of Proverbs speaks about hedgehogs—'The hedgehogs are a feeble folk, who have made their homes in the rocks.'[13] Nothing is feebler than a Christian; nothing weaker than a monk, who for wrong may take no vengeance nor even indulge mild feelings of annoyance, however concealed within his breast.

The man who in his moral ascent possesses simple innocence and yet the gift of wisdom has Satan crushed like a poisonous viper beneath his feet. And, as a stag browsing upon high pastures, his quick intelligence feeds upon the lofty mysteries revealed by the prophets and apostles.

There, with deep compunction, he will make the thoughts of the psalms his own. He will sing them no longer as verses composed by a prophet, but as born of his own prayers. At least he should use them as intended for his own mouth, and know that they were not fulfilled temporarily in the prophet's age and circumstances, but are being fulfilled in his daily life. There are times when a man understands God's Scriptures with the clarity with which a surgeon understands the body when he opens up the marrow and the veins. These are the times when our experience seems to show us the meaning by practical proof before we understand it intellectually.

For example, if we have the same attitudes of heart wherein the Psalmist wrote or sang his psalms, we shall become like the authors and be aware of the meaning before we have thought it out

instead of after. The force of the words strikes us before we have
rationally examined them. And when we use the words, we remember, by a kind of meditative association, our own circumstances and struggles, the results of our negligence or earnestness,
the mercies of God's providence or the temptations of the devil, the
subtle and slippery sins of forgetfulness or human frailty or un-
thinking ignorance. All these feelings we find expressed in the
psalms. We see their texts reflected in the clear glass of our own
moral experience. And with that experience to teach us, we do not
hear the words so much as discern the meaning intuitively. We will
not merely recite them like texts committed to memory, but bring
them out from the depths of the heart as an expression of moral
reality.

So the mind shall attain that purest of pure prayers to which
our earlier Conference led, so far as the Lord deigned to grant us;
the prayer which looks to see no visual image, uses no mind nor
words; the prayer wherein, like a spark leaping from a fire, the
mind is rapt upward; and, destitute of the aid of the senses or of
anything visible or material, pours forth its prayer to God with
groanings and sighs that cannot be uttered."

12. Germanus: "You have most clearly explained the system
of spiritual discipline for which I asked, and perfect prayer itself.
There can be nothing more sublime than to fold the recollection of
God into the little space of a meditation upon a single verse, to
summarize all the prayerful feelings in one sentence.

Now, we beg you to expound our one remaining problem. You
have given us this verse as a kind of formula. How can we keep it
permanently before us? By God's grace we have been liberated
from the stupidities of secular thoughts—how may we grasp spiritual thoughts and never let them go?

13. When the mind has begun to take the meaning of a psalm,
it passes on unawares and unintentionally to some other text of
Scripture. When it has just begun to meditate upon that text and
has half considered it, its attention is caught by another passage
and it forgets all about the earlier matter for meditation. And so it
goes on, hopping from text to text, from psalm to psalm, from
Gospel to Epistle and thence to a prophetic book and thence to a
narrative in the historical books of the Old Testament; meandering vaguely through the Bible, choosing nothing and grasping
nothing on purpose, considering no text to its depth; the mind
becomes a dilettante, a taster of spiritual meanings, not a creator
or owner of them. At the time of the office it totters about like a

drunkard, its worship ever inadequate. During the prayers it is thinking about a psalm or lesson. During the singing of the psalter, it is thinking about something quite outside the text of the psalm. During the lesson, it is thinking about something that has to be done, or remembering something that has been done. So it receives or rejects nothing in a disciplined and orderly manner, but seems to be knocked about by haphazard assaults, powerless to keep or to linger over the text which pleases it.

We therefore need to know how to worship adequately by these means, and how permanently to hold this verse which you gave us as a formula. Then our feelings would not rise and fall hither and thither under their own impetus, but would respond to the control of the will."

14. Isaac: "I think that enough was said on this subject in our earlier discussion. But because you want me to repeat it, I will give a brief summary on how to make the heart stable.

Three things make the wandering mind stop wandering: watching, meditation, prayer, when used purposefully and assiduously. This is only possible if the anxieties and worries of this life are first put away, through tirelessly engaging in work undertaken not for monetary gain, but for the religious needs of the coenobium. This is the only way to obey St. Paul's command, 'Pray without ceasing.'

He prays too little, who only prays when he is on his knees.

But he never prays, who while on his knees is in his heart roaming far afield.

Therefore what we wish to be while praying, we ought to be before we begin to pray. The praying mind cannot help being fashioned by its earlier condition, cannot help its earlier thoughts lifting it upward to heaven or pulling it downward to earth."

*   *   *   *

Thus far Abba Isaac, to our wonder, gave his second Conference on the nature of prayer. He gave his teaching about meditating on that one little verse, as an outline for beginners. Germanus and I admired the teaching and wanted to follow it, for we believed it to be a short and easy way. But when we tried it, we found it harder to observe than our previous method of wandering haphazardly through the Bible and meditating on a variety of different texts.

*   *   *   *

However, it is certain that a man is not incapable of perfection or purity of heart because he cannot read. Perfection and purity are available for anyone who uses one brief text—if he uses it with a purpose of heart strong and unwavering towards God.

JOHN CLIMACUS

Ladder of Divine Ascent

We have very little definite knowledge of the life of John "Climacus" ("John of the Ladder"), other than the fact that he lived in the late sixth and early seventh centuries, spent many years as a solitary in the Sinai, and served for a short period as the abbot of the monastery at Mt. Sinai.

His Ladder of Divine Ascent *is a seminal work of the Eastern Christian monastic tradition. Focusing principally on the practices of asceticism and the cultivation of virtues, the work is notable for its acute psychological insight and its kindly but relentless pursuit of the illusions that ensnare human beings devoted to the spiritual life. For John Climacus, contemplation is the summit to which all is directed, but he devotes his work more to the practical steps of spiritual growth than to the experience of prayer itself. These traits are well illustrated in the following excerpt, "Step 23" of his spiritual ladder.*

Step 23

On mad pride

1. Pride is denial of God, an invention of the devil, the despising of men, the mother of condemnation, the offspring of praise, a sign of sterility, flight from divine assistance, the precursor of madness, the herald of falls, a foothold for satanic possession, source of anger, door of hypocrisy, the support of demons, the guardian of sins, the patron of unsympathy, the rejection of compassion, a bitter inquisitor, an inhuman judge, an opponent of God, a root of blasphemy.

2. The beginning of pride is the consummation of vainglory; the middle is the humiliation of our neighbour, the shameless

parade of our labours, complacency in the heart, hatred of exposure; and the end is denial of God's help, the extolling of one's own exertions, fiendish character.

3. Let all of us who wish to avoid this pit listen: this passion often finds food in gratitude, for at first it does not shamelessly advise us to deny God. I have seen people who thank God with their mouth but mentally magnify themselves. And this is confirmed by that Pharisee who said ironically: God, I thank Thee.[1]

4. Where a fall has overtaken us, there pride has already pitched its tent; because a fall is an indication of pride.

5. A venerable man said to me: 'Suppose that there are twelve shameful passions. If we deliberately love one of them (I mean, pride), it will fill the place of the remaining eleven.'

6. A haughty monk contradicts violently, but a humble one cannot even look one in the face.

7. The cypress does not bend to live on earth; nor does a lofty-hearted monk do so to acquire obedience.

8. A proud person grasps at authority, because otherwise he cannot, or rather, does not want to be utterly lost.

9. God resists the proud.[2] Who then can have mercy on them? Every proud-hearted man is unclean before God.[3] Who then can cleanse such a person?

10. The proud are corrected by falling into sin. It is a devil which spurs them on. But apostasy is madness. In the first two cases people have often been healed by men, but the last is humanly incurable.

11. He who refuses reproof shows his passion (pride), but he who accepts it is free of this fetter.

12. An angel[4] fell from heaven without any other passion except pride, and so we may ask whether it is possible to ascend to heaven by humility alone without any other of the virtues.

13. Pride is loss of wealth and sweat. They cried but there was none to save, no doubt because they cried with pride. They cried to the Lord and He heard them not,[5] no doubt because they were not trying to cut out the faults against which they prayed.

14. A most learned old man spiritually admonished a proud brother, but he in his blindness said: 'Excuse me, Father, I am not proud.' The wise old man said to him: 'What clearer proof of this passion could you have given us, son, than to say, "I am not proud"?'

15. Such people can make good use of submission, a more rigorous and humiliating life, and the reading of the supernatural

feats of the Fathers. Perhaps even then, there will be little hope of salvation for those suffering from this malady.

16. It is shameful to be proud of the adornments of others, but utter madness to fancy one deserves God's gifts. Be exalted only by such merits as you had before your birth. But what you got after your birth, as also birth itself, God gave you. Only those virtues which you have obtained without the co-operation of the mind belong to you, because your mind was given you by God. Only such victories as you have won without the co-operation of the body have been accomplished by your efforts, because the body is not yours but a work of God.

17. Do not be self-confident until you hear the final sentence passed upon yourself, bearing in mind the guest who got as far as joining in the marriage feast and then was bound hand and foot and cast out into the outer darkness.[6]

18. Do not lift up your neck, creature of earth! For many, though holy and spiritual, were cast from heaven.

19. When the demon of pride gets a foothold in his servants, he appears to them either in sleep or in a waking vision, as though in the form of a holy angel or some martyr, and gives them a revelation of mysteries, or a free bestowal of spiritual gifts, so that these unfortunates may be deceived and completely lose their wits.

20. Even if we endure a thousand deaths for Christ, even so we shall not repay all that is due. For the blood of God, and the blood of his servants are quite different, and I am thinking here of the dignity and not of the actual physical substance.

21. We should constantly be examining and comparing ourselves with the holy Fathers and the lights who lived before us, and we should then find that we have not yet entered upon the path of the ascetic life, and have not kept our vow in holy fashion, and in disposition are still living in the world.

22. A monk, properly speaking, is he whose soul's eye does not look haughtily, and whose bodily feeling is unmoved.

23. A monk is he who calls his enemies to combat like wild beasts, and provokes them as they flee from him.

24. A monk experiences unceasing rapture of mind and sorrow of life.

25. A monk is one who is conditioned by virtues as others are by pleasures.

26. A monk possesses unfailing light in the eye of the heart.

27. A monk has an abyss of humility into which he has plunged and suffocated every evil spirit.

28. Forgetfulness of our sins is the result of conceit, for the remembrance of them leads to humility.

29. Pride is utter penury of soul, under the illusion of wealth, imagining light in its darkness. The foul passion not only blocks our advance, but even hurls us down from the heights.

30. The proud man is a pomegranate, rotten inside, while outwardly radiant with beauty.

31. A proud monk has no need of a devil; he has become a devil and enemy to himself.

32. Darkness is foreign to light; and a proud person is foreign to every virtue.

33. In the hearts of the proud, blasphemous words will find birth, but in the souls of the humble, heavenly contemplations.

34. A thief abominates the sun, as a proud man scorns the meek.

35. I do not know how it is, but the proud for the most part remain ignorant of their real selves, and they imagine that they are victorious over their passions, and they only realize their poverty when they depart from this life.

36. The man enmeshed in pride will need the help of God, for the salvation of men cannot avail him.

37. I once caught this mad imposter as it was rising in my heart bearing on its shoulders its mother, vainglory. Roping them with the noose of obedience and thrashing them with the whip of humility, I demanded how they got access to me. At last, when flogged, they said: We have neither beginning nor birth, for we are the originators of all the passions. Contrition of heart that is born of obedience is our real enemy; we cannot bear to be subject to anyone; that is why we fell from heaven, though we had authority there.

In brief, we are the parents of all that opposes humility; for everything which furthers humility opposes us. Our power extends to all short of heaven, so where will you run from our presence? We often accompany patience under dishonour, and obedience and freedom from anger, and lack of resentment, and service of one's neighbour. Our offspring are the sins of spiritual people: anger, calumny, spite, irritability, shouting, blasphemy, hypocrisy, hatred, envy, disputing, self-will, disobedience.

There is only one thing in which we have no power to meddle; and we shall tell you this, for we cannot bear your blows: If you keep up a sincere condemnation of yourself before the Lord you can count us as weak as a cobweb. For pride's saddle-horse, as you see, is vainglory on which I am mounted. But holy humility and self-accusation laugh at both the horse and its rider, happily singing the song of victory: Let us sing to the Lord, for gloriously has He been glorified: horse and rider He has thrown into the sea[7] and into the abyss of humility.

This is the twenty-third step. He who mounts it (if any can mount it) will be strong.

MACARIUS OF EGYPT
Spiritual Homilies

Of unknown authorship, the Spiritual Homilies *were attributed for many centuries to Macarius, a fourth century hermit and desert father who became a spiritual guide for many in a life of almost sixty years (c. 330–390) in the desert of Scete. Although it is now known that Macarius himself did not write these homilies, they are authentic representatives of the great ideals of Egyptian desert monasticism.*

Be attentive to this name of Our Lord, Jesus Christ, in contrition of heart; when your lips are moving, draw it to yourself and do not lead it into your mind only to repeat it, but think of your invocation: "Our Lord Jesus, the Christ, have mercy on me"; then in repose you will see His divinity reposing on you.

Part II Notes

St. Athanasius
1. Gen. 25:27.
2. Matt. 4:20.
3. Acts 4:35.
4. Matt. 19:21.
5. Matt. 6:34.
6. II Thess. 3:10.
7. Matt. 6:7; I Thess. 5:17.

8. I Cor. 15:10.
9. Hosea 4:12.
10. Ps. 118:7.
11. Rom. 8:3–4.
12. Eph. 6:11.
13. I Cor. 9:27.
14. II Cor. 12:10.
15. Phil. 3:14.
16. I Kings 18:15.
17. Rom. 8:38.
18. Ps. 27:3.
19. Ps. 68:1.
20. Ps. 118:10.
21. Rom. 8:32.

Wisdom of the Desert

1. "Lord have mercy on me a sinner." This is the basis for the "Prayer of Jesus," frequently repeated and universally practised in Oriental monasticism.

John Cassian

1. In the year 399.
2. Gen. 1:26.
3. Rom. 1:23; Jer. 2:11.
4. II Cor. 5:16.
5. I Cor. 15:28.
6. John 17:21–6; I John 4:10.
7. Ps. 70:1.
8. Ps. 36:11.
9. Deut. 6:7.
10. Matt. 5:3; Ps. 74:21.
11. Ps. 40:17.
12. Ps. 104:18.
13. Prov. 30:26.

John Climacus

1. St. Luke xviii, 11.
2. James iv, 6.
3. Proverbs xvi, 5.
4. I.e. Lucifer.
5. Psalm xvii, 42.
6. St. Matthew xxii, 13.
7. Exodus xv, 1.

Part III

PATRISTIC DOCTRINES OF SPIRITUALITY

And what is this God? I asked the earth and it answered: "I am not he," and all things that are in the earth made the same confession . . . I said to all the things that throng about the gateways of the senses: "Tell me of my God, since you are not he; tell me something of him." And they cried out in a great voice: "He made us." My question was my gazing upon them, and their answer was their beauty. . . . I asked the whole frame of the universe about my God, and it answered me: "I am not he, but he made me!"

St. Augustine (354-430)

47

ST. GREGORY OF NYSSA

The Life of Moses

One of the three great Cappadocian Fathers of the fourth century (the other two were Gregory's brother St. Basil the Great and their mutual friend St. Gregory Nazianzen), Gregory of Nyssa (c. 335–394) has come to be regarded increasingly as the most brilliant and subtle thinker among them. Many of his works are devoted to spirituality. Normally he develops his ideas by commenting on the "spiritual sense" of scriptural texts. Perhaps his best known works of this type are the Commentary on the Canticle of Canticles *and his* Life of Moses, *from which the following selection is taken.*

A key concept of Gregory's spirituality is the doctrine of progress, epektasis, *according to which all of the spiritual life is a continual growth, a "straining ahead" in the sense of St. Paul: "Forgetting the past, I strain ahead for what is still to come . . ." (Phil. 3:13).* Philosophical not empirical or psychological

In following the course of our exegesis we have allowed ourselves to be drawn into a spiritual interpretation of the text. Let us now return to our main topic. Here we have a man who affirms, according to the inspired word, that he has enjoyed so many visions in which he has seen God clearly, so much so that he describes them as being face to face, as one might talk to a friend. How can a man who has enjoyed this still ask God to show Himself, as though He Who was constantly visible had not yet appeared to him, and as though he had never enjoyed that grace which we believe he did in virtue of the inspired word? The voice from heaven does indeed grant his request, and does not refuse to bless him with this favor. Yet at the same time it leads him once more to despair insofar as it reveals that what he is seeking surpasses human nature. God, however, tells him that there is a place with Him, and in the place a rock, and a *hole of the rock* (Exod. 33.21); and here He wishes Moses to stay. And then the Lord puts His hand over the mouth of the hole, and He calls to Moses as he passes by. At this call, Moses

49

comes out of *the hole of the rock* and sees His *back* (Exod. 33.23); and thus he feels he has seen Him Whom he sought, so that the promise made by the voice of God was not proven false.

Now if we considered this merely in its literal sense, the meaning would remain very difficult for us to discover, and it would give us an idea that is incompatible with the divine nature. For we may not speak of front and back save of things which have dimension. But the dimensions of every body are limited. Hence if you imagine that God has dimension, you cannot avoid giving Him a corporeal nature. Further, all bodies are composites; and composites exist by means of the union of their various parts. Hence a composite cannot be incorruptible. And what is corruptible cannot be eternal, since corruption is simply the separation of the parts of a composite.

If then we were to take this text about God's back literally, we would be logically forced into an absurd conclusion. Front and back are said of dimension; dimension applies only to bodies; and bodies, like all composites, are essentially corruptible. What is corruptible cannot be eternal. Thus if you were completely dependent on the literal meaning, you would be logically forced to admit corruption in God. Yet God is incorporeal and incorruptible.

What meaning then will do justice to the sacred text if we reject the obvious meaning? And if this text which is part of the entire context forces us to seek another interpretation, then surely we must interpret all of it in the same way. For what we understand of a part must necessarily apply to the whole; for every whole is a coalescence of parts. Thus the place with God, the rock in that place, Moses' going to the spot that is called *the hole of the rock*, Moses' entrance, and the placing of the divine hand over the mouth of the hole, the call of Moses, and his vision of God—all this would more suitably be interpreted in an allegorical sense.

What then is the meaning of the passage? All heavy bodies that receive a downward motion, even if they receive no further impulse after the first contact, are rapidly carried downwards of themselves, provided that any surface on which they are moving is graded and sloping, and that they meet no obstacle to interrupt their motion. So too, the soul moves in the opposite direction, light and swiftly moving upwards once it is released from sensuous and earthly attachments, soaring from the world below up towards the heavens. And if nothing comes from above to intercept its flight, seeing that it is of the nature of Goodness to attract those who raise their eyes towards it, the soul keeps rising ever higher and higher, stretching with its desire for heavenly things *to those that are before* (Phil. 3.13), as the Apostle tells us, and thus it will always continue to soar ever higher. For because of what it has already attained, the soul does not wish to abandon the heights that lie beyond it. And thus the soul moves ceaselessly upwards, always reviving its tension for its onward flight by means of the progress it has already realized. Indeed, it is only spiritual activity that nourishes its force by exercise; it does not slacken its tension by action but rather increases it.

This is the reason why we say that the great Moses, moving ever forwards, did not stop in his upward climb. He set no limit to his rise to the stars. But once he had put his foot upon the ladder on which the Lord had leaned (Gen. 28.13), as Jacob tells us, he constantly kept moving to the next step; and he continued to go ever higher because he always found another step that lay beyond the highest one that he had reached.

Moses refused to pose as the son of the Egyptian princess. He became the avenger of the Jews. He moved out to a deserted spot which was untroubled by human existence. He allows a herd of tame animals to find pasture within his soul. He saw the light of the fire. As he moves towards the flame he unburdens himself by removing his sandals. He restored liberty to his family and his race. He saw his enemies sink and drown beneath the waves. He lived out of doors under the cloud; assuaged his thirst at the rock; harvested bread from heaven; then he fought the foreign foe by lifting up his hands; he heard the trumpet sound; he entered into the darkness; he penetrated the secret recesses of that tabernacle not made by human hand; he learnt the secrets of the divine priesthood; he destroyed the idol; he besought God; he restored the Law, smashed because of the sins of the Jews; he shone in glory. And yet, though raised to such heights, he is still restless with desire, is more and more dissatisfied, and still thirsts for that which had filled him to capacity. And just as though he had received nothing, he still begs God to give him more; he asks God to show Himself to him, not now by way of analogy, but as He is in Himself.

What Moses was experiencing, I think, was a longing which filled his soul for the Supreme Good; and this longing was constantly being intensified by his hope in the Transcendent, arising from the beauty which he had already glimpsed; and this hope constantly inflamed his desire to see what was hidden because of all that he had attained at each stage. Thus it is that the ardent lover of beauty, constantly receiving an image, as it were, of what he longs for, wants to be filled with the very impression of the archetype. The bold demand of the soul that climbs the hills of desire tends towards the direct enjoyment of Beauty, and not merely through mirrors or reflections.

In refusing Moses' request, the voice of God in a sense grants it, by pointing out in a few words an infinite abyss of contemplation. For God in his bounty granted that his desire would be fulfilled; but He did not promise that his desire would ever cease or be fully satisfied. Indeed He would not have shown Himself to His servant if the vision would have been such as to terminate Moses' desire; for the true vision of God consists rather in this, that the soul that looks up to God never ceases to desire Him. For this reason He says: *Thou canst not see my face: for man shall not see me and live* (Exod. 34.20). Now this does not mean that the vision could cause the death of those who enjoy it. For how could the face of life ever become the cause of death for those who approach it? Rather, since the divinity by its very nature is life-giving, and since it is characteristic of it to transcend all knowledge, it follows that the man who thinks that God can be known does not really have life; for he has been falsely diverted from true Being to something devised by his own imagination. For the true Being is true Life, and cannot be known by us. If then this life-giving nature transcends knowledge, what our minds attain in this case is surely not life. And that which is not life is naturally incapable of producing life. Thus it is that Moses' desire is filled by the very fact that it remains unfulfilled.

By these words, then, Moses is taught that the divine is by its very nature infinite and cannot be circumscribed by any definite term. For if we think of the divine nature as being limited, we must necessarily think of some reality which is outside of this limit. Everything that is limited is limited by something else. Thus birds are limited by the air, and fishes by the sea. The fish is limited on every side by the water, and the bird in the same way by the air; the term of limitation for the fish consists in the surface of the water that surrounds him, and this is his receptacle; and so too for the bird, the air about it, which is its receptacle. In the same way, if we conceive of God as being limited we must necessarily grant that His nature is received into something else. Now the container is greater than the thing contained, as logical demonstration can show. But everyone agrees that the divine nature is essential Beauty. And that which is different from Beauty must be some-

thing that is not beautiful. Now if, as we have shown, the container must be greater than the thing contained, it follows that those who conceive of God as limited must conceive Him as being received by evil. Granting too that the thing contained is always smaller than the container, it should follow that what is greater is also superior. Hence anyone who imagines that the divine nature is limited makes beauty inferior to its opposite. But this is absurd.

We can conceive then of no limitation in an infinite nature; and that which is limitless cannot by its nature be understood. And so every desire for the Beautiful which draws us on in this ascent is intensified by the soul's very progress towards it. And this is the real meaning of seeing God: never to have this desire satisfied. But fixing our eyes on those things which help us to see, we must ever keep alive in us the desire to see more and more. And so no limit can be set to our progress towards God.

ST. GREGORY THE GREAT

Homily on Ezechiel

In a period of cultural and political decline and chaos, Gregory the Great (elected Pope in 1590) was a bridge between the religious and secular culture of antiquity and the Middle Ages. His Homilies on Ezechiel *(593) are brilliant expressions of his faith in Christ, his understanding of the Church, and his dedication to the contemplative life.*

I know that often when I could not by myself understand something in Sacred Writ, I came to understand it when I was placed in the midst of my brothers.

ST. AUGUSTINE OF HIPPO

Confessions

The greatest and most influential of the Western Fathers, St. Augustine (354–430) treated in his works nearly all aspects of

Christian doctrine and experience. He made a definitive synthesis of Christianity with ancient culture that was to become normative for the entire Middle Ages and in many ways for the Christian Church ever since.

In the realm of spirituality, St. Augustine drew on Neoplatonic philosophy in order to explain the gradual rise of man from the distractions of the material world, in which he finds himself immersed, to union with God. The following text, taken from Book X of his Confessions, *is a classic description of the Neoplatonic approach to spirituality that became the pattern for most Christian contemplatives.*

As the day now approached on which she was to depart this life (which day Thou knewest, we did not), it fell out—Thou, as I believe, by Thy secret ways arranging it—that she and I stood alone, leaning in a certain window, from which the garden of the house we occupied at Ostia could be seen; at which place, removed from the crowd, we were resting ourselves for the voyage, after the fatigues of a long journey. We then were conversing alone very pleasantly; and, "forgetting those things which are behind, and reaching forth unto those things which are before,"[1] we were seeking between ourselves in the presence of the Truth, which Thou art, of what nature the eternal life of the saints would be, which eye hath not seen, nor ear heard, neither hath entered into the heart of man.[2] But yet we opened wide the mouth of our heart, after those supernal streams of Thy fountain, "the fountain of life," which is "with Thee;"[3] that being sprinkled with it according to our capacity, we might in some measure weigh so high a mystery.

And when our conversation had arrived at that point, that the very highest pleasure of the carnal senses, and that in the very brightest material light, seemed by reason of the sweetness of that life not only not worthy of comparison, but not even of mention, we, lifting ourselves with a more ardent affection towards "the Selfsame,"[4] did gradually pass through all corporeal things, and even the heaven itself, whence sun, and moon, and stars shine upon the earth; yea, we soared higher yet by inward musing, and discoursing, and admiring Thy works; and we came to our own minds, and went beyond them, that we might advance as high as that region of unfailing plenty, where Thou feedest Israel[5] for ever with the food of truth, and where life is that Wisdom by whom all these things are made, both which have been, and which are to come; and she is not made, but is as she hath been, and so shall ever be; yea, rather, to "have been," and "to be hereafter," are not in her, but only "to be," seeing she is eternal, for to "have been" and "to be hereafter" are not eternal. And while we were thus speaking, and straining after her, we slightly touched her with the whole effort of our heart; and we sighed, and there left bound "the first-fruits of the Spirit;"[6] and returned to the noise of our own mouth, where the word uttered has both beginning and end. And what is like unto Thy Word, our Lord, who remaineth in Himself without becoming old, and "maketh all things new"?[7]

We were saying, then, If to any man the tumult of the flesh were silenced,—silenced the phantasies of earth, waters, and air,—silenced, too, the poles; yea, the very soul be silenced to herself, and go beyond herself by not thinking of herself,—silenced fancies and imaginary revelations, every tongue, and every sign, and whatsoever exists by passing away, since, if any could hearken, all these say, "We created not ourselves, but were created by Him who abideth for ever:" If, having uttered this, they now should be silenced, having only quickened our ears to Him who created them, and He alone speak not by them, but by Himself, that we may hear His word, not by fleshly tongue, nor angelic voice, nor sound of thunder, nor the obscurity of a similitude, but might hear Him—Him whom in these we love—without these, like as we two now strained ourselves, and with rapid thought touched on that Eternal Wisdom which remaineth over all. If this could be sustained, and other visions of a far different kind be withdrawn, and this one ravish, and absorb, and envelope its beholder amid these inward joys, so that his life might be eternally like that one moment of knowledge which we now sighed after, were not this "Enter thou into the joy of Thy Lord"?[8] And when shall that be? When we shall all rise again; but all shall not be changed.[9]

Such things was I saying; and if not after this manner, and in these words, yet, Lord, Thou knowest, that in that day when we were talking thus, this world with all its delights grew contemptible to us, even while we spake. Then said my mother, "Son, for myself, I have no longer any pleasure in aught in this life. What I want here further, and why I am here, I know not, now that my hopes in this world are satisfied. There was indeed one thing for which I wished to tarry a little in this life, and that was that I might see thee a Catholic Christian before I died. My God has exceeded this abundantly, so that I see thee despising all earthly felicity, made His servant,—what do I here?"

Soliloquies

Augustine: Lo, I have prayed to God.
Reason: Now what do you want to know?

A. All these things which I prayed for.
R. Sum them up briefly.

A. I desire to know God and the soul.
R. Nothing more?

A. Absolutely nothing.

DIONYSIUS THE AREOPAGITE

Mystical Theology   Knowing God -

In the late fifth or early sixth century, an unknown Syrian monk wrote a number of books under the pseudonym of Dionysius the Areopagite, a supposed Greek convert of St. Paul. Because of the profound content of these writings and because of their supposed closeness to the apostolic witness itself, they enjoyed an extraordinary influence on Christian thought and spirituality for well over a thousand years.

The Mystical Theology *of Dionysius became the classic expression of "apophatic mysticism," which stressed that God was totally beyond the power of the human intellect, and that contemplation was a "way of divine darkness" that could never be grasped in any adequate way by the human mind. The work is reproduced here in its entirety.*

CHAPTER I

What is the Divine Gloom

Trinity, which exceedeth all Being, Deity, and Goodness! Thou that instructeth Christians in Thy heavenly wisdom! Guide us to that topmost height of mystic lore which exceedeth light and more

[handwritten top margin: + He is more interested in true concepts than psychological experience or evidence from experience of man — Pre-empirical age Pre-psychology age —]

than exceedeth knowledge, where the simple, absolute, and unchangeable mysteries of heavenly Truth lie hidden in the dazzling
obscurity of the secret Silence, outshining all brilliance with the
intensity of their darkness, and surcharging our blinded intellects
with the utterly impalpable and invisible fairness of glories which
exceed all beauty! Such be my prayer; and thee, dear Timothy, I
counsel that, in the earnest exercise of mystic contemplation, thou
leave the senses and the activities of the intellect and all things
that the senses or the intellect can perceive, and all things in this
world of nothingness, or in that world of being, and that, thine
understanding being laid to rest, thou strain (so far as thou
mayest) towards an union with Him whom neither being nor
understanding can contain. For, by the unceasing and absolute
renunciation of thyself and all things, thou shalt in pureness cast
all things aside, and be released from all, and so shalt be led
upwards to the Ray of that divine Darkness which exceedeth all
existence.

These things thou must not disclose to any of the uninitiated,
by whom I mean those who cling to the objects of human thought,
and imagine there is no super-essential reality beyond, and fancy
that they know by human understanding Him that has made
Darkness His secret place. And, if the Divine Initiation is beyond
such men as these, what can be said of others yet more incapable
thereof, who describe the Transcendent Cause of all things by
qualities drawn from the lowest order of being, while they deny
that it is in any way superior to the various ungodly delusions
which they fondly invent in ignorance of this truth? That while it
possesses all the positive attributes of the universe (being the
universal Cause), yet in a stricter sense It does not possess them,
since It transcends them all, wherefore there is no contradiction
between affirming and denying that It has them inasmuch as It
precedes and surpasses all deprivation, being beyond all positive
and negative distinctions?

Such at least is the teaching of the blessed Bartholomew. 'For
he says that the subject-matter of the Divine Science is vast and yet
minute, and that the Gospel combines in itself both width and
straitness. Methinks he has shown by these his words how marvellously he has understood that the Good Cause of all things is
eloquent yet speaks few words, or rather none; possessing neither
speech nor understanding because it exceedeth all things in a
super-essential manner, and is revealed in Its naked truth to those
alone who pass right through the opposition of fair and foul, and

[handwritten right margin: or still profiting from meditation?]

[handwritten right margin: "those who are finding God in creation —?]

[handwritten right margin: He seems to undervalue this lack of vision but could also be stage of beginners. Takes a philosophic stance instead of process of development stand.]

[handwritten bottom margin: + philosopher not psychologist]

as in St. the purification of memory intellect will is in regard to founts of contemplation.

pass beyond the topmost altitudes of the holy ascent and leave behind them all divine enlightenment and voices and heavenly utterances and plunge into the Darkness where truly dwells, as saith the Scripture, that One Which is beyond all things. For not without reason[2] is the blessed Moses bidden first to undergo purification himself and then to separate himself from those who have not undergone it; and after all purification hears the many-voiced trumpets and sees many lights flash forth with pure and diverse-streaming rays, and then stands separate from the multitudes and with the chosen priests presses forward to the topmost pinnacle of the Divine Ascent. Nevertheless he meets not with God Himself, yet he beholds—not Him indeed (for He is invisible)—but the place wherein He dwells. And this I take to signify that the divinest and the highest of the things perceived by the eyes of the body or the mind are but the symbolic language of things subordinate to Him who Himself transcendeth them all. Through these things His incomprehensible presence is shown walking upon those heights of His holy places which are perceived by the mind; and then It breaks forth, even from the things that are beheld and from those that behold them, and plunges the true initiate unto the Darkness of Unknowing wherein he renounces all the apprehensions of his understanding and is enwrapped in that which is wholly intangible and invisible, belonging wholly to Him that is beyond all things and to none else (whether himself or another), and being through the passive stillness of all his reasoning powers united by his highest faculty to Him that is wholly Unknowable, of whom thus by a rejection of all knowledge he possesses a knowledge that exceeds his understanding.

CHAPTER II

How it is necessary to be united with and render praise
to Him Who is the cause of all and above all.

Unto this Darkness which is beyond Light we pray that we may come, and may attain unto vision through the loss of sight and knowledge, and that in ceasing thus to see or to know we may learn to know that which is beyond all perception and understanding (for this emptying of our faculties is true sight and knowledge), and that we may offer Him that transcends all things the praises of a transcendent hymnody, which we shall do by denying or removing all things that are—like as men who, carving a statue out of marble, remove all the impediments that hinder the clear perceptive of the latent image and by this mere removal display the hidden statue itself in its hidden beauty. Now we must wholly distinguish this negative method from that of positive statements. For when we were making positive statements[3] we began with the most universal statements, and then through intermediate terms we came at last to particular titles, but now ascending upwards from particular to universal conceptions we strip off all qualities in order that we may attain a naked knowledge of that Unknowing which in all existent things is enwrapped by all objects of knowledge, and that we may begin to see that super-essential Darkness which is hidden by all the light that is in existent things.

[margin, handwritten: Here again he speaks as a philosophe (logician) not a psychologist]

CHAPTER III

What are the affirmative expressions respecting God, and what are the negative.

Now I have in my *Outlines of Divinity* set forth those conceptions which are most proper to the affirmative method, and have shown in what sense God's holy nature is called single and in what sense trinal, what is the nature of the Fatherhood and Sonship which we attribute unto It; what is meant by the articles of faith concerning the Spirit; how from the immaterial and indivisible Good the interior rays of Its goodness have their being and remain immovably in that state of rest which both within their Origin and within themselves is co-eternal with the act by which they spring from It; in what manner Jesus being above all essence has stooped to an essential state in which all the truths of human nature meet; and all the other revelations of Scripture whereof my *Outlines of Divinity* treat. And in the book of the *Divine Names* I have considered the meaning as concerning God of the titles Good, Existent, Life, Wisdom, Power and of the other titles which the understanding frames, and in my Symbolic Divinity I have considered what are the metaphorical titles drawn from the world of sense and applied to the nature of God; what are the mental or material images we form of God or the functions and instruments of activity we attribute to Him; what are the places where He dwells and the robes He is adorned with; what is meant by God's anger, grief, and indignation, or the divine inebriation and wrath; what is meant by God's oath and His malediction, by His slumber and awaking, and all the other inspired imagery of allegoric symbolism. And I doubt not that you have also observed how far more copious are the last terms than the first for the doctrines of God's Nature and the

[margin, handwritten: So he obviously is meditating using his inner rational power.]

exposition of His Names could not but be briefer than the Symbolic Divinity.[4] For the more that we soar upwards the more our language becomes restricted to the compass of purely intellectual conceptions, even as in the present instance plunging into the Darkness which is above the intellect we shall find ourselves reduced not merely to brevity of speech but even to absolute dumbness both of speech and thought. Now in the former treatises the course of the argument, as it came down from the highest to the lowest categories, embraced an ever-widening number of conceptions which increased at each stage of the descent, but in the present treatise it mounts upwards from below towards the category of transcendence, and in proportion to its ascent it contracts its terminology, and when the whole ascent is passed it will be totally dumb, being at last wholly united with Him Whom words cannot describe. But why is it, you will ask, that after beginning from the highest category when one method was affirmative we begin from the lowest category where it is negative? Because, when affirming the existence of that which transcends all affirmation, we were obliged to start from that which is most akin to It, and then to make the affirmation on which the rest depended; but when pursuing the negative method, to reach that which is beyond all negation, we must start by applying our negations to those qualities which differ most from the ultimate goal. Surely it is truer to affirm that God is life and goodness than that He is air or stone, and truer to deny that drunkenness or fury can be attributed to Him than to deny that we may apply to Him the categories of human thought.

CHAPTER IV

That He Who is the Pre-eminent Cause of everything sensibly perceived is not Himself any one of the things sensibly perceived.

We therefore maintain that the universal Cause transcending all things is neither impersonal nor lifeless, nor irrational nor without understanding: in short, that It is not a material body, and therefore does not possess outward shape or intelligible form, or quality, or quantity, or solid weight; nor has It any local existence which can be perceived by sight or touch; nor has It the power of perceiving or being perceived; nor does It suffer any vexation or disorder through the disturbance of earthly passions, or any feebleness through the tyranny of material chances, or any want of light; nor any change, or decay, or division, or deprivation, or ebb and flow, or anything else which the senses can perceive. None of these things can be either identified with it or attributed unto It.

CHAPTER V

That He Who is the Pre-eminent Cause of everything intelligibly perceived is not Himself any one of the things intelligibly perceived.

Once more, ascending yet higher we maintain that It is not soul, or mind, or endowed with the faculty of imagination, conjecture, reason, or understanding; nor is It any act of reason or understanding; nor can It be described by the reason or perceived by the understanding, since It is not number, or order, or greatness, or littleness, or equality, or inequality, and since It is not immovable nor in motion, or at rest, and has no power, and is not power or light, and does not live, and is not life; nor is It personal essence, or eternity, or time; nor can It be grasped by the understanding, since It is not knowledge or truth; nor is It kingship or wisdom; nor is It one, nor is It unity, nor is It Godhead[5] or Goodness; nor is It a Spirit, as we understand the term, since It is not Sonship or Fatherhood; nor is It any other thing such as we or any other being can have knowledge of; nor does It belong to the category of non-existence or to that of existence; nor do existent beings know It as it actually is, nor does It know them as they actually are;[6] nor can the reason attain to It to name It or to know It; nor is it darkness, nor is It light, or error, or truth;[7] nor can any affirmation or negation apply to it; for while applying affirmations or negations to those orders of being that come next to It, we apply not unto It either affirmation or negation, inasmuch as It transcends all affirmation by being the perfect and unique Cause of all things, and transcends all negation by the pre-eminence of Its simple and absolute nature—free from every limitation and beyond them all.

Part III Notes

St. Augustine of Hippo

1. Phil. 3:13.
2. I Cor. 2:9; Is. 64:4.

3. Ps. 36:9.
4. Ps. 4:8.
5. Ps. 80:5.
6. Rom. 8:23.
7. Wisdom 7:27.
8. Matt. 25:21.
9. See I Cor. 15:51.

Dionysius the Areopagite

1. No writings of St. Bartholomew are extant. Possibly Dionysius is inventing, but not necessarily.

2. In the following passage we find the three stages tabulated by later mystical theology: purgation, illumination, union.

3. Namely, in the same author's works *The Divine Names* and the *Outlines of Divinity*.

4. The *Symbolical Divinity* was an attempt to spiritualize "popular" theology; the *Divine Names* sought to spiritualize philosophical theology; and the present treatise is a direct essay in Spiritual Theology.

5. Dionysius explains in the *Divine Names* (II, 7) that "Godhead" is the property of deified men, and so belongs to relativity.

6. It knows only Itself, and there knows all things in their Super-Essence—*sub specie aeternitatis*.

7. Truth is an Object of Thought. Therefore, being beyond objectivity, the ultimate Reality is not Truth. But still less is it Error.

Part IV

THE SPIRIT OF
MEDIEVAL MONASTICISM

Write my name, most gentle Jesus, beneath your sweet-sounding name in the book of life. Tell my soul: "You are mine; I your salvation, have acknowledged you; you will no longer be called 'Abandoned' but your name will be 'My will is in her,' so that my heritage may be with you forever in the land of the living."

St. Gertrude of Helfta (1256-1301)

ST. BENEDICT OF NURSIA

Rule

St. Benedict of Nursia (480–547), the great legislator of monasticism in the West, founded several monastic foundations in Italy, of which the most durable was the monastery of Monte Cassino.

Originally written for the monks of this monastery, Benedict's Rule gradually spread in the centuries following his death to nearly all monasteries in Western Europe. By the tenth century it had no significant competitors as a guide for monastic life. The Rule is characterized as a "middle way" between the rigorist asceticism of the Fathers of the Desert and the laxity that Benedict felt was so prevalent among ill-disciplined monks in his day.

Prologue

Son, listen to the precepts of your master; take them to your heart willingly. If you follow the advice of a tender father and travel the hard road of obedience, you will return to God, from whom by disobedience you have gone astray.

I address my discourse to all of you who will renounce your own will, enter the lists under the banner of obedience, and fight under the lead of your lawful sovereign, Christ the Lord.

First, I advise that you should implore the help of God to accomplish every good work you undertake; that he, who has now vouchsafed to rank us in the number of his children, may be no more grieved at our doing amiss. For we ought always to use his grace so faithfully in his service, as to give him no occasion to disinherit his children like an angry parent, or to punish for eternity his servants, like a master incensed at their crimes—servants who have refused to follow him in the way to glory.

Let us then exert ourselves now. The Scripture awakens us, saying: "Now it is the hour to arise from sleep"; and with eyes wide open to the light of heaven, and ears receptive to the word of God, let us hear what his voice repeats to us every day. "Today if you will hear his voice, harden not your hearts." And again, "He who hath ears to hear, let him hear what the Spirit saith unto the churches." What does he say? "Come, my children, hearken unto me and I will teach you the fear of the Lord." "Run while ye have the light of life, that the darkness of death overtake you not."[1]

The Lord, seeking to draw from the crowd one faithful servant, asks: "What man is he that desireth life and would fain see good days?"[2] If you reply: "It is I," God answers: "If you will possess the true and everlasting life, keep your tongue from evil and your lips from speaking guile. Depart from evil and do good: seek peace and pursue it. And when you have done this, then my eyes shall be open upon you, and my ears shall listen to your prayers, and even before you call upon me I will say: 'Behold, I am here.' " Dearest brethren, can we imagine anything more tender than this invitation of our Lord? See, in his goodness, he points out to us the way of life.

Let us then gird up our loins; let us walk by faith and try to serve him with good works; and thereby let us advance in his ways with the Gospel as our guide, that we may deserve to behold him who has called us to his kingdom. If we want to fix our dwelling there, we cannot arrive thereto without running in the ways of virtue. But let us enquire of the Lord with the prophet: "Lord who shall dwell in thy tabernacle, or who shall rest upon thy holy hill?" Brethren, let us hear the Lord's answer to the question, an answer which shows the way to the heavenly tabernacle: "He that walketh without blame and does right: he that speaketh truth in his heart; he that hath kept his tongue from guile, hath done no evil to his neighbour, and hath not believed slander of his neighbour."[3] He who drives the tempter and his temptations far from his heart, defeats his malice, and dashes his rising thoughts against the Rock Christ. He who fears the Lord without growing proud of his virtue and humbly acknowledges that what is good in him does not proceed from himself. He who gives God his due, and with the prophet blesses the work of God in himself: "Not unto us, O Lord, not unto us, but unto thy name give the glory." The apostle Paul found nothing of his own to boast of in his preaching: "By the grace of God (says he) I am what I am," and again, "He that glories, let him glory in the Lord." On this account our Lord in the Gospel tells us: "He that heareth these words of mine and doeth them, I will make him like the wise man who hath built his house upon a rock. The floods came and the winds blew, and they beat upon that house, and it fell not, for it was founded upon a rock."[4]

Our Lord expects that our works should ever correspond with these declarations of Scripture. Therefore, in consideration of the evils which we have to redress, he has given us the days of our life, and prolongs them to afford us an opportunity of making peace with him. "Dost thou not know," says the Apostle, "that the patience of God inviteth thee to repentance?" For our tender Lord assures us: "I will not the death of a sinner, but that he should be converted and live."[5]

When we enquired of the Lord about the person who should dwell in his tabernacle, we were informed what conditions were necessary for it; and it is now ours to perform those conditions.[6] Therefore our hearts and bodies are to be prepared to fight under his command; and we must beseech God to supply with his grace what it is impossible for nature to effect alone. Moreover, if we desire to avoid the pains of hell, and to compass eternal life, we must, while we have time in the body and ability to use the opportunity of a religious life, make haste and practise now the virtues which will serve us for all eternity.

To conclude: I am to erect a school for beginners in the service of the Lord: which I hope to establish on laws not too difficult or grievous. But if, for reasonable cause, for the retrenchment of vice or preservation of charity, I require some things which may seem too austere, you are not thereupon to be frightened from the ways of salvation. Those ways are always strait and narrow at the beginning. But as we advance in the practices of religion and in faith, the heart insensibly opens and enlarges through the wonderful sweetness of his love, and we run in the way of God's commandments. If then we keep close to our school and the doctrine we learn in it, and persevere in the monastery till death, we shall here share by patience in the passion of Christ and hereafter deserve to be united with him in his kingdom. Amen.

1. *Of the several sorts of monks*

It is well-known that there are four sorts of monks.

The first is of coenobites, who dwell in convents under the direction of a rule and an abbot.

The second is of anchorites, or hermits. These are not men who have hurried away into solitary cells with the indiscreet zeal of beginners, but have served a mature probation in monasteries, and there learnt by the example and help of their fellow-monks how to fight the devil; and thereafter are sufficiently appointed, without any other help than that of God, to enter the wilderness and fight a single combat against the sins of the flesh and the ill thoughts of the mind.

The third kind of monks, a pernicious kind, is that of the Sarabaites. These, without any probation of rule or experience (which test men as a furnace tests gold), live up to the practice of the world. Like lead in a furnace, they live softly and pliably: and by their very tonsure they are reproached of their infidelity to God. They dwell two or three together, or one alone; shepherdless, in no other fold but that of their own will, have no other law but what is agreeable and pleasing; they measure the proportion of holiness by their own choice and ideas, and call unlawful what they dislike.

The last sort is of those called Gyrovagi or Wanderers, whose whole life is a ramble from province to province, staying three or four days in each place; ever in motion and never settled, slaves to their pleasures, mere epicures, worse even than the Sarabaites.

The wretched ways of all these are fitter to be buried in oblivion than to be the subject of our discourse, and I pass them over. My aim is with God's help to give rules to the most vigorous kind, that of the Coenobites.

2. *What qualifications are required for an abbot?*

An abbot qualified to govern a monastery, ought always to remember the name he bears, and to maintain by his good life the title of superior: for he is esteemed to supply the place of Christ in the monastery, being called by his name; according to the apostle: "Ye have received the spirit of the adoption of sons, whereby we cry Abba, Father";[7] and therefore the abbot ought not to teach, establish, or command anything contrary to the law of the Lord, but so to deliver his ordinances and teaching that they may work on the minds of his disciples like a leaven or seasoning of divine justice.

Let the abbot always remember that at the dreadful day of judgement he is accountable for the obedience of his disciples as for his own teaching. He is to remember that whatever the Father of the family finds ill in the flock, shall lie at the shepherd's door. He shall not be declared guiltless in the Lord's judgement unless he has taken all the pains he can for a disobedient and turbulent flock. If he has used his utmost care to cut out their sins, he may say to the Lord with the prophet: "I have not hid thy justice within my heart: I have declared thy truth and thy salvation: but they have despised and rejected me."[8] And eternal death shall be the punishment of them that have been disobedient to his care.

When anyone takes upon him the office of abbot, he is to instruct his disciples in two ways. That is: he is to lay before them what is good and holy, more by example than by words: to teach the law of the Lord by word of mouth to such as are of a quicker comprehension, and by example to those of harder hearts and meaner capacities. He ought to create by his conduct an aversion from the thing which he condemns in his discourse; then he will not himself prove a castaway while he preaches to others, and will avoid God's reproach: "Wherefore dost thou declare my righteousness and take my testament into thy mouth? For thou hatest discipline, yea and hast rejected my exhortation"; and, "thou hast seen a mote in thy brother's eye, and hast not seen the beam in thine own."[9]

He is not to be partial, or to love one more than another, unless upon consideration of greater virtue or obedience. He is not to prefer the freeborn monk above the slave, except some other reasonable cause intervene. In such case it is allowable that the abbot should dispose of persons as he judges expedient and fair. Otherwise everyone is to keep his proper place; because, whether slaves or freeborn, we are all one in Christ, and we have all enlisted in the same service under one common Lord who is no respecter of persons. The only reason why God puts one man above another is because the one lives a better life and is humble. Therefore the abbot's charity must extend equally to all, and his discipline be impartial, to each according to his merits.

In his teaching the abbot is ever to observe this rule of the apostle: "Reprove, beseech, correct":[10] which consists in a judicious timing: to mix gentleness with sternness: at one time to show the severity of a master, at another the tenderness of a father: to use rigour with the irregular and the turbulent, but win to better things the obedient, mild, and patient. I warn him to reprove and chastise the careless or contemptuous.

Nor is he to dissemble the faults of those that go amiss, but to do his utmost to root them out as they begin to grow; always mindful of the danger of Eli the priest of Shiloh. Those who are of nobler character and are more capable of understanding, he is to admonish twice. But mere profligates, stubborn, proud, or disobedient, the moment they begin to do amiss, must be reclaimed by the rod. The abbot must know what is written: "The fool is not corrected by words": and, "strike thy son with the rod, and thou shalt deliver his soul from death."[11]

The abbot ought ever to remember what he is and what is meant by the name he bears, and to know that more is required of him to whose charge more is committed. Let him reflect how difficult and perplexing a business he undertakes, at once to gov-

ern many souls and to be subject to as many humours to suit
himself to everyone with regard to their capacity and condition; to
win some by fair means, others by reprimands, others by dint of
reason: that he may not suffer damage to his flock, but rather
rejoice at the increase and improvement of it.

Above all, he is not to dissemble or undervalue the care of souls
committed to his charge, for the sake of temporal concerns, which
are earthly, transitory, and fleeting; but ever to reflect that the
government of souls is his business, and that he is accountable for
them. And if perhaps the monastery have too little money, he is not
to be disturbed thereat; but to remember how it is written: "Seek ye
first the kingdom of God and his righteousness, and all these things
shall be added unto you"; and again, "Nothing is wanting to them
that fear him."[12]

Let him further reflect that he has undertaken the care of
souls, and is to prepare his accounts: let him be sure that at the day
of judgement he will be answerable for as many souls as he has
brothers, as well as for his own. If he is ever in dread of the severe
examination which he is to undergo for the sheep committed to
him, he will be as careful about himself as he is about his charges:
and so he will together cure the sins of others by his government,
and amend the faults in his own life.

3. *The manner of assembling the community in council*

Whenever any matter of moment is to be debated in the
monastery, the abbot is to assemble the whole community, and to
lay open the business before them: and after having heard their
opinions, and maturely debated with himself, he may resolve on
what he judges most profitable.

We have for this reason ordained that the whole community
shall be assembled, because God often reveals what is best to the
young. The brothers shall give their opinion with humility and
submission, and not maintain their judgement with vehemence,
but leave all to the disposal of the abbot, and jointly assent to what
he decides fit. Yet, as it is the duty of the disciple to obey his master,
so it is no less the part of the master to decide according to the rules
of equity and prudence.

All are to observe the Rule as their guide, and no one is rashly
to deviate from it. No one in the monastery is to be biased by his
self-will, nor may anyone argue with his abbot with heat when at
home, or at all when abroad. If he does, he shall be liable to regular
chastisement. Nevertheless the abbot himself is to act in every-

thing with a regard to the Rule and in fear of God; knowing that in all his proceedings he is to give an account before the truly impartial Judge.

If any matter of lesser consequence is to be decided for the advantage of the house, he is only to consult the elders: according as it is written: "Do thou nothing without counsel, and thou shalt not repent when thou hast done."[13]

4. *Of the instruments of good works*

First, to love the Lord God with all the heart, with all the soul, and
    with all the strength.
Next, to love the neighbour as oneself.
Next, not to kill.
Not to commit adultery.
Not to steal.
Not to covet.
Not to bear false witness.
To honour all men.
Not to do to another what we would not have done to ourselves.
To renounce oneself, in order to follow Christ.
To chastise the body.
Not to seek after pleasure.
To love fasting.
To relieve the poor.
To clothe the naked.
To visit the sick.
To bury the dead.
To help those that are in trouble.
To comfort the afflicted.
To eschew the ways of the world.
To prefer nothing before the love of Christ.
Not to give way to anger.
Not to lay up revenge.
Not to cover deceit in the heart.
Not to make a pretended peace.
Not to forsake charity.
Not to swear, for fear of being perjured.
To speak truth from the heart as well as the mouth.
Not to return evil for evil.
Not to do an injury: but to bear one with patience.
To love our enemies.
Not to return curse for curse, but rather a blessing for it.

To suffer persecution for righteousness' sake.

Not to be proud.

Not given to wine.

Not given to too much eating.

Not to sleepiness.

Not to laziness.

Not to complaining.

Not to detraction.

To repose all trust in God.

To attribute all the good we have in us God, and not to ourselves.

To acknowledge all evil to be our own, and to impute it to ourselves.

To fear the day of judgement.

To dread hell.

To long in the spirit for eternal life.

To keep death every day before our eyes.

To keep a continual watch over our actions.

To be convinced that God sees us wherever we are.

To dash evil thoughts, as soon as they arise in the heart, against
the Rock Christ; and to discover them to our spiritual father.

To preserve the tongue from evil and wicked talk.

Not to love much talk.

Not to love vain talk, or such as occasions laughter.

Not to love much or raucous laughter.

To listen willingly to the reading of holy books.

To use frequent prayer.

To confess to God every day in prayer, with tears and sighs, our
past offences.

To amend those sins for the future.

Not to accomplish the desires of the flesh.

To hate our own will.

In all things to obey the abbot's command, although (which God
forbid) he act contrary himself: being mindful of the precept of
the Lord which bids us: "Do what they say, not what they do."[14]

Not to want to be called a saint before we are, but first to be so, that
it may be said of us with greater truth.

Every day to live up to the commandments of God.

To love chastity.

To hate nobody.

Not to be addicted to jealousy.

Not to be envious.

Not to love contention.

To avoid ambition.

To venerate the elders.

To love the younger.

To pray for our enemies, for the love of Christ.

To be reconciled to those who have quarrelled with us, before the sun go down.

And never to despair of God's mercy.

These are the instruments of spiritual progress. If day and night we employ them, and at the day of judgement commend them into the hands of God, we shall be crowned with the reward he has promised "which neither eye hath seen nor ear hath heard, nor hath it entered into the heart of man what things God hath prepared for them that love him."[15]

The best place to practise these things is the monastery with its seclusion—provided that we remain steadily in the community and do not leave it.

5. *Of obedience*

The first degree of humility is a prompt and ready obedience. This is fitting for them who love Christ above all else. By reason of the holy duty they have undertaken, or for fear of hell, or for eternal glory, they make no more delay to comply, the very instant anything is appointed them, than if God himself had given the command. Of these the Lord said: "At the very sound of my voice he hath obeyed me." And again he declared to them that teach: "He that heareth you, heareth me."[16]

They who are of this temper abandon all, even to their very will; instantly clear their hands and leave unfinished what they had begun; so that the command is carried out in the moment it is uttered. Master and disciple are lent wings by the fear of God and the longing for eternal life, and so the command is obeyed in a flash.

It is for the sake of obedience that they enter into the narrow way of which the Lord said: "Narrow is the way that leadeth unto life."[17] The "narrowness" of the way is opposite to the broad way suggested by self-will and desire and pleasure: and they follow it by delighting to dwell in a community, to be subject to their abbot, and to follow the judgement of another. Such men live up to the practice of our Lord, who tells us: "I came not to do mine own will, but the will of him that sent me."[18]

This obedience will be pleasing to God and man, when it is performed with no fear, no delay, no coldness, no complaint, no reply. The obedience we pay to superiors is paid to God: for he tells us: "He that heareth you, heareth me." And it is to be done with willing heart, "because God loveth a cheerful giver."[19] When the disciple obeys unwillingly, with a grudge in heart or mouth, though he does the thing, yet he is so far from being pleasing to God, who sees reluctance in the heart, that he acquires no merit, but only incurs the penalty of those that murmur, till he has made a due atonement.

6. *Of silence*

Let us do as the prophet says: "I said, I will take heed unto my ways, that I offend not with my tongue. I have set a guard upon my mouth. I held my tongue, and was humbled, and kept silence from good words."[20] Here the prophet shows that if, for the sake of silence, we ought sometimes not to speak what is good; much more are we obliged to avoid all evil talk, for fear of the punishment due to sin. Therefore, frequent leave to talk is not to be granted to those who are advanced in perfection, although the subject be good and holy and edifying. Because it is written: "In much talk you shall not avoid sin"; and elsewhere, "Life and death are in the power of the tongue."[21] It belongs to the master to speak and teach, it is the duty of the disciple to hear and obey.

And therefore, if anything is to be asked from the superior, it must be with humility and submission. As for scurrility, idle jests or silly talk, I order that they be never heard in the monastery.

7. *Of humility*

Brethren, the Scripture asserts that "everyone that exalteth himself shall be humbled, and he that humbleth himself shall be exalted." It shows us thereby that all exaltation is in some measure the pride which the prophet tells us he took care to shun: "O Lord, my heart is not exalted, nor mine eyes lifted up: I have not aspired to great things, nor wonders above myself." And his reason for it is: because (says he): "If I had not thought humbly of myself but had exalted my soul, thou wouldst have driven away my soul like an infant weaned from the breast of its mother."[22]

Therefore, brethren, if we want to attain true humility, and come quickly to the top of that heavenly ascent to which we can only mount by lowliness in this present life, we must ascend by good works, and erect the mystical ladder of Jacob, where angels ascending and descending appeared to him. That ascent and descent means that we go downward when we exalt ourselves, and rise when we are humbled. The ladder represents our life in this world, which our Lord erects to heaven when our heart is humbled. And the sides of the ladder represent our soul and body, sides between which God has placed several rungs of humility and discipline, whereby we are to ascend if we would answer his call.

The first degree, then, of humility is, to have the fear of God ever before our eyes: never to forget what is his due, and always to remember his commands: to revolve in the mind how hell burns those who have contemned God, and how God has prepared eternal life for them that fear him: to preserve ourselves from the sins and vices of thought, of the tongue, the eyes, hands, feet, self-will and fleshly desires. Man ought to think that God always looks down from heaven upon him, and that all he does lies open to his sight, is daily told him by the angels. The prophet shows this truth, when he describes God as present in our thoughts, "searching the heart and reins"; and, "Our Lord knows the thoughts of men"; and, again, "Thou hast understood my thoughts a great way off": and, "The thought of man shall confess to thee." That he may ever watch the perverseness of his thoughts, let the right-minded brother continually repeat in the language of his heart: "Then I shall be without blemish before him, if I keep myself from mine iniquity."[23]

As for our own will, we are forbidden to pursue it by these words of the Scripture: "Turn away from thine own will": and we are required to ask of God in prayer, that his will may be done in us. We have reason to be convinced that we ought not to be guided by our own will, when we take account of what the Scripture tells us: "There are ways which to men appear to be right, whose endings nevertheless plunge us into the very depth of hell." And again, when we reflect fearfully upon the character given to the negligent: "They are corrupt and become abominable in their own pleasures."

As regards our sensual desires, we must remember that God is ever present; as the prophet says to the Lord: "All my desire lies open before thee."[24] So unlawful desires are to be carefully avoided, because death lurks behind the door at the very entrance to pleasure: whence the Scripture forbids us to "pursue our lusts."[25]

If then the eyes of the Lord observe both the good and the wicked, and God looks down from heaven upon the sons of men, to see if there be any that understand or seek after God; and again, if night and day our guardian angels give an account of what we do to the Lord; we must, every moment, be on our guard, lest God, at any time, should surprise us, as the Psalmist terms it, "leaning towards evil and rendered unprofitable"; and sparing us in this life (because he is good and waits for our becoming better) should reproach us in the next: "These things didst thou do, and I kept silence."[26]

The second degree of humility is, if anyone, not wedded to his own will, finds no pleasure in the compassing of his desires; but fulfils with his practice the word of our Lord: "I came not to do mine own will, but the will of him that sent me." The Scripture also says: "Pleasure hath its penalty, but need winneth a crown."[27]

The third degree of humility is, when anyone submits himself with obedience to his superior for the sake of the love of God, after the example of the Lord, of whom the apostle says: "He was made obedient even unto death."

The fourth degree of humility is, when anyone, in the practice of obedience, meets with hardships, contradictions, or affronts, and yet bears them all with a quiet conscience and with patience, and continues to persevere. The Scripture says: "He who perseveres to the end, the same shall be saved," and again: "Let your heart be strengthened, and wait for our Lord." And to show that the faithful servant ought to suffer every trial for God, the Scripture speaks in the person of those that suffer: "For thy sake we are killed all the day long: we are accounted as sheep for the slaughter." And afterwards, in full assurance of their reward, they say with happiness, "But in all these things we are conquerors through him that loved us." In another place the Scripture tells us: "Thou, O God, hast proved us: thou hast tried us with fire, as silver is tried. Thou hast led us into the snare, and loaded us with afflictions." And to show that we ought to live under a superior, it goes on, "Thou hast set men over our heads."[28]

So these sufferers live up to the command of God, bearing injuries and adversity with patience. But more: Struck on one cheek they offer the other. They give away their coat to him that takes away their cloak. Forced to walk one mile, they go two. They bear with false brethren, like Paul the apostle. They bless them that curse them.

The fifth degree of humility is, humbly to confess to the abbot every unlawful thought as it arises in the heart, and the hidden sins we have committed. The Scripture advises this, saying: "Reveal your way to God and hope in him": and again: "Confess to God because he is good: for his mercy endureth for ever."[29] And in the prophet: "I have made known my sin to thee, and have not covered my iniquities. I have said, I will declare to God my own iniquities against myself: and thou hast forgiven the wickedness of my heart."[30]

The sixth degree of humility is, if a monk be content with anything though never so vile and contemptible; and to think himself inadequate, and unworthy to succeed in whatever he is commanded to do; saying with the prophet: "I was brought to nothing and knew nothing. I am become like a brute beast before thee, yet I am always with thee."[31]

The seventh degree of humility is, when one does not merely call oneself the least and most abject of all mankind, but believes it, with sincerity of heart: humbling oneself and saying with the prophet: "I am a worm and no man: a scorn of men, and the outcast of the people." "I have been exalted, humbled, and confounded." And again: "It is good for me that thou hast humbled me, that I may learn to keep thy commandments."[32]

The eighth degree of humility is, when a monk does nothing but what is countenanced by the constitutions of the monastery, or the example of the elders.

The ninth degree of humility is, when a monk controls his tongue and keeps silence till a question be asked. For the Scripture teaches that "in much talk you will not avoid sinning"; and "the talkative man shall live out his life haphazardly."[33]

The tenth degree of humility is, not easily to lay hold on occasions of laughing. For it is written: "He who laughs loud is a fool."[34]

The eleventh degree of humility is, when a monk discourses with moderation and composure, mixing humility with gravity; speaking few words, but home, and to the purpose; not raising the voice. "The wise man is known because he speaks little."[35]

The twelfth degree of humility is, when the monk's inward humility appears outwardly in his comportment. And wherever he be, in the divine office, in the oratory, in the monastery, in the garden, on a journey, in the fields—wherever he is sitting, walking or standing, he is to look down with bowed head conscious of his guilt, imagining himself ready to be called to give account at the dread judgement: repeating in his heart what the publican in the Gospel said with eyes downcast: "Lord, I am not worthy, sinner that I am, to lift up my eyes to heaven"; and with the prophet "I am bowed down and humbled on every side."[36]

After he has climbed all these degrees of humility, the monk will quickly arrive at the top, the charity that is perfect and casts out all fear. And then, the virtues which first he practised with anxiety, shall begin to be easy for him, almost natural, being grown habitual. He will no more be afraid of hell, but will advance by the love of Christ, by good habits, and by taking pleasure in goodness. Our Lord, by the Holy Spirit, will deign to show this in the servant who has been cleansed from sin.

ST. SYMEON THE NEW THEOLOGIAN
Practical and Theological Precepts

Educated in Constantinople by his uncle, a courtier, Symeon (949–1022) became a monk and eventually an abbot and founder of a monastery near the capital of the Byzantine Empire. Frequently persecuted and vilified for his ideas and for the strictness of his teaching, Symeon left behind a rich and varied collection of writings on the spiritual life, noted for the intensity of spiritual experience which they express.

He who stands in the sea up to his knees or waist sees quite well what is outside the water; but when he plunges into the depths and is wholly covered by water, he can no longer see anything outside and he only perceives that he is wholly in the depths of the sea. That is what happens to those who advance in the spiritual way and enter the perfection of spiritual knowledge and contemplation.

ST. ANSELM
Proslogium

St. Anselm (1033–1109) is a transitional figure between patristic theology and the great scholastic writers of the high Middle Ages. A monk at the famous Norman monastery of Bec, Anselm was named its abbot in 1078. Appointed Archbishop of Canterbury in 1093, Anselm engaged in numerous struggles with the Norman rulers as they attempted to bring England fully under their control.

Despite his accomplishments in ecclesiastical administration, Anselm is best remembered for his philosophical and theological works. In his time theology, philosophy, and prayer were still intertwined in a single Christian synthesis. This synthesis is mirrored in his Proslogium, *a work principally devoted to philosophical proofs for the existence of God, but grounded (as the following selection shows) in a more than intellectual thirst for the knowledge of the divine.*

CHAPTER I

Up now, slight man! flee, for a little while, thy occupations; hide thyself, for a time, from thy disturbing thoughts. Cast aside, now, thy burdensome cares, and put away thy toilsome business. Yield room for some little time to God; and rest for a little time in him. Enter the inner chamber of thy mind; shut out all thoughts save that of God, and such as can aid thee in seeking him; close thy door and seek him. Speak now, my whole heart! speak now to God, saying, I seek thy face; thy face, Lord, will I seek (Psalms xxvii. 8). And come thou now, O Lord my God, teach my heart where and how it may seek thee, where and how it may find thee.

Lord, if thou art not here, where shall I seek thee, being absent? But if thou art everywhere, why do I not see thee present? Truly thou dwellest in unapproachable light. But where is unapproachable light, or how shall I come to it? Or who shall lead me to that light and into it, that I may see thee in it? Again, by what marks, under what form, shall I seek thee? I have never seen thee, O Lord, my God; I do not know thy form. What, O most high Lord, shall this man do, an exile far from thee? What shall thy servant do, anxious in his love of thee, and cast out afar from thy face? He pants to see thee, and thy face is too far from him. He longs to come to thee, and thy dwelling-place is inaccessible. He is eager to find thee, and knows not thy place. He desires to seek thee, and does not know thy face. Lord, thou art my God, and thou art my Lord, and never have I seen thee. It is thou that hast made me, and hast made me anew, and hast bestowed upon me all the blessings I enjoy; and not yet do I know thee. Finally, I was created to see thee, and not yet have I done that for which I was made.

O wretched lot of man, when he hath lost that for which he was made! O hard and terrible fate! Alas, what has he lost, and what has he found? What has departed, and what remains? He has lost the blessedness for which he was made, and has found the misery for which he was not made. That has departed without which nothing is happy, and that remains which, in itself, is only miserable. Man once did eat the bread of angels, for which he hungers now; he eateth now the bread of sorrows, of which he knew not then. Alas! for the mourning of all mankind, for the universal lamentation of the sons of Hades! He choked with satiety, we sigh with hunger. He abounded, we beg. He possessed in happiness, and miserably forsook his possession; we suffer want in unhappiness, and feel a miserable longing, and alas! we remain empty.

Why did he not keep for us, when he could so easily, that whose lack we should feel so heavily? Why did he shut us away from the light, and cover us over with darkness? With what purpose did he rob us of life, and inflict death upon us? Wretches that we are, whence have we been driven out; whither are we driven on? Whence hurled? Whither consigned to ruin? From a native country into exile, from the vision of God into our present blindness, from the joy of immortality into the bitterness and horror of death. Miserable exchange of how great a good, for how great an evil! Heavy loss, heavy grief-heavy all our fate!

But alas! wretched that I am, one of the sons of Eve, far removed from God! What have I undertaken? What have I accomplished? Whither was I striving? How far have I come? To what did I aspire? Amid what thoughts am I sighing? I sought blessings, and lo! confusion. I strove toward God, and I stumbled on myself. I sought calm in privacy, and I found tribulation and grief, in my inmost thoughts. I wished to smile in the joy of my mind, and I am compelled to frown by the sorrow of my heart. Gladness was hoped for, and lo! a source of frequent sighs!

And thou too, O Lord, how long? How long, O Lord, dost thou forget us; how long dost thou turn thy face from us? When wilt thou look upon us, and hear us? When wilt thou enlighten our eyes, and show us thy face? When wilt thou restore thyself to us? Look upon us, Lord; hear us, enlighten us, reveal thyself to us. Restore thyself to us, that it may be well with us,—thyself, without whom it is so ill with us. Pity our toilings and strivings toward thee, since we can do nothing without thee. Thou dost invite us; do thou help us. I beseech thee, O Lord, that I may not lose hope in sighs, but may breathe anew in hope. Lord, my heart is made bitter by its desolation; sweeten thou it, I beseech thee, with thy consolation. Lord, in hunger I began to seek thee; I beseech thee that I may not cease to hunger for thee. In hunger I have come to thee; let me not go unfed. I have come in poverty to the Rich, in misery to the Compassionate; let me not return empty and despised. And if, before I eat, I sigh, grant, even after sighs, that which I may eat. Lord, I am bowed down and can only look downward; raise me up that I may look upward. My iniquities have gone over my head; they overwhelm me; and, like a heavy load, they weigh me down. Free me from them; unburden me, that the pit of iniquities may not close over me.

Be it mine to look up to thy light, even from afar, even from the depths. Teach me to seek thee, and reveal thyself to me, when I seek thee, for I cannot seek thee, except thou teach me, nor find thee, except thou reveal thyself. Let me seek thee in longing, let me long for thee in seeking; let me find thee in love, and love thee in finding. Lord, I acknowledge and I thank thee that thou hast created me in this thine image, in order that I may be mindful of thee, may conceive of thee, and love thee; but that image has been so consumed and wasted away by vices, and obscured by the smoke of wrong-doing, that it cannot achieve that for which it was made, except thou renew it, and create it anew. I do not endeavor, O Lord, to penetrate thy sublimity, for in no wise do I compare my understanding with that; but I long to understand in some degree thy truth, which my heart believes and loves. For I do not seek to understand that I may believe, but I believe in order to understand. For this also I believe,—that unless I believed, I should not understand.

MECHTILD OF MAGDEBURG

The Flowing Light of the Godhead

From childhood on, Mechtild (c.1210–1285) was favored with powerful mystic experiences. In 1230 she became a Beguine at Magdeburg in Germany. She remained there for forty years, under the direction of Dominican friars, until old age and hostility forced her into retirement in the convent of Helfta, where St. Gertrude was a younger contemporary. The results of her mystical experiences are summarized in The Flowing Light of the Godhead, *in the form of a dialogue between Mechtild and Christ.*

Lord! Now am I a naked soul and thou a God most glorious! Our twofold intercourse is love eternal which can never die. Now comes a blessed stillness welcome to both. He gives himself to her and she to him. What shall now befall her, the soul knows: therefore am I comforted. Where two lovers come secretly together, they must often part, without parting.

ST. BERNARD OF CLAIRVAUX

On Loving God

St. Bernard of Clairvaux (1090–1153) was undoubtedly the most influential single figure in the twelfth century of Western Christianity. Under his influence, the return to primitive Benedictinism instituted by Robert of Molesmes and his companions at Citeaux spread with amazing rapidity throughout Europe. The writings of Bernard ushered in the golden age of medieval spirituality. His own viewpoint is characterized by the primacy of love, by an emphasis on the ecstacy of the soul transformed into the likeness of God, and by the importance of humility and obedience. Because of Bernard's extensive involvement in the Church politics of his time, his writings quickly took on a renown throughout Western Christianity and continued to exert an influence for many centuries. The following selections are taken from his treatise De Diligendo Deo *(On Loving God).*

You wish me to tell you why and how God should be loved. My answer is that God himself is the reason why he is to be loved. As for how he is to be loved, there is to be no limit to that love. Is this sufficient answer? Perhaps, but only for a wise man. As I am indebted, however, to the unwise also, it is customary to add something for them after saying enough for the wise. Therefore for the sake of those who are slow to grasp ideas I do not find it burdensome to treat of the same ideas more extensively if not more profoundly. Hence I insist that there are two reasons why God should be loved for his own sake: no one can be loved more righteously and no one can be loved with greater benefit. Indeed, when it is asked why God should be loved, there are two meanings

possible to the question. For it can be questioned which is rather
the question: whether for what merit of his or for what advantage
to us is God to be loved. My answer to both questions is assuredly
the same, for I can see no other reason for loving him than himself.
So let us see first how he deserves our love.

HOW GOD IS TO BE LOVED FOR HIS OWN SAKE

God certainly deserves a lot from us since he gave himself[1] to
us when we deserved it least. Besides, what could he have given us
better than himself? Hence when seeking why God should be loved,
if one asks what right he has to be loved, the answer is that the
main reason for loving him is "He loved us first."[2] Surely he is
worthy of being loved in return when one thinks of who loves,
whom he loves, how much he loves. Is it not he whom every spirit
acknowledges,[3] saying: "You are my God, for you do not need my
possessions."[4] This divine love is sincere, for it is the love of one
who does not seek his own advantage.[5] To whom is such love
shown? It is written: "While we were still his enemies, he reconciled us to himself."[6] Thus God loved freely, and even enemies.
How much did he love? St John answers that: "God so loved the
world that he gave his only-begotten Son."[7] St Paul adds: "He did
not spare his only Son, but delivered him up for us."[8] The Son also
said of himself: "No one has greater love than he who lays down his
life for his friends."[9] Thus the righteous one deserved to be loved by
the wicked, the highest and omnipotent by the weak. Now someone says: "This is true for man but it does not hold for the angels."
That is true because it was not necessary for the angels, for he who
came to man's help in time of need, kept the angels from such a
need, and he who did not leave man in such a state because he loved
him, out of an equal love gave the angels the grace not to fall into
that state.

II. I think that they to whom this is clear see why God ought to be
loved, that is, why he merits to be loved. If the infidels conceal these
facts, God is always able to confound their ingratitude by his
innumerable gifts which he manifestly places at man's disposal.
For, who else gives food to all who eat, sight to all who see, and air
to all who breathe? It would be foolish to want to enumerate; what I
have just said cannot be counted. It suffices to point out the chief
ones: bread, sun and air. I call them the chief gifts, not because they
are better but because the body cannot live without them. Man's
nobler gifts—dignity, knowledge, and virtue—are found in the

higher part of his being, in his soul. Man's dignity is his free will by which he is superior to the beasts and even dominates them. His knowledge is that by which he acknowledges that this dignity is in him but that it is not of his own making. Virtue is that by which man seeks continuously and eagerly for his Maker and when he finds him, adheres to him with all his might.

Each of these three gifts has two aspects. Dignity is not only a natural privilege, it is also a power of domination, for the fear of man hangs over all the animals on earth. Knowledge is also twofold, since we understand this dignity and other natural qualities are in us, yet we do not create them ourselves. Finally, virtue is seen to be twofold, for by it we seek our Maker and once we find him, we adhere to him so closely we become inseparable from him. As a result, dignity without knowledge is unprofitable, without virtue it can be an obstacle. The following reasoning explains both these facts. What glory is there in having something you do not know you have? Then, to know what you have but to be ignorant of the fact that you do not have it of yourself, for glory here, but not before God.[10] The Apostle says to him who glorifies himself: "What have you that you have not received? And if you have received it, how can you boast of it as if you had not received it?"[11] He does not say simply: "How can you boast of it," but adds: "as if you had not received it," to show the guilt lies not in boasting of something but in treating it as if it was not a gift received. This is rightly called vainglory, for it lacks the solid base of truth. St Paul marks the difference between true and vain glory: "He who boasts, let him boast in the Lord,"[12] that is, in the truth, for the Lord is truth.[13]

There are two facts you should know: first what you are; secondly, that you are not that by your own power, lest you fail to boast at all or do so in vain. Finally, if you do not know yourself, do as is written: "Go follow the flocks of your companions."[14] This is really what happens. When a man, promoted to a high dignity, does not appreciate the favor received, because of his ignorance he is rightly compared to the animals with whom he shares his present state of corruption and mortality.[15] It also happens when a man, not appreciating the gift of reason, starts mingling with the herds of dumb beasts to the extent that, ignoring his own interior glory, he models his conduct on the object of his senses. Led on by curiosity, he becomes like any other animal since he does not see he has received more than they. We should, therefore, fear that ignorance which gives us a too low opinion of ourselves. But we should fear no less, but rather more, that which makes us think ourselves better than we are. This is what happens when we deceive ourselves thinking some good is in us of ourselves. But indeed you should detest and avoid even more than these two forms of ignorance that presumption by which you, knowingly and on purpose, seek your glory in goods that are not your own and that you are certain are not in you by your own power. In this you are not ashamed to steal the glory of another. Indeed, the first kind of ignorance has no glory; the second kind has, but not in God's sight.[16] But the third evil, which is committed full knowingly, is a usurpation of divine rights. This arrogance is worse and more dangerous than the second kind of ignorance, in which God is ignored, because it makes us despise him. If ignorance makes beasts of us, arrogance makes us like demons. It is pride, the greatest of sins, to use gifts as if they were one's by natural right and while receiving benefits to usurp the benefactor's glory.

For this reason, virtue is as necessary as dignity and knowledge, being the fruit of both. By virtue the Maker and Giver of all is sought and adhered to, and rightly glorified in all good things. On the other hand, the man who knows what is good yet does not do it will receive many strokes of the lash.[17] Why? Because, "He did not want to understand to do well;"[18] worse again, "While in bed he plotted evil."[19] He strives like a wicked servant to lay hold of and even to steal his good Lord's glory for qualities which the gift of knowledge tells him most certainly are not from himself. Hence it follows that dignity without knowledge is quite useless and that knowledge without virtue is damnable. But the virtuous man, for whom knowledge is not harmful or dignity unfruitful, lifts up his voice to God and frankly confesses: "Not to us, O Lord, not to us, but to your name give glory;"[20] meaning, "O Lord, we attribute no part of our dignity or knowledge to ourselves: we ascribe it all to your name whence all good comes."

But see now, in trying to show that they who do not know Christ are sufficiently informed by natural law,[21] seen in the perfection of man's mind and body, to be obliged to love God for his own sake, we have lost sight of our subject. To state briefly what has been said, we repeat: is there an infidel who does not know that he has received the necessities for bodily life, by which he exists, sees, and breathes, from him who gives food to all flesh,[22] who makes his sun rise on the good and the bad, and his rain fall on the just and the unjust?[23] Who, again, can be wicked enough to think the author of his human dignity, which shines in his soul, is any other than he who says in the book of Genesis: "Let us make man to our own image and likeness?"[24] Who can think that the giver of knowledge is somebody different from him who teaches man knowledge?[25] Or again, who believes he has received or hopes to receive the gift of virtue from any other source than the hand of the Lord of virtue? Hence God deserves to be loved for his own sake even by the infidel who, although he is ignorant of Christ yet knows himself. Everyone, therefore, even the infidel, is inexcusable if he fails to love the Lord his God with all his heart, all his soul, all his might.[26] For an innate justice, not unknown to reason, cries interiorly to him that he ought to love with his whole being to one to whom he owes all that he is. Yet it is difficult, impossible for a man, by his own power of free will, once he has received all things from God, to turn wholly to the will of God and not rather to his own will and keep these gifts for himself as his own, as it is written: "All seek what is their own,"[27] and further: ". . . man's feelings and thoughts are inclined to evil."[28]

III. The faithful, on the contrary, know how totally they need Jesus and him crucified.[29] While they admire and embrace in him that charity which surpasses all knowledge,[30] they are ashamed at failing to give what little they have in return for so great a love and honor. Easily they love more who realize they are loved more: "He loves less to whom less is given."[31] Indeed, the Jew and Pagan are not spurred on by such a wound of love as the Church experiences, who says: "I am wounded by love,"[32] and again: "Cushion me about with flowers, pile up apples around me, for I languish with love."[33] The Church sees King Solomon with the diadem his mother had placed on his head.[34] She sees the Father's only Son carrying his cross, the Lord of majesty, slapped and covered with spittle; she sees the Author of life and glory pierced by nails, wounded by a lance, saturated with abuse, and finally laying down his precious life for his friends. As she beholds this, the sword of love transfixes all the more her soul, making her repeat: "Cushion me about with flowers, pile up apples around me, for I languish with love.". . .

VIII. Love is one of the four natural passions. There is no need to name them, for they are well known. It would be right, however, for that which is natural to be first of all at the author of nature's service. That is why the first and greatest commandment is: "You shall love the Lord, your God. . . ."[35]

THE FIRST DEGREE OF LOVE: MAN LOVES HIMSELF
FOR HIS OWN SAKE

Since nature has become more fragile and weak, necessity obliges man to serve it first. This is carnal love by which a man loves himself above all for his own sake. He is only aware of himself; as St Paul says: "What was animal came first, then what was spiritual."[36] Love is not imposed by a precept; it is planted in nature. Who is there who hates his own flesh? Yet should love, as it happens, grow immoderate, and, like a savage current, burst the banks of necessity, flooding the fields of delight, the overflow is immediately stopped by the commandment which says: "You shall love your neighbor as yourself."[37] It is just indeed that he who shares the same nature should not be deprived of the same benefits, especially that benefit which is grafted in that nature. Should a man feel overburdened at satisfying not only his brethren's just needs but also their pleasures, let him restrain his own if he does not want to be a transgressor. He can be as indulgent as he likes for himself providing he remembers his neighbor has the same rights. O man, the law of life and order[38] imposes on you the restraint of temperance, lest you follow after your wanton desires[39] and perish, lest you use nature's gifts to serve through wantonness the enemy of the soul. Would it not be more just and honorable to share them with your neighbor, your fellow man, than with your enemy? If, faithful to the Wiseman's counsel, you turn away from sensual delights and content yourself with the Apostle's teaching on food and clothing,[40] you will soon be able to guard your love against "carnal desires which war against the soul"[41] and I think you will not find it a burden to share with those of your nature that which you have withheld from the enemy of your soul. Then your love will be sober and just if you do not refuse your brother that which he needs of what you have denied yourself in pleasure. Thus carnal love becomes social when it is extended to others.

What would you do if, while helping out your neighbor, you find yourself lacking what is necessary for your life? What else can you do than to pray with all confidence to him "who gives abundantly and bears no grudges,[42] who opens his hand and fills with blessings every living being?"[43] There is no doubt that he will assist us willingly in time of need, since he helps us so often in time of plenty. It is written: "Seek first the kingdom of God and his justice, and the rest will be added thereto."[44] Without being asked he promises to give what is necessary to him who withholds from himself what he does not need and loves his neighbor. This is to seek the kingdom of God and implore his aid against the tyranny of sin, to prefer the yoke of chastity and sobriety rather than let sin reign in your mortal flesh.[45] And again, it is only right to share nature's gifts with him who shares that nature with you.

Nevertheless, in order to love one's neighbor with perfect justice, one must have regard to God. In other words, how can one love one's neighbor with purity, if one does not love him in God? But it is impossible to love in God unless one loves God. It is necessary, therefore, to love God first; then one can love one's neighbor in God. Thus God makes himself lovable and creates whatever else is good. He does it this way. He who made nature protects it, for nature was created in a way that it must have its creator for protector. The world could not subsist without him to whom it owes its very existence. That no rational creature may ignore this fact concerning itself or dare lay claim through pride to benefits due the creator, by a deep and salutary counsel, the same creator wills that man be disciplined by tribulations so that when man fails and God comes to his help, man, saved by God, will render God the honor due him. It is written: "Call to me in the day of sorrow; I will deliver you, and you shall honor me."[46] In this way, man who is animal and carnal, and knows how to love only himself, yet starts loving God for his own benefit, because he learns from frequent experience that he can do everything that is good for him in God and that without God he can do nothing good.

THE SECOND DEGREE OF LOVE: MAN LOVES GOD FOR HIS OWN BENEFIT

IX. Man, therefore, loves God, but for his own advantage and not yet for God's sake. Nevertheless, it is a matter of prudence to know what you can do by yourself and what you can do with God's help to keep from offending him who keeps you free from sin. If man's tribulations, however, grow in frequency and as a result he frequently turns to God and is frequently freed by God, must he not end, even though he had a heart of stone in a breast of iron, by realizing that it is God's grace which frees him and come to love God not for his own advantage but for the sake of God?

THE THIRD DEGREE OF LOVE: MAN LOVES GOD FOR GOD'S SAKE

Man's frequent needs oblige him to invoke God more often and approach him more frequently. This intimacy moves man to taste and discover how sweet the Lord is.[47] Tasting God's sweetness entices us more to pure love than does the urgency of our own needs. Hence the example of the Samaritans who said to the woman who had told them the Lord was present: "We believe now not on account of what you said; for we have heard him and we know he is truly the Savior of the world."[48] We walk in their footsteps when we say to our flesh, "Now we love God, not because of your needs; for we have tasted and know how sweet the Lord is." The needs of the flesh are a kind of speech, proclaiming in transports of joy the good things experienced. A man who feels this way will not have trouble in fulfilling the commandment to love his neighbor. He loves God truthfully and so loves what is God's. He loves purely and he does not find it hard to obey a pure commandment, purifying his heart, as it is written, in the obedience of love.[49] He loves with justice and freely embraces the just commandment. This love is pleasing because it is free. It is chaste because it does not consist of spoken words but of deed and truth. It is just because it renders what is received. Whoever loves this way, loves the way he is loved, seeking in turn not what is his but what belongs to Christ, the same way Christ sought not what was his, but what was ours, or rather, ourselves. He so loves who says: "Confess to the Lord for he is good."[50] Who confesses to the Lord, not because he is good to him but because the Lord is good, truly loves God for God's sake and not for his own benefit. He does not love this way of whom it is said: "He will praise you when you do him favors."[51] This is the third degree of love: in it God is already loved for his own sake.

THE FOURTH DEGREE OF LOVE: MAN LOVES HIMSELF FOR THE SAKE OF GOD

X. Happy the man who has attained the fourth degree of love, he no longer even loves himself except for God. "O God, your justice is like the mountains of God."[52] This love is a mountain, God's towering peak. Truly indeed, it is the fat, fertile mountain.[53] "Who will climb the mountain of the Lord?"[54] "Who will give me the wings of a dove, that I may fly away to find rest?"[55] This place is made peaceful, a dwelling-place in Sion."[56] Alas for me, my exile has been lengthened."[57] When will flesh and blood, this vessel of clay, this earthly dwelling, understand the fact? When will this sort of affection be felt that, inebriated with divine love, the mind may forget itself and become in its own eyes like a broken dish,[58] hastening towards God and clinging to him, becoming one with him in spirit, saying: "My flesh and my heart have wasted away; O God of my heart, O God, my share for eternity."[59] I would say that man is blessed and holy to whom it is given to experience something of this sort, so rare in life, even if it be but once and for the space of a moment. To lose yourself, as if you no longer existed, to cease completely to experience yourself, to reduce yourself to nothing is not a human sentiment but a divine experience. If any mortal, suddenly rapt, as has been said, and for a moment is admitted to this, immediately the world of sin envies him, the evil of the day disturbs him, the mortal body weighs him down, the needs of the flesh bother him, the weakness of corruption offers no support, and sometimes with greater violence than these, brotherly love calls him back. Alas, he has to come back to himself, to descend again into his being, and wretchedly cry out: "Lord, I suffer violence,"[60] adding: "Unhappy man that I am, who will free me from this body doomed to death?"[61]

All the same, since Scripture says God made everything for his own purpose,[62] the day must come when the work will conform to and agree with its Maker. It is therefore necessary for our souls to reach a similar state in which, just as God willed everything to exist for himself, so we wish that neither ourselves nor other beings to have been nor to be except for his will alone; not for our pleasure. The satisfaction of our wants, chance happiness, delights us less than to see his will done in us and for us, which we implore every day in prayer saying: ". . . your will be done on earth as it is in heaven . . ." O pure and sacred love! O sweet and pleasant affection! O pure and sinless intention of the will, all the more sinless and pure since it frees us from the taint of selfish vanity, all the more sweet and pleasant, for all that is found in it is divine. It is deifying to go through such an experience. As a drop of water seems to disappear completely in a big quantity of wine, even assuming the wine's taste and color; just as red, molten iron becomes so much like fire it seems to lose its primary state; just as the air on a sunny day seems transformed into sunshine instead of being lit up; so it is necessary for the saints that all human feelings melt in a mysterious way and flow into the will of God. Otherwise, how will God be all in all[63] if something human survives in man? No doubt, the substance remains though under another form, another glory, another power. When will this happen? Who will see it? Who will possess it? "When shall I come and when shall I appear in God's presence?"[64] O my Lord, my God, "My heart said to you: my face has sought you; Lord, I will seek your face."[65] Do you think I shall see your holy temple?[66]

I do not think that can take place for sure until the word is fulfilled: "You will love the Lord your God with all your heart, all your soul, and all your strength,"[67] until the heart does not have to think of the body and the soul no longer has to give it life and feeling as in this life. Freed from this bother, its strength is established in the power of God. For it is impossible to assemble all these and turn them toward God's face as long as the care of this weak and wretched body keeps one busy to the point of distraction. Hence it is in a spiritual and immortal body, calm and pleasant, subject to the spirit in everything, that the soul hopes to attain the fourth degree of love, or rather to be possessed by it; for it is in God's hands to give it to whom he wishes, it is not obtained by human efforts. I mean he will easily reach the highest degree of love when he will no longer be held back by any desire of the flesh or upset by troubles as he hastens with the greatest speed and desire toward the joy of the Lord. All the same, do we not think the holy martyrs received this grace, at least partially, while they were still in their victorious bodies? The strength of this love seized their souls so entirely that, despising the pain, they were able to expose their bodies to exterior torments. No doubt, the feeling of intense pain could only upset their calm; it could not overcome them.

ISAAC OF STELLA

Sermons

Born in England, Isaac (c. 1100–1168) eventually emigrated to France, was ordained a priest, and joined the abbey of Citeaux about 1145. Shortly thereafter he was named the abbot of a newly formed Cistercian community at Stella. His Sermons, addressed to monks, stress the themes of Christ's self-emptying and our participation in his life through the Mystical Body and our adoptive sonship.

Any care or delight which does not lie in God alone, except love of our neighbor for God's sake, is superfluous and adulterous, alien to our reason for existence as human beings, contrary to God's plan for us and to our duties toward him.

RICHARD OF ST. VICTOR

Benjamin Major

A native of Scotland, Richard of St. Victor (c. 1120–1173) was prior of the great monastery and school of St. Victor near Paris. He was the first theologian to attempt systematic treatises on mystical theology, in his Benjamin Minor *(c. 1160) and his* Benjamin Major *(c. 1165).*

True to the theological tradition of his time, Richard casts these treatises in the form of symbolic interpretations of Scripture (in this case the story of Jacob and his sons from Genesis), but in fact his true interest lies in the coherent presentation of a doctrine describing the growth and development of the life of prayer. Influenced both by the Augustinian and the Dionysian traditions, Richard attempts a synthesis of views and betrays a marked interest in the experiential psychology of the spiritual life. His works exerted great influence, directly and indirectly, on most later spiritual writers in the West.

CHAPTER III (Bk. I)

Of the properties of contemplation and of how it differs from meditation or thinking

In order that we may more easily understand and rightly judge those things which are to be said about contemplation, we ought first to seek to determine or to define what it is and how it differs from thinking or meditation. For we must realize that we may regard one and the same object in one way by thinking, examine it in another way by meditation, and wonder at it in yet another by contemplation. Although at times these three may agree in studying the same object, they differ greatly in method. Thought[1] and meditation may approach one and the same matter in different ways and contemplation in yet a third and widely divergent manner. Thinking, slow-footed, wanders hither and thither along bypaths, caring not where they will lead. Meditation with great mental industry, plods along the steep and laborious road keeping the end in view. Contemplation on a free wing, circles around with great nimbleness wherever the impulse takes it. Thinking crawls along, meditation marches and sometimes runs, contemplation flies around and when it wills, it hovers upon the height. Thinking is without labour and bears no fruit. Meditation labours and has its fruit. Contemplation abides untoiling and fruitful. Thinking roams about, meditation investigates, contemplation wonders. Thinking arises from the imagination, meditation from the reason, contemplation from the intelligence. Behold these three: imagination, reason, intelligence. Intelligence takes the highest place, imagination the lowest, reason lies between them. Everything which comes under the view of the lower sense, comes necessarily also under the view of the higher sense. Hence it follows that everything which is grasped by the imagination, is also, together with much that is above it, grasped by the reason. So also, all that the imagination and reason include, together with those things which they cannot include, fall under the view of the intelligence. Behold then how wide is the extent of the ray of contemplation, for it embraces all things. And it is right that one and the same thing may, by one man, be considered thoughtfully, by another meditatively, by another contemplatively, yet not by a different road but by a different movement. Thinking moves from one thing to another rambling aimlessly. Meditation is perseveringly intent on one thing only. Contemplation sheds the light of a single ray upon innumerable objects. The depth of the mind is given expanse and immensity by the intelligence and the point of the contemplating soul is sharpened that it may become capable of understanding many things, and acute to penetrate subtleties. Contemplation can never exist without some degree of liveliness in the intelligence. For as it is the work of the intelligence which fastens the eye of the mind upon material things, so by that same power, from that one intuition of material things the eye is dilated to comprehend innumerable objects. Therefore whenever the soul of the contemplative is enlarged to take in lower things, as often as it is raised to the heights and sharpened to penetrate inscrutable things, or with marvellous nimbleness carried away by innumerable interests, almost without respite, so often you may be quite sure that this is the work of the power of the intelligence. This is said on account of those who think that these lower powers are unworthy of the regard of the intelligence, or of being considered in any way to belong to contemplation. But in a special and strict sense, contemplation is so called when it treats of sublime things where the soul makes use of the pure intelligence. But nevertheless contemplation always deals with *things*, either manifested according to their nature or known intimately by study or made clear by revelation.

CHAPTER IV (Bk. I)

Definition of contemplation, meditation and thinking,
individually

It seems that they may be defined thus: Contemplation is a free and clear vision of the mind fixed upon the manifestation of wisdom in suspended wonder. Or indeed as it appeared to a distinguished theologian of our times who defined it thus: Contemplation is the clear and free glance of the soul bearing intently upon objects of perception, to its furthest limits. Meditation however, is an industrious attention of the mind concentrated diligently upon the investigation of some object. Or thus: meditation is the careful look of the soul zealously occupied in the search of truth. But thinking is the careless glance of the soul prone to restless wandering. It will thus be seen that all three have this in common and it is almost of their essence, that they are the sight of the soul. Where nothing is discerned by the mind they cannot be thus named or declared to exist. It is common to contemplation as to meditation that they are occupied with useful things, and engaged chiefly and intensively in the study of wisdom or knowledge. But in this they differ greatly from thinking, which is wont at all times to relax in vain and frivolous considerations, throwing off the bridle of discretion to interfere or rush headlong into everything. Contemplation and thinking have this in common that by free motion and according to spontaneous impulse they move hither and thither and are not hindered by any obstacle or difficulty from following their course. In this they differ greatly from meditation which always is intent, however laborious the effort and notwithstanding difficulties of the mind, to grasp hard things, to break through obstacles and penetrate hidden things. Yet it often happens that in the wanderings of our thinking, the soul meets with something which it passionately desires to know and presses on strongly towards it. But if the mind satisfying its desire applies itself with zeal to this kind of investigation it already exceeds the bounds of thinking by thinking, and thought passes over into meditation. The same thing happens in the case of meditation. For when a truth has been long sought, and is at last discovered, the mind usually receives it greedily, wonders at it with exultation and for a long time rests therein in wonder. And this already shows meditation exceeding its bounds and passing over into contemplation. For it is the property of contemplation to adhere with wonder to the object which brings it joy. And in this it differs both from meditation and thinking. For thought, as we have said, always moves about hither and thither with uncertain steps, but meditation always tends to its final object, proceeding deliberately.

CHAPTER II (Bk. V)

In what ways all contemplation occurs, namely by the widening, the raising and the abstraction or ecstasy of the mind[1]

It seems to me that the character of contemplation varies in three ways. Sometimes it effects an enlarging of the mind, sometimes a raising and sometimes an abstraction of the mind. The enlarging of the mind is when the gaze of the soul expands widely and is intensely sharpened, but this in no way goes beyond the limit of human effort. The raising of the mind is when the activity of the intelligence, divinely illuminated, transcends the limits of human effort but does not go over into ecstasy, so that what it sees is above its powers, but the soul does not withdraw from its accustomed ways of knowing. The alienation of the mind (or ecstasy) is when the memory of things present withdraws from the mind and it moves by a transfiguration divinely wrought, into a strange state of soul unattainable by human effort. These three modes of contemplation are experienced by those who deserve to be raised to the height of that grace. The first is caused by human effort, the third only by divine grace, the middle one by a mingling of both, namely, human industry and divine grace. . . .

CHAPTER V (Bk. V)

That ecstasy of the human mind can have three causes

We have, I think, to relate ecstasy of the human mind to three causes. For it comes to pass that sometimes through greatness of devotion, or great wonder, or exceeding exultation, the mind cannot possess itself in any way, and being lifted up above itself, passes into ecstasy. The human mind is raised above itself by the greatness of its devotion, when it is kindled with such fire of heavenly desire that the flame of inner love flares up beyond human bearing. And the soul melted like wax is released from its former state, and vapourized as smoke, ascends upwards and is breathed forth to the heavens.

The human soul is led up above herself by wonder, when radiant with infused heavenly light and lost in wonder at the supreme beauty of God, she is torn from the foundation of her being. Like flashing lightning, the deeper she is cast down in self-depreciation in the face of the beauty she sees, so much the higher and the more rapidly does she rebound in her desire for the highest, and carried away above herself, she is lifted up to the heavens. The mind of man is abstracted from itself by excess of joy and exultation, when its inmost self, drunk with the abundance of interior sweetness, indeed wholly inebriated, forgets altogether what it is and what it will be, and is brought to this going forth of ecstasy by the greatness of its religious fervour, and in this condition of wonderful happiness, is suddenly transformed into a heavenly state.

Therefore if we have not yet experienced this kind of ecstasy, what should we feel about ourselves but that we are not loved and do not love in this degree? Whoever you are, if you loved fully and perfectly perhaps the perfection of your love, the urge of your burning desire would carry you away into this kind of ecstasy which we have partly described above. Again, if you were truly worthy of divine love, if you showed yourself fit for so great an honour, perhaps he would enlighten the eyes of your intelligence so greatly with the effulgence of his light and inebriate the desire of your heart with such a taste of his intimate sweetness, that thereby he would carry you up above yourself and lift you up to divine things by ecstasy. . . .

ST. GERTRUDE OF HELFTA

Spiritual Exercises

A German nun and mystic, Gertrude was educated at the convent of Helfta from the age of five. After her spiritual "conversion" in 1281, she was the recipient of many visions and interior mystical graces. She is a great representative of bridal mysticism and devotion to the Heart of Jesus.

Carried away one day by the excess of her love, she said to the Lord: "Would, O Lord, that I might have a fire that could liquefy my soul so that I could pour it totally out like a libation unto thee!" The Lord answered: "Thy will is such a fire."

ST. GREGORY OF SINAI

Instructions to Hesychasts

The mid-fourteenth century saw a revival and codification of methods of asceticism and prayer within the monasticism of the Eastern Church. Because of attacks from without and from within, the monks of Mt. Athos and other Greek-speaking monastic centers were impelled to explain and justify their mode of life. Chief among the proponents of hesychasm in this period were St. Gregory Palamas (c. 1296–1359) and St. Gregory of Sinai (c. 1295–1346). The following quotations from the latter author give a clear insight into the precise yet simple methodology advocated by hesychast writers for the attaining of union with God.

1. *How to sit in the cell*

Sitting in your cell, remain patiently in prayer, according to the precept of the Apostle Paul (Rom. xii. 12; Col. iv. 2). Collect your mind into your heart and send out thence your mental cry to our Lord Jesus, calling for His help and saying: 'Lord Jesus Christ, have mercy upon me.' Do not give in to faint-heartedness and laziness, but labour in your heart and drive your body, seeking the Lord in your heart. Compel yourself by every means to do this work, for 'The kingdom of heaven suffereth violence, and the violent take it by force' (Matt. xi. 12), as the Lord said, showing that this attainment demands severe labour and spiritual struggle.

2. *How to say the prayer*

Some of the fathers taught that the prayer should be said in full: 'Lord, Jesus Christ, Son of God, have mercy upon me.' Others advised saying half, thus: 'Jesus, Son of God, have mercy upon me', or 'Lord Jesus Christ, have mercy upon me', or to alternate, sometimes saying it in full and sometimes in a shorter form. Yet it is not advisable to pander to laziness by changing the words of the prayer too often, but to persist a certain time as a test of patience. Again, some teach the saying of the prayer with the lips, others with and in the mind. In my opinion both are advisable. For at times the mind, left to itself, becomes wearied and too exhausted to say the prayer mentally; at other times the lips get tired of this work. Therefore both methods of prayer should be used—with the lips and with the mind. But one should appeal to the Lord quietly and without agitation, so that the voice does not disturb the attention of the mind and does not thus break off the prayer, until the mind is accustomed to doing this and, receiving force from the Spirit, firmly prays within on its own. Then there will be no need to say the prayer with the lips; indeed, it will be impossible, for he who reaches this stage is fully content with mental doing of the prayer and has no wish to leave it.

3. *How to hold the mind*

You should know that no one can hold the mind by himself, if it be not held by the Spirit. For it cannot be held, not because of its mobile nature but because, through neglect, it has acquired the habit of turning and wandering hither and thither. When through transgressing the commandments of Him who has regenerated us (in baptism) we became separated from God, we lost our union with Him and destroyed in our feeling a mental feeling of Him. A mind thus inclined and withdrawn from God is led captive everywhere. And there is no way of regaining its stability except by repenting to God and uniting with Him, by frequent and patient prayers, and by mentally confessing our sins to Him each day. God immediately forgives those who ask forgiveness in humility and contrition and who ceaselessly invoke His holy name. When through this working at prayer the action of the prayer becomes established in the heart, then prayer begins to keep the mind near by, fills it with joy and does not let it be made captive. However, wanderings of thoughts occur even after this, for thoughts submit fully only to those who are perfect in the Holy Spirit and who, through Jesus Christ, have attained a state free from wanderings.

4. *How to drive away thoughts*

No beginner can ever drive away a thought if God does not drive it away. Only the strong are capable of struggling with them and banishing them. But even they do not achieve this by themselves, but with God's help rise up to wrestle with them, armed with His weapons. So, when thoughts come, call to our Lord Jesus, often and patiently, and they will retreat; for they cannot bear the warmth of the heart produced by prayer, and flee as if scorched by fire. John of the Ladder tells us to flog our foes with the name of Jesus; for our God is fire, devouring evil. The Lord is quick to help, and will speedily revenge those who wholeheartedly call to Him day and night.—But he who does not possess the action of prayer can conquer thoughts in another manner, by imitating Moses. For if he rises up and lifts his eyes and hands to heaven (Exod. xvii. 11) God drives thoughts away. After this he should again sit down and patiently resume his prayer.—This method is for a man who has not yet attained the action of prayer. But even a man who already possesses the action of prayer, when bodily passions, such as laziness and lust, grievous and violent passions, stir in him, often gets up and raises his hands to seek help against them. Still, to avoid illusion he does not do this for long, but after a while sits down again, to prevent the enemy from seducing his mind by showing him some phantom. For only the pure and perfect can have a mind safe from harm, even though the mind be safe from downfall no matter where it is, whether high or low, in the heart or elsewhere.

5. *How to psalmodise*

Some say one should psalmodise often, others—not often, again others—not at all. But I advise you neither to psalmodise so frequently as to cause unrest, nor to leave it off altogether, lest you fall into weakness and negligence, but to follow the example of those who psalmodise infrequently. For, in the words of simple wisdom, moderation is best in all things. To psalmodise much is good for those who follow active life, since they are ignorant of mental occupations and lead a life of labour. But it is not good for those who practise silence, for whom it is more fitting to abide in God alone, praying in their heart and refraining from thought. For, according to John of the Ladder, silence means setting aside thoughts about things, whether of the senses or the mind. Moreover, if it uses up all its energy in too much psalmody, the mind will not have force enough steadily and patiently to remain in prayer. John of the Ladder further advises that at night it is better to give more time to prayer and less to psalmody.—So also must you do. When, sitting in your cell, you see that prayer is acting and does not cease its movement in your heart, never abandon it to get up for psalmody, until it leaves you of its own accord. For otherwise, leaving God within, you will address yourself to Him from without, thus passing from the higher to the lower. Moreover, in this way you will disturb the mind, and remove it from its peaceful calm. Silence, in accordance with its name, has in itself such actions as work in peace and quiet. For our God is peace, being above all speech and tumult.

In accordance with our mode of life, our psalmody too should be angelic and not carnal. Oral psalmody is a sign of the mental cry within and is given us lest we become lazy and coarse, to bring us to the state in which in truth we should be. Those who are ignorant of prayer (have not experienced its power and action)—this prayer which, according to St. John of the Ladder, is the source of virtues watering, like plants, the powers of our soul—such people should psalmodise much, psalmodise without measure, be always occupied with various works and never know rest from them, until, through much intensive laborious work, they enter into the state of contemplation, having acquired the action of mental prayer within them.—The work of silence is one thing and that of a cenobite another; but each, abiding in that to which he has been called, shall be saved. Therefore I hesitate to write to you, because of the weak ones, for I know that you move among them. He who works at the prayer from hearsay or reading and has no instructor, works in vain. According to the words of the fathers, he who has tasted grace must psalmodise sparingly, and must concentrate on the practice of prayer. However, if he is attacked by laziness, let him psalmodise or read the writings of the fathers. A ship has no need of oars when the wind swells the sails, for then the wind gives it sufficient power easily to navigate the salt sea of passions. But when the wind dies and the ship stops, it has to be set in motion by oars or by a tugboat.

As an argument against this, some people point to holy fathers who performed all-night watches, spending all their time in psalmody. Our reply to this is, that not all travelled by the same road, or followed the same rule to the end. Many passed from active life to contemplation and, having ended their works, kept Sabbath according to spiritual law and rejoiced in God alone; and they were fed by the Divine sweetness of grace which would not allow them to psalmodise or think of anything else. They remained always in a state beyond mind, having attained the end of desires, even if only in part. Others kept to a life of action to the end and attained salvation, dying in the hope of receiving their reward in the future. Some have at death received a testimony of their salvation, or exuded a sweet aroma after death, in token thereof. These latter are those who have preserved the grace of baptism but who, owing to the captivity or ignorance of the mind, failed to taste while alive the palpable though mysterious communion with that grace. Yet others successfully practise the one and the other, that is psalmody and prayer, and spend their life in this way, richly endowed with grace, which moves all things to activity and makes them overcome all obstacles. Others again, although they were simple people, kept silence to the end, and being one became one with the One God, finding contentment in the one prayer. To the perfect all is possible through Jesus Christ Who is their strength—to Whom be glory for ever and ever. Amen.

6. *How to partake of food*

What shall we say of the belly, the queen of passions? If you can slay it or half kill it, keep a tight hold. It has mastered me, beloved, and I serve it as a slave and a vassal. It is the colleague of the demons and the home of passions. Through it we fall, and through it we rise again, when it behaves itself. Through it we have lost the first Divine rank and the second. For after the old corruption we have been renewed in Christ; but now we have once more fallen away from God, through neglect of commandments (whose observance would preserve and restore grace to us); and without knowing it, we puff ourselves up, imagining that we are with God.

According to the fathers, physical nourishment may differ greatly: one man needs little, another much to sustain his natural strength, and each reaches satisfaction as regards food in accordance with his strength and habit. But the practiser of silence should always be starved, never allowing himself to eat his fill. For when the stomach is heavy and, through this, the mind is clouded, a man cannot practise prayer with purity and firmness. Under the influence of the vapours produced by much food he becomes drowsy and longs to lie down and sleep—and this leads to innumerable dreams filling his mind in sleep.

Thus a man who strives after salvation and forces himself, for the sake of the Lord, to lead a life of silence, should be satisfied, in my opinion, with one litra (three-quarters of a pound) of bread; three or four cups of water or wine a day, and a little of any other victuals which may be to hand. He must not let himself eat to satiety; so that, through such wise use of food, that is through eating all kinds of food, on the one hand he may avoid boastfulness and on the other may not show disdain of God's creations, which are most excellent; and he thanks God for everything. Such is the reasoning of the wise! To those whose faith is weak, abstinence in food is most salutary and the Apostle orders such men to eat herbs (Rom. xiv. 2), for they do not believe that God will preserve them.

What shall I say to you? You have asked for a ruling, and a ruling is usually hard, especially for you in your old age. The young cannot always keep to a definite weight and measure, so how will you keep to it? You should be free in partaking of food. When you happen to be overcome, repent, blaming yourself—and make new efforts. And never cease behaving in this way, falling and rising again, and with this blaming yourself alone and no one else—and you will find peace, wisely attaining victory through downfalls. Yet do not exceed the limit which we have established above.— This you should do, for no other victuals strengthen the body as much as do bread and water. Therefore the Prophet, counting all the rest as nothing, merely said: Son of man! Thou shalt eat bread by weight and shalt drink water by measure (Ezek. iv. 9, etc.).

The partaking of food has three degrees: abstinence, adequacy and satiety. To abstain, means to remain a little hungry after eating; to eat adequately, means neither to be hungry, nor weighed down; to be satiated, means to be slightly weighed down. But eating beyond satiety is the door to belly-madness, through which lust comes in. But you, firm in this knowledge, choose what is best for you, according to your powers, without overstepping the limits: for the perfect, according to the Apostle, ought 'both to be full and to be hungry ... and do all things through Christ which strengtheneth' (Phil. iv. 12, 13).

7. Of illusion and other subjects

See, I want to impart to you true knowledge of *illusion*, so that you should guard against it, and not cause great harm to yourself and ruin your soul through ignorance. For human self-will is easily inclined to the enemies' side, especially in the case of the inexperienced, since these are more assiduously pursued by them. All around, near to beginners and the self-willed, the demons are wont to spread the nets of thoughts and pernicious fantasies and prepare moats for their downfall, since their city is still in the hands of the barbarians. It is not to be wondered at, if any one of them goes astray or loses his reason, or accepts or has accepted illusion, or sees something foreign to truth, or says something unseemly, through lack of experience and ignorance. Often a man, while discoursing about truth in his ignorance, says one thing instead of another, not knowing how to express the true state of affairs correctly, and by this unwise action horrifies his listeners and brings abuse and ridicule on the heads of hesychasts. There is nothing strange in the fact that beginners make mistakes even after much labour: this has happened to many who sought God, both now and in the past.

Remembrance of God or mental prayer is higher than all other works; as the love of God, it stands at the head of all virtues. But a man who is arrogant and shameless in his efforts to enter into God and worship Him with purity, and who attempts to acquire God in himself, is easily destroyed by the demons if this be allowed them. For, daringly and presumptuously seeking that which does not correspond to his state, he strives in his pride to attain it before its time. The merciful Lord, seeing how hasty we are as regards things which are above us, often prevents us from falling into temptation, in order that each of us, realising his arrogance, should by himself turn to right action before making himself an object of abuse and ridicule for the demons, and of lamentation for men. Especially is this so, if a man seeks this marvellous doing with patience and humility, with obedience and asking the guidance of the experienced, so as to avoid reaping tares instead of wheat, gall instead of sweetness, and finding ruin instead of salvation. For the strong and the perfect should always wrestle alone with the demons, ceaselessly wielding against them the sword of the Spirit, 'which is the word of God' (Eph. vi. 17). But the weak and the beginners use flight as their stronghold, with reverence and fear, refusing to join combat and not daring to be involved in it before their time—and in this way they escape death.

But you, if you are truly practising silence hoping to be with God, and you see something either sensory or spiritual, within or without, be it even the image of Christ or of an angel or some saint, or if an imaginary light pervades your mind, in no way accept it. The mind has in itself a natural power of dreaming and can easily build fantastic images of what it desires in those who do not apprehensively pay attention, and so cause themselves harm. Memories, too, of good and bad things will often suddenly imprint their images in the mind, and thus entice it to dreaming. Then the man to whom this happens becomes a dreamer instead of a hesychast. Therefore beware, and avoid being enticed into believing something, however good it may be, without questioning the experienced and making thorough investigation, and then you will suffer no harm. Always be displeased with such images and keep your mind colourless, formless and imageless. It has often happened that even things sent by God, as a test before victory, have turned into harm for many. Our Lord wishes to test our self-will, to see whither it inclines. But a man who has seen something, whether with mind or senses, even if this thing be from God, and who accepts it without questioning the experienced, easily falls or will fall into temptation, since he is quick to accept thoughts. Therefore a beginner should pay attention to the action of the heart, which is not led astray, and refuse to accept anything else until his passions are pacified. God is not angry with him who keeps careful attention on himself if, through fear of temptation, he refuses to accept what comes from Him, without questioning and due investigation. On the contrary, He praises his wisdom, although He has been wroth with some.

One should not, however, question everyone, but only him who has been entrusted with the guidance of others, whose life shines, and who is himself 'poor, yet making many rich', according to the Gospels (2 Cor. vi. 10). Many inexperienced men have done harm to many unwise people, for which they will be judged after death. For not everyone has the right to guide others, but only those who have been endowed with Divine discernment, according to the Apostle (1 Cor. xii. 10), namely that discerning of spirits which separates good from evil by the sword of the word. Each man has his own reason and his natural discernment, either practical or scientific, but not all have discerning of spirits. Therefore the wise Sirach says: 'Be in peace with many: nevertheless have but one counsellor of a thousand' (Ecclus. vi. 6). It is hard to find a guide unerring either in deeds, words or understanding. That a man is unerring can be recognised if he has testimony from the Scriptures both for practice and for understanding, and is humbly wise in the realms of wisdom. For it is no small labour to know truth clearly and to keep clean from what is opposed to grace. For the devil is wont to present his illusion in the guise of truth, especially to beginners, transforming his deceit into something spiritual.

Therefore, a man striving to attain pure prayer in silence must proceed towards it with great trepidation, lamenting and begging the guidance of the experienced, constantly shedding tears for his sins, in sorrowful contrition and with a fearful apprehension of being cast into hell or of falling away from God and being separated from Him now or in time to come. For the devil, seeing a man leading a life of lamentation, hastens to him, fearing the advent of humility born of weeping. But if someone dreams of reaching on high with conceit, moved, not by true desire, but by the suggestion of Satan, the latter easily enslaves him in his nets. Therefore the safest armour is to remain in prayer and lamentation so as not to fall from the joy of prayer into self-conceit, but to keep oneself unharmed by choosing the joy of sorrow. For prayer free of illusion is warmth, when joined with prayer to Jesus, Who brings fire to the soil of our heart; this warmth scorches passions like tares, and brings joy and quiet to the heart, coming neither from the right nor the left, nor from above, but issuing forth in the heart itself like a spring of water from the life-giving Spirit. It is this prayer alone that you should wish to find and attain in the heart, keeping your mind free from dreams and stripped of all thoughts and reasonings. And be not afraid, for He Who said: 'Be of good cheer; it is I; be not afraid;' (Matt. xiv. 27) is Himself with us, He Whom we seek and Who always protects us. So in calling to God we must neither fear nor sigh.

If some people have gone astray through damage to their mind, you must know that they have incurred this through self-will and pride. For if a man seeks God with obedience, questioning and wise humility, he will always be protected from harm by the grace of Christ, Who desires all men to be saved. If temptation assails such a man, this occurs to test and crown him, and is accompanied by speedy help from God Who has allowed this, since His ways are inscrutable. For, as the fathers say, he who lives rightly and is faultless in his behaviour with all men, holding himself from sycophancy and presumption, will not be harmed, even if a whole army of demons put innumerable temptations in his way. But those who act with self-will and self-confidence are easily subject to harm. Therefore the practiser of silence should always keep to the royal road. For excess in anything is usually accompanied by conceit, which is followed by illusion.

In keeping silence, there are three virtues we should practise strictly and verify each hour whether we constantly abide in them, lest we be robbed by forgetfulness, and move outside them. They are: abstinence, not talking, and self-belittlement, i.e. humility. They support and protect one another; prayer is born of them and grows without ceasing.

The beginning of the action of grace in prayer manifests itself differently, for, according to the Apostle, the Spirit divides his gifts severally 'as he will' (1 Cor. xii. 11). To some there comes the spirit of fear, rending the mountains of passions and breaking in pieces the rocks—hardened hearts—such fear that the flesh seems to be pierced by nails and numbed as in death. Others quake, being filled with joy—what the fathers called the leaping of joy. In yet others, pre-eminently in those who have achieved success in prayer, God produces a subtle and serene glow of light when Christ comes to dwell in the heart (Eph. iii. 17) and to shine mysteriously in the spirit. Therefore God spoke to Elijah on the mount of Horeb (1

Kings xix. 12) and said that the Lord is not in this or that—not in some individual actions of beginners—but in a subtle glow of light[1] which shows the perfection of prayer.

8. *Question:*
    What is a man to do when the demon takes the form of an angel of light and tries to seduce him?

Answer:
    In this case a man needs great power of discernment to discriminate rightly between good and evil. So in your heedlessness, do not be carried away too quickly by what you see, but be weighty (not easy to move) and, carefully testing everything, accept the good and reject the evil. Always you must test and examine, and only afterwards believe. Know that the actions of grace are manifest and the demon, in spite of his transformations, cannot produce them, namely, meekness, friendliness, humility, hatred of the world, cutting off passion and lust—which are the effects of grace. Works of the demons are: arrogance, conceit, intimidation and all evil. By such actions you will be able to discern whether the light shining in your heart is of God or of Satan. Lettuce looks like mustard, and vinegar in colour like wine; but when you taste them the palate discerns and defines the difference between each. In the same way the soul, if it has discernment, can discriminate by mental taste the gifts of the Holy Spirit from the fantasies and illusions of Satan.

ST. GREGORY PALAMAS

On the Blessed Hesychasts

Monk of Mount Athos and later Archbishop of Thessalonica, St. Gregory Palamas (c. 1296–1359) was a great defender of hesychasm against attacks led by the monk Barlaam of Calabria. His writings, written during one of its most flourishing periods, provide us with a summary of the principles of Eastern monasticism.

He who purifies his body by self mastery, who by love makes anger and lust an occasion for virtue, and who teaches the mind, cleansed by prayer, to stand before God, will receive and see in himself the grace promised to the pure in heart.

Part IV Notes

St. Benedict of Nursia

1. Rom. 13:11; Ps. 95:8; Matt. 11:15; Rev. 2:7; Ps. 34:11; John 12:35.
2. Ps. 34:12–15.
3. Ps. 15:1–3.
4. Ps. 115:1; I Cor. 15:10; II Cor. 10:17; Matt. 7:24–5.
5. Rom. 2:4; Ezek. 33:11.
6. The Oxford manuscript of the Rule ends the Prologue here with: "and if we perform that duty, we doubtless shall become the heirs of heaven." But other manuscripts of the *Rule* suggest that this shorter version of the Prologue was not original.
7. Rom. 8:15.
8. Ps. 40:10; Isa. 1:2.
9. Ps. 50:16–17; Matt. 7:3.
10. II Tim. 4:2.
11. Prov. 18:2; 29:19; 23:13–14.
12. Matt. 6:33; Ps. 34:10.
13. Ecclesiasticus 32:19.
14. Matt. 23:3.
15. I Cor. 2:9.
16. Ps. 18:44; Luke 10:16.
17. Matt. 7:14.
18. John 6:38.
19. II Cor. 9:7.
20. Ps. 39:1–2.
21. Prov. 10:19 and 18:21.
22. Luke 14:11; Ps. 131:1–2.
23. Ps. 7:9; 94:11 139:1; 76:10; 18:23.
24. Ecclesiasticus 18:30; Prov. 16:25; Ps. 14:1; 38:9.
25. Ecclesiasticus 18:30.
26. Prov. 15:3; Ps. 14:3; 53:2–3; 50:21.
27. John 6:38. The second text is not from the Bible but from (e.g.) *Acta Martyrum.*
28. Matt. 10:22; Ps. 27:14; Rom. 8:36–7; Ps. 66:10–12.
29. Ps. 37:5; 106:1.
30. Ps. 32:5.
31. Ps. 73:21–2.
32. Ps. 22:6; 88:15; 119:71.

33. Prov. 10:19; Ps. 140:11.
34. Ecclesiasticus 21:20.
35. From the *Sentences of Sixtus*, a book of proverbs and moral sayings.
36. Luke 18:13; Ps. 119:107.

St. Bernard of Clairvaux

1. Gal. 1:4.
2. I Jn. 4:9–10.
3. I Jn. 4:2.
4. Ps. 16:2.
5. I Cor. 13:5.
6. Rom. 5:10.
7. Jn. 3:16.
8. Rom. 8:32.
9. Jn. 15:13.
10. Rom. 4:2.
11. I Cor 4:7.
12. I Cor. 1:31; II Cor 10:17; Cf. Jer 9:23–24.
13. Jn. 14:6.
14. Cant. 1:6–7.
15. Ps. 49:13.
16. Rom. 4:2.
17. Luke 12:47.
18. Ps. 36:4.
19. Ps. 36:5.
20. Ps. 115:1.
21. Cf. Rom 1:19ff; 2:14–15.
22. Ps. 136:25.
23. Mt 5:45.
24. Gen 1:26.
25. Ps 94:10.
26. Mk 12:30.
27. Phil 2:21.
28. Gen 8:21.
29. 1 Cor 2:2.
30. Eph 3:19.
31. Luke 7:43, 47; cf. 12:48.
32. Cant. 2:5; cf. 4:9.
33. Cant. 2:5.
34. Cant. 3:11.
35. Matt. 22:37.
36. I Cor. 15:46.
37. Matt. 22:39.
38. Sir. 45:6.
39. Sir. 18:30.
40. I Tim. 6:8.
41. I Pet. 2:11.
42. James 1:5.

43. Ps. 145:16.
44. Matt 6:33; Luke 12:31.
45. Rom. 6:12.
46. Ps. 50:15.
47. Ps. 34:9.
48. Jn. 4:42.
49. I Pet. 1:22.
50. Ps. 118:1.
51. Ps. 49:19.
52. Ps. 36:7.
53. Ps. 68:16.
54. Ps. 24:3.
55. Ps. 55:7.
56. Ps. 76:3.
57. Ps. 120:5.
58. Ps. 31:13.
59. Ps. 73:26.
60. Is. 38:14.
61. Rom. 7:24.
62. Prov. 16:14; cf. Rev. 4:11.
63. I Cor. 15:28.
64. Ps. 42:3.
65. Ps. 27:8.
66. Ps. 27:4.
67. Mark 12:30.

Richard of St. Victor

Book I

1. Richard uses *cogitatio*, for a vague kind of thinking, in contrast to sustained thought which he calls meditation.

Book V

1. Richard throughout this treatise uses the terms *dilatatio, sublevatio* and *alienatio mentis*. But for the third, he also uses *excessus mentis*, with the same meaning. It will be translated 'abstraction' where this is more suitable to render the shade of meaning.

St. Gregory of Sinai

1. The English version of I Kings xix. 12 has 'still small voice'; the nearest English equivalent to the Slavonic version is 'subtle and serene wafting of wind'. Although this text is under reference, the literal translation of the passage which has been rendered as 'subtle glow of light' would be 'subtle and serene wafting of light'.

Part V

EXTRA-MONASTIC MOVEMENTS IN MEDIEVAL SPIRITUALITY

Prayer is the means whereby we rightly **understand the** fullness of joy that is coming to us; it is true **longing, and sure** trust too.

Julian of Norwich (c. 1342–1420)

ST. FRANCIS OF ASSISI

Rule of 1221

St. Francis of Assisi (1182–1226) introduced new elements into the religious life by his emphasis on the literal imitation of Christ's poverty and on a missionary sensitivity. His simple, unstructured, yet radical mentality is well illustrated in the following quotations from his Rule *of 1221, an early attempt to describe and regulate the life of his followers. Although this* Rule *was superseded by later developments–particularly by his approved* Rule *of 1223–it allows a glimpse into the primitive idea of the Franciscan foundation.*

In the name of the Father and of the Son and of the Holy Spirit. Amen. This is the life Brother Francis asked to be permitted him and approved by the lord Pope Innocent. The Pope granted his request and approved the Rule for him and for his friars, present and to come.

Brother Francis and his successors as head of this Order must promise obedience and reverence to his holiness Pope Innocent and his successors. The other friars are bound to obey Brother Francis and his successors.

CHAPTER I

*The friars are to live in obedience,
without property, and in chastity*

The Rule and life of the friars is to live in obedience, in chastity and without property, following the teaching and the footsteps of our Lord Jesus Christ who says, *If thou wilt be perfect, go, sell what thou hast, and give to the poor, and thou shalt have treasure in heaven; and come, follow me* (Mt. 19:21); and, *If anyone wishes to come after me, let him deny himself, and take up his cross, and follow me* (Mt. 16:24). Elsewhere he says, *If anyone comes to me and does not hate his father and mother, and wife and children, and brothers and sisters, yes, and even his own life, he cannot be my disciple* (Lk. 14:26). *And everyone who has left house, or brothers, or sisters, or father, or mother, or wife, or children, or lands, for my name's sake, shall receive a hundredfold, and shall possess life everlasting* (Mt. 19:29).

CHAPTER II

Of the reception and clothing of the friars

If anyone is inspired by God to live our life and comes to our brothers, they should welcome him; and if they see that he is determined to profess our Rule, they should bring him to their minister as soon as possible, being very careful not to interfere in his temporal affairs in any way. The minister, for his part, should receive him kindly and encourage him and tell him all about our way of life. When that has been done, the candidate should sell all his possessions and give the money to the poor, if he is willing and able to do so in conscience and without hindrance. The friars and their ministers, however, should be careful not to interfere in his affairs in any way; they must not accept any money from him, either personally or through an intermediary. But if they are in want, the friars could accept other material goods for their needs, just like the rest of the poor, but not money.

When the postulant returns, the minister should clothe him as a novice for a year, giving him two tunics without a hood, a cord and trousers, and a caperon[1] reaching to the cord. When the year fixed for the novitiate is over, he should be allowed to profess obedience; and once that has been done, he may not change to another Order, or wander about beyond the limits of obedience, as the pope has commanded.[2] The Gospel tells us, *No one, having put his hand to the plough and looking back, is fit for the kingdom of God* (Lk. 9:62).

If anyone who seeks admission to the Order cannot dispose of his property without hindrance, although he is spiritually minded to do so, he should leave it all behind him, and that is enough.

No candidate may be received contrary to the norms and prescriptions of the Church.

The friars who have already made their profession of obedience may have one habit with a hood and, if necessary, another without a hood. They may also have a cord and trousers. All the friars must wear poor clothes and they can patch them with pieces of sackcloth and other material, with God's blessing. As our Lord tells us in the Gospel, *Those who wear fine clothes and live in luxury are in the houses of kings* (Lk. 7:25).

And even though people may call them hypocrites, the friars should never cease doing good. They should avoid expensive clothes in this world in order that they may have something to wear in the kingdom of heaven (Mt. 22:11).

CHAPTER VI

Recourse to the ministers, and let none of the friars be called "Prior"

The friars who cannot observe the Rule, no matter where they are, must have recourse to their minister as soon as possible and tell him all about it. The minister should do his best to provide for them as he would like provision to be made for himself, if he were in similar circumstances.

No one is to be called "Prior". They are all to be known as "Friars Minor" without distinction, and they should be prepared to wash one another's feet.

CHAPTER VII

Work and the service of others

The friars who are engaged in the service of lay people for whom they work should not be in charge of money or of the cellar. They are forbidden to accept positions of authority in the houses of their employers, or to take on any job which would give scandal or make them lose their own souls. They should be the least and subordinate to everyone in the house.

The friars who have a trade should work at it, provided that it is no obstacle to their spiritual progress and can be practised without scandal. The Psalmist tells us, *You shall eat the fruit of your handiwork; happy shall you be, and favoured* (127:2); and St Paul adds, *If any man will not work, neither let him eat* (2 Thess. 3:10). Everyone should remain at the trade and in the position in which he was called. In payment they may accept anything they need, except money. If necessary, they can go for alms like the rest of the friars. They are allowed to have the tools which they need for their trade.

All the friars must work hard doing good, as it has been said, "Always be doing something worthwhile; then the devil will al-

ways find you busy,"[3] and, "Idleness is the enemy of the soul."[4] And
so those who serve God should be always busy praying or doing
good.

No matter where they are, in hermitages or elsewhere, the
friars must be careful not to claim the ownership of any place, or
try to hold it against someone else. Everyone who comes to them,
friend or foe, rogue or robber, must be made welcome.

And all the friars, no matter where they are or in whatever
situation they find themselves, should, like spiritually minded
men, diligently show reverence and honour to one another *without
murmuring* (1 Pet. 4:9). They should let it be seen that they are
happy in God, cheerful and courteous, as is expected of them, and
be careful not to appear gloomy or depressed like hypocrites.

CHAPTER VIII

The friars are forbidden to take money

Our Lord tells us in the Gospel, *Take heed and guard yourselves from all covetousness* (Lk. 12:15) and malice; and *Take heed
of the cares of this life* (Lk. 21:34) and the anxieties of the world.
And so all the friars, no matter where they are or where they go,
are forbidden to take or accept money in any way or under any
form, or have it accepted for them, for clothing or books, or as
wages, or in any other necessity, except to provide for the urgent
needs of those who are ill. We should have no more use or regard for
money in any of its forms than for dust. Those who think it is worth
more or who are greedy for it, expose themselves to the danger of
being deceived by the devil. We have left everything we had behind
us; we must be very careful now not to lose the kingdom of heaven
for so little. If ever we find money somewhere, we should think no
more of it than of the dust we trample under our feet, for it is vanity
of vanities, and all vanity (Eccles. 1:2).

If any of the friars collects or keeps money, except for the needs
of the sick, the others must regard him as a fraud and a thief and a
robber and a traitor, who keeps a purse,[5] unless he is sincerely
sorry. The friars are absolutely forbidden to take money as alms, or
have it accepted for them; so too they cannot ask for it themselves,
or have others ask for it, for their houses or dwelling places. It is
also forbidden to accompany anyone who is collecting money for
their houses.

The friars are free to engage in any other activity which is not
contrary to our Rule, with God's blessing. But if there are lepers in

urgent need, the friars may beg alms for them, only they must be on their guard against money. So too, they should not undertake long journeys for mere temporal reasons.

CHAPTER IX

Begging alms

The friars should be delighted to follow the lowliness and poverty of our Lord Jesus Christ, remembering that of the whole world we must own nothing; *but having food and sufficient clothing, with these let us be content* (1 Tim. 6:8), as St Paul says. They should be glad to live among social outcasts, among the poor and helpless, the sick and the lepers, and those who beg by the wayside. If they are in want, they should not be ashamed to beg alms, remembering that our Lord Jesus Christ, the Son of the living, all-powerful God *set his face like a very hard rock* (Is. 50:7) and was not ashamed. He was poor and he had no home of his own and he lived on alms, he and the Blessed Virgin and his disciples.

If people insult them and refuse to give them alms, they should thank God for it, because they will be honoured before the judgement-seat of our Lord Jesus Christ for these insults. The shame will be imputed to those who cause it, not to those who suffer it. Alms are an inheritance and a right which is due to the poor because our Lord Jesus Christ acquired this inheritance for us. The friars who are busy begging alms will receive a great reward themselves, besides enriching those who give them. Everything people leave after them in this world is lost, but for their charity and almsgiving they will receive a reward from God.

The friars should have no hesitation about telling one another what they need, so that they can provide for one another. They are bound to love and care for one another as brothers, according to the means God gives them, just as a mother loves and cares for her son. As St Paul says: *Let not him who eats despise him who does not eat, and let not him who does not eat judge him who eats* (Rom. 14:3). In case of necessity the friars, no matter where they are, can eat any ordinary food, just as our Lord tells us about King David who *ate the loaves of proposition, which he could not lawfully eat, but only the priests* (Mk 2:26). And they should remember those other words of the Lord: *Take heed to yourselves, lest your hearts be overburdened with self-indulgence and drunkenness and the cares of this life, and that day come upon you suddenly as a snare. For come it will upon all who dwell on the face of all the earth* (Lk. 21:34-35).

In times of urgent need, the friars may provide for themselves
as God gives them the opportunity, because necessity knows no
law.

CHAPTER XXII

An exhortation to the friars

Remember the words of our Lord, *Love your enemies, do good to
those who hate you* (Mt. 5:44). Our Lord Jesus Christ himself, in
whose footsteps we must follow (cf. 1 Pet. 2:21), called the man who
betrayed him his friend, and gave himself up of his own accord to
his executioners. Therefore, our friends are those who for no reason
cause us trouble and suffering, shame or injury, pain or torture,
even martyrdom and death. It is these we must love, and love very
much, because for all they do to us we are given eternal life.

We must hate our lower nature with its vices and sins; by
living a wordly life, it would deprive us of the love of our Lord Jesus
Christ and of eternal life, dragging us down with it into hell. By our
own fault we are corrupt, wretched, strangers to all good, willing
and eager only to do evil, as our Lord says in the Gospel: *Out of the
heart of men come evil thoughts, adulteries, immorality, murders,
thefts, covetousness, wickedness, deceit, shamelessness, jealousy,
blasphemy, pride, foolishness. All these things come from within,
from the heart of man, and it is these that make a man unclean* (Mk
7:21-22).

We have left the world now and all we have to do is to be
careful to obey God's will and please him. We must be very careful,
or we will turn out to be like the earth by the wayside, or the stony
or thorn-choked ground, as our Lord tells us in the Gospel: *The seed
is the word of God. And those by the wayside are they who have
heard; then the devil comes and takes away the word from their
heart, that they may not believe and be saved. Now those upon the
rock are they who, when they have heard, receive the word with joy;
and these have no root, but believe for a while, and in time of
temptation fall away. And that which fell among thorns, these are
they who have heard, and as they go their way are choked by the
cares and riches and pleasures of life, and their fruit does not ripen.
But that upon good ground, these are they who, with a right and
good heart, having heard the word, hold it fast, and bear fruit in
patience* (Lk. 8:11-15).

And so we friars should *leave the dead to bury their own dead*
(Mt. 8:22), as the Lord says. We should beware especially of the

malice and wiles of Satan; his only desire is to prevent man from raising his mind and heart to his Lord and God. He goes about, longing to steal man's heart away under the pretext of some good or useful interest, and obliterate the words and commandments of God from his memory. By the anxieties and worries of this life he tries to dull man's heart and make a dwelling for himself there, as our Lord put it: *But when the unclean spirit has gone out of man, he roams through dry places in search of rest, and finds none. Then he says, "I will return to my house which I have left"; and when he has come to it, he finds the place unoccupied, swept and decorated. Then he goes and takes with him seven other spirits more evil than himself, and they enter in and dwell there; and the last state of that man becomes worse than the first* (Mt. 12:43-45). And so we must all keep close watch over ourselves or we will be lost and turn our minds and hearts from God, because we think there is something worth having or doing, or that we will gain some advantage.

In that love which is God (cf. 1 Jn. 4:16), I entreat all my friars, ministers and subjects, to put away every attachment, all care and solicitude, and serve, love, honour, and adore our Lord and God with a pure heart and mind;[6] this is what he seeks above all else. We should make a dwelling-place within ourselves where he can stay, he who is the Lord God almighty, Father, Son, and Holy Spirit. He himself tells us: *Watch, then, praying at all times, that you may be accounted worthy to escape all these things that are to be, and to stand before the Son of Man* (Lk. 21:36). *When you stand up to pray* (Mk 11:25), say *Our Father who art in heaven* (Mt. 6:9). Let us adore him with a pure heart for *we must always pray and not lose heart* (Lk. 18:1); it is such men as these the Father claims for his worshippers. *God is spirit, and they who worship him must worship in spirit and truth* (Jn 4:24). We should turn to him as to *the shepherd and guardian of our souls* (1 Pet. 2:25). He says, *I am the good shepherd* (Jn 10:11). *I feed my sheep and I lay down my life for my sheep* (Jn 10:15). *All you are brothers. And call no one on earth your father; for one is your Father, who is in heaven. Neither be called masters; for one only is your Master, the Christ* (Mt. 23:8–10) who is in heaven.

If you abide in me, and if my words abide in you, ask whatever you will and it shall be done to you (Jn 15:7). *For where two or three are gathered together for my sake, there am I in the midst of them* (Mt. 18:20). *Behold I am with you even unto the consummation of the world* (Mt. 28:20). *The words that I have spoken to you are spirit and life* (Jn 6:64). *I am the way, and the truth, and the life* (Jn 14:6).

And so we must hold fast to the words, the life, the teaching, and the holy Gospel of our Lord Jesus Christ. Of his own goodness, he prayed to his Father for us and made his name known to us, as he said: Father, *I have manifested thy name to the men whom thou hast given me; because the words that thou hast given me, I have given to them. And they have received them, and have known of a truth that I came forth from thee, and they have believed that thou didst send me. I pray for them; not for the world do I pray, but for those whom thou hast given me, because they are thine, and all things that are mine are thine.*

Holy Father, keep in thy name those whom thou hast given me, that they may be one even as we are. These things I speak in the world, in order that they may have my joy made full in themselves. I have given them thy word; and the world has hated them because they are not of the world, even as I am not of the world. I do not pray that thou take them out of the world, but that thou keep them from evil. Sanctify them in truth. Thy word is truth.

Even as thou hast sent me into the world, so I also have sent them into the world. And for them I sanctify myself, that they also may be sanctified in truth. Yet not for these only do I pray, but for those also who through their word are to believe in me, that they may be perfectly made one, *and that the world may know that thou hast sent me, and that thou hast loved them even as thou hast loved me.* I will reveal thy name to them *in order that the love with which thou hast loved me be in them, and I in them. Father, I will that where I am, they also whom thou hast given me may be with me in order that they may behold my glory* (Jn 17:6–26) in thy kingdom.

ST. BONAVENTURE

Journey of the Mind to God

Theologian, cardinal, and successor of St. Francis as minister-general of the Friars Minor, St. Bonaventure (1221–1274) teaches a method of contemplation colored by the lyrical warmth of the Franciscan movement and by the probing analytical method characteristic of the new scholastic theology.

The following excerpt from his Journey of the Mind to God *(1259) is a summary of this Franciscan method of meditation.*

PROLOGUE

1. At the outset I invoke the Source whence all enlightenment descends to man, the Father of light from whom is "every best gift and every perfect gift."[1] Through the Son of God, our Lord Jesus Christ, I appeal to the Eternal Father that by the intercession of the most holy Virgin Mary, Mother of the same God and Lord, Christ Jesus, and by that of Blessed Francis, our guide and father, He might impart to us the "spirit of wisdom and revelation"[2] so as to direct our feet in the ways of that peace which surpasseth all understanding. It was the gospel of this peace our Lord Jesus Christ preached; it was peace such as this He gave to men. Following in the footsteps of the Master, our father St Francis, went through life preaching peace at the beginning and end of every discourse, wishing peace to all whom he met on the way, and sighing after ecstatic peace in every elevation of his mind like a citizen of that Jerusalem, whereof it is said by that Man of Peace who was peaceful with them that hated peace: "Seek ye those things which are for the peace of Jerusalem."[3] For he knew that only in peace stands the throne of Solomon, as it is written: "In peace is his dwelling-place, and his habitation is in Sion."[4]

2. Inspired by the example of the Blessed Francis, I sought after this peace with ardent longing—I, a sinner, who, though in all respects unworthy, have succeeded, the seventh in the order of time, to the general ministry of the brethren. It happened that as this desire came vehemently to me, and I longed for peace, God led me, in the thirty-third year after the death of Francis, to Mount Alvernia as to a place of quiet. While I abode there and was pondering over certain elevations of the human mind to God, the associations of the place brought before me that miracle which on this very spot had happened to the Blessed Francis when he saw a winged Seraph in the image of the Crucified. It occurred to me that the vision vouchsafed to St Francis typified the uplifting of our father in contemplation and the manner of his rapture suggested itself to my mind.

3. The six wings in which the Seraph was enveloped may rightly be understood to signify the six downpourings of heavenly light by means of which the soul is disposed to progress, as by steps or degrees, along the way that leads to peace through the ecstatic transports of Christian Wisdom. This road to final peace is none other than the most fervent love of the Crucified which so transformed Paul, when caught up to the third heaven,[5] that he could say: "With Christ I am nailed to the cross: I live, now not I, but

Christ liveth in me."[5] This same love of the Crucified so absorbed
the mind of Francis also that it revealed itself in the flesh inasmuch as he bore the most sacred Stigmata of the Passion in his
body for two years before his death. This vision of the six seraphic
wings, therefore, symbolises the six degrees of illumination which,
beginning with created things, lead up even to God to whom there
is no access save through the Crucified. "He that entereth not by
the door into the sheepfold, but climbeth up another way, the same
is a thief and a robber."[7] "But he that entereth in by the door shall
go in and out and shall find pasture." Wherefore John writes in the
Apocalypse: "Blessed are they that wash their robes in the Blood of
the Lamb: that they may have a right to the tree of life, and may
enter in by the gates into the city."[8] This is tantamount to saying
that no one can enter the heavenly Jerusalem who enters not
through the Blood of the Lamb as through a portal. No man is in
any way disposed for divine contemplations which lead to mental
transports and unheard of things unless he be, like the prophet
Daniel, a "man of desires." In two ways are such desires enkindled
in us: through the cry of prayer that ascends from anguish of heart,
and by the splendour of high thought which turns the eyes of the
mind directly and intently upon the rays of divine light.

4. Wherefore, to the groanings of prayer to God through
Christ crucified, in whose Blood we are cleansed from the defile-
ments of sin,[9] I first of all invite the reader, lest he should per-
chance think that reading will suffice without unction, speculation
without devotion, research without admiration, circumspection
without exultation, industry without piety, knowledge without
charity, intelligence without humility, study without divine grace,
or speculation without divinely inspired wisdom. To those, therefore, who are disposed by divine grace, the pious and humble, the
contrite and devout, to those who are anointed with the oil of divine
gladness, to the lovers of divine Wisdom and to those inflamed with
the desire thereof, and who wish to go apart in order to taste and
magnify and appreciate God, I offer the following speculations, at
the same time warning them that it is of little or no avail to look in
the mirror of creation unless the mirror of our minds be cleaned
and polished. First then, O man of God, thou must exercise thyself
in holy compunction, experiencing the prick of conscience, before
thou may raise thy eyes to the rays of divine Wisdom reflected in
her mirror, lest haply, from gazing on these rays, thou fall into a
deeper pit of darkness.

5. I have thought it well to divide this treatise into seven chapters and I have prefixed a title to each for the easier understanding of the things treated therein. I entreat my readers that they will regard the intention of the writer more than his work, the meaning of what is said more than the manner of its saying, truth more than elegance of style, exercise of the affections more than erudition of mind. Those who will do this must not hurry lightly over the pages but must slowly set to work and deeply ponder over their content.

CHAPTER I

Degrees of the Soul's Ascent

1. "Happy the man whose help is from Thee, when he hath set pilgrimages in his heart through the Valley of Tears, to the goal he hath fixed."[10] Since happiness is nothing else but the enjoyment of the Supreme Good, and the Supreme Good is above us, no one can be happy who does not rise beyond himself. This raising up of man is to be understood, of course, of mind and heart and not of body, and since there is question of reaching above himself on the part of man, he must be helped by supernatural strength and be lifted up by a higher power that stoops to raise him. However much then a man's inward steps are ordered and progress made, it is of no avail unless accompanied by help from on high. But divine aid is at hand for those who seek it with a devout and humble heart, and sigh for it in this Valley of Tears; this is done by fervent prayer. Prayer is, therefore, the source and origin of every upward progress that has God for goal. Wherefore, Dionysius in his "Mystical Theology," wishing to instruct us in these transcendent workings of the soul sets down prayer as the first condition. Let us each, therefore, have recourse to prayer and say to our Lord God: "Lead me, O Lord, on Thy path, that I may walk in Thy truth. Let my heart rejoice that it feareth Thy name."

2. By so praying we are led to discern the degrees of the soul's ascent to God. For, inasmuch as, in our present condition, this universe of things is a ladder whereby we may ascend to God, since among these things some are God's footprints, some God's image, some corporeal, some spiritual, some temporal, some eternal, and, hence, some outside of us, and some inside, it follows that if we are to attain to the contemplation of the First Principle and Source of all things, in Himself altogether spiritual, eternal, and above us,

we must begin with God's footprints which are corporeal, temporal and outside us and so enter on the Way that leads to God. We enter in within our own souls, which are images of the eternal God, spiritual and interior to us, and this is to enter into the Truth of God. Finally, we must reach out beyond and above ourselves to the region of the eternal and supereminently spiritual and look to the First Principle of all, and that is to enjoy the knowledge of God in reverential contemplation of His Majesty.

3. Here we have the three days' journey in the wilderness: "The Lord God of the Hebrews hath called us: we will go three days' journey into the wilderness, to sacrifice unto the Lord, our God."[11] Here we have also the threefold illumination of the day in Genesis when the Lord divided the light from darkness, when the first was evening as it were, the second morning and the third was noon-day. We have also that triple existence of things, first in matter, then in mind and finally in the divine art, as it is written: "Let it be made, He accomplished, and it was made."[12] Finally, there is reference to the triple substance of Christ, who is the Way to God, that is, to the corporeal, the spiritual and the divine.

4. In direct relation with this threefold progress of the soul to God, the human mind has three fundamental attitudes or outlooks. The first is towards corporeal things without, and in this respect it is designated as animal or simply sensual; the next is where it enters in within itself to contemplate itself, and here it ranks as spirit; the third is where its upward glance is beyond itself, and then it is designated "mens" or mind. In all three ways the human soul must prepare to raise itself to God so that it may love Him with the whole mind, with all its heart, and with its whole soul,[13] for in this consists the fullness of the Law and the highest Christian Wisdom.

5. But since every one of the aforesaid modes is doubled, according as we come to consider God as Alpha, and as Omega,[14] or according as we come to contemplate God in each as in and through a mirror, or because each of these modes of contemplation may be joined with another, or operative simply and purely in itself, so it is necessary that these three primary grades should be raised to the number six; whence, as God completed the universal world in six days, and rested on the seventh, so the smaller world of man is led in the most orderly way, by six successive grades of illumination, to the quiet of contemplation. A symbol of this may be seen in the six steps that led to the throne of Solomon;[15] in the six-winged Seraphim which Isaiah beheld in vision;[16] in the six days after

which God called Moses from the midst of darkness;[17] and in the six days after which, as we read in Matthew, Christ led His disciples up into a mountain, and was transfigured before them.[18]

6. Corresponding to the six degrees of the soul's ascent to God there are within the soul six kinds of faculties or powers by which we rise from depths to the heights, from external to things internal, from things of time to those of eternity, to wit, sense, imagination, reason, intellect, intelligence, and the fine point or apex of the soul. These powers we have implanted in us by nature; by sin deformed, they are reformed through grace; and they must be purified by justice, exercised by knowledge, and made perfect by wisdom.

7. In his primitive constitution man was created by God capable of untroubled contemplation, and for that reason was placed by God in a "garden of delights." But, turning his back on the true light in order to pursue the mutable good, he found himself, through his own fault, diminished and removed from his pristine stature. With him the whole human race through original sin was afflicted in a twofold manner: the human mind by ignorance and the human body by concupiscence. As a result man, blinded and bent down, sits in darkness and sees not the light of heaven, unless he be strengthened against concupiscence by grace with justice, and against ignorance by knowledge with wisdom. All this is done by Jesus Christ, "who of God is made unto us wisdom and justice and sanctification and redemption."[19] He, being the Power and Wisdom of God, the Incarnate Word full of grace and truth, is the Author of both grace and truth. He it is who infuses the grace of charity which, when it comes "from a pure heart, and a good conscience, and an unfeigned faith," is capable of ordering the whole soul according to the threefold aspect above mentioned. He also taught the knowledge of truth according to the triple mode of theology: by symbolic theology in which He teaches us how we might rightly use sensible things, by theology properly so called wherein we learn the use of things intelligible, and by mystical theology through contact with which we may be raised aloft to things unspeakable.

8. Whoso, therefore, would set out in quest of God must first leave aside such sins as deform nature, and engage in the exercise of the aforesaid powers of his soul. By prayer he may hope for grace which will readjust his powers in harmony; in a holy life he must seek for purifying justice; in meditation he will seek that knowledge which enlighteneth; in contemplation he will acquire perfect-

ing wisdom. Therefore, just as no one comes to wisdom save through grace, justice, and knowledge, so no one comes to contemplation save by clear-sighted meditation, by a holy life and devout prayer. As grace is the foundation of an upright will, and of a clear-sighted enlightened reason, so we must first pray, then live holily, and, thirdly, we must look long and attentively at the manifestations of truth; and so attending, we must rise, step by step, until we reach the high mountain where God of gods is seen in Sion.

ST. THOMAS AQUINAS

Summa Theologica, IIa-IIae

Born near Naples into a noble family, Thomas Aquinas (1225–1274) studied as a child under the Benedictines at Monte Cassino. After a bitter struggle against the wishes of his family, he joined the newly founded Dominican Order at the age of eighteen, and pursued a brilliant career as a student at Cologne and Paris. Later he taught at Paris and at various other study-houses of his Order.

The most important speculative theologian of the high Middle Ages, Thomas was intensely interested in questions concerning the spiritual life. The following selections drawn from the Summa Theologica *(1265–1272) illustrate this interest as it was translated into the dialectical method of medieval scholarly discourse.*

Q. 180   ARTICLE 7

Whether There Is Delight in Contemplation?

We proceed thus to the Seventh Article:—

Obj. 1. It would seem that there is no delight in contemplation. For delight belongs to the appetitive power; whereas contemplation resides chiefly in intellect. Therefore it would seem that there is no delight in contemplation.

Obj. 2. Further, all strife and struggle is a hindrance to delight. Now there is strife and struggle in contemplation. For Gregory says (*Hom. xiv, in Ezech.*) that *when the soul strives to contemplate God, it is in a state of struggle; at one time it almost overcomes, because by understanding and feeling it tastes something of the incomprehensible light, and at another time it almost succumbs, because even while tasting, it fails.* Therefore, there is no delight in contemplation.

Obj. 3. Further, delight is the result of a perfect operation, as stated in [Aristotle's] *Ethic.* x. 4. Now the contemplation of wayfarers is imperfect, according to 1 Cor. xiii. 12, *We see through a glass in a dark manner.* Therefore, seemingly there is no delight in the contemplative life.

Obj. 4. Further, a lesion of the body is an obstacle to delight. Now contemplation causes a lesion of the body; wherefore it is stated (*Gen xxxii*) that after Jacob had said (*verse 30*) *"I have seen God face to face"* ... *he halted on his foot (31)* ... *because he touched the sinew of his thigh and it shrank (32).* Therefore seemingly there is no delight in contemplation.

On the contrary, It is written of the contemplation of wisdom (Wis. viii, 16): *Her conversation hath no bitterness, nor her company any tediousness, but joy and gladness:* and Gregory says (*Hom. xiv, in Ezech.*) that the *contemplative life is sweetness exceedingly lovable.*

I answer that, There may be delight in any particular contemplation in two ways. First by reason of the operation itself, because each individual delights in the operation which befits him according to his own nature or habit. Now contemplation of the truth befits a man according to his nature as a rational animal: the result being that *all men naturally desire to know*, so that consequently they delight in the knowledge of truth. And more delightful still does this become to one who has the habit of wisdom and knowledge, the result of which is that he contemplates without difficulty. Secondly, contemplation may be delightful on the part of its object, in so far as one contemplates that which one loves; even as bodily vision gives pleasure, not only because to see is pleasurable in itself but because one sees a person whom one loves. Since, then, the contemplative life consists chiefly in the contemplation of God, of which charity is the motive . . . it follows that there is delight in the contemplative life, not only by reason of the contemplation itself, but also by reason of the Divine love.

In both respects the delight thereof surpasses all human delight, both because spiritual delight is greater than carnal pleasure (as stated above, when we were treating of the passions), and because the love whereby God is loved out of charity surpasses all love. Hence it is written (Ps. xxxiii. 9): *O taste and see that the Lord is sweet.*

Reply Obj. 1. Although the contemplative life consists chiefly in an act of the intellect, it has its beginning in the appetite, since it is through charity that one is urged to the contemplation of God. And since the end corresponds to the beginning, it follows that the term also and the end of the contemplative life has its being in the appetite, since one delights in seeing the object loved, and the very delight in the object seen arouses a yet greater love. Wherefore Gregory says (*Hom. xiv, in Ezech.*) that *when we see one whom we love, we are so aflame as to love him more.* And this is the ultimate perfection of the contemplative life, namely that the Divine truth be not only seen but also loved.

Reply Obj. 2. Strife or struggle arising from the opposition of an external thing hinders delight in that thing. For a man delights not in a thing against which he strives: but in that for which he strives; when he has obtained it, other things being equal, he delights yet more: wherefore Augustine says (*Conf. viii, 3*) that *the more peril there was in the battle, the greater the joy in the triumph.* But there is no strife or struggle in contemplation on the part of the truth which we contemplate, though there is on the part of our defective understanding and our corruptible body which drags us down to lower things, according to Wis. ix. 15, *The corruptible body is a load upon the soul, and the earthly habitation presseth down the mind that museth upon many things.* Hence it is that when man attains to the contemplation of truth, he loves it yet more, while he hates the more his own deficiency and the weight of his corruptible body, so as to say with the Apostle (Rom. vii. 24): *Unhappy man that I am, who shall deliver me from the body of this death?* Wherefore Gregory say (*Hom. xiv, in Ezech.*): *When God is once known by desire and understanding, He withers all carnal pleasure in us.*

Reply Obj. 3. The contemplation of God in this life is imperfect in comparison with contemplation in heaven; and in like manner the delight of the wayfarer's contemplation is imperfect as compared with the delight of contemplation in heaven, of which it is written (Ps xxxv. 9): *Thou shalt make them drink of the torrent of Thy pleasure.* Yet, though the contemplation of Divine things which is to be had by wayfarers is imperfect, it is more delightful than all other contemplation, however perfect, on account of the excellence of that which is contemplated. Hence the Philosopher [Aristotle] says *(De Part. Animal i. 5): We may happen to have our own little theories about those sublime beings and godlike substances, and though we grasp them but feebly, nevertheless so elevating is the knowledge that they give us more delight than any of those things that are round about us:* and Gregory says in the same sense *(loc. cit.): The contemplative life is sweetness exceedingly lovable; for it carries the soul away above itself, it opens heaven and discovers the spiritual world to the eyes of the mind.*

Reply Obj. 4. After contemplation Jacob halted with one foot, *because we need to grow weak in the love of the world ere we wax strong in the love of God,* as Gregory says *(loc. cit.) Thus when we have known the sweetness of God, we have one foot sound while the other halts; since every one who halts on one foot leans only on that foot which is sound.*

Q. 182, ARTICLE 1

Whether the Active Life is More Excellent Than the Contemplative?

We proceed thus to the First Article:—

Obj. 1. It would seem that the active life is more excellent than the contemplative. For *that which belongs to better men would seem to be worthier and better,* as the Philosopher says *(Top. iii. 1).* Now the active life belongs to persons of higher rank, namely prelates, who are placed in a position of honor and power; wherefore Augustine says *(De Civ. Dei, xix. 19)* that *in our actions we must not love honor or power in this life.* Therefore it would seem that the active life is more excellent than the contemplative.

Obj. 2. Further, in all habits and acts, direction belongs to the more important; thus the military art, being the more important, directs the art of the bridle-maker. Now it belongs to the active life to direct and command the contemplative, as appears from the words addressed to Moses (Exod. xix. 21), *Go down and charge the people, lest they should have a mind to pass the fixed limits to see the Lord.* Therefore the active life is more excellent than the contemplative.

Obj. 3. Further, no man should be taken away from a greater thing in order to be occupied with lesser things: for the Apostle says (1 Cor. xii. 31): *Be zealous for the better gifts.* Now some are taken away from the state of the contemplative life to the occupations of the active life, as in the case of those who are transferred to the state of prelacy. Therefore it would seem that the active life is more excellent than the contemplative.

On the contrary, Our Lord said (Luke x. 42): *Mary hath chosen the best part, which shall not be taken away from her.* Now Mary figures the contemplative life. Therefore the contemplative life is more excellent than the active.

I answer that, Nothing prevents certain things being more excellent in themselves, whereas they are surpassed by another in some respect. Accordingly we must reply that the contemplative life is simply more excellent than the active: and the Philosopher proves this by eight reasons (*Ethic. x. 7, 8*). The first is, because the contemplative life becomes man according to that which is best in him, namely the intellect, and according to its proper objects, namely things intelligible; whereas the active life is occupied with externals. Hence Rachel, by whom the contemplative life is signified, is interpreted *the vision of the principle,* whereas as Gregory says (*Moral. vi. 37*) the active life is signified by Lia who was blear-eyed.—The second reason is because the contemplative life can be more continuous, although not as regards the highest degree of contemplation, wherefore Mary, by whom the contemplative life is signified, is described as *sitting* all the time *at the Lord's feet.* —Thirdly, because the contemplative life is more delightful than the active; wherefore Augustine says (*De Verb. Dom. Serm. ciii*) that *Martha was troubled, but Mary feasted.* Fourthly, because in the contemplative life man is more self-sufficient, since he needs fewer things for that purpose; wherefore it was said (Luke x. 41):

Martha, Martha, thou are careful and art troubled about many things.—Fifthly, because the contemplative life is loved more for its own sake, while the active life is directed to something else. Hence it is written (Ps. xxvi. 4): *One thing I have asked of the Lord, this will I seek after, that I may dwell in the house of the Lord all the days of my life, that I may see the delight of the Lord.*—Sixthly, because the contemplative life consists in leisure and rest, according to Ps. xlv. 11, *Be still and see that I am God.*—Seventhly, because the contemplative life is according to Divine things, whereas active life is according to human things; wherefore Augustine says (*De Verb. Dom. Serm. civ*): *"In the beginning was the Word": to Him was Mary hearkening: "The Word was made flesh": Him was Martha serving.*—Eighthly, because the contemplative life is according to that which is most proper to man, namely his intellect; whereas in the works of the active life the lower powers also, which are common to us and brutes, have their part; wherefore (Ps xxxv. 7) after the words, *Men and beasts Thou wilt preserve, O Lord,* that which is special to man is added (verse 10): *In thy light we shall see light.*

Our Lord adds a ninth reason (Luke x. 42) when He says: *Mary has chosen the best part, which shall not be taken away from her,* which words Augustine (*De Verb. Dom. Serm. ciii*) expounds thus: *Not—Thou hast chosen badly but —She has chosen better. Why better? Listen —Because it shall not be taken away from her. But the burden of necessity shall at length be taken from thee: whereas the sweetness of truth is eternal.*

Yet in a restricted sense and in a particular case one should prefer the active life on account of the needs of the present life. Thus too the Philosopher says (*Top. iii. 2*): *It is better to be wise than to be rich, yet for one who is in need, it is better to be rich.* . . .

Reply Obj. 1. Not only the active life concerns prelates, they should also excel in the contemplative life; hence Gregory says (*Pastor. ii. 1*): *A prelate should be foremost in action, more uplifted than others in contemplation.*

Reply Obj. 2. The contemplative life consists in a certain liberty of mind. For Gregory says (*Hom. iii, in Ezech.*) that *the contemplative life obtains a certain freedom of mind, for it thinks not of temporal but of eternal things.* And Boëthius says (*De Consol.*

v. 2): *The soul of man must needs be more free while it continues to gaze on the Divine mind, and less so when it stoops to bodily things.* Wherefore it is evident that the active life does not directly command the contemplative life, but prescribes certain works of the active life as dispositions to the contemplative life; which it accordingly serves rather than commands. Gregory refers to this when he says (*loc. cit. in Ezech.*) that *the active life is bondage, whereas the contemplation life is freedom.*

Reply Obj. 3. Sometimes a man is called away from the contemplative life to the works of the active life on account of some necessity of the present life, yet not so as to be compelled to forsake contemplation altogether. Hence Augustine says (*De Civ. Dei, xix. 19*): *The love of truth seeks a holy leisure, the demands of charity undertake an honest toil*, the work namely of the active life. *If no one imposes this burden upon us we must devote ourselves to the research and contemplation of truth, but if it be imposed on us, we must bear it because charity demands it of us. Yet even then we must not altogether forsake the delights of truth, lest we deprive ourselves of its sweetness, and this burden overwhelm us.* Hence it is clear that when a person is called from the contemplative to the active life, this is done by way not of subtraction but of addition.

WALTER HILTON

The Scale of Perfection

Little is known of the life of Walter Hilton (d. 1396), other than the fact that he had led the life of a hermit for some years before eventually joining the Augustinian Canons at Thurgarton in Nottinghamshire, England. His Scale of Perfection *is a masterpiece of spiritual writing that has influenced many subsequent spiritual writers. Together with the* Cloud of Unknowing *and the* Revelations *of Julian of Norwich, it sums up the great medieval English contribution to spirituality.*

The opening of the spiritual eyes is a glowing darkness and rich nothingness. . . . It may be called: Purity of soul and spiritual rest, inward stillness and peace of conscience, refinement of thought and integrity of soul, a lively consciousness of grace and solitude of heart, the wakeful sleep of the spouse and the tasting of heavenly joys, the ardor of love and brightness of light, the entry into contemplation and reformation in feeling. . . .

Inward fears, doubts and perplexities will almost reduce the soul to despair. It will seem to be forsaken by God and abandoned into the hands of the devil, but it will retain a small secret trust in the goodness and mercy of God.

THE CLOUD OF UNKNOWING

Fourteenth-century England saw the flourishing of a number of important writers on spirituality. They are distinguished, as a group, by their avoidance of theological speculation and their concentration on practical suggestions for growth in prayer and the spiritual life. Here we are able to present selections from two of these English works: The Cloud of Unknowing, *and Mother Julian's* Revelations of Divine Love.

The anonymous author of The Cloud of Unknowing *is thought to have been a late fourteenth-century hermit who lived in the northeast Midlands of England. His works bear witness to the late-medieval revival of apophatic mysticism. Interesting affinities with Oriental hesychasm are evident, although they are probably the result of shared influences rather than of any direct contact between the two movements.*

As a practical guide for contemplative prayer, The Cloud *has rarely been surpassed. The following chapters give a taste of the delightful style of the author and an insight into the method of contemplation he teaches.*

CHAPTER III

How the work of contemplation shall be done;
of its excellence over all other works.

This is what you are to do: lift your heart up to the Lord, with a gentle stirring of love desiring him for his own sake and not for his gifts. Center all your attention and desire on him and let this be the sole concern of your mind and heart. Do all in your power to forget everything else, keeping your thoughts and desires free from involvement with any of God's creatures or their affairs whether in general or in particular. Perhaps this will seem like an irresponsible attitude, but I tell you, let them all be; pay no attention to them.

What I am describing here is the contemplative work of the spirit. It is this which gives God the greatest delight. For when you fix your love on him, forgetting all else, the saints and angels rejoice and hasten to assist you in every way—though the devils will rage and ceaselessly conspire to thwart you. Your fellow men are marvelously enriched by this work of yours, even if you may not fully understand how; the souls in purgatory are touched, for their suffering is eased by the effects of this work; and, of course, your own spirit is purified and strengthened by this contemplative work more than by all others put together. Yet for all this, when God's grace arouses you to enthusiasm, it becomes the lightest sort of work there is and one most willingly done. Without his grace, however, it is very difficult and almost, I should say, quite beyond you.

And so diligently persevere until you feel joy in it. For in the beginning it is usual to feel nothing but a kind of darkness about your mind, or as it were, a *cloud of unknowing*. You will seem to know nothing and to feel nothing except a naked intent toward God in the depths of your being. Try as you might, this darkness and this cloud will remain between you and your God. You will feel frustrated, for your mind will be unable to grasp him, and your heart will not relish the delight of his love. But learn to be at home in this darkness. Return to it as often as you can, letting your spirit cry out to him whom you love. For if, in this life, you hope to feel and see God as he is in himself it must be within this darkness and this cloud. But if you strive to fix your love on him forgetting all else, which is the work of contemplation I have urged you to begin, I am confident that God in his goodness will bring you to a deep experience of himself.

CHAPTER IV

Of the simplicity of contemplation; that it may not be acquired through knowledge or imagination.

I have described a little of what is involved in the contemplative work but now I shall discuss it further, insofar as I understand it, so that you may proceed securely and without misconceptions.

This work is not time-consuming even though some people believe otherwise. Actually it is the shortest you can imagine; as brief as an atom, which, as the philosophers say, is the smallest division of time. The atom is a moment so short and integral that the mind can scarcely conceive it. Nevertheless it is vastly important, for of this minute measure of time it is written: "You will be held responsible for all the time given you." This is entirely just because your principal spiritual faculty, the will, needs only this brief fraction of a moment to move toward the object of its desire.

If you were now restored by grace to the integrity man possessed before sin you would be complete master of these impulses. None would ever go astray, but would fly to the one sole good, the goal of all desire, God himself. For God created us in his image and likeness, making us like himself, and in the Incarnation he emptied himself of his divinity becoming a man like us. It is God, and he alone, who can fully satisfy the hunger and longing of our spirit which transformed by his redeeming grace is enabled to embrace him by love. He whom neither men nor angels can grasp by knowledge can be embraced by love. For the intellect of both men and angels is too small to comprehend God as he is himself.

Try to understand this point. Rational creatures such as men and angels possess two principal faculties, a knowing power and a loving power. No one can fully comprehend the uncreated God with his knowledge; but each one, in a different way, can grasp him fully through love. Truly this is the unending miracle of love: that one loving person, through his love, can embrace God, whose being fills and transcends the entire creation. And this marvelous work of love goes on forever, for he whom we love is eternal. Whoever has the grace to appreciate the truth of what I am saying, let him take my words to heart, for to experience this love is the joy of eternal life while to lose it is eternal torment.

He who with the help of God's grace becomes aware of the will's constant movements and learns to direct them toward God will never fail to taste something of heaven's joy even in this life and, certainly in the next, he will savor it fully. Now do you see why I rouse you to this spiritual work? You would have taken to it naturally had man not sinned, for man was created to love and everything else was created to make love possible. Nevertheless, by the work of contemplative love man will be healed. Failing in this work he sinks deeper into sin further and further from God, but by persevering in it he gradually rises from sin and grows in divine intimacy.

Therefore, be attentive to time and the way you spend it. Nothing is more precious. This is evident when you recall that in one tiny moment heaven may be gained or lost. God, the master of time, never gives the future. He gives only the present, moment by moment, for this is the law of the created order, and God will not contradict himself in his creation. Time is for man, not man for time. God, the Lord of nature, will never anticipate man's choices which follow one after another in time. Man will not be able to excuse himself at the last judgment, saying to God: "You overwhelmed me with the future when I was only capable of living in the present."

But now I see that you are discouraged and are saying to yourself: "What am I to do? If all he says is true, how shall I justify my past? I am twenty-four years old and until this moment I have scarcely noticed time at all. What is worse, I could not repair the past even if I wanted to, for according to his teaching such a task is impossible to me by nature even with the help of ordinary grace. Besides I know very well that in the future, either through frailty or laziness, I will probably not be any more attentive to the present moment than I have been in the past. I am completely discouraged. Please help me for the love of Jesus."

Well have you said "for the love of Jesus." For it is in his love that you will find help. In love all things are shared and so if you love Jesus, everyting of his is yours. As God he is the creator and dispenser of time; as man he consciously mastered time; as God and man he is the rightful judge of men and their use of time. Bind yourself to Jesus, therefore, in faith and love, so that belonging to him you may share all he has and enter the fellowship of those who love him. This is the communion of the blessed and these will be your friends: our Lady, St. Mary, who was full of grace at every moment; the angels, who are unable to waste time; and all the blessed in heaven and on earth, who through the grace of Jesus employ every moment in love. See, here is your strength. Understand what I am saying and be heartened. But remember, I warn you of one thing above all. No one can claim true fellowship with Jesus, his Mother, the angels, and the saints, unless he does all in his power with the help of grace to be mindful of time. For he must do his share however slight to strengthen the fellowship as it strengthens him.

And so do not neglect this contemplative work. Try also to appreciate its wonderful effects in your own spirit. When it is genuine it is simply a spontaneous desire springing suddenly toward God like spark from fire. It is amazing how many loving desires arise from the spirit of a person who is accustomed to this work. And yet, perhaps only one of these will be completely free from attachment to some created thing. Or again, no sooner has a man turned toward God in love when through human frailty he finds himself distracted by the remembrance of some created thing or some daily care. But no matter. No harm is done; for such a person quickly returns to deep recollection.

And now we come to the difference between the contemplative work and its counterfeits such as daydreaming, fantasizing, or subtle reasoning. These originate in a conceited, curious, or romantic mind whereas the blind stirring of love springs from a sincere and humble heart. Pride, curiosity, and daydreaming must be sternly checked if the contemplative work is to be authentically conceived in singleness of heart. Some will probably hear about this work and suppose that by their own ingenious efforts they can achieve it. They are likely to strain their mind and imagination unnaturally only to produce a false work which is neither human nor divine. Truly, such a person is dangerously deceived. And I fear that unless God intervenes with a miracle inspiring him to abandon these practices and humbly seek reliable counsel he will most certainly fall into mental aberrations or some great spiritual evil of the devil's devising. Then he risks losing both body and soul eternally. For the love of God, therefore, be careful in this work and never strain your mind or imagination, for truly you will not succeed this way. Leave these faculties at peace.

Do not suppose that because I have spoken of darkness and of a cloud I have in mind the clouds you see in an overcast sky or the darkness of your house when your candle fails. If I had, you could with a little imagination picture the summer skies breaking through the clouds or a clear light brightening the dark winter. But this isn't what I mean at all so forget this sort of nonsense. When I speak of darkness, I mean the absence of knowledge. If you are unable to understand something or if you have forgotten it, are you not in the dark as regards this thing? You cannot see it with your mind's eye. Well, in the same way, I have not said "cloud," but *cloud of unknowing*. For it is a darkness of unknowing that lies between you and your God.

CHAPTER V

That during contemplative prayer all created things and their works must be buried beneath the cloud of forgetting.

If you wish to enter into this cloud, to be at home in it, and to take up the contemplative work of love as I urge you to, there is something else you must do. Just as the *cloud of unkowing* lies above you, between you and your God, so you must fashion a *cloud of forgetting* beneath you, between you and every created thing. The *cloud of unknowing* will perhaps leave you with the feeling that you are far from God. But no, if it is authentic, only the absence of a *cloud of forgetting* keeps you from him now. Every time I say "all creatures," I refer not only to every created thing but also to all their circumstances and activities. I make no exception. You are to concern yourself with no creature whether material or spiritual nor with their situation and doings whether good or ill. To put it briefly, during this work you must abandon them all beneath the *cloud of forgetting*.

For although at certain times and in certain circumstances it is necessary and useful to dwell on the particular situation and activity of people and things, during this work it is almost useless. Thinking and remembering are forms of spiritual understanding in which the eye of the spirit is opened and closed upon things as the eye of a marksman is on his target. But I tell you that everything you dwell upon during this work becomes an obstacle to union with God. For if your mind is cluttered with these concerns there is no room for him.

Yes, and with all due reverence, I go so far as to say that it is equally useless to think you can nourish your contemplative work by considering God's attributes, his kindness or his dignity; or by thinking about our Lady, the angels, or the saints; or about the joys of heaven, wonderful as these will be. I believe that this kind of activity is no longer of any use to you. Of course, it is laudable to reflect upon God's kindness and to love and praise him for it; yet it is far better to let your mind rest in the awareness of him in his naked existence and to love and praise him for what he is in himself.

CHAPTER VI

A short explanation of contemplation in the form of a dialogue.

Now you say, "How shall I proceed to think of God as he is in himself?" To this I can only reply, "I do not know."

With this question you bring me into the very darkness and *cloud of unknowing* that I want you to enter. A man may know completely and ponder thoroughly every created thing and its works, yes, and God's works, too, but not God himself. Thought cannot comprehend God. And so, I prefer to abandon all I can know, choosing rather to love him whom I cannot know. Though we cannot know him we can love him. By love he may be touched and embraced, never by thought. Of course, we do well at times to ponder God's majesty or kindness for the insight these meditations may bring. But in the real contemplative work you must set all this aside and cover it over with a *cloud of forgetting*. Then let your loving desire, gracious and devout, step bravely and joyfully beyond it and reach out to pierce the darkness above. Yes, beat upon that thick *cloud of unknowing* with the dart of your loving desire and do not cease come what may.

CHAPTER VII

How a person should conduct himself during prayer
with regard to all thoughts, especially those arising
from curiosity and natural intelligence.

It is inevitable that ideas will arise in your mind and try to distract you in a thousand ways. They will question you saying, "What are you looking for, what do you want?" To all of them you must reply, "God alone I seek and desire, only him."

If they ask, "Who is this God?", tell them that he is the God who created you, redeemed you, and brought you to this work. Say to your thoughts, "You are powerless to grasp him. Be still." Dispel them by turning to Jesus with loving desire. Don't be surprised if your thoughts seem holy and valuable for prayer. Probably you will find yourself thinking about the wonderful qualities of Jesus, his sweetness, his love, his graciousness, his mercy. But if you pay attention to these ideas they will have gained what they wanted of you, and will go on chattering until they divert you even more to the thought of his passion. Then will come ideas about his great kindness, and if you keep listening they will be delighted. Soon you will be thinking about your sinful life and perhaps in this connection you will recall some place where you have lived in the past, until suddenly, before you know it, your mind is completely scattered.

And yet, they were not bad thoughts. Actually, they were good and holy thoughts, so valuable, in fact, that anyone who expects to advance without having meditated often on his own sinfulness, the Passion of Christ, and the kindness, goodness, and dignity of God, will most certainly go astray and fail in his purpose. But a person who has long pondered these things must eventually leave them behind beneath a *cloud of forgetting* if he hopes to pierce the *cloud of unknowing* that lies between him and his God. So whenever you feel drawn by grace to the contemplative work and are determined to do it, simply raise your heart to God with a gentle stirring of love. Think only of God, the God who created you, redeemed you, and guided you to this work. Allow no other ideas about God to enter your mind. Yet even this is too much. A naked intent toward God, the desire for him alone, is enough.

If you want to gather all your desire into one simple word that the mind can easily retain, choose a short word rather than a long one. A one-syllable word such as "God" or "love" is best. But choose one that is meaningful to you. Then fix it in your mind so that it will remain there come what may. This word will be your defense in conflict and in peace. Use it to beat upon the cloud of darkness above you and to subdue all distractions, consigning them to the *cloud of forgetting* beneath you. Should some thought go on annoying you demanding to know what you are doing, answer with this one word alone. If your mind begins to intellectualize over the meaning and connotations of this little word, remind yourself that its value lies in its simplicity. Do this and I assure you these thoughts will vanish. Why? Because you have refused to develop them with arguing. . . .

CHAPTER XXXVI

Of the kind of meditations common to contemplatives.

The meditation of those who are continually occupied in the work of contemplation . . . is more like a sudden intuition or obscure certainty. For example, they will suddenly be intuitively aware of their sinfulness or God's goodness, but without having made any conscious effort to realize this through reading or other means. Insight like this is more divine than human in origin.

Actually, at this point I would not be concerned if you ceased to meditate altogether on your fallen nature or the goodness of God. I am assuming, of course, that you are drawn by grace and have asked advice about leaving these practices behind. For then it is quite sufficient to focus your attention on a simple word such as *sin* or *God* (or another one you might prefer) and without the intervention of analytical thought allow yourself to experience directly the reality it signifies. Do not use clever logic to examine or explain this word to yourself nor allow yourself to ponder its ramifications as if this sort of thing could possibly increase your love. I do not believe reasoning ever helps in the contemplative work. This is why I advise you to leave these words whole, like a lump, as it were.

When you think of sin, intend nothing in particular but only yourself, though nothing particular in yourself either. For I believe that a dark generalized awareness of sin (intending only yourself but in an undefined way, like a lump) should incite you to the fury of a caged wild animal. Anyone looking at you, however, would not notice any change in your expression, and suppose that you were quite calm and composed. Sitting, walking, lying down, resting, standing, or kneeling, you would appear completely relaxed and peaceful.

CHAPTER XXXVII

Of the kind of personal prayers common to contemplatives.

The skilled contemplative, then, does not depend on discursive reasoning in the same way as beginners and those a little advanced in contemplation must do. His insights arise spontaneously without the help of intellectual processes, as direct intuitions of truth. Something similar may be said of his prayers, too. I am speaking now of his personal prayers, not the liturgical worship of the Church, though I do not mean to imply that liturgical prayer is neglected. On the contrary, the true contemplative has the highest esteem for the liturgy and is careful and exact in celebrating it, in continuity with the tradition of our fathers. But I am speaking now about the contemplative's personal private prayers. These, like his meditations, are wholly spontaneous and not dependent on specific methods of preparation.

Contemplatives rarely pray in words but if they do, their words are few. The fewer the better, as a matter of fact; yes, and a word of one syllable is more suited to the spiritual nature of this work than longer ones. For now the contemplative must hold himself continually poised and alert at the highest and most sovereign point of the spirit.

Let me try to illustrate what I mean with an example from real life. A man or woman terrified by sudden disaster is forced by the circumstances to the limits of his personal resources, and marshals all his energy into one great cry for help. In extreme situations like this, a person is not given to many words nor even to long ones. Instead, summoning all his strength, he expresses his desperate need in one loud cry: "Help!" And with this one little word he effectively arouses the attention and assistance of others.

In a similar way, we can understand the efficacy of one little interior word, not merely spoken or thought, but surging up from the depths of a man's spirit, the expression of his whole being. (By depths I mean the same as height, for in the realm of the spirit height and depth, length and breadth, are all the same.) And so this simple prayer bursting from the depths of your spirit touches the heart of Almighty God more certainly than some long psalm mumbled mindlessly under your breath. This is the meaning of that saying in Scripture: "A short prayer pierces the heavens."

CHAPTER XXXVIII

How and why a short prayer pierces the heavens.

Why do you suppose that this little prayer of one syllable is powerful enough to piece the heavens? Well, it is because it is the prayer of a man's whole being. A man who prays like this prays with all the height and depth and length and breadth of his spirit. His prayer is high, for he prays in the full power of his spirit; it is deep, for he has gathered all his understanding into this one little word; it is long, for if this feeling could endure he would go on crying out forever as he does now; it is wide, because with universal concern he desires for everyone what he desires for himself.

It is with this prayer that a person comes to understand with all the saints the length and breadth and height and depth of the eternal, gracious, almighty, and omniscient God, as St. Paul says.[1] Not completely, of course, but partially and in that obscure manner characteristic of contemplative knowledge. Length speaks of God's eternity, breadth of his love, height of his power, depth of his wisdom. Little wonder, then, that when grace so transforms a person to this image and likeness of God, his creator, his prayer is so quickly heard by God. And I feel sure that God will always hear and help a man who prays to him like this; yes, even though he be a sinner and, as it were, God's enemy. For if grace moves him to utter this anguished cry from the depths and height and length and breadth of his being, God will hear him.

Let me illustrate what I am saying with another example. Imagine that in the dead of night you heard your worst enemy cry out with his whole being "Help!" or "Fire!" Even though this man were your enemy would you not be moved to compassion by the agony of that cry and rush to help him? Yes, of course you would; and though it were in the dead of winter you would still hasten to quench the fire or calm his distress. My God! If grace can so transform a mere man to where he can forget his hatred and have such compassion for his enemy, what shall we not expect from God when he hears a person cry out to him from the height and depth and length and breadth of his whole being. For by nature God is the fullness of all that we are by participation. God's mercy belongs to the essence of his being; that is why we say he is all-merciful. Surely then we can confidently hope in him.

CHAPTER XXXIX

How the advanced contemplative prays; what prayer is;
and what words are most suited to the nature of
contemplative prayer.

We must pray, then, with all the intensity of our being in its height and depth and length and breadth. And not with many words but in a little word of one syllable.

But what word shall we use? Certainly the most appropriate word is one which reflects the nature of prayer itself. And what word is that? Well, let us first try to determine the nature of prayer and then perhaps we will be in a better position to decide.

In itself, prayer is simply a reverent, conscious openness to God full of the desire to grow in goodness and overcome evil. Now we know that all evil, either by instigation or deed, is summed up in the one word "sin." So when we ardently desire to pray for the destruction of evil let us say and think and mean nothing else but this little word "sin." No other words are needed. And when we intend to pray for goodness, let all our thought and desire be contained in the one small word "God." Nothing else and no other words are needed, for God is the epitome of all goodness. He is the source of all good, for it constitutes his very being.

Don't be surprised that I place these two words before all others. If I knew of any smaller words which so adequately expressed all that is good and evil, or had God taught me any others, I would certainly use them. And I advise you to do the same. Do not be anxious to investigate the nature of words or you will never get down to your task of learning to be a contemplative. For I assure you, contemplation is not the fruit of study but a gift of grace.

Even though I have recommended these two little words, you need not necessarily make them your own unless grace also inclines you to choose them. But if, through the attraction of Gods grace, you do find them meaningful, then by all means fix them firmly in your mind whenever you feel drawn to pray with words because they are short and simple. If you do not feel inclined to pray with words, then forget even these.

I think you will find that the simplicity in prayer which I so highly recommend will not inhibit its frequency because, as I explained earlier, this prayer is prayed in the length of the spirit which means that it is unceasing until it is answered. Our illustration confirms this. For when a person is terrified and in great distress, he will keep crying "Help!" or "Fire!" until someone hears his plea and comes to his aid.

CHAPTER XL

That during contemplation a person leaves aside all meditations on the nature of virtue and vice.

As I have explained already, you must immerse your being in the spiritual reality signified by the word "sin," yet without dwelling on any particular kind of sin such as pride, anger, envy, greed, sloth, gluttony, or lust, or on whether it is mortal or venial sin. For to a contemplative, what does the kind or gravity of the sin matter? In the light of contemplation anything that separates him from God, however slightly, appears as a grievous evil and robs him of inner peace.

Let yourself experience sin as a *lump*, realizing that it is yourself, but without defining it precisely. Then cry out in your heart this one word "sin," "sin," "sin," or "help," "help," "help." God can teach you what I mean through experience far better than I can with words. For it is best when this word is wholly interior without a definite thought or actual sound. Yet occasionally, you will be so satiated with the meaning of sin that the sorrow and burden of it will flow over your body and soul and you may burst out with the word itself.

All this is equally true of the little word "God." Immerse yourself in the spiritual reality it speaks of yet without precise ideas of God's works whether small or great, spiritual or material. Do not consider any particular virtue which God may teach you through grace, whether it is humility, charity, patience, abstinence, hope, faith, moderation, chastity, or evangelical poverty. For to a contemplative they are, in a sense, all the same. He finds and experiences all of them in God, who is the source and essence of all goodness. A contemplative has come to realize that if he posses-

ses God he possesses all goodness and this is why he desires nothing in particular but only the good God himself. And so you must also do, insofar as you can, with his grace. Let this little word represent to you God in all his fullness and nothing less than the fullness of God. Let nothing except God hold sway in your mind and heart.

And because, as long as you are in this mortal life, you will always feel to some extent the burden of sin as part and parcel of your being, you will be wise to alternate between these two words, "God" and "sin." Keep in mind this general principle: if you possess God you will be free of sin and when you are free of sin you possess God.

CHAPTER XLIII

That a man must lose the radical self-centered
awareness of his own being if he will reach
the heights of contemplation in this life.

Be careful to empty your mind and heart of everything except God during the time of this work. Reject the knowledge and experience of everything less than God, treading it all down beneath the *cloud of forgetting.* And now also you must learn to forget not only every creature and its deeds but yourself as well, along with whatever you may have accomplished in God's service. For a true lover not only cherishes his beloved more than himself but in a certain sense he becomes oblivious of himself on account of the one he loves.

And this is what you must learn to do. You must come to loathe and regret everything that occupies your mind except God, for everything is an obstacle between you and him. It is little wonder that you should eventually hate to think about yourself in view of your deep realization of sin. This foul, wretched lump called sin is none other than yourself and though you do not consider it in detail, you understand now that it is part and parcel of your very being and something that separates you from God.

And so reject the thought and experience of all created things but most especially learn to forget yourself, for all your knowledge and experience depends upon the knowledge and feeling of yourself. All else is easily forgotten in comparison with one's own self. See if experience does not prove me right. Long after you have successfully forgotten every creature and its works, you will find

that a naked knowing and feeling of your own being still remains
between you and your God. And believe me, you will not be perfect
in love until this, too, is destroyed.

CHAPTER XLIV

*How a person shall dispose himself so as to destroy
the radical self-centered awareness of his being.*

And now you ask me how you shall destroy this naked knowing and feeling of your own being. Perhaps you finally realize that
if you destroyed this, every other obstacle would be destroyed. If
you really do understand this you have done well. But to answer
you I must explain that without God's special grace, freely given,
and without perfect correspondence to his grace on your part, you
can never hope to destroy the naked knowing and feeling of your
being. Perfect correspondence to his grace consists in a strong,
deep, interior sorrow.

But it is most important to moderate this sorrow. You must be
careful never to strain your body or spirit irreverently. Simply sit
relaxed and quiet but plunged and immersed in sorrow. The sorrow
I speak of is genuine and perfect, and blessed is the man who
experiences it. Every man has plenty of cause for sorrow but he
alone understands the deep universal reason for sorrow who experiences *that he is*. Every other motive pales beside this one. He
alone feels authentic sorrow who realizes not only *what he is* but
that he is. Anyone who has not felt this should really weep, for he
has never experienced real sorrow. This sorrow purifies a man of
sin and sin's punishment. Even more, it prepares his heart to
receive that joy through which he will finally transcend the knowing and feeling of his being.

When this sorrow is authentic it is full of reverent longing for
God's salvation, for otherwise no human being could sustain it.
Were he not somehow nourished by the consolation of contemplative prayer, a man would be completely crushed by the knowing
and feeling of his being. For as often as he would have a true
knowing and a feeling of God in purity of spirit (insofar as that is
possible in this life) and then feels that he cannot—for he constantly finds his knowing and feeling as it were occupied and filled
with a foul, stinking lump of himself, which must always be hated
and despised and forsaken, if he shall be God's perfect disciple,
taught by him alone on the mount of perfection—he almost de-
spairs for the sorrow that he feels, weeping, lamenting, writhing,

cursing, and blaming himself. In a word, he feels the burden of himself so tragically that he no longer cares about himself if only he can love God.

And yet in all this, never does he desire to not-be, for this is the devil's madness and blasphemy against God. In fact, he rejoices that he is and from the fullness of a grateful heart he gives thanks to God for the gift and the goodness of his existence. At the same time, however, he desires unceasingly to be freed from the knowing and feeling of his being.

Everyone must sooner or later realize in some manner both this sorrow and this longing to be freed. God in his wisdom will teach his spiritual friends according to the physical and moral strength of each to sustain this truth and in accordance with each one's progress and openness to his grace. He will instruct them little by little until they are completely one in the fullness of his love—that fullness possible on earth with his grace.

CHAPTER XLVI

A helpful instruction on the avoidance of snares;
that in contemplation one should rely more
on joyful enthusiasm than sheer brute force.

For the love of God, then, be careful and do not imprudently strain yourself in this work. Rely more on joyful enthusiasm than on sheer brute force. For the more joyfully you work, the more humble and spiritual your contemplation becomes, whereas when you morbidly drive yourself, the fruits will be gross and unnatural. So be careful. Surely anyone who presumes to approach this lofty mountain of contemplative prayer through sheer brute force will be driven off with stones.[2] Stones as you know are hard, dry things that hurt terribly when they strike. Certainly morbid constraint will also hurt your health, for it is lacking the dew of grace and therefore completely dry. Besides it will do great harm to your foolish mind, leading it to flounder in diabolical illusions. So I say again, avoid all unnatural compulsion and learn to love joyfully with a sweet and gentle disposition of body and soul. Wait with gracious and modest courtesy for the Lord's initiative and do not impatiently snatch at grace like a greedy greyhound suffering from starvation.

I speak half playfully now, but try to temper the loud, crude sighing of your spirit and pretend to hide your heart's longing from the Lord. Perhaps you will scorn this as childish and frivolous but believe me, anyone who has the light to understand what I mean and the grace to follow it will experience, indeed, the delight of the Lord's playfulness. For like a father frolicking with his son, he will hug and kiss one who comes to him with a child's heart.

CHAPTER XLVII

*How one grows to the refinement of purity of spirit;
how a contemplative manifests his desire to God
in one way and to men in another.*

Don't be put off if I seem to speak childishly and foolishly and as if I lacked sound judgment. I do so purposely, for I believe that the Lord himself has inspired me over the last few days to think and feel as I do and to tell some of my other good friends what I now tell you.

One reason I have for advising you to hide your heart's desire from God is because when you hide it I think he actually sees it more clearly. By hiding it you will actually achieve your purpose and see your desire fulfilled sooner than by any means you could devise to attract God's attention. A second reason is that I wish you to outgrow dependence on your inconstant emotions and come to experience God in the purity and depth of your spirit. And finally, I want to help you tie the spiritual knot of burning love that will bind you to God in a communion of being and desire. For as you know, God is spirit and whoever desires to be united with him must enter into the truth and depth of a spiritual communion far transcending any earthly figure.

Obviously, God is all-knowing and nothing material or spiritual can actually be concealed from him, but since he is spirit, something thrust deep into the spirit is more clearly evident to him than something alloyed with emotions. And this is because the spiritual is connatural with him. For this reason I believe that to the extent that our desire is rooted in the emotions, it is more remote from God than if it awakened gently in the joyful composure of a pure, deep spirit.

Now you may understand better why I counsel you playfully to cover and conceal your desire from God. I am not suggesting that you hide it completely, for that would be the counsel of a fool and an impossible task besides. But I bid you, use your ingenuity to hide it from him as best you can. Why do I say this? Because I want you to cast it deep into your spirit far from the contagion of capricious emotions which render it less spiritual and more remote from God.

Moreover, I know that as your heart grows in purity of spirit, it is less dominated by the flesh and more intimately united to God. He will see you more clearly and you will become a source of delight to him. Of course, his vision is not literally affected by this or that for it is immutable. What I am trying to convey to you is that when your heart is transformed in purity of spirit, it becomes connatural with him, for he is spirit.

There is one other reason I have in advising you to conceal your longing from God. You and I and many like us are so inclined to misunderstand a spiritual reality and conceive it literally. Perhaps had I urged you to show your heart's desire to God, you would have demonstrated it physically either in gesture, sound, word, or some other strenuous activity such as you might employ to manifest a secret feeling of your heart to a human friend. But this would only render your contemplative work less simple and refined, for we show things to man in one way and to God in another.

CHAPTER XLVIII

That God desires to be served by a man in body and soul;
that he will glorify both; and how to distinguish
between good and evil spiritual delights.

My intention in all this is certainly not to discourage you from praying out loud when the Holy Spirit inspires you to do so. And if the joy of your spirit overflows to your senses so that you begin to speak to God as you might to a man, saying such things as "Jesus," "sweet Jesus," and the like, you need not stifle your spirit. God forbid that you should misunderstand me in this matter. For truly, I do not mean to deter you from external expressions of love. God forbid that I should separate body and spirit when God has made them a unity. Indeed, we owe God the homage of our whole person, body and spirit together. And fittingly enough he will glorify our whole person, body and spirit, in eternity. In anticipation of this eternal glory, God will sometimes inflame the senses of his devout friends with unspeakable delight and consolation even here in this life. And not just once or twice but perhaps very often as he judges best. This delight, however, does not originate outside the person, entering through the windows of his faculties, but wells up from an excess of spiritual joy and true devotion of spirit. Comfort and delight like this need never be doubted or feared. In a word, I believe that anyone who experiences it will not be able to doubt its authenticity.

But I advise you to be wary of other consolations, sounds, joys, or delights originating from external sources which you cannot identify, for they may be either good or evil, the work of a good angel or the work of the devil. But if you avoid vain sophistry and unnatural physical and emotional stress in the ways I have taught you (or in better ways that you may discover), it will not matter if they are good or evil, for they will be unable to harm you. Why is your security so insured? Because the source of authentic consolation is the reverent, loving desire that abides in a pure heart. This is the work of Almighty God wrought without recourse to techniques and therefore it is free of the fantasy and error liable to befall a man in this life.

As for other comforts, sounds, and delights, I will not go into the criteria for discerning whether they are good or evil just now, because I do not believe it is necessary. They are discussed thoroughly in another man's work which is far superior to anything I could write or say. You can find all I have said and all you need to know treated much better there. But what of that? I will go on anyway, for it does not weary me to reply to your heart's desire which seeks understanding of the interior life. This desire you manifested to me before in words and now I see it clearly in your actions.

One thing I will say regarding those sounds and delights which you perceive through your natural faculties and which may or may not be evil. Learn to be continually occupied in the blind, reverent, joyful longing of contemplative love as I have taught you. If you do this I am certain that this love itself will enable you to discern unerringly between good and evil. It is possible that these experiences may throw you off guard in the beginning because they are so unusual. But the blind stirring of love will steady your heart and you will give them no credence until they are approved of from within by the Holy Spirit or from without by the counsel of a wise spiritual father.

CHAPER XLIX

That the essence of all perfection is a good will; sensible consolations are not essential to perfection in this life.

And so you may confidently rely on this gentle stirring of love in your heart and follow wherever it leads you, for it is your sure guide in this life and will bring you to the glory of the next. This little love is the essence of a good life and without it no good work is possible. Basically, love means a radical personal commitment to God. This implies that your will is harmoniously attuned to his in an abiding contentedness and enthusiasm for all he does.

A good will like this is the essence of the highest perfection. The delight and consolations of sense and spirit, regardless how sublime, are but accidental to this and wholly dependent on it. I say they are accidental because it matters very little whether or not a person experiences them. They are incidental to life on earth but in eternity they will be essential elements of man's final glory, just as his body (which feels them now) will be united actually and essentially forever with his spirit. But on earth the kernel of all consolation is the inner reality of a good will. Moreover, I feel certain that a person who has matured in the perfecting of his will (at least insofar as he may in this life) experiences no earthly delight or consolation that he would not willingly and joyfully renounce if God so wished.

CHAPTER L

What is meant by pure love; that some people
experience little sensible consolation while others
experience a great deal.

I hope you see now why it is so important that we concentrate our whole energy and attention on this gentle stirring of love in the will. With all due reverence for God's gifts, it is my opinion that we should be quite careless of all delights and consolations of sense or spirit, regardless of how pleasurable or sublime they may be. If they come, welcome them but do not rest in them for fear of growing weak; believe me, you will expend a good deal of energy if you remain long in sweet feelings and tears. Possibly too, you may begin to love God on their account and not for himself. You will know whether or not this is happening if you become upset and irritable when you do not experience them. Should you find this to be the case, then your love is not yet chaste or perfect. When love is chaste and perfect, it may allow the senses to be nourished and strengthened by sweet emotions and tears, but it is never troubled if God permits them to disappear. It continues to rejoice in God all the same.

Some people experience a measure of consolation almost always while others only rarely. But God in his great wisdom determines what is best for each one. Some people are so spiritually fragile and delicate that unless they were always strengthened

with a little sensible consolation, they might be unable to endure
the various temptations and sufferings that afflict them as they
struggle in this life against their enemies from within and without.
And there are others so frail physically that they are unable to
purify themselves through rigorous discipline. Our Lord in his
great kindness purifies these people spiritually through consolations and tears. Yet there are others so spiritually virile that they
find enough consolation in the reverent offering of this gentle,
little love and in the sweet harmony of their hearts with God's.
They find such spiritual nourishment within that they need little
other comfort. Which of these people is holier or nearer to God, only
he knows. I certainly do not.

CHAPTER LXXIV

*That anyone disposed toward contemplation will recognize
something akin to his own spirit when he reads
this book and that only such a person should be
allowed to read or hear this book.*

Should it seem that the way of prayer I have described in this
book is unsuited to you spiritually or temperamentally, feel perfectly free to leave it aside and with wise counsel seek another in
full confidence. In that case I trust you will hold me excused for all I
have written here. Truly, I wrote only according to my simple
understanding of these things and with no other purpose than that
of helping you. So read it over two or three times. The more often
you read it the better, for that much more shall you grasp of its
meaning. Parts that seemed difficult and obscure at first may
perhaps become obvious and clear as you read it again.

It seems to me that anyone whom grace has drawn to contemplation will not read this book (or hear it read) without feeling that
it speaks of something akin to his own spirit. Should you feel this
way and find it helpful, thank God with all your heart and for love
of him pray for me.

I sincerely hope you will do this. But I am very serious when I
ask you, for the love of God, not to share this book with anyone else
unless you are convinced he is a person who will understand and
appreciate it. . . .

I really do not want worldly gossips, flatterers and fault-finders, talebearers and busybodies, or the plainly curious—educated or not—to get hold of this book. I never intended to write for these folk and do not even want them to hear about it. I do not doubt that some of them may be fine people, perhaps even very fervent in the active life, but this book is not suited to their needs.

CHAPTER LXXV

Of certain signs by which a man may determine whether or not God is drawing him to contemplation.

I would like to make clear that not everyone who reads this book (or hears it read) and finds it pleasantly interesting is therefore called to contemplation. The inner excitement he feels may not be so much the attraction of grace as the arousal of natural curiosity. But I will give you some signs for testing this inspiration so as to find its real source.

In the first place, let a man examine himself to see if he has done all in his power to purify his conscience of deliberate sin according to the precepts of Holy Church and the advice of his spiritual father. If he is satisfied on this account, all is well. But to be more certain, let him see if he is habitually more attracted to this simple contemplative prayer than to any other spiritual devotion. And then, if his conscience leaves him no peace in any exterior or interior work he does unless he makes this secret little love fixed upon the *cloud of unknowing* his principal concern, it is a sign that God is calling him to this work. But if these signs are lacking, I assure you, he is not.

I am not saying that those who are being called to contemplation will feel the stirring of love continually and permanently right from the beginning, for such is not the case. In fact, the young contemplative apprentice may often completely cease to experience it for various different reasons. Sometimes God will withdraw it so that he will not begin to presume it is his own doing, or that he can control it as he likes. Presumption like this is pride. Whenever the feeling of grace is withdrawn, pride is the cause. Not necessarily because one has actually yielded to pride, but because if this grace were not withdrawn from time to time pride would surely take root. God in his mercy protects the contemplative in this way, though some foolish neophytes will think he has turned enemy to them. They fail to see how true is his friendship. At other times God may withdraw this gift when the young apprentice grows careless and begins to take it for granted. If this happens he will very likely be overwhelmed with bitter pangs of remorse. But occasionally our Lord may delay in giving it back, so that having been lost and found again it may be the more deeply appreciated.

One of the most obvious and certain signs by which a person may know if he has been called to this work is the attitude he detects in himself when he has found again the lost gift of grace. For if after long delay and inability to do this work he feels his desire for it renewed with greater passion and a deeper longing of love—so much so that (as I often think) the sorrow he felt at its loss seems like nothing at all beside his joy at finding it again—he need have no fear of error in believing that God is calling him to contemplation, regardless of what sort of person he is now or has been in the past. It is not what you are nor what you have been that God sees with his all-merciful eyes, but what you desire to be. St. Gregory declares that "all holy desires heighten in intensity with the delay of fulfillment, and desire which fades with delay was never holy desire at all." For if a man experiences less and less joy when he discovers anew the sudden presence of great desires he had formerly pursued, his first desire was not holy desire. Possibly he felt a natural tendency toward the good but this should not be confused with holy desire. St. Augustine explains what I mean by holy desire when he says that "the entire life of a good Christian is nothing less than holy desire."

My dear friend, I bid you farewell now with God's blessing and mine. May God give you and all who love him true peace, wise counsel, and his own interior joy in the fullness of grace. Amen.

JULIAN OF NORWICH

Revelations of Divine Love

Mother Julian of Norwich (1342–c.1420) was the recipient of sixteen unforgettable revelations or "shewings" in May 1373, while she was recovering from a serious illness. Later she became an

*anchoress, living alone in a cell attached to a Benedictine church.
Her fame as a spiritual counselor was widespread, and though she
describes herself as "a simple, unlettered creature," she was clearly
a woman of keen intellect, brilliant imagination, and deep spiritual
sensitivity. She is one of the greatest English mystics.*

*These qualities are illustrated in one of her most famous vi-
sions, which is recounted in Chapter 51 of her book,* Revelations of
Divine Love.

CHAPTER LI

*God's answer to this doubt of hers, given in the wonderful
illustration of a lord and his servant; God wills that we
should wait for him, for it was nearly twenty years before
Julian understood this example; Christ sits at the
Father's right hand; how this is to be understood*

And then, in his courtesy, our Lord answered me, by giving me
the mysterious and wonderful illustration of the lord who had a
servant. And he helped me to understand the significance of each of
them. In the lord and in the servant alike I saw a twofold truth
expressed; I saw it first in my spirit in physical outline, and then it
was shown more spiritually without any such outline.

The first time I saw physically before me two people, a lord and
his servant. And God showed me its spiritual meaning. The lord is
sitting down quietly, relaxed and peaceful; the servant is standing
by his lord, humble and ready to do his bidding. And then I saw the
lord look at his servant with rare love and tenderness, and quietly
send him to a certain place to fulfil his purpose. Not only does that
servant go, but he starts off at once, running with all speed, in his
love to do what his master wanted. And without warning he falls
headlong into a deep ditch, and injures himself very badly. And
though he groans and moans and cries and struggles he is quite
unable to get up or help himself in any way. To crown all, he could
get no relief of any sort: he could not even turn his head to look at
the lord who loved him, and who was so close to him. The sight of
him would have been of real comfort, but he was temporarily so
weak and bemused that he gave vent to his feelings, as he suffered
his pains.

His pain was sevenfold. First of all there was the severe bruis-
ing which resulted from his fall, and was hurting very much; then

there was the sheer weight of his body; thirdly there was the consequent weakness following these two factors; fourthly his mind was shocked, and he could not see the reason for it all—so that he almost forgot the love that had spurred him on; and there was the fifth and further fact that he could not get up; moreover, in the sixth place—and this I found quite extraordinary—he was quite alone: wherever I looked, high and low, far and near, I could see none to help him; and lastly there was the hard rough surface on to which he had fallen.

I was greatly surprised to see with what humility this servant endured such suffering and I sought most carefully to find some fault in him, and to know if his lord regarded him as blameworthy. And, in truth, I could see neither. Basically it was his own good will and great longing that had caused his fall; he was still as loyal and goodhearted as when he stood before his lord, ready to do his bidding. And it is thus that his master always sees him. But now the sense in which he regarded him was twofold. There was the obvious primary one, humble, gentle, compassionate, and pitying—this was the first; and there was the second one, inner and more spiritual, which when it was showed me helped me to enter into the mind of his lord. He was delighting in the thought of the well-earned rest and great honour which in his abundant generosity he was planning to give his servant. This was all part of the inner significance, and it led me back to think of the first, not however to the exclusion of the second. It was as though his thoughtful lord were saying, 'Here is my servant whom I love. What hurt and discomfort he has known in my service—and all out of love for me, due to his own generous nature! Surely it would be right to reward him for all this terror and fright, this hurt, injury, and grief? Ought I not to give him something that will more than compensate him, and indeed, be even more worth having than his own previous health? If I did otherwise I should be showing no gratitude at all!'

I began to see now an inner, spiritual significance attaching to the lord's words. The natural consequence of his great goodness and worth was that his much beloved servant should be truly and gladly rewarded beyond anything he could have had had he not fallen. Yes, indeed, further; his fall and subsequent suffering were to be transformed into great and superlative honour and everlasting joy.

At this point the picture vanished, and our Lord then enlightened me with regard to this revelation. Yet for all his guidance, my puzzlement over the illustration never left me. I thought that it had been given as an answer to my request, yet at the same time I was unable to find a wholly satisfying meaning in it. The *servant* stood for Adam, as I shall be saying, but on the other hand there were many characteristics that could not possibly be ascribed to him. So there I had to leave it, a large part unknown. The full meaning of this marvellous illustration was not at that time shown me. Yet hidden deep down in this great picture are three particular attributes of the revelation. Indeed I now began to understand that every revelation was full of deep secrets. So I will now speak of those three qualities which bring some relief to my mind.

The first quality is the literal meaning of the words as I then received them; the second is the inner significance that I have discovered since; the third is the whole revelation itself, which, from beginning to end—covering the contents of this book—God in his goodness brings to mind, often and freely. As I understand it these three are so much one that I cannot—indeed, may not— separate them. And by these three-and-one I have been taught to believe and trust that our Lord God, through the same goodness by which he first revealed it, and for the same reason, will later in similar fashion make it known to us when he so wills.

After twenty years (all but three months) from the time of the revelation I received inner enlightenment, as I am going to tell: 'It is for you to consider all the details and circumstances shown in the illustration; even if you think they are vague and unimportant.' I assented wholeheartedly and eagerly, and began to give close attention to all the points and details that had been shown at that time, as far as my ability to understand would allow. I began with the lord and the servant as I saw them: how and where the lord sat; the colour and cut of his clothes; his appearance, and his innate nobility and goodness; and how and where the servant stood, what his clothes were like, and their colour and style; his outward bearing and his inner goodness and loyalty.

The *lord* who was sitting in solemn state, quietly and peacefully, I took to be God. The *servant* who stood before his lord I understood to be Adam. There was shown at that time just one man and his fall; to make us understand that God sees Everyman and his fall. In the sight of God everyman is one man, and one man is everyman. This man's strength was injured, and he was much weakened. His senses too were confused, for he turned away from looking at his lord. However his will was still sound in God's sight, for I saw that our Lord commended and approved his will. But he was prevented from seeing this about his will, and therefore was in great sorrow and distress. He could not see clearly his loving lord, so gentle and kind towards him, nor could he see how he really stood in the eyes of that same loving master. Well do I know that when we are really certain about these two things, even here we can savour something of their peace and rest, while in heaven by God's bountiful grace we shall enjoy them in their fullness.

At this time I began to learn how it is that God can still behold us in our sin. I went on to see that it is only pain that blames and punishes, but that our gracious Lord comforts and sympathizes, for he is ever kindly disposed towards our soul, and, loving us, longs to bring us to his bliss. It was a simple sort of place where the lord was sitting. It was the earth, bare, deserted, lonely, wild. His clothes were full and flowing and seemly. Their colour was the blue of the sky, restrained but beautiful; his countenance full of pity; his face was a light tan in colour and he had regular features; his eyes were dark, beautiful, and true, filled with loving compassion. There was deep and generous insight, full of eternity and heaven. And I thought that the love with which he ceaselessly regarded his servant, especially when he fell, would melt our own hearts with love and break them for very joy. This lovely gaze displayed a wonderful and fitting blend of compassion and pity, of joy and blessedness. The latter surpassed the former as the heaven does the earth. Pity was earthly, blessedness heavenly. The compassion and pity was that of the Father when his most loved creation, Adam, fell; the joy and blessedness was in his own beloved Son who is equal with the Father. The merciful gaze of his loving eyes ranged the whole earth, and went down with Adam into hell; his continuing pity kept Adam from eternal death. Mercy and pity dwell thus with mankind until at last we come to heaven. But man in this life is blind and cannot see God, our Father, as he is. And whenever he wills of his goodness to show himself to man, he shows himself in great simplicity, as man. All the same I saw quite clearly that we ought to know and believe that the Father is not man.

But his sitting on the bare, deserted, *earth* means this: he made man's soul to be his own city and his home. Of all his works this is the one that most pleases him. When man fell into sorrow and pain, he became unfit to serve in that noble office, yet our kind Father would prepare no other place for himself, but would sit upon the earth, waiting for mankind (itself compounded of earth), until such time as, by his grace, his beloved son had restored his city to its noble beauty through his tremendous effort.

The *blue* of his clothes symbolized his constancy; the tone of that distinguished *face* and the *dark eyes* combined to show his serious intent; the *ample nature* of his clothes, beautiful and radiant, suggested that he had within himself all heaven, all joy, all happiness. This first struck me when I was speaking of being 'helped to enter into the mind of his lord', for I saw him rejoicing at the honour to which he intended to restore his servant.

I still had cause to marvel as I beheld this lord and his servant. I saw the lord sitting in solemn state, and his servant standing reverently before him. In the servant there is a twofold significance, outward and inner. Outwardly he was dressed simply, like a man ready for work, and he stood very near his lord, not straight in front of him, but slightly to the side, on the left. He was wearing a single white coat, old and worn, stained with sweat, tight and short, coming just below the knee, threadbare, almost worn out, ready to fall apart any moment. I was very surprised at this for I thought it was most unsuitable garb for a much loved servant to wear in the presence of his honoured lord. But I realized that there was in him a fundamental love, a love for his lord equal to that of his lord for him. The servant was wise enough to know that there was but one thing to do to be worthy of his master. And for love, regardless of himself or the consequences, the servant at once started off, and ran at the bidding of his lord, to do whatever was his will, and that brought him honour. Outwardly he looked as if he had been working hard for a long time, but to my inner understanding he seemed to be a beginner, new to hard work, a servant who had never been sent out before.

There was an earthly treasure which the lord loved. I wondered what it might be, and the answer came to mind, 'It is a repast, lovely and pleasing to the lord.' For though the lord was sitting down as any man would, I could see no food or drink to give him. This was surprising in itself. Still more surprising was the fact that this great man had no servant but one, and him he sent off. I went on looking, wondering what sort of work the servant had to do. Then I understood: he was off to do work that was the hardest and most exhausting possible. He was to be a gardener, digging and banking, toiling and sweating, turning and trenching the ground, watering the plants the while. And by keeping at this work he would make sweet streams to flow, fine abundant fruits to grow; he would bring them to his lord, and serve them to his taste. And he would not return till he had prepared the meal just as he knew his master would like it. Then he would take it, and the appropriate refreshment, bearing them with due ceremony to his lord. And all the time the lord would be sitting where he had left him, waiting for the servant he had sent out.

I still puzzled where the servant came from. I saw that in the lord there was everlasting life and every goodness, except the treasure that was in the earth. And that treasure too had its being in the wonderful depth of his eternal love. But its worth to him depended on the servant's careful preparation of it, and his setting it before him, personally. All around the master was nothing but wilderness. I did not understand all that this example meant, so I still puzzled where the servant came from.

In the *servant* is represented the second Person of the Trinity; and in the *servant* again Adam, or in other words, Everyman. When I speak of the *Son* I am thinking of the Godhead which is equal to the Father's, and when I say the *servant* I have Christ's human nature in mind. He is the true Adam. The *nearness* of the servant has to do with the Son, and the *standing on the left side* refers to Adam. The *lord* is God the Father, the *servant* is the Son, Jesus Christ; the Holy Spirit is the *love* that is common to them both.

When Adam *fell*, God's Son fell. Because of the true unity which had been decreed in heaven, God's Son could not be dissociated from Adam. By *Adam* I always understand *Everyman*. Adam fell from life to death, first into the depths of this wretched world, and then into hell. God's Son fell, with Adam, but into the depth of the Virgin's womb—herself the fairest daughter of Adam—with the intent of excusing Adam from blame both in heaven and on earth. And with a mighty arm he brought him out of hell. By the servant's *wisdom* and *goodness* the Son is understood. The *poor clothes* of the workman standing near the left is a reference to human nature, and Adam, and all the subsequent mischief and weakness. In all this the good Lord showed his own Son and Adam as one man. Our virtue and goodness are due to Jesus Christ, our weakness and blindness to Adam; and both were shown in the one servant. In this way we can see how our good Lord Jesus has taken upon himself all our blame, and that, as a result, our Father cannot and will not blame us more than his own dear Son, Jesus Christ. So the servant, before he came to this world *stood before* his Father, ready for his will and against the time he should be *sent* to do that most worthy deed by which mankind was brought back to heaven. And this, notwithstanding he is God, equal with his Father in respect of his Godhead. In his future purpose he was

to be Man, to save man by fulfilling his Father's will. So he stood
before his Father as a servant, deliberately, making himself responsible for us.

He started off with all eagerness at his Father's will, and at
once he fell low, into the Virgin's womb, regardless of himself or his
hard lot. The *white coat* is his flesh; its being *single* the fact that
there is nothing separating Godhead and human nature; its *tight
fit* is poverty, its *age* is Adam's wearing of it, its *sweat stains*
Adam's toil, its *shortness*, the work the servant did. And I saw the
Son saying in effect, 'Dear Father, I stand before you in Adam's
stead, ready to start off and run. My will is to go to earth and bring
you honour, whenever you wish to send me. How long am I to desire
this?' The Son knew with absolute certainty when the Father's will
would be, and how long he would have to wait for it. But this he
knew in respect of his Godhead, for he is the wisdom of the Father.
His query however was made in virtue of his manhood. For all the
humanity that will be saved by his blessed incarnation and passion
is included in Christ's humanity; for he is the head, and we are his
members. To us members are unknown the day and time when all
these temporary griefs and sorrows will be done away, and joy and
blessedness be eternally achieved. To know this hour the whole
company of heaven is longing! The way to heaven for those of us
who are not yet members is by longing and desire. And we saw this
longing and desire in the servant's *standing* before his lord, or
rather in the Son's standing before his Father in Adam's coat. The
heartfelt desire that mankind has to be saved appeared in Jesus.
Jesus is everyone that will be saved, and everyone that will be
saved is Jesus—all through the charity of God; and through virtue,
obedience, humility and patience, on our part.

Moreover, in this wonderful example there is teaching for me
which is like beginning the ABC. It gives me some inkling of our
Lord's meaning. The secrets of this whole revelation are hidden in
it—though of course each individual revelation is full of secrets.
That the Father *sits* is a sign of his Godhead: it shows rest and
peace, for in the Godhead there can be no activity. That he showed
himself *lord* is a sign of his authority over our humanity. The
servant's *standing* means however that he is active, and the *left
side* shows he was not worthy to stand on an equal footing with the
lord. The *starting* is a reference to his Godhead, the *running* to his
humanity, for the Godhead started from the Father to enter the
Virgin's womb, falling, as it were, to take our human nature upon
himself. Thereby he accepted great hurt, the hurt which was our

flesh, in which from the first he experienced mortal pain. By his *standing reverently* before his lord but not in front of him, we are to understand that his garb was not suitable for the presence of his lord; indeed he could not stand in front of him all the while he was a labourer. Nor could he sit or rest peacefully until he had properly won that peace by his own hard work. The *left side* means that the Father deliberately allowed his own son to suffer in his human nature Everyman's pain, without sparing him. By his *coat ready to fall apart* is understood the assault, the flogging, the thorns, the nails, the pulling and pushing, the tearing of his tender flesh. I had already seen this in part at least, when I saw how his flesh had been torn from the skull and had hung in pieces. Then the bleeding had stopped, and it began to dry up, and adhered again to the bone. The *agony* and *struggling, groaning* and *moaning* suggest that he could never rise up again in all his power from the moment of his *fall* into the Virgin's womb until his body had been slain and he had yielded his soul (and with it all humanity) into his Father's hands.

From now on he began to show his power. He went down to hell, and there he raised up from the lowest depths that great mass which was his by right, united to him in high heaven. His body lay in the grave until Easter Day. Thereafter it never lay again. For there was rightly ended all the agony and struggling, the moaning and groaning. And our filthy, dying flesh which the Son of God took upon himself, like Adam's old *coat, tight, threadbare,* and too *short,* the Saviour transformed into something beautiful, fresh, bright and splendid, eternally spotless, *full and flowing,* fairer and richer than even the clothing I had seen on the Father. His clothing was blue, but Christ's was of a harmony and beauty the like and wonder of which I just cannot describe. It could not be more magnificent. Now the lord sits, not on an earthly desert, but on his throne in heaven, as he should. Now the Son stands, no longer a servant before the lord, bowed, shabby, and half-clad, but straight before him as his Father, clothed in rich and blessed amplitude, crowned with priceless splendour. We are his crown, the crown which is the Father's joy, the Son's honour, the Holy Spirit's pleasure, the endless, blessed wonder of all heaven. Now sits the Son, the labourer no longer standing on the Father's left, but sitting at the Father's right, in eternal peace and rest. (We do not mean, of course, that the Son sits literally on the right hand, side by side as people sit here! As I see it there is nothing of this sort in the Holy Trinity. 'To sit at the Father's right hand' means that he enjoys the highest dignity with the Father.) Now is the Bridegroom, God's

Son, resting with his beloved wife, the beautiful Virgin, eternally joyful. Now sits the Son, true God and true man, at rest and in peace in his own *city*, that city prepared for him in the eternal purpose of the Father. And the Father in the Son, and the Holy Spirit in the Father and in the Son.

NICHOLAS OF CUSA

The Vision of God

Nicholas of Cusa (1401–1464) studied with the Brethern of the Common Life in Holland, at the Universities of Heidelberg and Padua, and eventually became a versatile scientist, lawyer, classicist, promoter of political and ecclesiastical unity and Cardinal of the Church. His work on The Vision of God *was written for a Benedictine community to which he had often retired for prayer and reflection.*

And while observing how that gaze [of God] never leaves anyone, one may see that it takes such diligent care of each one as though it cared only for him, and for no other, and this to such a degree that one on whom it rests cannot even conceive that it takes care of any other. One will also see that it takes the same most diligent care of the least of creatures as of the greatest, and of the whole universe.

THE REVIVAL OF NEOPLATONIC MYSTICISM IN THE RHINELAND

As was the case in England, the fourteenth century in the Rhineland also witnessed a revival of apophatic mysticism under the influence of Dionysius the Areopagite. The Rhenish authors, however, were much more inclined than their English contemporaries to theoretical questions and daring mystical speculation. The Rhenish movement is here represented by a few brief selections from Meister Eckhart, O.P. (c. 1260–1327), Blessed Henry Suso, O.P. (c. 1295–1366), and Blessed Jan van Ruysbroeck (1293– 1381). These authors are distinguished by their insistence on the traditional themes of Neoplatonic contemplation and by their combination of these themes with a spirit of analysis and reflection deriving from medieval scholasticism. Eckhart was the most original and daring of these authors, Suso the most intimate and personal of them, and Ruysbroeck probably the most profound and complete in the development of his ideas.

MEISTER ECKHART, O.P.

Sermons

DISTINCTIONS ARE LOST IN GOD

Qui audit me, non confundetur (Ecclesiasticus 24:30)

The eternal wisdom of the Father says: "He that heareth me is not ashamed. (If he is ashamed, it is of his shame.) He who acts in me sins not. He that reveals me and fears me shall have eternal life." There is matter enough for one sermon in any of these three statements.

I shall discuss the first—that the eternal wisdom says: "He that heareth me is not ashamed." To hear the wisdom of the Father, one must be "in," at home, and alone.[1]

Three things there are that hinder one from hearing the eternal Word. The first is corporeality, the second, number, and the third, time. If a person has overcome these three, he dwells in eternity, is alive spiritually and remains in the unity, the desert of solitude, and there he hears the eternal Word. Our Lord says: "No man heareth my word or teaching until he hath forsaken selfhood."[2] The hearing of God's Word requires complete self-surrender. He who hears and that which is heard are identical constituents of the eternal Word. What the eternal Father teaches in his own Being, Nature, and Godhead—which he is always revealing through his only begotten Son. He teaches that we are to be identical with him.

To deny one's self is to be the only begotten Son of God and one who does so has for himself all the properties of that Son. All God's acts are performed and his teachings conveyed through the Son, to the point that we should be his only begotten Son. And when this is accomplished in God's sight, he is so fond of us and so fervent that he acts as if his divine Being might be shattered and he himself annihilated if the whole foundations of his Godhead were not revealed to us, together with his nature and being. God makes haste to do this, so that it may be ours as it is his. It is here that God finds joy and rapture in fulfillment and the person who is thus within God's knowing and love becomes just what God himself is.

If you love yourself, you love everybody else as you do yourself. As long as you love another person less than you love yourself, you will not really succeed in loving yourself but if you love all alike, including yourself, you will love them as one person and that person is both God and man. Thus he is a just and righteous person who, loving himself, loves all others equally.

Some people say: "I prefer my friends who are good to me to other people"—but they are wrong and this is not the perfect way. Nevertheless, we have to make the best of it, just as people do who have to sail over the sea with a cross wind and yet manage to get over. Well, it is like this with one who has his preferences in people, as naturally one will. If I care for other people as I do for myself, then what happens to them, whether for better or for worse, let it mean life or death, I should be glad to take it on myself. That is true friendship.

Speaking to this point, St. Paul says: "I could wish to be cut off eternally from God for my friends' sake and for God's sake."[3] To be cut off from God for an instant is to be cut off from him forever, and to be cut off from God at all is the pain of hell. What, then, does St. Paul mean by saying that he could wish to be cut off from God? The authorities question whether or not St. Paul, when he made this remark, was already perfect or only on the road to perfection. I say that he was already quite perfect, for otherwise he would not have said it and now I shall explain why St. Paul could say that he could wish to be cut off from God.

Man's last and highest parting occurs when, for God's sake, he takes leave of god.[4] St. Paul took leave of god for God's sake and gave up all that he might get from god, as well as all he might give—together with every idea of god. In parting with these, he parted with god for God's sake and yet God remained to him as God is in his own nature—not as he is conceived by anyone to be—nor yet as something yet to be achieved—but more as an "is-ness," as God really is. Then he neither gave to God nor received anything from him, for he and God were a unit, that is, pure unity. Thus one becomes that real person, for whom there can be no suffering, any more than the divine essence can suffer. As I have often said, there is something in the soul so closely akin to God that it is already one with him and need never be united to him. It is unique and has nothing in common with anything else. It has no significance [for this world?] whatsoever—none! Anything created is nothing but that Something is apart from and strange to all creation. If one were wholly this, he would be both uncreated and unlike any creature. If any corporeal thing or anything fragile were included in that unity, it, too, would be like the essence of that unity. If I should find myself in this essence, even for a moment, I should regard my earthly selfhood as of no more importance than a manure worm.

God gives to all things alike and as they proceed from God they are alike. Angels, men, and creatures all flow out of God in whom their prime origin is. Take them as they first emanate from him and you will find them all alike but, if they are alike in this temporal sphere, in eternity and in God they are the much more so. A flea, to the extent that it is in God, ranks above the highest angel in his own right. Thus, in God, all things are equal and are God himself.

In this likeness or identity God takes such delight that he pours his whole nature and being into it. His pleasure is as great, to take a simile, as that of a horse, let loose to run over a green heath where the ground is level and smooth, to gallop as a horse will, as fast as he can over the greensward—for this is a horse's pleasure and expresses his nature. It is so with God. It is his pleasure and rapture to discover identity, because he can always put his whole nature into it—for he is this identity itself.

A question is raised about those angels who live with us, serving and guarding us, as to whether or not they have less joy in identity than the angels in heaven have and whether they are hindered at all in their [proper] activities by serving and guarding us. No! Not at all! Their joy is not diminished, nor their equality, because the angel's work is to do the will of God and the will of God is the angel's work. If God told an angel to go to a tree and pick off the caterpillars, the angel would be glad to do it and it would be bliss to him because it *is* God's will.

Always to be ready to do God's will is to be ready for nothing else than what God is and wills. Such a person, being ill, would not wish to be well. Pain would be a pleasure to him and all the manifold of things would be an empty unity to him who is ready to do God's will. Indeed, if the pains of hell should follow, they would be joy and bliss—for he would be empty, having denied himself, and whatever might happen would not touch him. If my eye is to distinguish colors, it must first be free from any color impressions. If I see blue or white, the seeing of my eyes is identical with what is seen. The eye by which I see God is the same as the eye by which God sees me. My eye and God's eye are one and the same—one in seeing, one in knowing, and one in loving.

To love as God loves, one must be dead to self and all created things, and have as little regard for self as for one who is a thousand miles away. His life is an identity and a unity and there is no distinction in him. This person must have denied himself and the whole world. If anyone owned the whole world and gave it up as freely as he received it, God would give it back to him and eternal life to boot.

And if there were another person who had nothing but good will and he thought: "Lord, if this whole world were mine and two more with it, [or as many more as you please] I would give them up and myself too as completely as it was before I received them"— then God would return to him as much as he had given away with his own hands. There is still another person, who has nothing whatever, material or spiritual, to give away or forsake; he has given away and forsaken most of all. To him who even for one instant completely denies himself, shall all things be given, but if a person were to deny himself for twenty years and then return to selfishness even for a moment, it would be as if he had never denied himself at all. One who has denied himself and keeps denying himself and never even casts a glance on what he has given up, and remains steady, immovably and unchangeably what he is—he alone has really denied himself.

That we too may remain steady and unchangeable in the eternal Father, may God help us and the eternal wisdom too. Amen.

BLESSED ARE THE POOR

Beati Pauperes spiritu, quia ipsorum est regnum Coelorum
(Matthew 5:3)

Blessedness opened the mouth that spake wisdom and said: "Blessed are the poor in spirit, for theirs is the kingdom of heaven." All the angels and all the saints and all that were ever born must

keep silence when the eternal wisdom of the Father speaks; for all
the wisdom of angels and creatures is pure nothing, before the
bottomless wisdom of God. And this wisdom has spoken and said
that the poor are blessed.

Now, there are two kinds of poverty. One is external poverty
and it is good, and much to be praised in people who take it upon
themselves willingly, for the love of our Lord Jesus Christ, for he
himself practiced it in the earthly realm. Of this poverty I shall say
nothing more, for there is still another kind of poverty, an inward
poverty, with reference to which, this saying of our Lord is to be
understood: "Blessed are the poor in spirit, or of spirit."

Now, I pray you that you may be like this, so that you may
understand this address; for, by the eternal truth, I tell you that if
you haven't this truth of which we are speaking in yourselves, you
cannot understand me.

Certain people have asked me what this poverty is. Let us
answer that.

Bishop Albert says: "To be poor is to take no pleasure in
anything God ever created," and that is well said. But we shall say
it better and take "poverty" in a higher sense. He is a poor man who
wants nothing, knows nothing, and has nothing. I shall speak of
these three points.

In the first place, let us say that he is a poor man who wants
nothing. Some people do not understand very well what this
means. They are people who continue very properly in their penances and external practices of piety (popularly considered of great
importance—may God pardon it!) and still they know very little of
the divine truth. To all outward appearances, these people are to be
called holy, but inwardly they are asses, for they understand not at
all the true meaning of the divine reality. They say well that to be
poor is to want nothing, but they mean by that, living so that one
never gets his own way in anything, but rather so disposes himself
as to follow the all-loving will of God. These persons do no evil in
this, for they mean well, and we should praise them for that—may
God keep them in his mercy!

I tell you the real truth, that these people are not poor, nor are
they even like poor people. They pass for great in the eyes of people
who know no better. Yet I say that they are asses, who understand
the truth of the divine not at all. For their good intentions they may
possibly receive the Kingdom of Heaven, but of this poverty, of
which I shall now speak, they have no idea.

If I were asked, then, what it is to be a poor man who wants
nothing, I should answer and say: As long as a person keeps his
own will, and thinks it his will to fulfill the all-loving will of God,
he has not that poverty of which we are talking, for this person has
a will with which he wants to satisfy the will of God, and that is not
right. For if one wants to be truly poor, he must be as free from his
creature will as when he had not yet been born. For, by the everlasting truth, as long as you will do God's will, and yearn for
eternity and God, you are not really poor; for he is poor who wills
nothing, knows nothing, and wants nothing.

Back in the Womb from which I came, I had no god and merely
was, myself. I did not will or desire anything, for I was pure being, a
knower of myself by divine truth. Then I wanted myself and nothing else. And what I wanted, I was and what I was, I wanted, and
thus, I existed untrammeled by god or anything else. But when I
parted from my free will and received my created being, then I had
a god. For before there were creatures, God was not god, but,
rather, he was what he was. When creatures came to be and took on
creaturely being, then God was no longer God as he is in himself,
but god as he is with creatures.

Now we say that God, in so far as he is only god, is not the
highest goal of creation, nor is his fullness of being as great as that
of the least of creatures, themselves in God. And if a flea could have
the intelligence by which to search the eternal abyss of divine
being, out of which it came, we should say that god, together with
all that god is, could not give fulfillment or satisfaction to the flea!
Therefore, we pray that we may be rid of god, and taking the truth,
break into eternity, where the highest angels and souls too are
like what I was in my primal existence, when I wanted what I was,
and was what I wanted. Accordingly, a person ought to be poor in
will, willing as little and wanting as little as when he did not exist.
This is how a person is poor, who wills nothing.

Again, he is poor who knows nothing. We have sometimes said
that man ought to live as if he did not live, neither for self, nor for
the truth, nor for God. But to that point, we shall say something
else and go further. The man who is to achieve this poverty shall
live as having what was his when he did not live at all, neither his
own, nor the truth, nor god. More: he shall be quit and empty of all
knowledge, so that no knowledge of god exists in him; for when a
man's existence is of God's eternal species, there is no other life in
him: his life is himself. Therefore we say that a man ought to be

empty of his own knowledge, as he was when he did not exist, and let God achieve what he will and be as untrammeled by humanness as he was when he came from God.

Now the question is raised: In what does happiness consist most of all? Certain authorities have said that it consists in loving. Others say that it consists in knowing and loving, and this is a better statement. But we say that it consists neither in knowledge nor in love, but in that there is something in the soul, from which both knowledge and love flow and which, like the agents of the soul, neither knows nor loves. To know this is to know what blessedness depends on. This something has no "before" or "after" and it waits for nothing that is yet to come, for it has nothing to gain or lose. Thus, when God acts in it, it is deprived of knowing that he has done so. What is more, it is the same kind of thing that, like God, can enjoy itself. Thus I say that man should be so disinterested and untrammeled that he does not know what God is doing in him. Thus only can a person possess that poverty.

The authorities say that God is being, an intelligent being who knows everything. But I say that God is neither a being nor intelligent and he does not "know" either this or that. God is free of everything and therefore he is everything. He, then, who is to be poor in spirit must be poor of all his own knowledge, so that he knows nothing of God, or creatures, or of himself. This is not to say that one may not desire to know and to see the way of God, but it *is* to say that he may thus be poor in his own knowledge.

In the third place, he is poor who has nothing. Many people have said that this is the consummation, that one should possess none of the corporeal goods of this world, and this may well be true in case one thus becomes poor voluntarily. But this is not what I mean.

Thus far I have said that he is poor who does not want to fulfill the will of god but who so lives that he is empty of his own will and the will of god, as much so as when he did not yet exist. We have said of this poverty that it is the highest poverty. Next, we said that he is poor who knows nothing of the action of god in himself. When a person is as empty of "knowledge" and "awareness" as God is innocent of all things, this is the purest poverty. But the third poverty is most inward and real and I shall now speak of it. It consists in that a man *has* nothing.

Now pay earnest attention to this! I have often said, and great authorities agree, that to be a proper abode for God and fit for God to act in, a man should also be free from all [his own] things and [his own] actions, both inwardly and outwardly. Now we shall say something else. If it is the case that a man is emptied of things, creatures, himself and god, and if still god could find a place in him to act, then we say: as long as that [place] exists, this man is not poor with the most intimate poverty. For God does not intend that man shall have a place reserved for *him* to work in, since true poverty of spirit requires that man shall be emptied of god and all his works, so that if God wants to act in the soul, he himself must be the place in which he acts—and that he would like to do. For if God once found a person as poor as this, he would take the responsibility of his own action and would himself be the *scene* of action, for God is one who acts within himself. It is here, in this poverty, that man regains the eternal being that once he was, now is, and evermore shall be.

There is the question of the words of St. Paul: "All that I am, I am by the grace of God,"[5] but our argument soars above grace, above intelligence, and above all desire. (How is it to be connected with what St. Paul says?) It is to be replied that what St. Paul says is true, not that this grace was in him, but the grace of God had produced in him a simple perfection of being and then the work of grace was done. When, then, grace had finished its work, Paul remained as he was.

Thus we say that a man should be so poor that he is not and has not a place for God to act in. To reserve a place would be to maintain distinctions. *Therefore I pray God that he may quit me of god*, for [his] unconditioned being is above god and all distinctions. It was here [in unconditioned being] that I was myself, wanted myself, and knew myself to be this person [here before you], and therefore, I am my own first cause, both of my eternal being and of my temporal being. To this end I was born, and by virtue of my birth being eternal, I shall never die. It is of the nature of this eternal birth that I *have been* eternally, that I *am* now, and *shall be* forever. What I am as a temporal creature is to die and come to nothingness, for it came with time and so with time it will pass away. In my eternal birth, however, everything was begotten. I was my own first cause as well as the first cause of everything else. If I had willed it, neither I nor the world would have come to be! If I had not been, there would have been no god. There is, however, no need to understand this.

A great authority says: "His bursting forth is nobler than his efflux."[6] When I flowed forth from God, creatures said: "He is a god!" This, however, did not make me blessed, for it indicates that

I, too, am a creature. In bursting forth, however, when I shall be free within God's will and free, therefore of the will of god, and all his works, and even of god himself, then I shall rise above all creature kind, and I shall be neither god nor creature, but I shall be what I was once, now, and forevermore. I shall thus receive an impulse which shall raise me above the angels. With this impulse, I receive wealth so great that I could never again be satisfied with a god, or anything that is a god's, nor with any divine activities, for in bursting forth I discover that God and I are One. Now I am what I was and I neither add to nor subtract from anything, for I am the unmoved Mover, that moves all things. Here, then, a god may find no "place" in man, for by his poverty the man achieves the being that was always his and shall remain his eternally. Here, too, God is identical with the spirit and that is the most intimate poverty discoverable.

If anyone does not understand this discourse, let him not worry about that, for if he does not find this truth in himself he cannot understand what I have said—for it is a discovered truth which comes immediately from the heart of God. That we all may so live as to experience it eternally, may God help us! Amen.

From Sermon "Honor Thy Father"

The shell must be cracked apart if what is in it is to come out, for if you want the kernel you must break the shell. And therefore if you want to discover nature's nakedness you must destroy its symbols, and the farther you get in, the nearer you come to its essence. When you come to the One that gathers all things up into itself, there you must stay.

BLESSED HENRY SUSO, O.P.

Little Book of Truth

CHAPTER IV

Concerning the correct return which a self-abandoned man
should make through the only-begotten son

The Disciple: I have well-understood the truth concerning the creatures' issuing forth. I would now like to hear about the awakening, how a man should return through Christ and attain his salvation.

The Truth: It is important to know that Christ, the Son of God, has something in common with all men and something particular, not possessed by other men. He has a human nature in common with all men. He was truly a man. He assumed human nature but not a human personality. By this is meant that Christ assumed human nature in the indivisibility of the substance, which the theologian of Damascus calls "in atomo."[1] This means the common human nature which he adopted in the pure blood of the blessed body of Mary, from which he received the physical instrument.

And therefore human nature of itself has no right to claim—because Christ assumed it and not human personality—that every man could or should for this reason be God and man in the same manner as Christ was. He alone possessed the unique and incomprehensible dignity of assuming our nature in such purity that nothing of original sin, or of any other sin, ever touched him. Therefore he alone could redeem the sinful human race.

Secondly: The meritorious works which all other men do in true abandonment of themselves really lead them to the salvation which is the recompense of virtue. And this salvation consists in complete divine fruition, where all obstacles and otherness have been laid aside. But the union of the incarnation of Christ, because it takes place in a personal being, surpasses and exceeds the union of the souls of the blessed with God. Because, from the first moment when he was conceived as man, he was truly the Son of God, so that he had no other personality than that of the Son of God. But all other men have their natural personality in their natural being, and no matter how completely they are lost to themselves, or however fully they abandon themselves to the truth, it never occurs that they are transformed into the personality of the divine person and lose their own personality.

Thirdly: This man, Christ, also excels other men in that he is the head of the Church, just as the head of man is said to be in relation to his body, because it is written that all those whom he foreknew, he elected, that they may be made conformable to the image of the Son of God, so that he may be the first-born among many others.[2] And therefore, whoever earnestly desires to return and become a son with Christ, should turn with true self-

abandonment from himself to him. Then he will arrive at the place
to which he should go.

The Disciple: Lord, what is true self-abandonment?

The Truth: Observe with careful distinction these two words:
"self" and "abandonment." And if you can carefully weigh and
thoroughly penetrate their ultimate meaning, then you will
swiftly learn the truth.

Consider the first word, which is "self" or "me," and see what it
means. For this purpose, you must realize that every man has five
kinds of self.

The first "self" he has in common with a stone, and that is
existence. The second he has in common with a plant, and that is
growth. The third, with the animals, and that is feeling. The
fourth, with all men, is that he has a human nature like they. The
fifth, which belongs to him individually, is his personality, both
according to the essential and to the accidental.

Now what is it that leads a man astray and robs him of his
salvation? Only his last "self," by means of which man turns away
from God and towards himself, whereas he ought to return to him.
He thoughtlessly makes himself a "self" of his own. That is to say,
he blindly appropriates to himself what is God's, makes this his
goal, and eventually falls into sin.

But he who wishes to abandon this "self" completely should
cast three glances within. First, he should turn with a look that
sinks toward the nothingness of his own "self," and consider that
this "self" and the "self" of all things is nothing when left out and
shut out from the Something which is the only operating force.

The second look, which is not to be neglected, is that even in
the highest abandonment one's "self" always retains its own active
essence after the return, and that there, especially, it is not destroyed.

The third look takes place with the destruction and free surrender of one's self in all the things to which it had ever been led in
its state as a wild creature in shackled multiplicity against the
divine truth, in joy or sorrow, in action or inaction. This takes place
in such a way that he is lost irrevocably in the richness of power,
that he dies absolutely to himself, and becomes one with Christ in
eternity, so that at all times he acts in him, and receives all things
and contemplates all things in this simplicity.

And this surrendered "self" becomes a Christlike "I," as Scripture says of St. Paul: "For I through the Law have died to the Law
that I may live to God. With Christ I am nailed to the cross. It is

now no longer I that live, but Christ lives in me. And the life that I now live in the flesh, I live in the faith of the Son of God, who loved me and gave himself up for me" (Gal. 2:19-20). And this I call a well-balanced "self."

Now let us take the second word which he speaks: "Abandon." By this he means "forsake" or "despise." Of course, it is impossible for one to forsake oneself so that it becomes nothing at all, but only in one's contempt of oneself. Well for him who does this.

The Disciple: Praised be the truth! Dear Lord, tell me, does anything else remain to a blessed, self-abandoned man?

The Truth: It happens that when the good and faithful servant enters into the joy of his Lord, he becomes inebriated with the immeasurable abundance of the divine house. For he experiences in an ineffable manner what happens to a drunken man, who forgets himself, and is no longer himself. He is quite dead to himself, is entirely lost in God, has passed into him, and has become one spirit with him in all respects, like a little drop of water which is poured into a large portion of wine. Just as this is lost to itself, and draws to itself and into itself the taste and color of the wine, so it likewise happens to those who are in the complete possession of blessedness. All human desires fall away from them in an inexpressible manner, they melt away into themselves, and sink completely into the will of God.

If anything of man remained in man and was not entirely poured out of him, then the Scripture could not be true which says that God is to become all things to all things.[3] It is true that his being remains, but in a different form, in a different glory, and in a different capacity. And all this results from utter abandonment of self.

And he [St. Bernard] speaks further on the same topic: "But whether a man can ever be so self-abandoned in this life that he completely grasps this, and no longer, either in joy or sorrow, considers his own self, but only loves and seeks himself with the most perfect emotion for the sake of God, of this," he says, "I am not sure. Let those who have experienced it, come forward, for, as far as I can see, it is impossible."[4]

You can find the answer to your question in this conversation, because the true self-abandonment of such an exalted man in the world is formed and shaped after the self-abandonment of the blessed, of whom Scripture speaks, and is more or less similar to it in proportion as men are more or less united with God and have become one with him.

And note particularly what he [St. Bernard] says, that there they are deprived of their own being and are transformed into another form, into another glory, and into another force.

Now what else is this other strange form but the divine nature and the divine essence into which they flow and which flows into them, in order to be one with it?

What else is this glory than to be transfigured and glorified in the light of being, to which no man has access?

What else is this other power than that the divine strength and power are given to man through this personality and this union, to do and to leave undone all that belongs to his salvation? And so a man is dehumanized, as has been said.

The Disciple: Lord, is this possible on earth?

The Truth: This blessedness can be obtained in two ways. One way aims at the most perfect degree, which exceeds all possibility, and cannot be attained in this world because the body is included in man's nature, and the body's manifold tribulations stand in the way.

But blessedness in the sense of participated union is possible, although many men consider it impossible. And there is a reason for this, because neither mind nor reason can attain to it.

A theological work[5] states correctly that there is indeed one class of men, chosen and tried, who are of such a fully purified and godlike mind that virtues blossom forth in them as in God, because they are transformed and refined in the unity of their first exemplar. They arrive somehow at the full forgetfulness of this transient and temporal life, are transformed into the image of God, and are one with him.

All this holds true, however, only for those who have acquired this blessedness in the highest degree, or for a certain few men, very devout, who are still bodily on earth but spiritually in heaven.

JAN VAN RUYSBROECK

The Adornment of the Spiritual Marriage

CHAPTER XXIII

OF THE PAIN AND RESTLESSNESS OF LOVE

Of this inward demand and this invitation, and also because the creature lifts itself up and offers itself, and all that it can do, and yet can neither attain nor acquire the unity—of these things spring a ghostly pain. When the inmost part of the heart and the source of life have been wounded by love, and one cannot obtain that which one desires above all things, but must ever abide where one does not wish to be: from these two things pain comes forth. Here Christ is risen to the zenith of the conscience, and He sends His Divine rays into the hungry desires and into the longings of the heart; and this splendour burns and dries up and consumes all the moisture, that is, the strength and the powers of nature. The desire of the open heart, and the shining of the Divine rays, cause a perpetual pain.

If, then, one cannot achieve God and yet cannot and will not do without Him, from these two things there arise in such men tumult and restlessness, both without and within. And so long as a man is thus agitated, no creature, neither in heaven nor on earth, can give him rest or help him. In this state there are sometimes spoken from within sublime and salutary words, and singular teachings and wisdom are given. In this inward tumult one is ready to suffer all that can be suffered, that one may obtain that which one loves. This fury of love is an inward impatience which will hardly use reason or follow it, if it cannot obtain that which it loves. This inward fury eats a man's heart and drinks his blood. Here the sensible heat of love is fiercer than at any other stage in man's whole life; and his bodily nature is secretly wounded and consumed without any outward work, and the fruits of the virtues ripen more quickly than in all the degrees which have been shown heretofore.

In the like season of the year, the visible sun enters the sign of *Leo*, that is, the Lion, who is fierce by nature, for he is the lord over all beasts. So likewise, when a man comes to this way, Christ, the bright Sun, stands in the sign of the Lion, for the rays of His heat are so fierce that the blood in the heart of the impatient man must boil. And when this fierce way prevails, it masters and subdues all other ways and works; for it wills to be wayless, that is, without manner. And in this tumult a man sometimes falls into a desire and restless longing to be freed from the prison of his body, so that he may at once be united with Him Whom he loves. And he opens his inward eyes and beholds the heavenly house full of glory and joy, and his Beloved crowned in the midst of it, flowing forth towards His saints in abounding bliss; whilst he must lack all this. And therefrom there often spring in such a man outward tears and great longings. He looks down and considers the place of exile in which he has been imprisoned, and from which he cannot escape;

then tears of sadness and misery gush forth. These natural tears soothe and refresh the man's heart, and they are wholesome to the bodily nature, preserving its strength and powers and sustaining him through this state of tumult. All the manifold considerations and exercises according to ways or manner are helpful to the impatient man; that his strength may be preserved and that he may long endure in virtue.

CHAPTER XXIV

OF ECSTACIES AND DIVINE REVELATIONS

By this fierce ardour and this impatience some men are at times caught into the spirit, above the senses; and there words are spoken to them and images and similitudes shown to them, teaching them some truth of which they or other men have need, or else things that are to come. These are called revelations or visions. If they are bodily images, they are received in the imagination. This may be the work of an angel in man, through the power of God. If it be an intellectual truth, or a ghostly image, through which God reveals Himself in His unfathomableness, this is received in the understanding; and the man can clothe it in words in so far as it can be expressed in words. Sometimes a man may also be drawn above himself and above the spirit (but not altogether outside himself) into an Incomprehensible Good, which he shall never be able either to utter or to explain in the way in which he heard and saw; for in this simple act and this simple vision, to hear and to see are one. And none can work this in man, without intermediary and without the co-operation of any creature, save God alone. It is called RAP-TUS; which means, rapt away, or uplifted, or carried away. At times God grants to such men a sudden spiritual glimpse, like the lightning in the sky. It comes like a sudden glimpse of strange brightness, shining forth from the Simple Nudity. And thereby for an instant the spirit is raised above itself; but the light passes at once and the man returns to himself again. This is the work of God Himself; it is something very sublime; for those to whom it happens often become illuminated men.

Other things sometimes happen to those who live in the fierce ardour of love; for often another light shines into them, and this is the work of God through means. In this light the heart and the desirous powers uplift themselves towards that light; and, in the meeting with that light, the joy and the satisfaction are so great that the heart cannot contain them, but breaks out in a loud voice with cries of joy. And this is called the JUBILUS, or jubilation; that is, a joy which cannot be uttered in words. And one cannot contain oneself; but if one would go out with an opened and uplifted heart to meet this light the voice must follow, so long as this exercise and this light endure. Some inward men are at times taught in a dream by their guardian angels or by other angels, concerning many things of which they have need. Some men too are found who have many sudden intuitions, or inspirations, or imaginations, and also have miraculous dreams, and yet remain in their outward senses. But these know nothing of the tumult of love; for they dwell in outward multiplicity, and love has not wounded them. These things may be natural, or they may come from the devil, or from good angels, and therefore we may have faith in them so far as they accord with Holy Writ, and with the truth, but no more. If we trust them beyond this, we may easily be deceived.

CHAPTER XXXV

OF THE SECOND COMING OF CHRIST, OR, THE FOUNTAIN WITH THREE RILLS

Now we will speak further of the second manner of the coming of Christ, in those inward exercises by which a man is adorned, enlightened, and enriched in the three highest powers of the soul. This coming we will liken to a living fountain with three rills.

The fountain-head, from which the rills flow forth, is the fulness of Divine grace within the unity of our spirit. There grace dwells essentially; abiding as a brimming fountain, and actively flowing forth in rills into all the powers of the soul, each according to its need. These rills are special inflowings or workings of God in the higher powers, wherein God works by means of grace in many diverse ways.

CHAPTER XXXVI

THE FIRST RILL ADORNS THE MEMORY[1]

The first rill of grace, which God causes to flow forth in this coming, is a pure simplicity, shining in the spirit without differentiation. This rill takes its rise from the fountain within the unity of the spirit; and it flows straight downwards and pours through all the powers of the soul, the lower and the higher; and raises them above all multiplicity and all busyness and produces simplicity in a man; and shows and gives him the inward bond of unity of spirit.

Thus he is lifted up as regards his memory, and is freed from distracting images and from fickleness.

Now in this light, Christ demands a going out in conformity with this light and with this coming. So the man goes out, and knows and finds himself, through this simple light which has been poured into him, to be united and established and penetrated and confirmed, in the unity of his spirit or mind. Thereby the man is raised up and set in a new state, and he turns inwards, and fixes his memory upon the Nudity, above all the distractions of sensible images, and above multiplicity. Here the man possesses the essential and supernatural unity of his spirit, as his own dwelling-place and as his own eternal, personal heritage. He ever has a natural and supernatural tendency towards this same unity; and this same unity through the gifts of God and through simplicity of intention, shall have an eternal loving tendency towards that most high Unity, where, in the bond of the Holy Ghost, the Father and the Son are united with all saints. And thus the first rill, which demands unity, is satisfied.

CHAPTER XXXVII

THE SECOND RILL ENLIGHTENS THE UNDERSTANDING

Through inward charity and loving inclination and the faithfulness of God, there arises the second rill from the fulness of grace within the unity of the spirit; and it is a ghostly light which flows forth and shines into the understanding, discerning diverse things. For this light shows and proves in truth the distinctions between all the virtues; but this does not lie wholly in our power. For, even if we always had this light within our souls, it is God Who makes it to be silent and to speak, and He may show it and hide it, give it and take it away, in any time and place; for this light is His. And He therefore works in this light when He wills, and where He wills, and for whom He wills, and what He wills. These men have no need of revelations, neither of being caught up above the senses; for their life, and dwelling-place, their way, and their being, are in the spirit, above the senses and above sensibility. And there God shows to such men what is His good pleasure, and what is needful for them or for other men. Nevertheless God could, were such His will, deprive such men of their outward senses, and show them from within unknown similitudes and future things in many ways.

Now Christ wills that this man go out and walk in this light, in the way of this light. Therefore this enlightened man shall go out and shall mark his state and his life from within and from without, and see whether he is perfectly like unto Christ, according to His manhood and according to His Godhead. For we have been created in the image and after the likeness of God. And he shall raise his enlightened eyes, by means of the illuminated reason, to the intelligible Truth, and mark and behold in a creaturely way the most high Nature of God and the fathomless attributes which are in God: for to a fathomless Nature belong fathomless virtues and activities.

The most high Nature of the Godhead may thus be perceived and beheld: how it is Simplicity and Onefoldness, inaccessible Height and bottomless Depth, incomprehensible Breadth and eternal Length, a dark Silence, a wild Desert, the Rest of all saints in the Unity, and a common Fruition of Himself and of all saints in Eternity. And many other marvels may be seen in the abysmal Sea of the Godhead; and though, because of the grossness of the senses to which they must be shown from without, we must use sensible images, yet, in truth, these things are perceived and beheld from within, as an abysmal and unconditioned Good. But if they must be shown from without, it must be done by means of diverse similitudes and images, according to the enlightenment of the reason of him who shapes and shows them.

The enlightened man shall also mark and behold the attributes of the Father in the Godhead: how He is omnipotent Power and Might, Creator, Mover, Preserver, Beginning and End, the Origin and Being of all creatures. This the rill of grace shows to the enlightened reason in its radiance. It also shows the attributes of the Eternal Word: abysmal Wisdom and Truth, Pattern of all creatures and all life, Eternal and unchanging Rule, Seeing all things and Seeing Through all things, none of which is hidden from Him; Transillumination and Enlightenment of all saints in heaven and on earth, according to the merits of each. And even as this rill of radiance shows the distinctions between many things, so it also shows to the enlightened reason the attributes of the Holy Ghost: incomprehensible Love and Generosity, Compassion and Mercy, infinite Faithfulness and Benevolence, inconceivable Greatness, outpouring Richness, a limitless Goodness drenching through all heavenly spirits with delight, a Flame of Fire which burns all things together in the Unity, a flowing Fountain, rich in all savours, according to the desire of each; the Preparation of all saints for their eternal bliss and their entrance therein, an Embrace and Penetration of the Father, the Son, and all saints in fruitive Unity. All this is observed and beheld without differentiation or division in the simple Nature of the Godhead. And according to our perception these attributes abide as Persons do, in manifold distinctions. For between might and goodness, between generosity and truth, there are, according to our perception, great differences. Nevertheless all these are found in oneness and undifferentiation in the most high Nature of the Godhead. But the relations which make the personal attributes remain in eternal distinction. For the Father begets distinction. For the Father incessantly begets his Son, and Himself is unbegotten; and the Son is begotten, and cannot beget; and thus throughout eternity the Father has a Son, and the Son a Father. And these are the relations of the Father to the Son, and of the Son to the Father. And the Father and the Son breathe forth one Spirit, Who is Their common Will or Love. And this Spirit begets not, nor is He begotten; but must eternally pour forth, being breathed forth from both the Father and the Son. And these three Persons are one God and one Spirit. And all the attributes with the works which flow forth from them are common to all the Persons, for They work by virtue of Their Onefold Nature.

.   .   .   .   .   .

The incomprehensible richness and loftiness of the Divine Nature, its outpouring generosity toward all in common, fills a man with wonder. And, above all, he wonders at the universality of God and His outpouring upon all things. For he beholds the incomprehensible Essence as a common fruition of God and all saints. And he sees the Divine Persons as a common outpouring and a common activity in grace and in glory, in nature and above nature, in all places and at all times, in saints and in men, in heaven and on earth, in all creatures, rational, irrational, and material, according to the merits, the need, and the receptivity of each. And he beholds heaven and earth, sun and moon, the four elements, together with all creatures, and the course of the heavens, created for all in common. God, with all His gifts, is common to all: the angels are common: the soul is common to all its powers, to the whole body, to all its members, yet in each member is entire; for the soul cannot be divided, save by the reason. For though, according to the reason, the highest powers and the lowest, the spirit and the soul, are certainly divided; yet, in nature, they are one. So too God is whole and special to each, and yet common to all creation; for by

Him all things are; within Him and upon Him, heaven and earth and all nature depend. When a man thus considers the wonderful wealth and loftiness of the Divine Nature, and all the multiplicity of gifts which He gives and offers to His creatures, then there grows up within him a wonder at such manifold richness, at such loftiness, and at the immeasurable faithfulness of God to His creatures. And thence springs a particular inward gladness of the spirit, and a high trust in God, and this inward gladness envelops and drenches all the powers of the soul and the most inward part of the spirit.

CHAPTER XXXVIII

THE THIRD RILL ESTABLISHES THE WILL TO EVERY PERFECTION

From this gladness and the fulness of grace and the faithfulness of God, there is born and flows forth the third rill in this same unity of the spirit. This rill, like a fire, enkindles the will, and swallows up and consumes everything into unity. And it fills to the brim and flows through all the powers of the soul, with rich gifts and with a singular nobility: and it calls forth in the will a tender spiritual love without effort.

Now Christ says inwardly within the spirit by means of this burning brook: GO YE OUT by practices in conformity with these gifts and with this coming. By the first rill, which is a simple light, the memory has been lifted above sensible images, and has been grounded and established in the unity of the spirit. By the second rill, which is an inflowing light, understanding and reason have been enlightened, to know the diverse ways of virtue and of practice, and discern the mysteries of the Scriptures. By the third rill, which is an inpouring heat, the supreme will has been enkindled in tranquil love, and has been endowed with great riches. Thus has this man become spiritually enlightened; for the grace of God dwells like a fountainhead in the unity of his spirit; and its rills cause in the powers an outflowing with all the virtues. And the fountainhead of grace ever demands a flowing-back into the same source from whence the flood proceeds.

RAMON LULL

The Art of Contemplation

Ramon Lull (c. 1232–1315) stands as a bridge-person between the thought of medieval Europe and the Islamic tradition. A native of Majorca, Lull became a Franciscan after an irreligious youth spent as a Spanish courtier. Remarkably versatile, he devoted his life to voluminous writings, reform of the Church, preaching, Arabic scholarship, and missionary journeys to North Africa.

Written about 1280, his Art of Contemplation *is a practical manual inserted into* Blanquerna, *a long semiallegorical romance written in Lull's native Catalan. The hero of this romance (Blanquerna himself) rises to the papacy, effects great reforms in the Church, but eventually renounces his position in order to devote himself to the life of a hermit. The* Art of Contemplation *pretends to be a description of Blanquerna's manner of prayer in his hermitage.*

Lull's spiritual doctrine is marked by keen psychological interest and by a pervasive voluntarism—a mysticism of love and the will. Because of his profound contacts with Arabic learning, Lull brings to Christian spirituality new sensitivities and perhaps some awareness of the rich Islamic mystic tradition.

CHAPTER I

OF THE MANNER WHEREIN BLANQUERNA
CONTEMPLATED THE VIRTUES OF GOD

Blanquerna rose at midnight and gazed upon the heavens and the stars, and cast out all things from his thoughts, and fixed them upon the virtues of God. For he was fain to contemplate the goodness of God in all the sixteen virtues,[1] and the sixteen virtues in the goodness of God; for which cause, falling on his knees, and raising his hands to the heavens and his thoughts to God, he spake these words with his lips and pondered them in his soul with all the powers of his memory, understanding and will:

2. 'O Sovereign Good, Thou that art infinitely great in eternity, power, wisdom, love, virtue, truth, glory, perfection, justice, liberality, mercy, humility, dominion, patience! I adore Thee as I remember, comprehend, love and speak of Thee and of all these virtues herein named, which are one thing with Thyself, as Thou

art one with them, one very essence without difference soever.'

3. 'O Sovereign Good, that art so great, Sovereign Greatness, that art so good! Wert Thou not eternal, Thou wert not so great a good that my soul could fill its memory with remembrance of Thee, nor its understanding with understanding of Thee, nor its will with love of Thee. But since Thou art Infinite and Eternal Good, Thou canst fill my whole soul and every soul with infused grace and blessing, that memory, understanding and love may be given to Thee, O Infinite and Eternal Sovereign Good.'

4. Through the power which Blanquerna remembered in Sovereign goodness, he gained power and strength to raise his consideration above the firmament, and considered a greatness so exceeding great that it had infinite power of movement, like unto a flash of light shining in the six common directions—to wit, above and below, before and behind, to left and to right; and finding no limit, nor beginning nor end. As Blanquerna thus considered, he marvelled greatly, the more so when to the consideration of this goodness he joined that of eternity, which has neither beginning nor end. And while Blanquerna was wholly absorbed in this consideration, he remembered how great a good is that of Divine power, which can be so great and so everlasting, and whose knowledge and will are infinite and eternal, as are its virtue, truth, glory, perfection, justice, liberality, mercy, humility, dominion and patience.

5. As Blanquerna pursued his contemplation in this wise, his heart began to burn within him, and his eyes to weep, at the great joy which he had in remembering, understanding and loving such noble virtues in Sovereign goodness. But ere he could perfectly weep, his understanding descended to the level of the imagination, and he fell to thinking and doubting how it could be that, before the world was, God should have justice, liberality, mercy, humility, dominion; and, through the alliance of understanding and imagination, doubt chilled the warmth of his heart and the tears in his eyes grew fewer. So Blanquerna parted understanding and imagination and exalted the former above the latter, remembering how the Sovereign Good is infinite in all perfection, and how for this cause, through His own virtue and glory, He may have and can have to so great a degree of perfection all the virtues above named before the world was as well as now that the world is; only that, while the world was not, there was lacking any person who might receive from the Sovereign Good the grace and the influence of these above-named virtues.

6. Greatly now joyed the will of Blanquerna because his understanding had cast down the imagination which impeded its working and had soared aloft, leaving the imagination behind, to comprehend the infinite power of God, which in justice, liberality, and the like, must needs have been before the world was; for, were this not so, it would follow that in Sovereign Goodness there was defect of greatness, power, eternity and virtue. And since it is impossible that in God is any defect at all, for that cause the will set the heart of Blanquerna so fiercely on fire that his eyes were abundantly filled with tears.

7. While Blanquerna contemplated and wept, his memory, understanding and will conversed mentally with each other within his soul, and they found great delight in the virtues of God, as these words show: 'Memory,' said Understanding, 'what remembrance hast thou of the goodness, wisdom and love of God? And thou, O Will, what dost thou love in them?' Memory answered and said: 'When I consider in my remembrance how great a good it is to know oneself to be greater and nobler in knowledge and will than any beside, I feel not so high nor so great as when I remember the Sovereign Good, Who is infinite in knowledge and will. And when I consider eternity, power, virtue, truth, and the rest, then I feel myself to be magnified and exalted as I think upon these things.' With these words and many others did Memory reply to Understanding; and Will replied in like manner, saying that she felt not so great nor high when she loved the Sovereign Good because He is more loving and wise than any beside, as when she loved Him because of His infinite and eternal wisdom and love. After these words, Understanding said to Memory and Will that her own state was like to theirs in the contemplation of the Sovereign Good.

8. Memory, Understanding and Will agreed among themselves that they would contemplate the Sovereign Good in His virtue, truth and glory. Memory recalled the virtue of the Infinite Good, His virtue being infinite in truth and glory. Understanding comprehended that which Memory recalled, and Will loved that which Memory recalled and Understanding comprehended. Once again Memory turned to remembrance, and recalled the infinite truth of Sovereign Good, in the which truth are virtue and glory. And Understanding comprehended infinite glory, which is in virtue and truth, and our glorious Sovereign Good; and Will loved this wholly and in the unity of one actuality, in one and the same perfection.

9. Blanquerna enquired of his Understanding: 'If the Sovereign Good give me salvation, what wilt thou thereby comprehend?' Understanding answered: 'I shall comprehend the mercy and humility and liberality of God.' 'And thou, O Memory, if He condemn me, what wilt thou remember?' He answered: 'I shall remember the justice and dominion and perfection and power of God.' 'And thou, O Will, what wilt thou love?' He answered: 'I will love that which Memory recalls, so that I be in a place where I may love it; for the virtues which are in the Sovereign Good are worthy in themselves to be loved.'

10. After these words, Blanquerna remembered his sins, and comprehended how great a good it is that in God there is patience; for were there no patience in God, so soon as man sinned he would be punished and cast out from this world. And therefore he enquired of his Will: 'What thanks shall I render to the patience of God which has thus borne with me?' Will answered and said that he should love justice in his Sovereign Good, even were it possible that his Understanding should know that he was to be punished by damnation for his sins. Blanquerna was greatly pleased at the answer which Will had made; and with his mouth and with the three powers of his soul he praised and blessed patience in the Sovereign Good through all the Divine virtues.

11. In this wise did Blanquerna contemplate the Divine virtues, from midnight until the hour when he should ring for matins, and he gave thanks to God because He had humbled him by guiding him in his contemplation. And as he was about to cease from contemplation and to ring for matins, he began to bethink himself that he had not contemplated the Patience of God as highly as the other virtues, because he had contemplated it in relation to himself, as has been declared above. Therefore it behoved him to turn once more to contemplation, and he said that he adored and contemplated the Patience of God in that it was one self-same thing with Sovereign goodness and with all the other virtues, without difference soever. Wherefore Understanding greatly marvelled how patience could be one thing in essence with the remaining virtues. But Memory recalled that in God the virtues have no diversity the one from the other, but that, since their operations in the creatures are diverse, they themselves appear diverse, even as the reflection of a person appears when he looks into two mirrors, of which one is crooked and the other straight, yet the reflection itself is one, in each of the mirrors, without diversity soever.

RICHARD ROLLE

The Fire of Love

Born in Yorkshire, (c. 1300–1349) Richard Rolle studied at Oxford. Shortly after abandoning his studies, he became a hermit. Independent and extreme in his youth, Rolle eventually mellowed and died as the spiritual director of a convent of Cistercian nuns. His rich and varied writings, in English and Latin, are noted for their elaborate style as well as for the fervor of their content.

As far as my study of Scripture goes, I have found that to love Christ above all else will involve three things: warmth and song and sweetness. And these three, as I know from personal experience, cannot exist for long without there being great quiet.

THOMAS À KEMPIS

The Imitation of Christ

Thomas Hemerken of Kempen, or Thomas à Kempis (c. 1380–1471) was a member of the Brethren of the Common Life, an association of priests organized in the Netherlands in the late fourteenth century. Ordained a priest in 1413, Thomas spent much of his life copying books for the schools staffed by members of his order.

The Imitation of Christ is probably more a compilation than a truly original work. At any rate, it represents a new movement in medieval spirituality, away from concern with mystical prayer and toward a more practical concern with a spirituality of discipline and asceticism accessible to all who earnestly wish to follow Christ. This work has exerted great appeal through the ages, and has probably been read more widely than any other book except the Bible. A few chapters are here presented as a testimony to the work's importance and as an illustration of the more practical caste of much Catholic spirituality in the past 500 years.

CHAPTER XXXIII

Of Inconstancy of Heart, and of Having
Our Final Intention Directed unto God

My son, trust not to thy feeling, which now is; quickly shall it
be changed into another. As long as thou livest, thou art subject to
mutability,[1] even against thy will; so that thou art found one while
merry, another while sad; one while quiet, another while troubled;
now devout, then undevout; now diligent, then listless; now grave,
and then light.

2. But he that is wise and well instructed in the Spirit stand-
eth above these changeful things; not heeding what he feeleth in
himself or which way the wind of instability bloweth; but so that
the whole intention of his mind maketh progress to the due and
desired end. For thus he will be able to continue throughout one
and the self-same and unshaken; in the midst of so many various
issues the single eye of his intention being directed unceasingly
towards me.

And the purer the eye of the intention is,[2] with so much the
more constancy doth a man pass through divers storms.

But in many the eye of a pure intention waxeth dim, for their
regard is quickly drawn aside to some pleasurable object which
meeteth them. For it is rare to find one who is wholly free from all
blemish of self-seeking. So the Jews of old came to Bethany to
Martha and Mary, *not for Jesus' sake only, but that they might see
Lazarus.*[3]

The eye of our intention therefore is to be purged, that it may
be single and right;[4] and is to be directed towards Me, beyond all
the various objects which may come between.

CHAPTER XXXIV

That God Is Sweet above All Things, and in All Things,
to Him That Loveth Him

Behold, my God, and my all! What can I desire more, and what
happier thing can I long for? O sweet and delicious word! but to him
only who loveth the Word, not the world, nor the things that are in
the world.

My God, and my all! To him that understandeth, enough hath
been said; and to repeat it often, is delightful to him that loveth.
Forasmuch as when Thou art present, all things are delightful, but

when Thou art absent, all things are a loathing. Thou makest a
quiet heart, and great peace, and festal joy. Thou makest us to
think well of all circumstances, and in all to praise Thee; neither
can any thing please long without Thee; but if it must needs be
pleasant and of a good savour, Thy grace must be present, and it
must be seasoned with the seasoning of Thy wisdom. What will not
be of good savour unto him to whom Thou savourest well? And him
to whom Thou savourest not, what shall have power to please?

But the wise men of the world, and they also who relish the
things of the flesh, are found wanting in Thy Wisdom;[5] for in the
world is found the utmost vanity, and in the flesh is found death.
But they that follow Thee by the contempt of wordly things, and
mortification of the flesh, are known to be truly wise; for they are
brought over from vanity to truth, from the flesh to the spirit. To
these God savoureth well; and what good soever is found in creatures, they wholly refer unto the praise of their Maker. Different,
however, yea, very different is the savour of the Creator and of the
creature, of Eternity and of time, of Light uncreated and of light
received.

2. O everlasting Light, surpassing all created luminaries,
flash forth Thy lightning[6] from above, piercing all the most inward
parts of my heart. Make clean, make glad, make bright and make
alive my spirit, with all the powers thereof, that I may cleave unto
Thee in ecstasies of joy. O when will that blessed and desired hour
come, that Thou mayest satisfy me with Thy Presence, and be unto
me all in all! So long as this is not granted me I shall not have full
joy.

Still, alas! the old man doth live in me;[7] he is not wholly
crucified, is not perfectly dead. Still lusteth he mightily against the
Spirit, and stireth up inward wars, nor suffereth the kingdom of
the soul to be in peace.

*But Thou that rulest the power of the sea, and stillest the lifting
up of its waves,*[8] arise and help me! *Scatter the nations that desire
war;*[9] crush Thou them in Thy might. Display Thy wonderful
works, I beseech Thee, and let Thy right hand be glorified; for there
is no other hope or refuge for me, save in Thee, O Lord my God.[10]

CHAPTER XXXV

*That There Is No Security From
Temptation in This Life*

My son, thou art never secure in this life, but as long as thou
livest,[1] thou needest always spiritual armour. Thou dwellest

among enemies, and art fought against on the right hand and on the left.[2]

If therefore thou defend not thyself on every side with the shield of patience, thou wilt not be long without a wound. Moreover, if thou set not thy heart fixedly on Me, with a sincere wish to suffer all things for Me, thou wilt not be able to bear the heat of this combat, nor to attain to the palm of the blessed. Thou oughtest therefore manfully to go through all, and to use a strong hand against whatsoever withstandeth thee.

For to him that overcometh is manna given,[3] and for the indolent there remaineth much misery.

2. If thou seek rest in this life, how wilt thou then attain to the everlasting rest? Dispose not thyself for much rest, but for great patience. Seek true peace, not in earth, but in Heaven; not in men, nor in any other creature, but in God alone.

For the love of God thou oughtest cheerfully to undergo all things, that is to say, labours and pains; temptations, vexations, anxieties, necessities, infirmities, injuries, slanders, reproofs, humiliations; confusions, corrections, and despisings. These help to virtue; these are the trial of a novice in Christ; these frame the heavenly crown. I will give an everlasting reward for a short labour, and infinite glory for transitory confusion.

3. Thinkest thou that thou shalt always have spiritual consolations at thine own will? My saints had not such always, but they had many afflictions, and sundry temptations, and great forsakings. Nevertheless in all these they bore themselves up patiently, and trusted rather in God than in themselves; knowing that the *sufferings of this time are not worthy to be compared with winning the future glory.*[4] Wilt thou have that at once, which many after many tears and great labours have hardly obtained?

Wait for the Lord, behave thyself manfully, and be of good courage;[5] do not distrust, do not leave thy place, but steadily expose both body and soul for the glory of God. I will reward thee most plenteously; I will be with thee in every tribulation.[6]

Part V Notes

St. Francis of Assisi

1. The caperon was a kind of upper garment extending down to the cord. All that remains of it today is a narrow strip of cloth that is attached to the front of the novice's capuche.

2. In the Bull *Cum secundum consilium*, 1220.
3. St Jerome, Epistle 125.
4. St Anselm, Epistle 49.
5. Therefore one like Judas.
6. With a pure heart, with a pure mind, imply freedom from all self-seeking and attachment to earthly goods, not freedom from the guilt of sin. A man is pure if he lives for God alone, if there is no room in his heart for the desires of the Ego or attachment to the world and worldly goods.

St. Bonaventure

1. James i. 17.
2. Eph. i. 17.
3. Psalm cxxi. 6.
4. Psalm lxxv. 3.
5. II Cor. xii. 2.
6. Gal. ii. 20.
7. John x. i.
8. Apoc. xxii. 14.
9. Heb. i. 3.
10. Psalm lxxxiii. 6.
11. Exod. iii. 18.
12. Gen. i. 3.
13. Mark xii. 30.
14. Apoc. i. 8. St. Bonaventure's thought may be understood as follows: to see God *through* the mirror is to see Him through our understanding of the objects we investigate; the mind sees Him *in* the mirror when it sees Him actually at work in these objects. Thus the steps of the ascent, developed through the rest of the book, run as follows:
1. Seeing God through His traces in the universe
2. seeing God in His traces in the human act of perception
3. seeing God through His image in man's natural mental powers
4. seeing God in His image in man's soul reformed by grace
5. seeing God through His attribute of being
6. seeing God in His attribute of goodness.
15. I Kings x. 19.
16. Isaiah vi. 2.
17. Exod. xxiv. 16.
18. Matt. xvii. 1.
19. I Cor. i. 30.

The Cloud of Unknowing

1. Eph. 3:18.
2. Heb. 12:30; Exod. 19:30.

Meister Eckhart, O.P.

1. Cf. Matt. 6:6.
2. Cf. Luke 14:26.
3. Rom. 9:3.

4. Obviously, "god" means a human conception of God. This is a distinction Eckhart did not make explicit and his statements therefore sounded blasphemous to his contemporaries, even though they were intended in all piety.

5. I Cor. 15:10.

6. Probably Plato, *Timaeus* 40–41.

Blessed Henry Suso, O.P.

1. John Damascene, *De Fide Orthodoxa*, III, c. 11.
2. Rom. 8:29.
3. I Cor. 15:28.
4. St. Bernard, *De diligendo Deo*, chap. 15, n. 39.
5. St. Thomas Aquinas, *Summa Theologica*, I, q. 61, a. 5.

Jan van Ruysbroeck

1. It should be remembered that for the mediæval psychologist the term "memory" included all that we mean by "mind."

Ramon Lull

1. The sixteen "virtues" of God are goodness, greatness, and the fourteen other virtues enumerated in paragraph 2.

Thomas à Kempis

1. Job xiv. 2.
2. S. Matt. vi. 22.
3. S. John xii. 9.
4. S. Matt. vi. 22.
5. Cor. i. 26; Rom. viii. 5; 1 John ii. 16.
6. Psalm cxliv. 6.
7. Rom. vii.
8. Psalm lxxxix. 9.
9. Psalm lxviii. 30.
10. Psalm xxxi. 14.
11. Job vii. 1.
12. 2 Cor. vi. 7.
13. Rev. ii. 17.
14. Rom. viii. 18.
15. Psalm xxvii. 14.
16. Psalm xci. 15.

Part VI

COUNTER-REFORMATION SPIRITUALITY

The common sense of the ordinary soul is simply this: being perfectly satisfied with what it knows is suitable for it, and never attempting to tread beyond the boundaries laid out for it. It is not inquisitive about the way God acts. It is quite happy to submit to his will and makes no attempt to find out his intentions. It wants to know only what every moment says to it, listens to what God utters in the depths of its heart and does not ask what has been said to others.

Jean-Pierre de Caussade (1675-1751)

ST. IGNATIUS OF LOYOLA

Spiritual Exercises

St. Ignatius of Loyola (1491–1556), founder of the Jesuit Order, combined the military ardor of late-medieval Spain with the impassioned realism and humanism of the early northern Renaissance. In his Spiritual Exercises, *a manual for spiritual retreats, Ignatius attempted to lead his followers toward an "election" of God's will for their lives. The* Spiritual Exercises *are a typical product of devotio moderna, a movement in piety that stressed an intensely individual relation of the believer to Christ and an imaginative identification with His life, especially His passion. Earlier writers had seen the goal of perfection as theosis (divinization), contemplation, or transformation. Ignatius and many of his followers in modern spirituality have rather stressed that the aim of all spiritual life is the identification of the human will with the divine, regardless of experiential effects, contemplative knowledge, and the like. Ignatian spirituality and its offshoots are, therefore, intensely practical in orientation, geared especially to Christians busy with ministry and even profane tasks in their daily lives. The following excerpts from the* Spiritual Exercises *discuss such topics as the consciousness of sin, the "election" of God, and the discernment of spirits.*

FIRST PRINCIPLE AND FOUNDATION

Man was created to praise, reverence, and serve God our Lord, and by this means to save his soul; and the other things on the face of the earth were created for man's sake, and in order to aid him in the prosecution of the end for which he was created. Whence it follows, that man must make use of them in so far as they help him to attain his end, and in the same way he ought to withdraw himself from them in so far as they hinder him from it. It is therefore necessary that we should make ourselves indifferent to all created things, in so far as it is left to the liberty of our free-will to do so, and is not forbidden; in such sort that we do not for our part wish for health rather than sickness, for wealth rather than poverty, for honour rather than dishonour, for a long life rather than a

short one; and so in all other things, desiring and choosing only
those which most lead us to the end for which we were created.

FROM THE "FIRST WEEK"

THE FIRST EXERCISE

The First Exercise is a meditation by means of the three
powers of the soul upon the first, the second, and the third sin. It
contains in itself, after a preparatory prayer and two preludes,
three principal points and a colloquy.

The preparatory prayer is to ask our Lord God for grace that
all my intentions, actions, and operations may be ordained purely
to the service and praise of His Divine Majesty.

The first prelude is a composition of place, seeing the spot.
Here it is to be observed that in contemplation or meditation on
visible matters, such as the contemplation of Christ our Lord, Who
is visible, the composition will be to see with the eyes of the
imagination the corporeal place where the thing I wish to contemplate is found. I say the corporeal place, such as the Temple or
the mountain, where Jesus Christ or our Lady is found, according
to what I desire to contemplate. In meditation on invisible things,
such as the present meditation on sins, the composition will be to
see with the eyes of the imagination and to consider that my soul is
imprisoned in this corruptible body, and my whole self in this vale
of misery, as it were in exile among brute beasts; I say my whole
self, that is, soul and body.

The second prelude is to ask of God our Lord that which I wish
and desire. The petition ought to be according to the subject-
matter, *i.e.*, if the contemplation is on the Resurrection, the petition ought to be to ask for joy with Christ rejoicing; if it be on the
Passion, to ask for grief, tears, and pain in union with Christ in
torment; here it will be to ask for shame and confusion at myself,
seeing how many have been lost for one sole mortal sin, and how
many times I have merited to be lost eternally for my so many sins.

Before all the contemplations or meditations the preparatory
prayer must always be the same, without any alteration. There
must also be the two above-named preludes, which are changed
from time to time according to the subject-matter.

The first point will be to apply the memory to the first sin,
which was that of the angels; and then immediately to employ the
understanding on the same by turning it over in the mind: and
then the will, desiring to remember and understand the whole, in

order to put myself to the blush, and to be confounded, bringing my many sins into comparison with the one sole sin of the angels; and while they have gone to Hell for one sin, how often I have deserved the same for so many. I say, to bring to memory the sin of the angels, how they were created in grace, yet not willing to help themselves by the means of their liberty in the work of paying reverence and obedience to their Creator and Lord, falling into pride, they were changed from grace into malice, and hurled from Heaven to Hell; and then in turn to reason more in particular with the understanding, and thus in turn to move still more the affections by means of the will.

The second point will be to do the same, *i.e.*, to apply the three powers, to the sin of Adam and Eve; bringing before the memory how for that sin they did such long penance, and how much corruption came upon the human race, so many men being put on the way to Hell. I say, to bring to memory the second sin, that of our first parents; how, after Adam had been created in the plain of Damascus, and placed in the terrestrial Paradise, and Eve had been formed out of his rib, when they had been forbidden to eat of the tree of knowledge, yet eating of it, and so sinning, they were afterwards clothed in garments made of skins, and driven out of Paradise, lived without original justice, which they had lost, all their life long in many travails and much penance; and in turn with the understanding to discuss all this, making more especially use of the will, as has been said before.

The third point will be to do in like manner also in regard to the third sin, *i.e.*, the particular sin of some one person who for one mortal sin has gone to Hell; and many others without number have been condemned for fewer sins than I have committed. I say, to do the same in regard to the third particular sin, bringing before the memory the gravity and malice of sin committed by man against his Creator and Lord; then to discuss with the understanding, how in sinning and acting against the Infinite Goodness, such a person has justly been condemned for ever; and to conclude with acts of the will, as has been said.

Colloquy. Imagining Christ our Lord before us and placed on the Cross, to make a colloquy with Him, asking Him how, being our Creator, He had come to this, that He has made Himself Man, and from eternal life has come to temporal death, thus to die for my sins. Again, to look at myself, asking what I have done for Christ, what I am doing for Christ, what I ought to do for Christ; and then seeing Him that which He is, and thus fixed to the Cross, to give expression to what shall present itself to my mind.

The colloquy is made properly by speaking as one friend speaks to another, or as a servant to his master; at one time asking for some favour, at another blaming oneself for some evil committed, now informing him of one's affairs, and seeking counsel in them. And at the end let a *Pater noster* be said.

THE SECOND EXERCISE

The Second Exercise is a meditation upon sins; it contains, after the preparatory prayer and the two preludes, five points and a colloquy.

Let the preparatory prayer be the same.

The first prelude will be the same composition of place.

The second is to ask for what I desire; it will be here to beg great and intense grief, and tears for my sins.

The first point is the series of sins, that is to say, to recall to memory all the sins of my life, looking at them from year to year or from period to period. Three things help in this: the first, to behold the place and the house where I have dwelt; the second, the conversation I have had with others; the third, the calling in which I have lived.

The second point is to weigh the sins, looking at the foulness and the malice that every mortal sin committed contains in itself, even supposing that it were not forbidden.

The third point is to consider who I am, abasing myself by examples; first, how little I am in comparison with all men; secondly, what men are in comparison with all the angels and saints of Paradise; thirdly, to consider what all that is created is in comparison with God; then I alone, what can I be? fourthly, to consider all my corruption and foulness of body; fifthly, to see myself as an ulcer and abscess whence have issued so many sins and so many iniquities, and such vile poison.

The fourth point is to consider who God is, against Whom I have sinned, looking at His attributes, comparing them with their contraries in myself: His wisdom with my ignorance, His omnipotence with my weakness, His justice with my iniquity, His goodness with my malice.

The fifth point is an exclamation of wonder, with intense affection, running through all creatures in my mind, how they have suffered me to live, and have preserved me in life; how the angels, who are the sword of the Divine Justice, have borne with me, and have guarded and prayed for me; how the saints have been interceding and praying for me; and the heavens, the sun, the moon, the stars, and the elements, the fruits of the earth, the birds, the fishes, and the animals; and the earth, how it is it has not opened to swallow me up, creating new hells that I might suffer in them for ever.

The whole to conclude with a colloquy of mercy, reasoning and giving thanks to God our Lord, for having given me life till now, and proposing through His grace to amend henceforward. *Pater noster.*

FROM THE "SECOND WEEK"

INTRODUCTION TO THE CONSIDERATION OF STATES OF LIFE

Having already considered the example which Christ our Lord has given us for the first state, which consists in the observance of the Commandments, while He was obedient to His parents; and likewise the example He has given us for the second, which is that of evangelical perfection, when He remained in the Temple, leaving His adopted father, and His natural Mother, to apply Himself exclusively to the service of His Eternal Father; let us at the same time that we contemplate His life, begin to investigate and to ask in what kind of life or state His Divine Majesty wishes to make use of us.

And thus by way of some introduction to it, in the first Exercise that follows we will consider the intention of Christ our Lord, and on the other side that of the enemy of our human nature, and how we ought to dispose ourselves in order to arrive at perfection in whatever state or kind of life God shall give us to elect:

FOURTH DAY

The meditation on Two Standards, the one of Christ, our sovereign Leader and Lord: the other of Lucifer, the mortal enemy of our human nature.

The usual preparatory prayer.

The first prelude is the history: it will be here how Christ calls and desires all under His banner: Lucifer on the contrary under his.

The second prelude is a composition of place, seeing the spot: it will be here to see a vast plain of all the region round Jerusalem, where the Supreme general-Leader of all the good is Christ our Lord: and to imagine another plain in the country of Babylon, where the chief of the enemy is Lucifer.

The third prelude is to ask for what I want: it will be here to ask for knowledge of the deceits of the wicked chieftain, and for help to guard against them; and for knowledge of the true life which our Sovereign and true Leader points out, and for grace to imitate Him.

The first point is to imagine the chieftain of all the enemy as seated in that great plain of Babylon, as on a lofty throne of fire and smoke, in aspect horrible and fearful.

The second point is to consider how he summons together innumerable devils, how he disperses them some to one city, some to another, and so on throughout the whole world, omitting not any provinces, places, or states of life, or any persons in particular.

The third point is to consider the address which he makes, and how he warns them to lay snares and chains; telling them how they are first to tempt men to covet riches (as he is wont to do in most cases), so that they may more easily come to the vain honour of the world, and then to unbounded pride; so that the first step is riches, the second honour, the third pride; and from these three steps he leads them to all other vices.

In the same way, on the other hand, we are to consider the sovereign and true Leader, Christ our Lord.

The first point is to consider how Christ our Lord, in aspect fair and winning, takes His station in a great plain of the country near Jerusalem on a lowly spot.

The second point is to consider how the Lord of the whole world chooses out so many persons, Apostles, disciples, &c., and sends them throughout the whole world diffusing His sacred doctrine through all states and conditions of persons.

The third point is to consider the address which Christ our Lord makes to all His servants and friends, whom He sends on this expedition, recommending to them that they desire to help all, by guiding them first to the highest degree of poverty of spirit, and even to actual poverty, if it please His Divine Majesty, and He should choose to elect them to it: leading them, secondly, to a desire of reproaches and contempt, because from these two humility results; so that there are three steps: the first, poverty, opposed to riches; the second, reproaches and contempt, opposed to worldly honour; the third, humility, opposed to pride: and from these three steps let them conduct them to all other virtues.

A colloquy to our Lady to obtain for me grace from her Son and Lord that I may be received under His Standard. And first, in the highest degree of poverty of spirit, and not less in actual poverty, if it please His Divine Majesty, and He should choose to elect and receive me to it. Secondly, in bearing reproaches and insults, the better to imitate Him in these, provided only I can endure them without sin on the part of any person, or displeasure to His Divine Majesty; and after this an *Ave Maria*.

To ask the same from the Son, that He obtain for me this grace from the Father; and then to say an *Anima Christi*.

To ask the same from the Father, that He grant me this grace; and to say a *Pater noster*.

This Exercise will be made at midnight, and again early in the morning; and two repetitions of it will be made at the hours of Mass and Vespers, always finishing with the triple colloquy to our Lady, the Son, and the Father; and the meditation on the Classes, which follows, will be made during the hour before supper.

THE THREE CLASSES

On the same fourth day will be made the meditation on the Three Classes of men, in order to embrace that which is best.

The usual preparatory prayer.

The first prelude is the history, which is concerning three classes of men, each of which has acquired ten thousand ducats, not purely and duly for the love of God. They all desire to save their souls, and to find in peace God our Lord, ridding themselves of the burden and impediment to this end which they find in their affection to the money acquired.

The second prelude is a composition of place, seeing the spot: it will be here to see myself standing before God our Lord and all His saints, that I may desire and know that which is more pleasing to His Divine Goodness.

The third prelude is to ask for what I desire: it will be here to beg the grace to choose that which is most for the glory of His Divine Majesty, and for the salvation of my soul.

The first class would like to shake off the affection which they have for the money acquired, so as to find in peace God our Lord, and so as to know how to save their souls; but they take no means even up to the hour of death.

The second class desire to shake off the affection, but they wish to shake it off in such a way as to remain in possession of what they have gained, so that God must come to what they desire: and they do not determine to leave the money in order to go to God, even although this would be the best state for them.

The third class wish to shake off the affection, but they wish so to shake it off as to have no desire to retain the money, or not; so that they desire only to wish for it or not according as God our Lord shall give them to wish, and according as it shall seem to them better for the service and praise of His Divine Majesty; and meanwhile they wish to consider that they have actually left all, striving to wish neither for this nor for any other thing, unless it be only the service of God our Lord that move them to this wish, so that the desire of being able the better to serve God our Lord is what moves them to take or leave the money.

To make the same three colloquies as were made in the preceding contemplation of the Two Standards.

It is to be noted, that when we feel any affection or repugnance to actual poverty, when we are not indifferent to poverty or riches, it will help much to the rooting out of such an inordinate affection, to ask in our colloquies, even though it be against the flesh, that our Lord should choose us to actual poverty, protesting that we desire, petition, and ask for it, provided it be to the service and praise of His Divine Goodness. . . .

THE THREE DEGREES OF HUMILITY

The first degree of humility is necessary for eternal salvation; it is, that I so submit and humble myself, so far as I can, in all things to obey the law of God our Lord, in such wise that even though men should make me lord of all created things in this world, or for the sake of my own temporal life, I would not enter into deliberation about breaking a commandment, whether Divine or human, which bound me under mortal sin.

The second degree is more perfect humility than the first; it consists in finding myself in such a state as not to desire nor be more affected to have riches than poverty, to wish for honour than dishonour, to desire a long life than a short life, when the service of God our Lord and of the salvation of my soul are equal; and by this means never to enter into deliberation about committing a venial sin, neither for the sake of all created things, nor even if on that account men should deprive me of life.

The third degree is the most perfect humility; when, the first and second degree being included, and supposing equal praise and glory to the Divine Majesty, the better to imitate Christ our Lord, and to become actually more like to Him, I desire and choose rather poverty with Christ poor, than riches; contempt with Christ contemned, than honours; and I desire to be esteemed as useless and foolish for Christ's sake, Who was first held to be such, than to be accounted wise and prudent in this world.

And thus it will be very profitable for him who desires to obtain this third degree of humility, to make the above-mentioned triple colloquy of the Classes, imploring our Lord to be pleased to elect him to this third degree of greater and more perfect humility, in order the better to imitate and serve Him, if it be for the equal or greater service and praise of His Divine Majesty.

THE ELECTION
PRELUDE FOR MAKING THE ELECTION

In every good Election, as far as regards ourselves, the eye of our intention ought to be single, looking only to the end for which I was created, which is, for the praise of God our Lord, and for the salvation of my soul. And thus whatever I choose ought to be for this, that it should help me to the end for which I was created; not ordering and drawing the end to the means, but the means to the end. As, for example, it happens that many first choose to marry, which is a means, and secondarily to serve our Lord God in the married state, which service of God is the end. In the same way there are others that first desire to possess benefices and then to serve God in them. So these do not go straight to God, but wish God to come straight to their inordinate affections; thus they make of the end a means, and of the means an end; so that what they ought to take first they take last. For first we ought to make our object the desire to serve God, which is the end; and secondarily to receive the benefice, or marry, if it is more profitable to me; and this is the means to the end. Nothing then ought to move me to take these or other means, or to deprive myself of them, except only the service and praise of God our Lord and the eternal salvation of my soul.

CONSIDERATION FOR THE PURPOSE OF OBTAINING KNOWLEDGE OF THE MATTERS ABOUT WHICH AN ELECTION IS TO BE MADE, WHICH CONTAINS FOUR POINTS AND A NOTE.

I. It is necessary that all matters, about which we wish to make an Election, be indifferent or good in themselves, and that they prevail within our holy mother the Hierarchical Church, and that they be not bad, or in opposition to her.

II. There are some things which fall under an immutable

election, such as are the priesthood, matrimony, and the like; and
there are others which fall under a mutable election, as for example, receiving or abandoning benefices, and receiving or relin-
quishing temporal goods.

III. In an immutable election which has been made once for
all, there is no further case for election, because it cannot be undone,
as for example, matrimony, the priesthood, &c. It must only be
noticed, that if one has not made the election duly, ordinately, and
without inordinate affections, let him repent and take care to lead
a good life in his calling; and such an election is not seemingly a
vocation from Heaven, because it is an inordinate and irregular
election. And in this way many err, making for themselves a
vocation from Heaven out of an irregular or an evil election; for all
vocations from Heaven are always pure, untainted, free from admixture of the flesh, or of any other inordinate affection whatsoever.

IV. If anybody has made an election duly and ordinately in
matters which fall under a mutable election, having in no way
clung to the flesh or the world, there is no need of his making his
election anew, but let him perfect himself in that as far as possible.

Note.—It is to be observed that if such a mutable election was
not sincere nor well-ordered when made, then it is profitable to
make it duly, if any one desires to bring forth fruits that shall be
notable and very pleasing to God our Lord.

THREE TIMES, IN EACH OF WHICH A SOUND AND GOOD ELECTION MAY BE MADE

The first time is when God our Lord so moves and attracts the
will, that, without doubt or the power of doubting, such a devoted
soul follows what has been pointed out to it, as St. Paul and St.
Matthew did when they followed Christ our Lord.

The second time is when much light and knowledge is obtained by experiencing consolations and desolations, and by experience of the discernment of various spirits.

The third time is one of tranquillity: when one considers, first,
for what man is born, viz., to praise God our Lord, and to save his
soul; and when, desiring this, he chooses as the means to this end a
kind or state of life within the bounds of the Church, in order that
he may thereby be helped to serve God our Lord, and to save his
soul. I said a time of tranquillity; that is, when the soul is not
agitated by divers spirits, but enjoys the use of its natural powers

freely and quietly. If an election is not made in the first and second times, there are the two following methods of making it in this third time.

THE FIRST METHOD OF MAKING A SOUND AND GOOD ELECTION CONTAINS SIX POINTS

The first point is to propose to myself the matter about which I wish to make an election, as for example an office or benefice to be accepted or left, or any other thing which falls under a mutable election.

Secondly, it is necessary to keep as my aim the end for which I was created, which is to praise God our Lord, and to save my soul; and at the same time to find myself indifferent, without any inordinate affection; so that I be not more inclined or disposed to take than to leave the thing proposed, nor more disposed to leave it than to take it, but I must be, as it were, in equilibrium on a balance, ready to follow that which I shall feel to be more for the glory and praise of God our Lord and for the salvation of my soul.

The third point is to beg God our Lord that He may be pleased to move my will, and place in my soul that which I ought to do in regard to the matter proposed, which may be more to His praise and glory; turning over the matter well and faithfully in my mind, and making a choice in conformity with His most holy will and good pleasure.

The fourth point is to consider the matter, reasoning as to what advantages and profit will accrue to me if I hold the proposed office or benefice solely for the praise of our Lord God and the salvation of my soul; on the other hand, reasoning likewise on the inconveniences and dangers which there are in holding it. And then do the same in the second part, viz., view the advantages and profit in not holding it, and likewise, on the other hand, the inconvenience and dangers in not holding it.

The fifth point is, after I have thus turned over and reasoned on everything with regard to the matter proposed, to see to what side reason most inclines; and thus following the weightier motions of reason, and not any sensual ones, I must come to a decision about the matter proposed.

The sixth point is that, after having made such an election or decision, he who has made it must with great diligence betake himself to prayer, in the presence of God our Lord, and offer Him that election, that His Divine Majesty may be pleased to receive and confirm it, if it be to His greater service and praise.

THE SECOND METHOD OF MAKING A SOUND AND GOOD ELECTION
CONTAINS FOUR RULES AND A NOTE.

The first rule is that the love, which urges and causes me to choose such or such a thing, descend from on high from the love of God; so that he who chooses, feel first in himself that the love which he has more or less for the thing he chooses, is solely for the sake of his Creator and Lord.

The second rule is to place before my eyes a man whom I have never seen or known, and to consider what I, desiring all perfection for him, would tell him to do and choose for the greater glory of God our Lord, and the greater perfection of his soul; and acting so, to keep the rule which I lay down for another.

The third rule is to consider, as if I were at the point of death, what would be the form and measure which I should then desire to have observed in the proceeding of the present election; and regulating my conduct according to this, I must make my decision in all things.

The fourth rule is, viewing and considering what I shall find myself at the Day of Judgment, to think how I shall then wish to have decided in regard to the present matter; and the rule which I should then wish to have observed, I will now observe, that I may then find myself full of joy and pleasure.

Note.—Having observed all the preceding rules to secure my salvation and eternal repose, I will make my election and oblation to God our Lord according to the sixth point of the first method of making an election.

FROM THE "FOURTH WEEK"

CONTEMPLATION FOR OBTAINING LOVE

Two things are to be noticed here:

The first is, that love ought to be found in deeds rather than words.

The second is, that love consists in mutual interchange on either side, that is to say, in the lover giving and communicating with the beloved what he has or can give, and on the other hand, in the beloved sharing with the lover, so that if the one have knowledge, honour, riches, he share it with him who has them not, and thus the one share all with the other.

The usual preparatory prayer.

The first prelude is a composition of place, and it is here to see myself standing before God our Lord and His angels and saints who are interceding for me.

The second prelude is to ask for what I want. It will be here to ask for an interior knowledge of the many and great benefits I have received, that, thoroughly grateful, I may in all things love and serve His Divine Majesty.

The first point is to call to mind the benefits received, of my creation, redemption, and particular gifts, dwelling with great affection on how much God our Lord has done for me, and how much He has given me of that which He has; and consequently, how much He desires to give me Himself in so far as He can according to His Divine ordinance; and then to reflect in myself what I, on my side, with great reason and justice, ought to offer and give to His Divine Majesty, that is to say, all things that are mine, and myself with them, saying, as one who makes an offering, with great affection:

"Take, O Lord, and receive all my liberty, my memory, my understanding, and all my will, whatsoever I have and possess. Thou hast given all these things to me; to Thee, O Lord, I restore them: all are Thine, dispose of them all according to Thy will. Give me Thy love and Thy grace, for this is enough for me."

The second point is to consider how God dwells in creatures, in the elements giving them being, in the plants giving them growth, in animals giving them feeling, and in men giving them understanding, and so in me giving me being, life, feeling, and causing me to understand; making likewise of me a temple, since I am created to the likeness and image of His Divine Majesty; and then reflecting on myself in the same way as has been said in the first point, or in any other way that I shall feel to be better. And let the same be done with regard to each of the following points.

The third point is to consider how God works and labours for me in all created things on the face of the earth, that is, *habet se ad modum laborantis* [behaves like one that labours], as in the heavens, elements, plants, fruit, cattle, &c., giving them being, preserving them, giving them growth and feeling, &c., and then to reflect on myself.

The fourth point is to see how all good things and all gifts descend from above, as my limited power from the Supreme and Infinite Might on high, and in the same way, justice, goodness, pity, mercy, &c., just as the rays descend from the sun, and waters from the spring. Then to conclude by reflecting on myself, as has been said before.

To finish with a colloquy and *Pater noster*.

RULES FOR THE DISCERNMENT OF SPIRITS

RULES FOR IN SOME DEGREE PERCEIVING AND KNOWING
THE VARIOUS MOTIONS EXCITED IN THE SOUL; THE GOOD,
THAT THEY MAY BE ADMITTED; THE BAD, THAT THEY
MAY BE REJECTED: AND THESE RULES ARE MORE
SUITABLE FOR THE FIRST WEEK.

I. In the case of those who go from mortal sin to mortal sin, the enemy is generally wont to place before their eyes apparent pleasures, causing them to imagine sensual gratifications and pleasures, in order to keep them fast and to plunge them deeper in their vices and sins. The good spirit in such persons acts in the contrary manner, causing them to feel the stings and the remorse of conscience by the reproaches of reason.

II. In those who go on earnestly rooting out their sins, and advancing daily from good to better in the service of God our Lord, the contrary to what is set down in the first rule takes place; for now it belongs to the evil spirit to cause anxiety and sadness, and to place obstacles in the way, disquieting the soul by false reasons, so that it make no further progress; and it belongs to the good spirit to inspire it with courage and strength, to give it consolation, tears, inspirations, and peace, making things easy, and removing every impediment, that it may make progress in good works.

III. *On Spiritual Consolation.*—I call it consolation when there is excited in the soul some interior motion by which it begins to be inflamed with the love of its Creator and Lord, and when, consequently, it can love no created thing on the face of the earth in itself, but only in the Creator of them all. Likewise, when it sheds tears, moving it to the love of its Lord, whether it be from grief for its sins, or from the Passion of Christ our Lord, or from other things directly ordained to His service and praise. Finally, I call consolation every increase of hope, faith, and charity, and all interior joy, which calls and attracts man to heavenly things, and to the salvation of his own soul, rendering it quiet and tranquil in its Creator and Lord.

IV. *On Spiritual Desolation.*—I call desolation all that is contrary to what is set down in the third rule, as darkness and disquiet of soul, an attraction towards low and earthly objects, the disquiet of various agitations and temptations, which move it to diffidence, without hope and without love, when the soul finds itself slothful, tepid, sad, and, as it were, separated from its Creator and Lord. For as consolation is contrary to desolation, so the thoughts that spring from consolation are contrary to those that spring from desolation.

V. In time of desolation we must never make a change, but remain firm and constant in the resolutions and determination made on the day preceding this desolation, or in the preceding consolation. For as in consolation it is the good spirit that guides and directs us, so on desolation it is the bad spirit, by whose counsels we cannot find the way to any right decision.

VI. Although in desolation we ought not to change our former resolutions, it is very profitable vehemently to make change in ourselves in ways that oppose the desolation; as, for example, by insisting more on prayer and meditation, by frequent examination, and by increasing in some suitable manner our penances.

VII. Let him who is in desolation consider how our Lord, to try him, has left him to his natural powers, that he may resist the various agitations and temptations of the enemy; and to do so is always in his power, by the assistance of God, which always remains to him, though he may not clearly perceive it, as our Lord has withdrawn from him His great favour, great love and intense grace, leaving him, however, grace sufficient for his eternal salvation.

VIII. Let him who is in desolation strive to remain in patience, a virtue contrary to the troubles which harass him; and let him think that he will shortly be consoled, using all endeavours against the desolation in the way explained in the sixth rule.

IX. There are three principal reasons why we find ourselves in desolation. The first is because we are tepid, slothful, or negligent in our spiritual exercises, and thus on account of our faults spiritual consolation is removed from us. The second reason is that God may try how much we are worth, and how much we progress in His service and praise when deprived of such a bountiful pay, as it were, of consolations and special graces. The third reason is that He may give us a true knowledge whereby we may intimately feel that it is not in our power to acquire or retain great devotion, ardent love, tears, or any other spiritual consolation, but that all is a gift and favour of God our Lord, and to teach us not to build our nest in another's house, by allowing our intellect to be lifted up to any kind of pride or vainglory, by attributing to ourselves feelings of devotion or other kinds of spiritual consolation.

X. Let him who is in consolation think how he will be in future desolation, gaining fresh strength for it.

XI. Let him who is in consolation strive to humble and lower himself as far as he can, thinking how little he is worth in time of desolation without such a grace or consolation; on the other hand, he who is in desolation must remember that he can do much with sufficient grace to resist all his enemies, when he takes strength in his Creator and Lord.

XII. The enemy acts like a woman, inasmuch as he is weak in spite of himself, but strong in will; for as it is in the nature of a woman, quarrelling with a man, to lose courage and to take to flight when he shows himself undaunted; and on the contrary, if the man begin to take to flight and to lose courage, the rage, the spite, and the ferocity of the woman become very great, and altogether without bounds: so in the same manner it is in the nature of our enemy to become powerless and to lose courage (while his temptations take to flight), when the person who is exercising himself in spiritual matters shows a dauntless front to the temptations of the enemy, acting in a manner diametrically opposed to them; and on the contrary, if the exercitant begins to fear and to lose courage in sustaining temptation, there is no beast so fierce on the face of the earth as the enemy of our human nature in prosecuting with intense malice his wicked designs.

XIII. He also acts like a false lover, inasmuch as he wishes to remain hidden and undiscovered; for as this false man, speaking with an evil purpose, and paying court to the daughter of some honest father, or the wife of some honest man, wishes his conversations and insinuations to be kept secret, and, on the contrary, is much displeased when the daughter discovers to her father, or the wife to her husband, his deceitful words and his depraved intention, because he easily infers that he cannot succeed in the designs he has conceived; in the same way, when the enemy of our human nature obtrudes on a just soul his wiles and deceits, he wishes and desires that they be furtively received and kept secret, but he is very displeased when they are discovered to a good confessor or some other spiritual person who knows his frauds and malice, because he infers that he cannot succeed in the wicked design he had conceived, as his evident frauds are laid open.

XIV. He acts likewise as a military chief does in order to get possession of and to despoil the object of his desires. For as a leader and general, pitching his camp, and inspecting the strength and condition of some citadel, storms it on the weakest side; in the same way the enemy of our human nature prowls round and explores on all sides all our virtues, theological, cardinal, and moral, and where he finds us weakest, and in greatest need as regards our eternal salvation, there he makes his attack, and strives to take us by storm.

RULES TO THE SAME EFFECT, CONTAINING A FULLER DISCERNMENT
OF SPIRITS, AND MORE SUITABLE TO THE SECOND WEEK

I. It belongs to God and His angels to give in their motions true joy and spiritual gladness, removing all sadness and disturbance of mind occasioned by the enemy; while it belongs to him to fight against such joy and spiritual consolation, bringing forward pretended reasons, sophistries, and perpetual fallacies.

II. It belongs to God our Lord alone to grant consolation to the soul without any preceding cause for it, because it belongs to the Creator alone to go in and out of the soul, to excite motions in it, attracting it entirely to the love of His Divine Majesty. I say, without cause, that is, without any previous perception or knowledge of any object from which such consolation might come to the soul, by means of its own acts of the understanding and will.

III. When a cause has preceded, it is possible for the good as well as the bad angel to afford consolation to the soul, but with opposite intentions: the good angel for the advantage of the soul, that it may progress and advance from good to better; the bad angel for the contrary, that he may bring it henceforward to yield to his wicked and malicious designs.

IV. It belongs to the bad angel, transfiguring himself into an angel of light, to enter with the devout soul, and to come out his own way; that is to say, to begin by inspiring good and holy thoughts in conformity with the dispositions of the just soul, and afterwards gradually to endeavour to gain his end, by drawing the soul into his secret snares and perverse intentions.

V. We ought to be very careful to watch the course of such thoughts; and if the beginning, middle, and end are all good, leading to all that is good, this is a mark of the good angel; but if the thoughts suggested end in something bad or distracting, or less good than that which the soul had determined to follow, or if they weaken, disturb, or disquiet the soul, taking away the peace, the tranquillity, and the quiet she enjoyed before, it is clear sign that they proceed from the bad spirit, the enemy of our advancement and of our eternal salvation.

VI. When the enemy of our human nature has been discovered and recognized by his serpent's tail, and by the bad end to which he leads, it is profitable for him who has been thus tempted by him to examine afterwards the course of the good thoughts suggested to him, and their beginning, and to remark how little by little the enemy contrived to make him fall from the state of sweetness and spiritual delight he was in, until he brought him to his own depraved purpose; that by the experience and knowledge thus acquired and noted he may be on his guard for the future against his accustomed deceits.

VII. In the case of those who are making progress from good to better, the good angel touches the soul gently, lightly, and sweetly, as a drop of water entering into a sponge; and the evil spirit touches it sharply, and with noise and disturbance, like a drop of water falling on a rock. In the case of those who go from bad to worse, spirits touch it in the contrary manner: and the reason of this difference is the disposition of the soul, according as it is contrary or similar to these angels; for when it is contrary to them they enter with perceptible commotion and disturbance; but when it is similar to them, they enter in silence, as into their own house, through the open doors.

VIII. When there is consolation without any preceding cause, though there be no deceit in it, inasmuch as it proceeds only from God our Lord, as before explained, nevertheless the spiritual person to whom God gives this consolation ought with great watchfulness and care to examine and to distinguish the exact period of the actual consolation from the period which follows it, in which the soul continues fervent and feels the remains of the Divine favour and consolation lately received; for in this second period it often happens that by its own thoughts, from its own habits, and in consequence of its conceptions and judgments, whether by the suggestion of the good or evil spirit, it makes various resolves and plans, which are not inspired immediately by God our Lord; and hence it is necessary that they be thoroughly well examined before they receive entire credit and are carried out into effect.

FRAY LUIS DE GRANADA

Book of Prayer and Meditation

A Dominican steeped both in Thomist thought and in the Christian humanism of the Renaissance, Fray Luis de Granada (1504–1588) spent his life as a preacher and spiritual writer in Spain and Portugal. He was one of the first writers to offer a method of prayer accessible to the laity. He was strongly influenced by the fourteenth-century Rhineland mystics, and in turn his own writings exerted a great influence on St. Teresa of Avila.

What is it, Lord, that prevents our hearts from running to thee? What bonds could be so strong that they hold us captive and prevent us from reaching thee? If it is a love for the things of this world, how can such fragile and passing things hold back the impetus of our love for thee? Will a little blade of grass be sufficient to resist a stone that comes hurtling down a mountain side?

ST. TERESA OF AVILA

St. Teresa of Avila (1515–1582) was the foundress of the Discalced Carmelite reform in Spain. Beginning in 1562, she founded a great number of convents dedicated to contemplation throughout Spain. She was also instrumental, together with John of the Cross, in instigating the same Carmelite reform among the male branch of the Order. Her writings, notable for their simplicity and their passionate interest in a detailed description of human experience at prayer, have become classics of the prayer life.

The Life of Teresa of Jesus

CHAPTER XI

Gives the reason why we do not learn to love God perfectly in a short time. Begins, by means of a comparison, to describe four degrees of prayer, concerning the first of which something is here said. This is most profitable for beginners and for those who are receiving no consolations in prayer.

I shall now speak of those who are beginning to be the servants of love—for this, I think, is what we become when we resolve to follow in this way of prayer Him Who so greatly loved us. So great a dignity is this that thinking of it alone brings me a strange comfort, for servile fear vanishes at once if while we are at this first stage we act as we should. O Lord of my soul and my Good! Why, when a soul has resolved to love Thee and by forsaking everything does all in its power towards that end, so that it may the better employ itself in the love of God, hast Thou been pleased that it should not at once have the joy of ascending to the possession of this perfect love? But I am wrong: I should have made my complaint by asking why we ourselves have no desire so to ascend, for it is we alone who are at fault in not at once enjoying so great a dignity. If we attain to the perfect possession of this true love of God, it brings all blessings with it. But so niggardly and so slow are we in giving ourselves wholly to God that we do not prepare ourselves as we should to receive that precious thing which it is His Majesty's will that we should enjoy only at a great price.

I am quite clear that there is nothing on earth with which so great a blessing can be purchased; but if we did what we could to obtain it, if we cherished no attachment to earthly things, and if all our cares and all our intercourse were centred in Heaven, I believe there is no doubt that this blessing would be given us very speedily, provided we prepared ourselves for it thoroughly and quickly, as did some of the saints. But we think we are giving God everything, whereas what we are really offering Him is the revenue or the fruits of our land while keeping the stock and the right of ownership of it in our own hands. We have made a resolve to be poor, and that is a resolution of great merit; but we often begin to plan and strive again so that we may have no lack, not only of necessaries, but even of superfluities; we try to make friends who will give us these, lest we should lack anything; and we take greater pains, and perhaps even run greater risks, than we did before, when we had possessions of our own. Presumably, again, when we became nuns, or previously, when we began to lead spiritual lives and to follow after perfection, we abandoned all thought of our own importance;[1] and yet hardly is our self-importance wounded[2] than we quite forget that we have surrendered it to God and we try to seize it again, and wrest it, as they say, out of His very hands, although we had apparently made Him Lord of our will. And the same thing happens with everything else.

A nice way of seeking the love of God is this! We expect great handfuls of it, as one might say, and yet we want to reserve our affections for ourselves! We make no effort to carry our desires into effect or to raise them far above the earth. It is hardly suitable that people who act in this way should have many spiritual consolations; the two things seem to me incompatible. So, being unable to make a full surrender of ourselves, we are never given a full supply of this treasure. May His Majesty be pleased to give it to us little by little, even though the receiving of it may cost us all the trials in the world.

The Lord shows exceeding great mercy to him whom He gives grace and courage to resolve to strive after this blessing with all his might. For God denies Himself to no one who perseveres but gradually increases the courage of such a one till he achieves victory. I say "courage" because of the numerous obstacles which the devil at first sets in his path to hinder him from ever setting out upon it, for the devil knows what harm will come to him thereby and that he will lose not only that one soul but many more. If by the help of God the beginner strives to reach the summit of perfection, I do not believe he will ever go to Heaven alone but will always take many others with him: God treats him like a good captain, and gives him soldiers to go in his company. So many are the dangers and difficulties which the devil sets before him that if he is not to turn back he needs not merely a little courage but a very great deal, and much help from God.

To say something, then, of the early experiences of those who are determined to pursue this blessing and to succeed in this enterprise (I shall continue later with what I began to say about mystical theology, as I believe it is called): it is in these early stages that their labour is hardest, for it is they themselves who labour and the Lord Who gives the increase. In the other degrees of prayer the chief thing is fruition, although, whether at the beginning, in the middle or at the end of the road, all have their crosses, different as these may be. For those who follow Christ must take the way which He took, unless they want to be lost. Blessed are their labours, which even here, in this life, have such abundant recompense. I shall have to employ some kind of comparison, though, being a woman and writing simply what I am commanded, I should like to avoid doing so; but this spiritual language is so hard to use for such as, like myself, have no learning, that I shall have to seek some such means of conveying my ideas. It may be that my comparison will seldom do this successfully and Your Reverence will be amused to see how stupid I am. But it comes to my mind now that I have read or heard of this comparison: as I have a bad memory, I do not know where it occurred or what it illustrated, but it satisfies me at the moment as an illustration of my own.

The beginner must think of himself as of one setting out to make a garden in which the Lord is to take His delight, yet in soil most unfruitful and full of weeds. His Majesty uproots the weeds and will set good plants in their stead. Let us suppose that this is already done—that a soul has resolved to practise prayer and has already begun to do so. We have now, by God's help, like good gardeners, to make these plants grow, and to water them carefully, so that they may not perish, but may produce flowers which shall send forth great fragrance to give refreshment to this Lord of ours, so that He may often come into the garden to take His pleasure and have His delight among these virtues.

Let us now consider how this garden can be watered, so that we may know what we have to do, what labour it will cost us, if the gain will outweigh the labour and for how long this labour must be borne. It seems to me that the garden can be watered in four ways: by taking the water from a well, which costs us great labour; or by a water-wheel and buckets, when the water is drawn by a windlass (I have sometimes drawn it in this way: it is less laborious than the other and gives more water); or by a stream or a brook, which waters the ground much better, for it saturates it more thoroughly and there is less need to water it often, so that the gardener's labour is much less; or by heavy rain, when the Lord waters it with no labour of ours, a way incomparably better than any of those which have been described.

And now I come to my point, which is the application of these four methods of watering by which the garden is to be kept fertile, for if it has no water it will be ruined. It has seemed possible to me in this way to explain something about the four degrees of prayer to which the Lord, of His goodness, has occasionally brought my soul. May He also of His goodness grant me to speak in such a way as to be of some profit to one of the persons who commanded me to write this book,[3] whom in four months the Lord has brought to a point far beyond that which I have reached in seventeen years. He prepared himself better than I, and thus his garden, without labour on his part, is watered by all these four means, though he is still receiving the last watering only drop by drop; such progress is his garden making that soon, by the Lord's help, it will be submerged. It will be a pleasure to me for him to laugh at my explanation if he thinks it foolish.

Beginners in prayer, we may say, are those who draw up the water out of the well: this, as I have said, is a very laborious proceeding, for it will fatigue them to keep their senses recollected, which is a great labour because they have been accustomed to a life of distraction. Beginners must accustom themselves to pay no heed to what they see or hear, and they must practise doing this during hours of prayer; they must be alone and in their solitude think over their past life—all of us, indeed, whether beginners or proficients, must do this frequently. There are differences, however, in the degree to which it must be done, as I shall show later. At first it causes distress, for beginners are not always sure that they have repented of their sins (though clearly they have, since they have so sincerely resolved to serve God). Then they have to endeavour to meditate upon the life of Christ and this fatigues their minds. Thus far we can make progress by ourselves—of course with the help of God, for without that, as is well known, we cannot think a single good thought. This is what is meant by beginning to draw up water from the well—and God grant there may be water in it! But that, at least, does not depend on us: our task is to draw it up and to do what we can to water the flowers. And God is so good that when, for reasons known to His Majesty, perhaps to our great advantage, He is pleased that the well should be dry, we, like good gardeners, do all that in us lies, and He keeps the flowers alive without water and makes the virtues grow. By water here I mean tears—or, if there be none of these, tenderness and an interior feeling of devotion.

What, then, will he do here who finds that for many days he experiences nothing but aridity, dislike, distaste and so little desire to go and draw water that he would give it up entirely if he did not remember that he is pleasing and serving the Lord of the garden; if he were not anxious that all his service should not be lost, to say nothing of the gain which he hopes for from the great labour of lowering the bucket so often into the well and drawing it up without water? It will often happen that, even for that purpose, he is unable to move his arms—unable, that is, to think a single good thought, for working with the understanding is of course the same as drawing water out of the well. What, then, as I say, will the gardener do here? He will be glad and take heart and consider it the greatest of favours to work in the garden of so great an Emperor; and, as he knows that he is pleasing Him by so working (and his purpose must be to please, not himself, but Him), let him render Him great praise for having placed such confidence in him, when He has seen that, without receiving any recompense, he is taking such great care of that which He had entrusted to him; let him help Him to bear the Cross and consider how He lived with it all His life long; let him not wish to have his kingdom on earth or ever cease from prayer; and so let him resolve, even if this aridity should persist his whole life long, never to let Christ fall beneath the Cross. The time will come when he shall receive his whole reward at once. Let him have no fear that his labour will be lost. He is serving a good Master, Whose eyes are upon him. Let him pay no heed to evil thoughts, remembering how the devil put such thoughts into the mind of Saint Jerome in the desert.[4]

These trials bring their own reward. I endured them for many years; and, when I was able to draw but one drop of water from this blessed well, I used to think that God was granting me a favour. I know how grievous such trials are and I think they need more courage than do many others in the world. But it has become clear to me that, even in this life, God does not fail to recompense them highly; for it is quite certain that a single one of those hours in which the Lord has granted me to taste of Himself has seemed to me later a recompense for all the afflictions which I endured over a long period while keeping up the practice of prayer. I believe myself that often in the early stages, and again later, it is the Lord's will to give us these tortures, and many other temptations which present themselves, in order to test His lovers and discover if they can drink of the chalice and help Him to bear the Cross before He trusts them with His great treasures. I believe it is for our good that His Majesty is pleased to lead us in this way so that we may have a clear understanding of our worthlessness; for the favours which come later are of such great dignity that before He grants us them He wishes us to know by experience how miserable we are, lest what happened to Lucifer happen to us also.

What is there that Thou doest, my Lord, which is not for the greater good of the soul that Thou knowest to be already Thine and that places itself in Thy power, to follow Thee withersoever Thou goest, even to the death of the Cross, and is determined to help Thee bear that Cross and not to leave Thee alone with it? If anyone finds himself thus determined, there is nothing for him to fear. No, spiritual people, there is no reason to be distressed. Once you have reached so high a state as this, in which you desire to be alone and to commune with God, and abandon the pastimes of the world, the chief part of your work is done. Praise His Majesty for this and trust in His goodness, which never yet failed His friends. Close the eyes of your thought and do not wonder: "Why is He giving devotion to that person of so few days' experience, and none to me after so many years?" Let us believe that it is all for our greater good; let His Majesty guide us whithersoever He wills; we are not our own, but His. It is an exceeding great favour that He shows us when it is His pleasure that we should wish to dig in His garden, and we are then near the Lord of the garden, Who is certainly with us. If it be His will that these plants and flowers should grow, some by means of the water drawn from this well and others without it, what matter is that to me? Do Thou, O Lord, what Thou wilt, let me not offend Thee and let not my virtues perish, if, of Thy goodness alone, Thou hast given me any. I desire to suffer, Lord, because Thou didst suffer. Let Thy will be in every way fulfilled in me, and may it never please Thy Majesty that a gift so precious as Thy love be given to people who serve Thee solely to obtain consolations.

It must be carefully noted—and I say this because I know it by experience—that the soul which begins to walk resolutely in this way of mental prayer and can persuade itself to set little store by consolations and tenderness in devotion, and neither to be elated when the Lord gives them nor disconsolate when He withholds them, has already travelled a great part of its journey. However often it may stumble, it need not fear a relapse, for its building has been begun on a firm foundation.[5] Yes, love for God does not consist in shedding tears, in enjoying thse consolations and that tenderness which for the most part we desire and in which we find comfort, but in serving Him with righteousness, fortitude of soul and humility. The other seems to me to be receiving rather than giving anything.

As for poor women like myself, who are weak and lack fortitude, I think it fitting that we should be led by means of favours: this is the way in which God is leading me now, so that I may be able to suffer certain trials which it has pleased His Majesty to give me. But when I hear servants of God, men of weight, learning and intelligence, making such a fuss because God is not giving them devotion, it revolts me to listen to them. I do not mean that, when God gives them such a thing, they ought not to accept it and set a great deal of store by it, because in that case His Majesty must know that it is good for them. But I do mean that if they do not receive it they should not be distressed: they should realize that, as His Majesty does not give it them, it is unnecessary; they should be masters of themselves and go on their way. Let them believe that they are making a mistake about this: I have proved it and seen that it is so. Let them believe that it is an imperfection in them if, instead of going on their way with freedom of spirit, they hang back through weakness and lack of enterprise.

I am not saying this so much for beginners (though I lay some stress upon it, even for these, because it is of great importance that they should start with this freedom and determination): I mean it rather for others. There must be many who have begun some time back and never manage to finish their course, and I believe it is largely because they do not embrace the Cross from the beginning that they are distressed and think that they are making no progress. When the understanding ceases to work, they cannot bear it, though perhaps even then the will is increasing in power, and putting on new strength,[6] without their knowing it. We must realize that the Lord pays no heed to these things: to us they may look like faults, but they are not so. His Majesty knows our wretch-

edness and the weakness of our nature better than we ourselves
and He knows that all the time these souls are longing to think of
Him and to love Him. It is this determination that He desires in us.
The other afflictions which we bring upon ourselves serve only to
disturb our souls, and the result of them is that, if we find ourselves
unable to get profit out of a single hour, we are impeded from doing
so for four. I have a great deal of experience of this and I know that
what I say is true, for I have observed it carefully and have discussed it afterwards with spiritual persons. The thing frequently
arises from physical indisposition, for we are such miserable creatures that this poor imprisoned soul shares in the miseries of the
body, and variations of season and changes in the humours often
prevent it from accomplishing its desires and make it suffer in all
kinds of ways against its will. The more we try to force it at times
like these, the worse it gets and the longer the trouble lasts. But let
discretion be observed so that it may be ascertained if this is the
true reason: the poor soul must not be stifled. Persons in this
condition must realize that they are ill and make some alteration
in their hours of prayer; very often it will be advisable to continue
this change for some days.

They must endure this exile as well as they can, for a soul
which loves God has often the exceeding ill fortune to realize that,
living as it is in this state of misery, it cannot do what it desires
because of its evil guest, the body. I said we must observe discretion, because sometimes the same effects will be produced by the
devil; and so it is well that prayer should not always be given up
when the mind is greatly distracted and disturbed, nor the soul
tormented by being made to do what is not in its power. There are
other things which can be done—exterior acts, such as reading or
works of charity—though sometimes the soul will be unable to do
even these. At such times the soul must render the body a service
for the love of God, so that on many other occasions the body may
render services to the soul. Engage in some spiritual recreation,
such as conversation (so long as it is really spiritual), or a country
walk, according as your confessor advises. In all these things it is
important to have had experience, for from this we learn what is
fitting for us; but let God be served in all things. Sweet is His yoke,
and it is essential that we should not drag the soul along with us, so
to say, but lead it gently, so that it may make the greater progress.

I repeat my advice, then (and it matters not how often I say
this, for it is of great importance), that one must never be depressed
or afflicted because of aridities or unrest or distraction of the mind.

If a person would gain spiritual freedom and not be continually troubled, let him begin by not being afraid of the Cross and he will find that the Lord will help him to bear it; he will then advance happily and find profit in everything. It is now clear that, if no water is coming from the well, we ourselves can put none into it. But of course we must not be careless: water must always be drawn when there is any there, for at such a time God's will is that we should use it so that He may multiply our virtues.

CHAPTER XXIX

. . . describes certain great favours which the Lord showed her and the things which His Majesty said to her to reassure her and give her answers for those who opposed her.

I have strayed far from any intention, for I was trying to give the reasons why this kind of vision cannot be the work of the imagination. How could we picture Christ's Humanity by merely studying the subject or form any impression of His great beauty by means of the imagination? No little time would be necessary if such a reproduction was to be in the least like the original. One can indeed make such a picture with one's imagination, and spend time in regarding it, and considering the form and the brilliance of it; little by little one may even learn to perfect such an image and store it up in the memory. Who can prevent this? Such a picture can undoubtedly be fashioned with the understanding. But with regard to the vision which we are discussing there is no way of doing this: we have to look at it when the Lord is pleased to reveal it to us—to look as He wills and at whatever He wills. And there is no possibility of our subtracting from it or adding to it, or any way in which we can obtain it, whatever we may do, or look at it when we like or refrain from looking at it. If we try to look at any particular part of it, we at once lose Christ.

For two years and a half things went on like this and it was quite usual for God to grant me this favour. It must now be more than three years since He took it from me as a continually recurring favour,[1] by giving me something else of a higher kind, which I shall describe later. Though I saw that He was speaking to me, and though I was looking upon that great beauty of His, and experiencing the sweetness with which He uttered those words—sometimes stern words—with that most lovely and Divine mouth, and though, too, I was extremely desirous of observing the colour of His eyes, or

His height, so that I should be able to describe it, I have never been sufficiently worthy to see this, nor has it been of any use for me to attempt to do so; if I tried, I lost the vision altogether. Though I sometimes see Him looking at me compassionately, His gaze has such power that my soul cannot endure it and remains in so sublime a rapture that it loses this beauteous vision in order to have the greater fruition of it all. So there is no question here of our wanting or not wanting to see the vision. It is clear that the Lord wants of us only humility and shame, our acceptance of what is given us and our praise of its Giver.

This refers to all visions, none excepted. There is nothing that we can do about them; we cannot see more or less of them at will; and we can neither call them up nor banish them by our own efforts. The Lord's will is that we shall see quite clearly that they are produced, not by us but by His Majesty. Still less can we be proud of them: on the contrary, they make us humble and fearful, when we find that, just as the Lord takes from us the power of seeing what we desire, so He can also take from us these favours and His grace, with the result that we are completely lost. So while we live in this exile let us always walk with fear.

Almost invariably the Lord showed Himself to me in His resurrection body, and it was thus, too, that I saw Him in the Host. Only occasionally, to strengthen me when I was in tribulation, did He show me His wounds, and then He would appear sometimes as He was on the Cross and sometimes as in the Garden. On a few occasions I saw Him wearing the crown of thorns and sometimes He would also be carrying the Cross—because of my necessities, as I say, and those of others—but always in His glorified flesh. Many are the affronts and trials that I have suffered through telling this and many are the fears and persecutions that it has brought me. So sure were those whom I told of it that I had a devil that some of them wanted to exorcize me. This troubled me very little, but I was sorry when I found that my confessors were afraid to hear my confessions or when I heard that people were saying things to them against me. None the less, I could never regret having seen these heavenly visions and I would not exchange them for all the good things and delights of this world. I always considered them a great favour from the Lord, and I think they were the greatest of treasures; often the Lord Himself would reassure me about them. I found my love for Him growing exceedingly: I used to go to Him and tell Him about all these trials and I always came away from prayer comforted and with new strength. I did not dare to argue with my critics, because I saw that that made things worse, as they thought me lacking in humility. With my confessor, however, I did discuss these matters; and whenever he saw that I was troubled he would comfort me greatly.

As the visions became more numerous, one of those who had previously been in the habit of helping me and who used sometimes to hear my confessions when the minister was unable to do so, began to say that it was clear I was being deceived by the devil. So, as I was quite unable to resist it, they commanded me to make the sign of the Cross whenever I had a vision, and to snap my fingers at it[2] so as to convince myself that it came from the devil, whereupon it would not come again: I was not to be afraid, they said, and God would protect me and take the vision away. This caused me great distress: as I could not help believing that my visions came from God, it was a terrible thing to have to do; and, as I have said, I could not possibly wish them to be taken from me. However, I did as they commanded me. I besought God often to set me free from deception; indeed, I was continually doing so and with many tears. I would also invoke Saint Peter and Saint Paul, for the Lord had told me (it was on their festival that He had first appeared to me)[3] that they would prevent me from being deluded; and I used often to see them very clearly on my left hand, though not in an imaginary vision. These glorious Saints were in a very real sense my lords.

To be obliged to snap my fingers at a vision in which I saw the Lord caused me the sorest distress. For, when I saw Him before me, I could not have believed that the vision had come from the devil even if the alternative were my being cut to pieces. So this was a kind of penance to me, and a heavy one. In order not to have to be so continually crossing myself, I would carry a cross in my hand. This I did almost invariably; but I was not so particular about snapping my fingers at the vision, for it hurt me too much to do that. It reminded me of the way the Jews had insulted Him, and I would beseech Him to forgive me, since I did it out of obedience to him who was in His own place, and not to blame me, since he was one of the ministers whom He had placed in His Church. He told me not to worry about it and said I was quite right to obey, but He would see that my confessor learned the truth. When they made me stop my prayer He seemed to me to have become angry, and He told me to tell them that this was tyranny. He used to show me ways of knowing that the visions were not of the devil; some of these I shall describe later.

Once, when I was holding in my hand the cross of a rosary, He put out His own hand and took it from me, and, when He gave it back to me, it had become four large stones, much more precious than diamonds—incomparably more so, for it is impossible, of course, to make comparisons with what is supernatural, and diamonds seem imperfect counterfeits beside the precious stones which I saw in that vision. On the cross, with exquisite workmanship, were portrayed the five wounds.[4] He told me that henceforward it would always look to me like that, and so it did: I could never see the wood of which it was made, but only these stones. To nobody, however, did it look like this except to myself. As soon as they had begun to order me to test my visions in this way, and to resist them, the favours became more and more numerous. In my efforts to divert my attention from them, I never ceased from prayer; even when asleep I used to seem to be praying, for this made me grow in love. I would address my complaints to the Lord, telling Him I could not bear it. Desire and strive to cease thinking of Him as I would, it was not in my power to do so. In every respect I was as obedient as I could be, but about this I could do little or nothing, and the Lord never gave me leave to disobey. But, though He told me to do as I was bidden, He reassured me in another way, by teaching me what I was to say to my critics; and this He does still. The arguments with which He provided me were so conclusive that they made me feel perfectly secure.

Shortly after this, His Majesty began to give me clearer signs of His presence, as He had promised me to do. There grew within me so strong a love of God that I did not know who was inspiring me with it, for it was entirely supernatural and I had made no efforts to obtain it. I found myself dying with the desire to see God and I knew no way of seeking that life save through death. This love came to me in vehement impulses, which, though less unbearable, and of less worth, than those of which I have spoken previously, took from me all power of action. For nothing afforded me satisfaction and I was incapable of containing myself: it really seemed as though my soul were being torn from me. O sovereign artifice of the Lord, with what subtle diligence dost Thou work upon Thy miserable slave! Thou didst hide Thyself from me, and out of Thy love didst oppress me with a death so delectable that my soul's desire was never to escape from it.

No one who has not experienced these vehement impulses can possibly understand this: it is no question of physical restlessness within the breast, or of uncontrollable devotional feelings which occur frequently and seem to stifle the spirit. That is prayer of a much lower kind, and we should check such quickenings of emotion by endeavouring gently to turn them into inward recollection and to keep the soul hushed and still. Such prayer is like the violent sobbing of children: they seem as if they are going to choke, but if they are given something to drink their superabundant emotion is checked immediately. So it is here: reason must step in and take the reins, for it may be that this is partly accountable for by the temperament. On reflection comes a fear that there is some imperfection, which may in great part be due to the senses. So this child must be hushed with a loving caress which will move it to a gentle kind of love; it must not, as they say, be driven at the point of the fist. Its love must find an outlet in interior recollection and not be allowed to boil right over like a pot to which fuel has been applied indiscriminately. The fire must be controlled at its source and an endeavour must be made to quench the flame with gentle tears, not with tears caused by affliction, for these proceed from the emotions already referred to and do a great deal of harm. I used at first to shed tears of this kind, which left my brain so distracted and my spirit so wearied that for a day or more I was not fit to return to prayer. Great discretion, then, is necessary at first so that everything may proceed gently and the operations of the spirit may express themselves interiorly; great care should be taken to prevent operations of an exterior kind.

These other impulses are very different. It is not we who put on the fuel; it seems rather as if the fire is already kindled and it is we who are suddenly thrown into it to be burned up. The soul does not try to feel the pain of the wound caused by the Lord's absence. Rather an arrow is driven into the very depths of the entrails, and sometimes into the heart, so that the soul does not know either what is the matter with it or what it desires. It knows quite well that it desires God and that the arrow seems to have been dipped in some drug which leads it to hate itself for the love of this Lord so that it would gladly lose its life for Him. No words will suffice to describe the way in which God wounds the soul and the sore distress which He causes it, so that it hardly knows what it is doing. Yet so delectable is this distress that life holds no delight which can give greater satisfaction. As I have said, the soul would gladly be dying of this ill.

This distress and this bliss between them bewildered me so much that I was never able to understand how such a thing could be. Oh, what it is to see a wounded soul—I mean when it understands its condition sufficiently to be able to describe itself as wounded for so excellent a cause! It sees clearly that this love has come to it through no act of its own, but that, from the exceeding great love which the Lord bears it, a spark seems suddenly to have fallen upon it and to have set it wholly on fire. Oh, how often, when in this state, do I remember that verse of David: *Quemadmodum desiderat cervus ad fontes aquarum,*[5] which I seem to see fulfilled literally in myself!

When these impulses are not very strong they appear to calm down a little, or, at any rate, the soul seeks some relief from them because it knows not what to do. It performs certain penances, but is quite unable to feel them, while the shedding of its blood causes it no more distress than if its body were dead. It seeks ways and means whereby it may express something of what it feels for the love of God; but its initial pain is so great that I know of no physical torture which can drown it. There is no relief to be found in these medicines: they are quite inadequate for so sublime an ill.[6] A certain alleviation of the pain is possible, which may cause some of it to pass away, if the soul begs God to grant it relief from its ill, though it sees none save death, by means of which it believes it can have complete fruition of its Good. At other times the impulses are so strong that the soul is unable to do either this or anything else. The entire body contracts and neither arm nor foot can be moved. If the subject is on his feet, he remains as though transported and cannot even breathe: all he does is to moan—not aloud, for that is impossible, but inwardly, out of pain.

It pleased the Lord that I should sometimes see the following vision. I would see beside me, on my left hand, an angel in bodily form—a type of vision which I am not in the habit of seeing, except very rarely. Though I often see representations of angels, my visions of them are of the type which I first mentioned. It pleased the Lord that I should see this angel in the following way. He was not tall, but short, and very beautiful, his face so aflame that he appeared to be one of the highest types of angel who seem to be all afire. They must be those who are called cherubim:[7] they do not tell me their names but I am well aware that there is a great difference between certain angels and others, and between these and others still, of a kind that I could not possibly explain. In his hands I saw a long golden spear and at the end of the iron tip I seemed to see a point of fire. With this he seemed to pierce my heart several times so that it penetrated to my entrails. When he drew it out, I thought he was drawing them out with it and he left me completely afire with a great love for God. The pain was so sharp

that it made me utter several moans; and so excessive was the
sweetness caused me by this intense pain that one can never wish
to lose it, nor will one's soul be content with anything less than
God. It is not bodily pain, but spiritual, though the body has a share
in it—indeed, a great share. So sweet are the colloquies of love
which pass between the soul and God that if anyone thinks I am
lying I beseech God, in His goodness, to give him the same experience.[8]

During the days that this continued, I went about as if in a
stupor. I had no wish to see or speak with anyone, but only to hug
my pain, which caused me greater bliss than any that can come
from the whole of creation. I was like this on several occasions,
when the Lord was pleased to send me these raptures, and so deep
were they that, even when I was with other people, I could not
resist them; so, greatly to my distress, they began to be talked
about. Since I have had them, I do not feel this pain so much, but
only the pain of which I spoke somewhere before—I do not remember in what chapter. The latter is, in many respects, very
different from this, and of greater worth. But, when this pain of
which I am now speaking begins, the Lord seems to transport the
soul and to send it into an ecstasy, so that it cannot possibly suffer
or have any pain because it immediately begins to experience
fruition. May He be blessed for ever, Who bestows so many favours
on one who so ill requites such great benefits.

Interior Castle (First Mansion)

CHAPTER I

Treats of the beauty and dignity of our souls; makes a comparison by
the help of which this may be understood; describes the benefit
which comes from understanding it and being aware of the favours
which we receive from God; and shows how the door of this castle is
prayer.

While I was beseeching Our Lord to-day that He would speak
through me, since I could find nothing to say and had no idea how to
begin to carry out the obligation laid upon me by obedience, a
thought occurred to me which I will now set down, in order to have
some foundation on which to build. I began to think of the soul as if

it were a castle made of a single diamond or of very clear crystal, in which there are many rooms,[1] just as in Heaven there are many mansions.[2] Now if we think carefully over this, sisters, the soul of the righteous man is nothing but a paradise, in which, as God tells us, He takes His delight.[3] For what do you think a room will be like which is the delight of a King so mighty, so wise, so pure and so full of all that is good? I can find nothing with which to compare the great beauty of a soul and its great capacity. In fact, however acute our intellects may be, they will no more be able to attain to a comprehension of this than to an understanding of God; for, as He Himself says, He created us in His image and likeness.[4] Now if this is so—and it is—there is no point in our fatiguing ourselves by attempting to comprehend the beauty of this castle; for, though it is His creature, and there is therefore as much difference between it and God as between creature and Creator, the very fact that His Majesty says it is made in His image means that we can hardly form any conception of the soul's great dignity and beauty.[5]

It is no small pity, and should cause us no little shame, that, through our own fault, we do not understand ourselves, or know who we are. Would it not be a sign of great ignorance, my daughters, if a person were asked who he was, and could not say, and had no idea who his father or his mother was, or from what country he came? Though that is great stupidity, our own is incomparably greater if we make no attempt to discover what we are, and only know that we are living in these bodies, and have a vague idea, because we have heard it and because our Faith tells us so, that we possess souls. As to what good qualities there may be in our souls, or Who dwells within them, or how precious they are—those are things which we seldom consider and so we trouble little about carefully preserving the soul's beauty. All our interest is centred in the rough setting of the diamond, and in the outer wall of the castle—that is to say, in these bodies of ours.

Let us now imagine that this castle, as I have said, contains many mansions,[6] some above, others below, others at each side; and in the centre and midst of them all is the chiefest mansion where the most secret things pass between God and the soul. You must think over this comparison very carefully; perhaps God will be pleased to use it to show you something of the favours which He is pleased to grant to souls, and of the differences between them, so far as I have understood this to be possible, for there are so many of them that nobody can possibly understand them all, much less anyone as stupid as I. If the Lord grants you these favours, it will be a great consolation to you to know that such things are possible; and, if you never receive any, you can still praise His great goodness. For, as it does us no harm to think of the things laid up for us in Heaven, and of the joys of the blessed, but rather makes us rejoice and strive to attain those joys ourselves, just so it will do us no harm to find that it is possible in this our exile for so great a God to commune with such malodorous worms, and to love Him for His great goodness and boundless mercy. I am sure that anyone who finds it harmful to realize that it is possible for God to grant such favours during this our exile must be greatly lacking in humility and in love of his neighbour; for otherwise how could we help rejoicing that God should grant these favours to one of our brethren when this in no way hinders Him from granting them to ourselves, and that His Majesty should bestow an understanding of His greatness upon anyone soever? Sometimes He will do this only to manifest His power, as He said of the blind man to whom He gave his sight, when the Apostles asked Him if he were suffering for his own sins or for the sins of his parents.[7] He grants these favours, then, not because those who receive them are holier than those who do not, but in order that His greatness may be made known, as we see in the case of Saint Paul and the Magdalen, and in order that we may praise Him in His creatures.

It may be said that these things seem impossible and that it is better not to scandalize the weak. But less harm is done by their disbelieving us than by our failing to edify those to whom God grants these favours, and who will rejoice and will awaken others to a fresh love of Him Who grants such mercies, according to the greatness of His power and majesty. In any case I know that none to whom I am speaking will run into this danger, because they all know and believe that God grants still greater proofs of His love. I am sure that, if any one of you does not believe this, she will never learn it by experience. For God's will is that no bounds should be set to His works. Never do such a thing, then, sisters, if the Lord does not lead you by this road.

Now let us return to our beautiful and delightful castle and see how we can enter it. I seem rather to be talking nonsense; for, if this castle is the soul, there can clearly be no question of our entering it. For we ourselves are the castle: and it would be absurd to tell someone to enter a room when he was in it already! But you must understand that there are many ways of "being" in a place. Many souls remain in the outer court of the castle, which is the place occupied by the guards; they are not interested in entering it,

and have no idea what there is in that wonderful place, or who
dwells in it, or even how many rooms it has. You will have read
certain books on prayer which advise the soul to enter within itself:
and that is exactly what this means.

A short time ago I was told by a very learned man that souls
without prayer are like people whose bodies or limbs are paralysed:
they possess feet and hands but they cannot control them. In the
same way, there are souls so infirm and so accustomed to busying
themselves with outside affairs that nothing can be done for them,
and it seems as though they are incapable of entering within
themselves at all. So accustomed have they grown to living all the
time with the reptiles and other creatures to be found in the outer
court of the castle that they have almost become like them; and
although by nature they are so richly endowed as to have the power
of holding converse with none other than God Himself, there is
nothing that can be done for them. Unless they strive to realize
their miserable condition and to remedy it, they will be turned into
pillars of salt for not looking within themselves, just as Lot's wife
was because she looked back.[8]

As far as I can understand, the door of entry into this castle is
prayer and meditation: I do not say mental prayer rather than
vocal, for, if it is prayer at all, it must be accompanied by meditation. If a person does not think Whom he is addressing, and what he
is asking for, and who it is that is asking and of Whom he is asking
it, I do not consider that he is praying at all even though he be
constantly moving his lips. True, it is sometimes possible to pray
without paying heed to these things, but that is only because they
have been thought about previously; if a man is in the habit of
speaking to God's Majesty as he would speak to his slave, and never
wonders if he is expressing himself properly, but merely utters the
words that come to his lips because he has learned them by heart
through constant repetition, I do not call that prayer at all—and
God grant no Chritian may ever speak to Him so! At any rate,
sisters, I hope in God that none of you will, for we are accustomeed
here to talk about interior matters, and that is a good way of
keeping oneself from falling into such animal-like habits.[9]

Let us say no more, then, of these paralysed souls, who, unless
the Lord Himself comes and commands them to rise, are like the
man who had lain beside the pool for thirty years:[10] they are
unfortunate creatures and live in great peril. Let us rather think of
certain other souls, who do eventually enter the castle. These are
very much absorbed in wordly affairs; but their desires are good;

sometimes, though infrequently, they commend themselves to Our Lord; and they think about the state of their souls, though not very carefully. Full of a thousand preoccupations as they are, they pray only a few times a month, and as a rule they are thinking all the time of their preoccupations, for they are very much attached to them, and, where their treasure is, there is their heart also.[11] From time to time, however, they shake their minds free of them and it is a great thing that they should know themselves well enough to realize that they are not going the right way to reach the castle door. Eventually they enter the first rooms on the lowest floor, but so many reptiles get in with them that they are unable to appreciate the beauty of the castle or to find any peace within it. Still, they have done a good deal by entering at all.

You will think this is beside the point, daughters, since by the goodness of the Lord you are not one of these. But you must be patient, for there is no other way in which I can explain to you some ideas I have had about certain interior matters concerning prayer. May it please the Lord to enable me to say something about them; for to explain to you what I should like is very difficult unless you have had personal experience; and anyone with such experience, as you will see, cannot help touching upon subjects which, please God, shall, by His mercy, never concern us.

Fifth Mansion

CHAPTER II

. . . Explains the Prayer of Union by a delicate comparison.
Describes the effects which it produces in the soul.
Should be studied with great care.

You will suppose that all there is to be seen in this Mansion has been described already, but there is much more to come yet, for, as I said, some receive more and some less. With regard to the nature of union, I do not think I can say anything further; but when the soul to which God grants these favours prepares itself for them, there are many things to be said concerning what the Lord works in it. Some of these I shall say now, and I shall describe that soul's state. In order the better to explain this, I will make use of a comparison which is suitable for the purpose; and which will also show us how, although this work is performed by the Lord, and we can do nothing to make His Majesty grant us this favour, we can do a great deal to prepare ourselves for it.

You will have heard of the wonderful way in which silk is made—a way which no one could invent but God—and how it comes from a kind of seed which looks like tiny peppercorns[1] (I have never seen this, but only heard of it, so if it is incorrect in any way the fault is not mine). When the warm weather comes, and the mulberry-trees begin to show leaf, this seed starts to take life; until it has this sustenance, on which it feeds, it is as dead. The silkworms feed on the mulberry-leaves until they are full-grown, when people put down twigs, upon which, with their tiny mouths, they start spinning silk, making themselves very tight little cocoons, in which they bury themselves. Then, finally, the worm, which was large and ugly, comes right out of the cocoon a beautiful white butterfly.

Now if no one had ever seen this, and we were only told about it as a story of past ages, who would believe it? And what arguments could we find to support the belief that a thing as devoid of reason as a worm or a bee could be diligent enough to work so industriously for our advantage, and that in such an enterprise the poor little worm would lose its life? This alone, sisters, even if I tell you no more, is sufficient for a brief meditation, for it will enable you to reflect upon the wonders and the wisdom of our God. What, then, would it be if we knew the properties of everything? It will be a great help to us if we occupy ourselves in thinking of these wonderful things and rejoice in being the brides of so wise and powerful a King.

But to return to what I was saying. The silkworm is like the soul which takes life when, through the heat which comes from the Holy Spirit, it begins to utilize the general help which God gives to us all, and to make use of the remedies which He left in His Church—such as frequent confessions, good books and sermons, for these are the remedies for a soul dead in negligences and sins and frequently plunged into temptation. The soul begins to live and nourishes itself on this food, and on good meditations, until it is full grown—and this is what concerns me now: the rest is of little importance.

When it is full-grown, then, as I wrote at the beginning, it starts to spin its silk and to build the house in which it is to die. This house may be understood here to mean Christ. I think I read or heard somewhere that our life is hid in Christ, or in God (for that is the same thing), or that our life is Christ.[2] (The exact form of this[3] is little to my purpose.)

Here, then, daughters, you see what we can do, with God's favour. May His Majesty Himself be our Mansion as He is in this Prayer of Union which, as it were, we ourselves spin. When I say He will be our Mansion, and we can construct it for ourselves and hide ourselves in it, I seem to be suggesting that we can subtract from God, or add to Him. But of course we cannot possibly do that! We can neither subtract from, nor add to, God, but we can subtract from, and add to, ourselves, just as these little silkworms do. And, before we have finished doing all that we can in that respect, God will take this tiny achievement of ours, which is nothing at all, unite it with His greatness and give it such worth that its reward will be the Lord Himself. And as it is He Whom it has cost the most, so His Majesty will unite our small trials with the great trials which He suffered, and make both of them into one.

On, then, my daughters! Let us hasten to perform this task and spin this cocoon. Let us renounce our self-love and self-will, and our attachment to earthly things. Let us practise penance, prayer, mortification, obedience, and all the other good works that you know of. Let us do what we have been taught; and we have been instructed about what our duty is. Let the silkworm die—let it die, as in fact it does when it has completed the work which it was created to do. Then we shall see God and shall ourselves be as completely hidden in His greatness as is this little worm in its cocoon. Note that, when I speak of seeing God, I am referring to the way in which, as I have said, He allows Himself to be apprehended in this kind of union.

And now let us see what becomes of this silkworm, for all that I have been saying about it is leading up to this. When it is in this state of prayer, and quite dead to the world, it comes out a little white butterfly. Oh, greatness of God, that a soul should come out like this after being hidden in the greatness of God, and closely united with Him, for so short a time—never, I think, for as long as half an hour! I tell you truly, the very soul does not know itself. For think of the difference between an ugly worm and a white butterfly; it is just the same here. The soul cannot think how it can have merited such a blessing—whence such a blessing could have come to it, I meant to say, for it knows quite well that it has not merited it at all.[4] It finds itself so anxious to praise the Lord that it would gladly be consumed and die a thousand deaths for His sake. Then it finds itself longing to suffer great trials and unable to do otherwise. It has the most vehement desires for penance, for solitude, and for all to know God. And hence, when it sees God being offended, it becomes greatly distressed. In the following Mansion we shall treat of these things further and in detail, for, although the experiences of this Mansion and of the next are almost identical, their effects come to have much greater power; for, as I have said, if after God comes to a soul here on earth it strives to progress still more, it will experience great things.

To see, then, the restlessness of this little butterfly—though it has never been quieter or more at rest in its life! Here is something to praise God for—namely, that it knows not where to settle and make its abode. By comparison with the abode it has had, everything it sees on earth leaves it dissatisfied, especially when God has again and again given it this wine which almost every time has brought it some new blessing. It sets no store by the things it did when it was a worm—that is, by its gradual weaving of the cocoon. It has wings now: how can it be content to crawl along slowly when it is able to fly? All that it can do for God seems to it slight by comparison with its desires. It even attaches little importance to what the saints endured, knowing by experience how the Lord helps and transforms a soul, so that it seems no longer to be itself, or even its own likeness. For the weakness which it used to think it had when it came to doing penance is now turned into strength. It is no longer bound by ties of relationship, friendship or property. Previously all its acts of will and resolutions and desires were powerless to loosen these and seemed only to bind them the more firmly; now it is grieved at having even to fulfil its obligations in these respects lest these should cause it to sin against God. Everything wearies it, because it has proved that it can find no true rest in the creatures.

I seem to be enlarging on this subject and there is much more that I could say: anyone to whom God has granted this favour will realize that I have said very little. It is not surprising, then, that, as this little butterfly feels a stranger to things of the earth, it should be seeking a new restingplace. But where will the poor little creature go? It cannot return to the place it came from, for, as has been said, however hard we try, it is not in our power to do that until God is pleased once again to grant us this favour. Ah, Lord! What trials begin afresh for this soul! Who would think such a thing possible after it had received so signal a favour? But, after all,[5] we must bear crosses in one way or another for as long as we live. And if anyone told me that after reaching this state he had enjoyed continual rest and joy, I should say that he had not reached it at all, but that if he had got as far as the previous Mansion, he might possibly have experienced some kind of consolation the effect of which was enhanced by physical weakness, and perhaps even by the devil, who gives peace to the soul in order later to wage a far severer war upon it.

I do not mean that those who attain to this state have no peace: they do have it, and to a very high degree, for even their trials are of such sublimity and come from so noble a source that, severe though they are, they bring peace and contentment. The very discontent caused by the things of the world arouses a desire to leave it, so grievous that any alleviation it finds can only be in the thought that its life in this exile is God's will. And even this is insufficient to comfort it, for, despite all it has gained, the soul is not wholly resigned to the will of God, as we shall see later. It does not fail to act in conformity with God's will, but it does so with many tears and with great sorrow at being unable to do more because it has been given no more capacity. Whenever it engages in prayer, this is a grief to it. To some extent, perhaps, it is a result of the great grief caused by seeing how often God is offended, and how little esteemed, in this world, and by considering how many souls are lost, both of heretics and of Moors; although its greatest grief is over the loss of Christian souls, many of whom, it fears, are condemned, though so great is God's mercy that, however evil their lives have been, they can amend them and be saved.

Oh, the greatness of God! Only a few years since—perhaps only a few days—this soul was thinking of nothing but itself. Who has plunged it into such grievous anxieties? Even if we tried to meditate for years on end, we could not feel this as keenly as the soul does now. God help me! If I were able to spend many days and years in trying to realize how great a sin it is to offend God, and in reflecting that those who are damned are His children, and my brothers and sisters, and in meditating upon the dangers in which we live, and in thinking how good it would be for us to depart from this miserable life, would all that suffice? No, daughters; the grief I am referring to is not like that caused by these kinds of meditation. That grief we could easily achieve, with the Lord's help, by thinking a great deal about those things; but it does not reach to the depths of our being, as does this grief, which, without any effort on the soul's part, and sometimes against its will, seems to tear it to pieces and grind it to powder. What, then, is this grief? Whence does it come? I will tell you.

Have you not heard concerning the Bride (I said this a little while back,[6] though not with reference to the same matter) that God put her in the cellar of wine and ordained charity in her? Well, that is the position here. That soul has now delivered itself into His hands and His great love has so completely subdued it that it neither knows nor desires anything save that God shall do with it what He wills. Never, I think, will God grant this favour save to the soul which He takes for His very own. His will is that, without understanding how, the soul shall go thence sealed with His seal. In reality, the soul in that state does no more than the wax when a seal is impressed upon it—the wax does not impress itself; it is only prepared for the impress: that is, it is soft—and it does not even soften itself so as to be prepared; it merely remains quiet and consenting. Oh, goodness of God, that all this should be done at Thy cost! Thou dost require only our wills and dost ask that Thy wax may offer no impediment.

Here, then, sisters, you see what our God does to the soul in this state so that it may know itself to be His. He gives it something of His own, which is what His Son had in this life: He can grant us no favour greater than that. Who could have wanted to depart from this life more than His Son did? As, indeed, His Majesty said at the Last Supper: "With desire have I desired."[7] "Did not the painful death that Thou wert to die present itself to Thee, O Lord, as something grievous and terrible?" "No, because My great love and My desire that souls shall be saved transcend these pains beyond all comparison and the very terrible things that I have suffered since I lived in the world, and still suffer, are such that by comparison with them these are nothing."

I have often thought about this: I know that the torment which a certain person of my acquaintance[8] has suffered, and suffers still, at seeing the Lord offended, is so intolerable that she would far sooner die than suffer it. And, I reflected, if a soul which has so very little charity by comparison with Christ's that it might be said to be almost nothing beside His felt this torment to be so intolerable, what must the feelings of Our Lord Jesus Christ have been, and what a life must He have lived, if He saw everything and was continually witnessing the great offences which were being committed against His Father? I think this must certainly have caused Him much greater grief than the pains of His most sacred Passion; for there He could see the end of His trials; and that sight, together with the satisfaction of seeing our redemption achieved through His death, and of proving what love He had for His Father by suffering so much for Him, would alleviate His pains, just as, when those who have great strength of love perform great penances, they hardly feel them, and would like to do more and more, and everything that they do seems very small to them. What, then, would His Majesty feel when He found Himself able to prove so amply to His Father how completely He was fulfilling the obligation of obedience to Him and showing His love for His neighbour? Oh, the great delight of suffering in doing the will of God! But the constant sight of so many offences committed against His Majesty and so many souls going to hell must, I think, have been so painful to Him that, had He not been more than man, one day of that grief would have sufficed to put an end to any number of lives that He might have had, let alone to one.

BERNARDINE DE LAREDO

Physician, writer, devotional master and Franciscan lay-brother, Bernardine of Laredo (1482-1540) had a direct influence on the spirituality of Teresa of Avila. In his writings he stressed the accessibility of contemplation and the contemplative life for all people—religious or lay, married or single—who are prepared to give themselves fully to it.

The love which, by the great goodness of God, contemplative souls possess, in Infinite love, takes all fear from them and gives them security and true hope, in boundless charity, that they will never cease to will what God wills; hence, there is nought left for them to fear.

ST. JOHN OF THE CROSS

St. John of the Cross (1542–1591) collaborated with St. Teresa in reforming the Carmelite Order. Most famous for his writings on inner purifications (the "night of the senses" and the "night of the spirit"), John developed a classic description of growth in prayer from the first moments of conversion until the highest reaches of mystical union.
John's major works are all written in the form of very discursive commentaries on his own poems. The following selections describe several different phases of growth in the spiritual life.

The Ascent of Mount Carmel (Book I)

CHAPTER IV

The necessity of truly traversing this dark night of sense (mortification of the appetites) in journeying toward union with God.

1. The necessity of passing through this dark night (the mortification of the appetites and the denial of pleasure in all things) for the attainment of the divine union with God arises from the fact that all of man's attachments to creatures are pure darkness in God's sight. Clothed in these affections, a person will be incapable of the enlightenment and dominating fullness of God's pure and simple light, unless he rejects them. There can be no concordance between light and darkness; as St. John says: *Tenebrae eam non comprehenderunt* (The darkness could not receive the light). [Jn. 1:5]

2. The reason, as we learn in philosophy, is that two contraries cannot coexist in the same subject. Darkness, an attachment to creatures, and light, which is God, are contraries and bear no likeness toward each other, as St. Paul teaches in his letter to the Corinthians: *Quae conventio luci ad tenebras?* (What conformity is there between light and darkness?). [2 Cor. 6:14] Consequently, the light of divine union cannot be established in the soul until these affections are eradicated.

3. For a better proof of this, it ought to be kept in mind that an attachment to a creature makes a person equal to that creature; the firmer the attachment, the closer is the likeness to the creature, and the greater the equality. For love effects a likeness between the lover and the object loved. As a result David said of those who set their hearts upon their idols: *Similes illis fiant qui faciunt ea, et omnes qui confidunt in eis* (Let all who set their hearts on them become like them). [Ps. 113:8] He who loves a creature, then, is as low as that creature, and in some way even lower, because love not only equates, but even subjects the lover to the loved object.

By the mere fact, then, that a man loves something, his soul becomes incapable of pure union and transformation in God; for the baseness of a creature is far less capable of the sublimity of the Creator than is darkness of light.

All the creatures of heaven and earth are nothing when compared to God, as Jeremias points out: *Aspexi terram, et ecce vacua erat et nihil; et caelos, et non erat lux in eis* (I looked at the earth, and it was empty and nothing; and at the heavens, and I saw they had no light). [Jer. 4:23] By saying that he saw an empty earth, he meant that all its creatures were nothing and that the earth too was nothing. In stating that he looked up to the heavens and beheld no light, he meant that all the heavenly luminaries were pure darkness in comparison with God. All creatures in contrast to God are nothing, and a man's attachments to them are less than nothing, since these attachments are an impediment to and deprive the soul of transformation in God—just as darkness is nothing, and less than nothing, since it is a privation of light. A man who is in darkness does not comprehend the light, so neither will a person attached to creatures be able to comprehend God. Until a man is purged of his attachments he will not be equipped to possess God, neither here below through the pure transformation of love, nor in heaven through the beatific vision.

For the sake of greater clarity we shall be more specific.

4. We just asserted that all the being of creatures compared with the infinite being of God is nothing, and that, therefore, a man attached to creatures is nothing in the sight of God, and even less than nothing, because love causes equality and likeness and even brings the lover lower than the object of his love. In no way, then, is such a man capable of union with the infinite being of God. There is no likeness between what is not and what is.

To be particular, here are some examples:

All the beauty of creatures compared with the infinite Beauty of God is supreme ugliness. As Solomon says in Proverbs: *Fallax gratia, et vana est pulchritudo* (Comeliness is deceiving and beauty vain). [Prv. 31:30] So a person attached to the beauty of any creature is extremely ugly in God's sight. A soul so unsightly is incapable of transformation into the beauty which is God, because ugliness does not attain to beauty.

All the grace and elegance of creatures compared with God's grace is utter coarseness and crudity. That is why a person captivated by this grace and elegance of creatures becomes quite coarse and crude in God's sight. Accordingly, he is incapable of the infinte grace and beauty of God because of the extreme difference between the coarse and the infinitely elegant.

Now all the goodness of creatures in the world compared with the infinite goodness of God can be called evil, since nothing is good, save God only. [Lk. 18:19] A man, then, who sets his heart on the good things of the world becomes extremely evil in the sight of God. Since evil does not comprehend goodness, this person will be incapable of union with God, Who is supreme goodness.

5. All of the world's wisdom and human ability contrasted with the infinite wisdom of God is pure and utter ignorance, as St. Paul writes to the Corinthians: *Sapientia hujus mundi stultitia est apud Deum* (The wisdom of this world is foolishness in God's sight). [1 Cor. 3:19] Anyone, therefore, who values his knowledge and ability as a means of reaching union with the wisdom of God is highly ignorant in God's sight and will be left behind, far away from this wisdom. Ignorance does not grasp what wisdom is; and in God's sight those who think they have some wisdom are very ignorant. For the Apostle says of them in writing to the Romans: *Dicentes enim se esse sapientes, stulti facti sunt* (Taking themselves for wise men, they became fools). [Rom. 1:22]

Only those who set aside their own knowledge and walk in God's service like unlearned children receive wisdom from God. This is the wisdom about which St. Paul taught the Corinthians: *Si quis videtur inter vos sapiens esse in hoc saeculo, stultus fiat ut sit sapiens. Sapientia enim hujus mundi stultitia est apud Deum* (If anyone among you thinks he is wise, let him become ignorant so as to be wise. For the wisdom of this world is foolishness with God). [1 Cor. 3:18–19] Accordingly, a man must advance to union with God's wisdom by unknowing rather than by knowing.

6. All the sovereignty and freedom of the world compared with the freedom and sovereignty of the Spirit of God is utter slavery, anguish, and captivity.

A person, then, because he is attached to prelacies, or other such dignities, and to freedom of his appetites, and because he finds unacceptable God's holy teaching, that whoever wants to be the greater will be the least, and that whoever wants to be the least will become the greater [Lk. 22:26], is considered and treated by God as a base slave and prisoner, not as a son. For such a one, the royal freedom of spirit attained in divine union is impossible, because freedom has nothing to do with slavery. And freedom cannot abide in a heart dominated by the appetites—in a slave's heart; it dwells in a liberated heart, which is a son's heart. This is why Sara told her husband Abraham to cast out the bondwoman and her son, declaring that the bondwoman's son should not be an heir together with the free son. [Gn. 21:10]

7. All the delights and satisfactions of the will in the things of the world in contrast to all the delight that is God is intense suffering, torment, and bitterness. He who links his heart to these delights, then, deserves in God's eyes intense suffering, torment, and bitterness. He will not be capable of attaining the delights of the embrace of union with God, since he merits suffering and bitterness.

All the wealth and glory of creation compared with the wealth that is God is utter poverty and misery in the Lord's sight. The person who loves and possesses these things is completely poor and miserable before God, and will be unable to attain the richness and glory of the state of transformation in God; the miserable and poor is extremely distant from the supremely rich and glorious.

8. Divine Wisdom, with pity for these souls that become ugly, abject, miserable, and poor on account of their love for worldly things which in their opinion are rich and beautiful, exclaims in Proverbs: *O viri, ad vos clamito, et vox mea ad filios hominum. Intelligite, parvuli, astutiam, et insipientes, animadvertite. Audite quia de rebus magnis locutura sum.* And further on: *Mecum sunt divitiae et gloria opes superbae et justitia. Melior est fructus meus auro et lapide pretioso, et genimina mea argento electo. In viis justitiae ambulo, in medio semitarum judicii, ut ditem diligentes me, et thesauros eorum repleam.* The meaning of this passage is: O men, I cry to you, my voice is directed to the sons of men. Be attentive, little ones, to cunning and sagacity; and you ignorant, be careful. Listen, because I want to speak of great things. Riches and glory are mine, high riches and justice. The fruit you will find in me is better than gold and precious stones; and my generations (what will be engendered of Me in your souls) are better than choice silver. I walk along the ways of justice, in the midst of the paths of judgment, to enrich those who love me and fill their treasures completely. [Prv. 8:4–6; 18–21]

God speaks, here, to all those who are attached to the things of the world. He calls them little ones because they become as little as the things they love. He tells them, accordingly, to be cunning and careful, that He is dealing with great things, not small things, as they are; and that the riches and glory they love are with Him and in Him, not where they think; and that lofty riches and justice are present in Him. Although in their opinion the things of this world are riches, He tells them to bear in mind that His riches are more precious, that the fruit found in them will be better than gold and precious stones, and that what He begets in souls has greater value than cherished silver, which signifies every kind of affection possible in this life.

Book II

FROM CHAPTER XIV

Signs signifying a readiness for contemplation

. . . We shall state one reason which manifests how a loving, general knowledge and awareness of God in the soul is required before discontinuing discursive meditation.

If a man did not have this knowledge or attentiveness to God, he would, as a consequence, be neither doing anything nor receiving anything. Having left the discursive meditation of the sensitive faculties and still lacking contemplation (the general knowledge in which the spiritual faculties—memory, intellect, and will—are actuated and united in this passive, prepared knowledge), he would have no activity whatsoever relative to God. For a person can neither conceive nor receive knowledge already prepared for him save through either the sensitive or spiritual faculties. With the sensory faculties, as we affirmed, a person can make discursive meditation, seek out and form knowledge from the objects; and with the spiritual faculties he can enjoy the knowledge received without any further activity of the senses.

The difference between the functions of these two groups of faculties resembles that existing between toil and the enjoyment of the fruits of this toil; between the drudgery of the journey and the rest and quiet gladdening its end; or again between cooking a meal and eating without effort what has already been cooked and prepared; or it is like the difference between receiving a gift and profiting by it.

If the sensitive faculties are idle as to their work of discursive meditation, and the spiritual faculties as to the contemplation and knowledge received and formed in them, there is no basis for asserting that the soul is occupied.

This knowledge is a requisite, then, in order to leave the way of discursive meditation.

It is noteworthy that this general knowledge is at times so

recondite and delicate (especially when purer, simpler, and more perfect), spiritual, and interior that the soul does not perceive or feel it, even though employed with it.

This is especially so when, as we affirmed, this knowledge is clearer, simpler, and more perfect; and then this knowledge is still less perceptible when it shines upon a purer soul, one freer from the particular ideas and concepts apprehensible by the senses or intellect. Since the individual lacks the feelings of the sensitive part of the soul, by not possessing these particular ideas and concepts which the senses and intellect are accustomed to act upon, he does not perceive this knowledge.

For this reason the purer, simpler, and more perfect the general knowledge is, the darker it seems to be and the less the intellect perceives. On the other hand, the less pure and simple the knowledge is in itself, although it enlightens the intellect, the clearer and more important it appears to the individual, since it is clothed, wrapped, or commingled with some intelligible forms apprehensible to the intellect or the senses.

The following example is a clear illustration of this.

In observing a ray of sunlight stream through the window, we notice that the more it is pervaded with particles of dust, the clearer and more palpable and sensible it appears to the senses; yet obviously the sun ray in itself is less pure, clear, simple, and perfect in that it is full of so many specks of dust. We also notice that when it is more purified of these specks of dust it seems more obscure and impalpable to the material eye; and the purer it is, the more obscure and inapprehensible it seems to be. If the ray of sunlight should be entirely cleansed and purified of all dust particles, even the most minute, it would appear totally obscure and incomprehensible to the eye, since visible things, the object of the sense of sight, would be absent. Thus the eye would find no images on which to rest, because light is not the proper object of sight, but only the means through which visible things are seen. If there is nothing visible off which the ray of light can reflect, nothing will be seen. If the ray, then, were to enter through one window and go out another without striking any quantitative object, it would be invisible. Yet the ray of sunlight would be purer and cleaner than when, on account of being filled with visible objects, it is more manifestly perceived.

The spiritual light has a similar relationship to the intellect, the eye of the soul. This supernatural, general knowledge and light shines so purely and simply in the intellect and is so divested and freed of all intelligible forms (the objects of the intellect) that it is imperceptible to the soul. This knowledge, when purer, is even at times the cause of darkness, because it dispossesses the intellect of its customary lights, forms, and phantasies and effects a noticeable darkness.

When this divine light does not strike so forcibly, a person apprehends neither darkness, nor light, nor anything at all from heavenly or earthly sources. Thus he will sometimes remain in deep oblivion and afterwards will not realize where he was, nor what occurred, nor how the time passed. As a result it can and does happen that an individual will spend many hours in this oblivion, yet upon returning to self think that only a moment or no time at all has passed.

The purity and simplicity of the knowledge is the cause of this oblivion. While occupying a man's soul, it renders it simple, pure, and clear of all the apprehensions and forms through which the senses and memory were acting when conscious of time. And thus it leaves the soul in oblivion and unaware of time.

Although, as we asserted, this prayer lasts a long while, it seems of brief duration to the individual, since he has been united with pure knowledge which is independent of time. This is the short prayer which, it is said, pierces the heavens. [Ecclus. 35:21] It is short because it is not subject to time, and it penetrates the heavens because the soul is united with heavenly knowledge. When the individual returns to himself he observes the effects this knowledge produced in him without his having been aware of this. These effects are: an elevation of mind to heavenly knowledge, and a withdrawal and abstraction from all objects, forms, and figures as well as from the remembrance of them.

David declares that such was his experience upon returning to himself after this oblivion: *Vigilavi, et factus sum sicut passer solitarius in tecto* (I became conscious and discovered that I was like the solitary sparrow on the housetop). [Ps. 101:8] By solitary he refers to the withdrawal and abstraction from all things; by the housetop, to the mind elevated on high. The soul remains, in consequence, as though ignorant of all things, since it knows only God without knowing how it knows Him. For this reason the bride in the Canticle or Canticles, when she states that she went down to Him, numbers unknowing among the effects this sleep and oblivion produced in her, saying: *Nescivi* (I knew not). [Ct. 6:10–11]

As we mentioned, it seems to a person when occupied with this knowledge that he is idle because he is not at work with his senses or faculties. Nevertheless he must believe that he is not wasting time, for even though the harmonious interaction of his sensory and spiritual faculties ceases, his soul is occupied with knowledge in the way we explained. This is why, also in the Canticle of Canticles, the wise bride responded to one of her doubts: *Ego dormio et cor meum vigilat.* [Ct. 5:2] This was like saying: Though I (according to what I am) sleep, naturally, by ceasing to work, my heart watches, supernaturally, in its elevation to supernatural knowledge.

The Dark Night (Book II)

CHAPTER IX

Although this night darkens the spirit, it does so to give light.

1. It remains to be said, then, that even though this happy night darkens the spirit, it does so only to impart light concerning all things; and even though it humbles a person and reveals his miseries, it does so only to exalt him; and even though it impoverishes and empties him of all possessions and natural affection, it does so only that he may reach out divinely to the enjoyment of all earthly and heavenly things, with a general freedom of spirit in them all.

That elements be commingled with all natural compounds, they must be unaffected by any particular color, odor, or taste, and thus they can concur with all tastes, odors, and colors. Similarly, the spirit must be simple, pure, and naked as to all natural affections, actual and habitual, in order to be able to freely communicate in fullness of spirit with the divine wisdom, in which, on account of the soul's purity, the delights of all things are tasted in a certain eminent degree. Without this purgation the soul would be wholly unable to experience the satisfaction of all this abundance of spiritual delight. Only one attachment or one particular object to which the spirit is actually or habitually bound is enough to hinder the experience or reception of the delicate and intimate delight of the spirit of love which contains eminently in itself all delights.

2. Because of their one attachment to the food and fleshmeat they had tasted in Egypt [Ex. 16:3], the children of Israel were unable to get any taste out of the delicate bread of angels—the manna of the desert, which, as Scripture says, contained all savors

and was changed to the taste each one desired. [Wis. 16:20–21] Similarly the spirit, still affected by some actual or habitual attachment or some particular knowledge or any other apprehension, is unable to taste the delights of the spirit of freedom.

The reason is that the affections, sentiments, and apprehensions of the perfect spirit, because they are divine, are of another sort and are so eminent and so different from the natural that their actual and habitual possession demands the annihilation and expulsion of the natural affections and apprehensions; for two contraries cannot coexist in one subject.

Hence, that the soul pass on to these grandeurs, this dark night of contemplation must necessarily annihilate it first and undo it in its lowly ways by putting it in darkness, dryness, conflict, and emptiness. For the light imparted to the soul is a most lofty divine light which transcends all natural light and which does not belong naturally to the intellect.

3. That the intellect reach union with the divine light and become divine in the state of perfection, this dark contemplation must first purge and annihilate it of its natural light and bring it actually into obscurity. It is fitting that this darkness last as long as is necessary for the expulsion and annihilation of the intellect's habitual way of understanding which was a long time in use, and that the divine light and illumination take its place. Since that strength of understanding was natural to the intellect, the darkness it here suffers is profound, frightful, and extremely painful. This darkness seems to be substantial darkness, since it is felt in the deep substance of the spirit.

The affection of love which is bestowed in the divine union of love is also divine, and, consequently, very spiritual, subtle, delicate, and interior, exceeding every affection and feeling of the will and every appetite. The will, as a result, must be first purged and annihilated of all its affections and feelings in order to experience and taste through union of love this divine affection and delight, which is so sublime and which does not naturally belong to the will. The soul is left in a dryness and distress proportionate with its habitual natural affections (whether for divine or human things), so that every kind of demon may be debilitated, dried up, and tried in the fire of this divine contemplation, as when Tobias placed the fish heart in the fire [Tb. 6:8], and the soul may become pure and simple, with a palate purged and healthy and ready to experience the sublime and marvelous touches of divine love. After the expulsion of all actual and habitual obstacles, it will behold itself transformed in these divine touches.

4. Furthermore, in this union for which the dark night is a preparation, the soul in its communion with God must be endowed and filled with a certain glorious splendor embodying innumerable delights. These delights surpass all the abundance the soul can possess naturally, for nature, so weak and impure, cannot receive these delights, as Isaias says: *Eye has not seen, nor ear heard, nor has it entered the heart of man what He has prepared*, etc. [Is. 64:4] As a result the soul must first be set in emptiness and poverty of spirit and purged of every natural support, consolation, and apprehension, earthly and heavenly. Thus empty, it is truly poor in spirit and stripped of the old man, and thereby able to live that new and blessed life which is the state of union with God, attained by means of this night.

5. Extraneous to its common experience and natural knowledge, the soul will have a very abundant and delightful divine sentiment and knowledge of all divine and human things. It must then be refined and inured, as far as its common and natural experience goes (for the eyes by which it now views these things will be as different from those of the past as is spirit from sense and divine from human), and placed in terrible anguish and distress by means of this purgative contemplation. And the memory must be abstracted from all agreeable and peaceful knowledge and feel interiorly alien to all things, in which it will seem that all things are different than before.

This night withdraws the spirit from its customary manner of experience to bring it to the divine experience which is foreign to every human way. It seems to the soul in this night that it is being carried out of itself by afflictions. At other times a man wonders if he is not being charmed, and he goes about with wonderment over what he sees and hears. Everything seems so very strange even though he is the same as always. The reason is that he is being made a stranger to his usual knowledge and experience of things so that annihilated in this respect he may be informed with the divine, which belongs more to the next life than to this.

6. A man suffers all these afflictive purgations of spirit that he may be reborn in the life of the spirit by means of this divine inflow, and through these sufferings the spirit of salvation is brought forth in fulfillment of the words of Isaias: *In your presence, O Lord, we have conceived and been in the pains of labor and have brought forth the spirit of salvation.* [Is. 26:17–18]

Moreover, the soul should leave aside all its former peace, because it is prepared by means of this contemplative night to attain inner peace, which is of such a quality and so delightful that, as the Church says, it surpasses all understanding. [3rd Sun. of Advent, Epis. Phil. 4:7] That peace was not truly peace, because it was clothed with many imperfections; although to the soul walking in delight it seemed to be peace. It seemed to be a twofold peace, sensory and spiritual, since the soul beheld within itself a spiritual abundance. This sensory and spiritual peace, since it is still imperfect, must first be purged; the soul's peace must be disturbed and taken away. In the passage we quoted to demonstrate the distress of this night, Jeremias felt disturbed and wept over his loss of peace: *My soul is withdrawn and removed from peace.* [Lam. 3:17]

7. This night is a painful disturbance involving many fears, imaginings, and struggles within a man. Due to the apprehension and feeling of his miseries, he suspects that he is lost and that his blessings are gone forever. The sorrow and moaning of his spirit is so deep that it turns into vehement spiritual roars and clamoring, and sometimes he pronounces them vocally and dissolves in tears (if he has the strength and power to do so); although such relief is less frequent.

David, one who also had experience of this trial, refers to it very clearly in one of the psalms: *I was very afflicted and humbled; I roared with the groaning of my heart.* [Ps. 37:9] This roaring embodies great suffering. Sometimes due to the sudden and piercing remembrance of his wretchedness, a man's roaring becomes so loud and his affections so surrounded by suffering and pain that I know not how to describe it save by the simile holy Job used while undergoing this very trial: *as the overflowing waters so is my roaring.* [Jb. 3:24] As the waters sometimes overflow in such a way that they inundate everything, this roaring and feeling so increases that in seeping through and flooding everything, it fills all one's deep affections and energies with indescribable spiritual anguish and suffering.

8. These are the effects produced in the soul by this night which enshrouds the hopes one has for the light of day. The prophet Job also proclaims: *In the night my mouth is pierced with sufferings, and they that feed upon me do not sleep.* [Jb. 30:17] The mouth refers to the will pierced through by these sufferings which neither sleep nor cease to tear the soul to shreds. For these doubts and fears that penetrate the soul are never at rest.

9. This war or combat is profound because the peace awaiting the soul must be exceedingly profound; and the spiritual suffering is intimate and penetrating because the love to be possessed by the soul will also be intimate and refined. The more intimate and

highly finished the work must be, so the more intimate, careful, and pure must the labor be; and commensurate with the solidity of the edifice is the energy involved in the work. As Job says, the soul is withering within itself and its inmost parts boiling without any hope. [Jb. 30:16, 27]

Because in the state of perfection toward which it journeys by means of this purgative night, the soul must reach the possession and enjoyment of innumerable blessings of gifts and virtues in both its substance and its faculties, it must first in a general way feel a withdrawal, deprivation, emptiness, and poverty regarding these blessings. And a person must be brought to think that he is far removed from them, and become so convinced that no one can persuade him otherwise or make him believe anything but that his blessings have come to an end. Jeremias points this out when he says in the passage already cited: *I have forgotten good things.* [Lam. 3:17]

10. Let us examine now why this light of contemplation, which is so gentle and agreeable and which is the same light to which the soul must be united and in which it will find all its blessings in the desired state of perfection, produces such painful and disagreeable effects when in these initial stages it shines upon the soul.

11. We can answer this question easily by repeating what we already explained in part; that is, there is nothing in contemplation or the divine inflow which of itself can give pain, contemplation rather bestows sweetness and delight. The cause for not experiencing these agreeable effects is the soul's weakness and imperfection at the time, its inadequate preparation, and the qualities it possesses which are contrary to this light. Because of these the soul has to suffer when the divine light shines upon it.

CHAPTER X

Explains this purgation thoroughly by means of a comparison.

1. For the sake of further clarity in this matter, we ought to note that this purgative and loving knowledge or divine light we are speaking of, has the same effect on a soul that fire has on a log of wood. The soul is purged and prepared for union with the divine light just as the wood is prepared for transformation into the fire. Fire, when applied to wood, first dehumidifies it, dispelling all moisture and making it give off any water it contains. Then it gradually turns the wood black, makes it dark and ugly, and even

causes it to emit a bad odor. By drying out the wood, the fire brings to light and expels all those ugly and dark accidents which are contrary to fire. Finally, by heating and enkindling it from without, the fire transforms the wood into itself and makes it as beautiful as it is itself. Once transformed, the wood no longer has any activity or passivity of its own, except for its weight and its quantity which is denser than the fire. For it possesses the properties and performs the actions of fire: it is dry and it dries; it is hot and it gives off heat; it is brilliant and it illumines; and it is also light, much lighter than before. It is the fire that produces all these properties in the wood.

2. Similarly, we should philosophize about this divine, loving fire of contemplation. Before transforming the soul, it purges it of all contrary qualities. It produces blackness and darkness and brings to the fore the soul's ugliness; thus the soul seems worse than before and unsightly and abominable. This divine purge stirs up all the foul and vicious humors of which the soul was never before aware; never did it realize there was so much evil in itself, since these humors were so deeply rooted. And now that they may be expelled and annihilated they are brought to light and seen clearly through the illumination of this dark light of divine contemplation. Although the soul is no worse than before, neither in itself nor in its relationship with God, it feels undoubtedly so bad as to be not only unworthy that God should see it but deserving of His abhorrence; in fact, it feels that God now does abhor it.

This comparison illustrates many of the things we have been saying and shall say.

3. First, we can understand that the very loving light and wisdom into which the soul will be transformed is that which in the beginning purges and prepares it, just as the fire which transforms the wood by incorporating it into itself is that which was first preparing it for this transformation.

4. Second, we discern that the experience of these sufferings does not derive from this wisdom—for as the Wise Man says: *All good things come to the soul together with her* [Wis. 7:11]—but from the soul's own weakness and imperfection. Without this purgation it cannot receive the divine light, sweetness, and delight of wisdom, just as the log of wood until prepared cannot be transformed by the fire that is applied to it. And this is why the soul suffers so intensely. Ecclesiasticus confirms our assertion by telling what he suffered in order to be united with wisdom and enjoy it: *My soul wrestled for her, and my entrails were disturbed in acquiring her;*

therefore shall I possess a good possession. [Ecclus. 51:25, 29]

5. Third, we can infer the manner in which souls suffer in purgatory. The fire, when applied, would be powerless over them, if they did not have imperfections from which to suffer. These imperfections are the fuel which catches on fire, and once they are gone there is nothing left to burn. So it is here on earth; when the imperfections are gone, the soul's suffering terminates, and joy remains.

6. Fourth, we deduce that as the soul is purged and purified by this fire of love, it is further enkindled in love, just as the wood becomes hotter as the fire prepares it. A person, however, does not always feel this enkindling of love. But sometimes the contemplation shines less forcibly that he may have the opportunity to observe and even rejoice over the work being achieved, for then these good effects are revealed. It is as though one were to stop work and take the iron out of the forge to observe what is being accomplished. Thus the soul is able to perceive the good of which it was unaware while the work was proceeding. So too, when the flame stops acting upon the wood, there is a chance to see how much it has enkindled it.

7. Fifth, we can also gather from this comparison why, as we previously mentioned, the soul after this alleviation suffers again, more intensely and inwardly than before. After that manifestation and after a more exterior purification of imperfections, the fire of love returns to act more interiorly on the consumable matter of which the soul must be purified. The suffering of the soul becomes more intimate, subtle, and spiritual in proportion to the inwardness, subtlety, spirituality, and deep-rootedness of the imperfections which are removed. This more interior purgation resembles the action of fire upon wood: As the fire penetrates more deeply into the wood its action becomes stronger and more vehement, preparing the innermost part in order to gain possession of it.

8. Sixth, we discover the reason it seems to the soul that all blessings are past and that it is full of evil. For at this time it is conscious of nothing but its own bitterness; just as in the example of the wood, for neither the air nor anything else gives it more than a consuming fire. Yet, when other manifestations like the previous are made, the soul's joy will be more interior because of the more intimate purification.

9. Seventh, we deduce that when the purification is soon to return, even though the soul's joy is ample during these intervals (so much so that it sometimes seems, as we pointed out, that the

bitterness will never recur), there is a feeling, if it adverts (and sometimes it cannot help adverting), that some root remains. And this advertence does not allow complete joy, for it seems that the purification is threatening to assail it again. And when the soul does have this feeling, the purification soon returns. Finally, that more inward part still to be purged and illumined cannot be completely concealed by the portion already purified, just as there is a very perceptible difference between that inmost part of the wood still to be illumined and that which is already purged. When this purification returns to attack more interiorly, it is no wonder that once again the soul thinks all its good has come to an end and that its blessings are over. Placed in these more interior sufferings, it is blinded as to all exterior good.

The Spiritual Canticle

STANZAS 14 AND 15

Introduction

1. Since this little dove [the soul] was flying in the breeze of love above the flood waters of her loving fatigues and yearnings, which she has shown until now, and could find nowhere to alight, the compassionate father Noah, stretching out his merciful hand, caught her on her last flight and placed her in the ark of his charity. [Gn. 8:9] This occurred when in the stanza we just explained the Bridegroom said, "return, dove."

Finding in this recollection all that she desired and more than is expressible, the soul begins to sing the praises of her Beloved in the following stanzas. They apply to His grandeurs, which she experiences and enjoys in this union.

> My Beloved is the mountains,
> And lonely wooded valleys,
> Strange islands,
> And resounding rivers,
> The whistling of love-stirring breezes,
>
> The tranquil night
> At the time of the rising dawn,
> Silent music,

Sounding solitude,
The supper that refreshes, and deepens love.

2. Before commenting on these stanzas, we should call to mind for the sake of a clearer understanding of them, and those that follow, that this spiritual flight denotes a high state and union of love, in which, after much spiritual exercise, the soul is placed by God. This state is called spiritual espousal with the Word, the Son of God. And at the beginning, when this flight is experienced the first time, God communicates to the soul great things about Himself, beautifies her with grandeur and majesty, adorns her with gifts and virtues, and clothes her with the knowledge and honor of God, as the betrothed is clothed on the day of her betrothal.

Not only do her vehement yearnings and complaints of love cease, but, in being graced with the blessings mentioned, a state of peace and delight and gentleness of love begins in her. This state is indicated in these stanzas, in which she does no more than tell in song her Beloved's grandeurs, which she knows and enjoys in Him through this union of espousal. In the remaining stanzas she no longer speaks of sufferings and longings as she did before, but of the communion and exchange of sweet and peaceful love with her Beloved, because now in this state all those sufferings have ceased.

It should be noted that these two stanzas describe the most that God communicates to the soul at this time. Yet it must not be thought that He communicates to all those who reach this state everything declared in these two stanzas, or that He does so in the same manner and measure of knowledge and feeling. To some souls He gives more and to others less, to some in one way and to others in another, although all alike may be in this same state of spiritual espousal. But the greatest possible communication is recorded here because it includes everything else. The commentary follows.

Commentary on the two stanzas

3. In Noah's ark, as the divine Scripture says, there were many rooms for different kinds of animals, and all the food that could be eaten. [Gn. 6:14, 19–21] It should be noted that, similarly, the soul in her flight to the divine ark, the bosom of God, not only sees there the many mansions that His Majesty through St. John declared were in His Father's house [Jn. 14:2], but sees and knows there all the foods (all the grandeurs the soul can enjoy) included in

these two stanzas and signified by these common terms. These grandeurs in substance are as follows:

4. The soul sees and tastes abundance and inestimable riches in this divine union. She finds all the rest and recreation she desires, and understands secrets and strange knowledge of God, which is another one of the foods that taste best to her. She experiences in God an awesome power and strength which sweeps away every other power and strength. She tastes there a splendid spiritual sweetness and gratification, discovers true quiet and divine light, and tastes sublimely the wisdom of God reflected in the harmony of His creatures and works. She has the feeling of being filled with blessings and of being empty of evils and far removed from them. And above all she understands and enjoys inestimable refreshment of love which confirms her in love. These in substance are the affirmations of the two stanzas.

5. The bride says in these stanzas that the Beloved is all these things in Himself, and that He is so also for her, because in such superabundant communications from God, the soul experiences and knows the truth of St. Francis' prayer: *My God and my all.* Since God is all things to the soul and the good that is in all things, the communication of this superabundance is explained through its likeness to the goodness of the things mentioned in these stanzas, which we shall explain in our commentary on each of the verses. It should be known that what is explained here is present in God eminently and infintely, or better, each of these sublime attributes is God, and all of them together are God.

Inasmuch as the soul in this case is united with God, she feels that all things are God, as St. John experienced when he said: *Quod factum est, in ipso vita erat* (That which was made, had life in Him). [Jn. 1:4] It should not be thought that what the soul is said to feel here is comparable to seeing things by means of the light, or creatures by means of God; rather in this possession the soul feels that God is all things for her. Neither must it be thought that, because the soul has so sublime an experience of God, we are asserting that she has essential and clear vision of Him. This experience is nothing but a strong and overflowing communication and glimpse of what God is in Himself, in which the soul feels the goodness of the things mentioned in these verses, which we shall now comment upon.

6.   My Beloved is the mountains,
Mountains have heights and they are affluent, vast, beautiful,

graceful, bright, and fragrant. These mountains are what my Beloved is to me.

7.   And lonely wooded valleys,

Lonely valleys are quiet, pleasant, cool, shady, and flowing with fresh waters; in the variety of their groves and in the sweet song of the birds, they afford abundant recreation and delight to the senses, and in their solitude and silence they refresh and give rest. These valleys are what my Beloved is to me.

8.   Strange islands,

Strange islands are surrounded by water and situated across the sea, far withdrawn and cut off from communication with other men. Many things very different from what we have here are born and nurtured in these islands; they are of many strange kinds and powers never before seen by men, and they cause surprise and wonder in anyone who sees them. Thus, because of the wonderful new things and the strange knowledge (far removed from common knowledge) which the soul sees in God, she calls Him "strange islands."

A man is called strange for either of two reasons: He is withdrawn from people; or, compared with other men, he is singular and superior in his deeds and works. The soul calls God "strange" for these two reasons. Not only is He all the strangeness of islands never seen before, but also His ways, counsels, and works are very strange and new and wonderful to man.

It is no wonder that God is strange to men who have not seen Him, since He is also strange to the holy angels and to the blessed. For the angels and the blessed are incapable of seeing Him fully, nor will they ever be capable of doing so. Until the day of the Last Judgment they will see so many new things in Him concerning His deep judgments and His works of mercy and justice that they will forever be receiving new surprises and marveling the more. Hence not only men but also the angels can call Him strange islands. Only to Himself is He neither strange nor new.

9.   And resounding rivers,

Rivers have three properties: first they besiege and inundate everything they encounter; second, they fill up all the low and empty spots found along their path; third, they are so loud that they muffle and suppress every other sound. Since in this communication the soul has in God a delightful experience of these three properties, she says that her Beloved is resounding rivers.

As for the first property, it should be known that the soul is conscious at this time that the torrent of God's spirit is besieging and taking possession of her so forcibly that all the rivers of the world seem to have flooded in upon her and to be assailing her. She feels that all the actions and passions in which she was formerly occupied are drowned therein. This is not a torment to her, although it is a thing of tremendous force, because these rivers are rivers of peace, as God declared of this onslaught through Isaias: *Ecce ego declinabo super eam quasi fluvium pacis, et quasi torrentem inundantem gloriam* (See that I will descend and besiege her—the soul—like a river of peace and like a torrent overflowing with glory). [Is. 66:12] Hence this divine onslaught God causes in the soul is like a resounding river which fills everything with peace and glory.

The second property the soul experiences at this time is that of the divine water filling the low places of her humility and the voids of her appetites, as St. Luke says: *Exaltavit humiles. Esurientes implevit bonis* (He exalted the humble and filled the hungry with good things). [Lk. 1:52–53]

The third property she experiences in these resounding rivers of her Beloved is a spiritual clamor and outcry, louder than any other sound or call. This cry prevails against all other cries and its sound exceeds all the sounds of the world.

To explain how this comes about we will have to delay a short while.

10. This clamor or resounding of these rivers which the soul refers to here is such an abundant plenitude that she is filled with goods, and it is so powerful a force that she is possessed by it, for it seems to be not merely the sound of rivers but the sound of roaring thunder. Nevertheless this cry is a spiritual cry which does not contain these other material sounds, nor their pain and disturbance, but rather grandeur, strength, power, delight, and glory. It is like an immense interior clamor and sound which clothes the soul in power and strength.

This spiritual cry and noise was made in the souls of the Apostles when the Holy Spirit descended upon them like a mighty wind, as is related in the Acts of the Apostles. [Acts 2:2] To manifest the spiritual voice bestowed on them interiorly, that sound was heard exteriorly as of a fierce wind by all who were in Jerusalem. [Acts 2:5–6] This sound denoted what the Apostles received interiorly, a fullness of power and fortitude.

St. John says that while the Lord Jesus was praying to His Father in the conflict and anguish occasioned by His enemies, an interior voice came to Him from heaven, comforting Him in His humanity. The sound of this voice which the Jews heard as though coming from outside was so deep and loud that some said it had thundered and others that an angel from heaven had spoken. [Jn. 12:27–29] The reason is that that voice, which was heard as though coming from without, denoted and manifested the fortitude and strength which was interiorly bestowed on Christ in His humanity.

It must not be thought on this account that the soul fails to receive in its spirit the sound of the spiritual voice. It should be noted that the spiritual voice is the effect produced in the spirit, just as the sound in the ear and the knowledge in the spirit is an effect of the material voice. David meant this when he said: *Ecce dabit voci suae vocem virtutis* (Behold that God will give to His voice the voice of power). [Ps. 67:34] This power is the interior voice, because when David said He will give to His voice the voice of power he meant that to the exterior voice, heard from without, He will give the voice of power that is heard from within.

Hence it should be known that God is an infinite voice, and by communicating Himself to the soul in this way He produces the effect of an immense voice.

11. St. John heard this voice and says in the Apocalypse that the voice he heard from heaven *erat tamquam vocem aquarum et tamquam vocem tonitrui magni* (was like the voice of many waters and like the voice of a great thunder). [Ap. 14:2] That it might not be thought that because this voice was so great it was harsh and painful, he immediately adds that it was so gentle it sounded *sicut citharoedorum citharizantium in citharis suis* (like many harpers playing on their harps). [Ap. 14:2] And Ezechiel says that this sound as of many waters was *quasi sonum sublimis Dei* (like the sound of the most high God), that is, this infinite voice was communicated in a most lofty and gentle way. For as we said it is God Himself who communicates Himself by producing this voice in the soul. But He limits Himself in each soul, measuring out the voice of power according to the soul's capacity, and this voice produces great delight and grandeur. As a result He said to the bride in the Canticle: *Sonet vox tua in auribus meis, vox enim tua dulcis* (Let your voice sound in my ears, for your voice is sweet). [Ct. 2:14]

12.   The whistling of love-stirring breezes,

The soul refers to two things in this verse: the breezes and the whistling.

By "love-stirring breezes" is understood the attributes and graces of the Beloved which by means of this union assail the soul and lovingly touch it in its substance.

This most sublime and delightful knowledge of God and His attributes which overflows into the intellect from the touch these attributes of God produce in the substance of the soul, she calls the whistling of these breezes. This is the most exalted delight of all the soul here enjoys.

13. To understand this better it should be noted that just as two things are felt in the breeze (the touch and the whistling or sound), so in this communication of the Bridegroom two things are experienced: knowledge and a feeling of delight. As the feeling of the breeze delights the sense of touch, and its whistling the sense of hearing, so the sentiment of the Beloved's attributes are felt and enjoyed by the soul's power of touch, which is in its substance, and the knowledge of these attributes is experienced in its hearing, which is the intellect.

It should also be known that the love-stirring breeze is said to come when it wounds in a pleasant way by satisfying the appetite of the one desiring such refreshment, because the sense of touch is then filled with enjoyment and refreshment; and the hearing, through this delectable touch, experiences great pleasure and gratification in the sound and whistling of the breeze. The delight of hearing is much greater than that of feeling, because the sound in the sense of hearing is more spiritual; or, better, it more closely approaches the spiritual than does feeling. Consequently, the delight of hearing is more spiritual than that of feeling.

14. Since this touch of God gives intense satisfaction and enjoyment to the substance of the soul, and gently fulfills her desire for this union, she calls this union or these touches, love-stirring breezes. As we have said, the Beloved's attributes are lovingly and sweetly communicated in this breeze, and from it the intellect receives the knowledge of whistling.

She calls the knowledge a "whistling," because just as the whistling of the breeze pierces deeply into the hearing organ, so this most subtle and delicate knowledge penetrates with wonderful savoriness into the innermost part of the substance of the soul, and the delight is greater than all others.

The reason for the delight is that the already understood substance, stripped of accidents and phantasms, is bestowed. For this knowledge is given to that intellect which philosophers call the passive or possible intellect, and the intellect receives it passively without any efforts of its own. This knowing is the soul's main delight because it is pertinent to the intellect, and as theologians say fruition, the vision of God, is proper to the intellect.

Since this whistling refers to the substantial knowledge mentioned, some theologians think our Father Elias saw God in that whistling of the gentle breeze heard on the mount at the mouth of his cave. [3 Kgs. 19:11–13] Scripture calls it "the whistling of the gentle breeze," because knowledge was begotten in his intellect from the delicate spiritual communication. The soul calls this knowledge "the whistling of love-stirring breezes" because it flows over into the intellect from the loving communication of the Beloved's attributes. As a result she calls the knowledge "the whistling of the love-stirring breezes."

15. This divine whistling which enters through the soul's hearing is not only, as I have said, the understood substance, but also an unveiling of truths about the divinity and a revelation of His secrets. When Scripture refers to a communication of God which enters by hearing, this communication ordinarily amounts to a manifestation of these naked truths to the intellect, or a revelation of the secrets of God. These are pure spiritual revelations or visions, which are given only to the spirit without the service and help of the senses. Thus what is called the communication of God through hearing is very certain and lofty.

Accordingly, St. Paul in order to declare the height of his revelation did not say: *vidit arcana verba*, and still less: *gustavit arcana verba*, but: *audivit arcana verba quae non licet homini loqui* (he heard secret words which men are not permitted to utter). [2 Cor. 12:4] It is thought that he saw God there as our Father Elias also did in the whistling.

Since faith, as St. Paul also says [Rom. 10:17], comes through hearing, so too that which faith tells us, the understood substance, comes through spiritual hearing. The prophet Job indicates this clearly in speaking with God Who revealed Himself: *Auditu auris audivi te, nunc autem oculus meus videt te* (With the hearing of the ear I heard You and now my eye sees You). [Jb. 42:5] This passage points out clearly that to hear Him with the hearing of the soul is to see Him with the eye of the passive intellect. Consequently, he does not say I heard You with the hearing of my ears, but of my ear, nor, I saw You with my eyes, but with my eye, which is the intellect. This hearing of the soul, therefore, is the vision of the intellect.

16. It must not be thought that, because what the soul understands is the naked substance, there is perfect and clear fruition as in heaven. Although the knowledge is stripped of accidents, it is not for this reason clear, but dark, for it is contemplation, which in this life, as St. Dionysius says, is a ray of darkness. [Pseudo-Dionysius Areopagita, *De Mystica Theologia,* chap. 1] We can say that it is a ray and image of fruition, since it is in the intellect that fruition takes place.

This understood substance that the soul calls "whistling" is equivalent to "the eyes I have desired," of which the soul said, when they were being revealed to her, "Withdraw them, Beloved," because her senses could not endure them.

17. Because it seems to me that a passage from Job which confirms a great deal of what I said about this rapture and espousal is very appropriate, I will refer to it here, even though we may be detained some more, and I will explain its pertinent parts. First, I will cite the entire passage in Latin, and then render it in the vernacular, afterwards I will offer a brief explanation of what interests us. After this I shall go on with the commentary on the verses of the other stanza.

In the Book of Job, then, Eliphaz the Temanite speaks in the following way: *Porro ad me dictum est verbum absconditum et quasi furtive suscepit auris mea venas susurri ejus. In horrore visionis nocturnae quando solet sopor occupare homines, pavor tenuit me et tremor, et omnia ossa mea perterrita sunt; et cum spiritus, me praesente, transiret, inhorruerunt pili carnis meae. Stetit quidam, cujus non agnoscebam vultum, imago coram oculis meis, et vocem quasi aurae lenis audivi* (Truly a hidden word was spoken to me, and my ear as though by stealth received the veins of his whisper. In the horror of the nocturnal vision, when sleep usually occupies men, fear and trembling took hold of me and all my bones were disturbed; and as the spirit passed before me the hair of my flesh shriveled. There stood one before me whose countenance I knew not, an image before my eyes, and I heard the voice of a gentle wind.) [Jb. 4:12–16] The passage contains almost everything we have said about this rapture, from stanza 13 up to this point.

18. What Eliphaz, the Temanite, refers to (in saying that a hidden word was spoken to him) was given to the soul when, unable to endure it, she said, "Withdraw them, Beloved."

By saying that his ear, as though by stealth, received the veins of his whisper, he refers to the naked substance the intellect receives. The veins here denote the interior substance, and the whisper signifies that communication and touch of attributes by which the understood substance is imparted to the intellect. He calls the communication a "whisper" because it is very gentle, just as the soul calls it "love-stirring breezes" because it is lovingly bestowed. He says he received it as though by stealth because, as a stolen article is not one's own, so that secret from a natural viewpoint is foreign to man, for Eliphaz received what did not belong to him naturally. Thus it was unlawful for him to receive it just as it was unlawful for St. Paul to disclose the secret words he heard. [2 Cor. 12:4] Hence the other prophet twice declared: *My secret for myself.* [Is. 24:16]

In saying that in the horror of the nocturnal vision when sleep usually occupies men, fear and trembling took hold of him, he refers to the fear and trembling naturally caused in the soul by that rapturous communication, unendurable to nature, in the imparting of God's spirit. The prophet here indicates that just as men are oppressed and frightened by the vision they call a nightmare which occurs when they are about to sleep (at that moment between sleeping and waking, the point at which sleep begins), so at the time of this spiritual transport, between the sleep of natural ignorance and the wakefulness of supernatural knowledge, which is the beginning of the rapture or ecstasy, the communication of a spiritual vision gives rise to this fear and trembling.

19. And he adds that all his bones were terrified or disturbed, which amounts to saying that they were shaken and dislocated. He refers here to the great disjuncture of the bones which we said they suffer at this time. Daniel clearly indicates this when he says upon his vision of the angel: *Domine in visione tua dissolutae sunt compages meae* (Lord, upon seeing you the joints of my bones are loosed). [Dn. 10:16]

And in what he says next, that is, "and as the spirit passed before me" (by making my spirit pass beyond its natural limits and ways through the rapture we have mentioned), "the hair of my flesh shriveled," he attests to our teaching concerning the body: that in this transport, as in death, it remains frozen, and the flesh stiff.

20. And continuing: "there stood before me one whose countenance I knew not, an image before my eyes." He who stood before him was God, who communicated Himself in the manner mentioned. And he says that he did not know His countenance, to signify that in such a communication and vision, even though most sublime, the countenance and essence of God is neither known nor seen. Yet he says that it was an image before his eyes, because that knowledge of the hidden word was most high, like an image and trace of God, but he does not refer to the essential vision of God.

21. Then he concludes, saying: "and I heard the voice of a gentle wind." This voice of the gentle wind refers to the whistling of love-stirring breezes, which the soul says is her Beloved.

It must not be thought that these visits are always accompanied by natural tremblings and torments; for, as we said, these are found only in those who are beginning to enter the state of illumination and perfection and this kind of communication; in others they are very gentle.

The commentary continues:

22.   The tranquil night

In this spiritual sleep in the bosom of the Beloved, the soul possesses and relishes all the tranquility, rest, and quietude of the peaceful night; and she receives in God, together with this peace, a fathomless and obscure divine knowledge. As a result she says that her Beloved is a tranquil night to her.

23.   At the time of the rising dawn,

Yet she does not say that the tranquil night is equivalent to a dark night, but, rather, that it is like the night that has reached the time of the rising dawn. This quietude and tranquillity in God is not entirely obscure to the soul as is a dark night; but it is a tranquillity and quietude in divine light, in the new knowledge of God, in which the spirit elevated to the divine light is in quiet.

She very appropriately calls this divine light "the rising dawn," which means the morning. Just as the rise of morning dispels the darkness of night and unveils the light of day, so this spirit, quieted and put to rest in God, is elevated from the darkness of natural knowledge to the morning light of the supernatural knowledge of God. This morning light is not clear, as was said, but dark as night at the time of the rising dawn. Just as the night at the rise of dawn is not entirely night or entirely day, but is, as they say, at the break of day, so this divine solitude and tranquillity, informed by the divine light, has some share in that light, but not its complete clarity.

24. In this tranquillity the intellect is aware of being elevated, with strange newness, above all natural understanding to the divine light, just as a person who after a long sleep opens his eyes to the unexpected light.

I think David was referring to this knowledge when he said: *Vigilavi et factus sum sicut passer solitarius in tecto* (I have kept watch and am become like a solitary sparrow on the housetop). [Ps. 101:8] This was like saying: I opened the eyes of my intellect and found myself above all natural knowledge, without this knowledge and alone on the housetop, which is above all low things.

He says he became like the solitary sparrow, because in this contemplation the spirit has the traits of a solitary sparrow. There are five of these traits:

First, the sparrow ordinarily perches on the highest thing. And so the spirit at this stage is placed in the highest contemplation.

Second, it always turns its beak toward the wind. Thus the spirit ever turns the beak of its affection toward the Spirit of Love, Who is God.

Third, it is usually alone and allows no other bird close to it, for when another perches nearby it flies away. Thus the spirit in this contemplation is alone in regard to all things, stripped of them all, nor does it allow within itself anything other than solitude in God.

The fourth trait is that it sings very sweetly. And so does the spirit sing sweetly to God at this time, for the praises it renders Him are of the most delightful love, pleasant to the soul and precious in God's eyes.

The fifth is that it possesses no definite color. So neither does the perfect spirit, in this excess, have any color of sensible affection or self-love; it does not even have any particular consideration in either its lower or higher part, nor will it be able to describe the mode or manner of this excess, for what it possesses is an abyss of the knowledge of God.

25. Silent music,

In that nocturnal tranquillity and silence and in that knowledge of the divine light the soul becomes aware of Wisdom's wonderful harmony and sequence in the variety of His creatures and works. Each of them is endowed with a certain likeness of God and in its own way gives voice to what God is in it. So creatures will be for the soul a harmonious symphony of sublime music surpassing all concerts and melodies of the world.

She calls this music "silent" because it is tranquil and quiet knowledge, without the sound of voices. And thus there is in it the sweetness of music and the quietude of silence. Accordingly, she says that her Beloved is silent music because in Him she knows and enjoys this symphony of spiritual music. Not only is He silent music, but He is also

26.   Sounding solitude,

This is almost identical with silent music, for even though that music is silent to the natural senses and faculties, it is sounding solitude for the spiritual faculties. When these spiritual faculties are alone and empty of all natural forms and apprehensions, they can receive in a most sonorous way the spiritual sound of the excellence of God, in Himself and in His creatures. We said above that St. John speaks of this spiritual vision in the Apocalypse, that is: *the voice of many harpers playing on their harps.* [Jn. 14:2] This vision was spiritual and had nothing to do with material harps. It involved a knowledge of the praises that each of the blessed in his own degree of glory gives continually to God. This praise is like music, for as each one possesses God's gifts differently, each one sings His praises differently, and all of them together form a symphony of love, as of music.

27. In this same way the soul perceives in that tranquil wisdom that all creatures, higher and lower ones alike, according to what each in itself has received from God, raise their voice in testimony to what God is. She beholds that each in its own way, bearing God within itself according to its capacity, magnifies God. And thus all these voices form one voice of music praising the grandeur, wisdom, and wonderful knowledge of God.

This is the meaning of the Holy Spirit in the Book of Wisdom when He said: *Spiritus Domini replevit orbem terrarum, et hoc quod continet omnia, scientiam habet vocis* (The spirit of the Lord filled the whole earth, and this world which contains all things has knowledge of the voice). [Wis. 1:7] This voice is the sonorous solitude the soul knows here, that is, the testimony to God which, in themselves, all things give.

Since the soul does not receive this sonorous music without solitude and estrangement from all exterior things, she calls it "silent music" and "sounding solitude," which she says is her Beloved. And what is more:

28.   The supper that refreshes, and deepens love.

Supper affords lovers refreshment, satisfaction, and love. Since in this gentle communication the Beloved produces these three benefits in the soul, she calls it "the supper that refreshes, and deepens love."

It should be known that in the divine Scripture this term "supper" refers to the divine vision. Just as supper comes at the end of a day's work and at the beginning of the evening rest, this tranquil knowledge causes the soul to experience a certain end of her evils and the possession of good things in which her love of God is deepened more than before. As a result, He is the supper that refreshes by being the end of evils for her, and that deepens love by being to her the possession of all goods.

29. Yet for a better understanding of what this supper is to the soul—it is as we said her Beloved—we should note in this appropriate place what the beloved Bridegroom says in the Apocalypse:*I stand at the door and knock; if anyone opens, I shall enter and sup with him, and he with Me*. [Ap. 3:20] In this text He indicates that He carries His supper with Him, and it is nothing but His own very delights and savors that He himself enjoys. In uniting Himself with the soul He imparts them, and she likewise enjoys them. For such is the meaning of the words, *I shall sup with him, and he with Me*. Hence these words declare the effect of the divine union of the soul with God, in which God's very own goods are graciously and bounteously shared in common with His bride, the soul. He Himself is for her the supper that refreshes and enamors, for in being bounteous He refreshes her, and in being gracious He enamors her.

30. Before continuing with the commentary on the remaining stanzas, we ought to point out here that even though we have said that in this state of espousal the soul enjoys complete tranquillity and receives the most abundant communication possible in this life, it should be understood that this tranquillity refers only to the superior part (until the state of spiritual marriage the sensory part never completely loses the dross left from bad habits, or brings all its energies into subjection, as will be said later) and that this communication is the most abundant possible to the state of espousal. In the spiritual marriage there are striking advantages over this state of espousal, for although the bride, the soul, enjoys so much good in these visits of the state of espousal, still she suffers from her Beloved's withdrawals and from disturbances and afflictions in her sensory part and from the devil; all of these cease in the state of marriage.

ST. JOHN EUDES

The Life and Kingdom of Jesus in Christian Souls

One of the greatest spiritual figures in seventeenth-century France, St. John Eudes (1601–1680) spent many years as an Oratorian preacher and confessor. Wishing to dedicate his energies more fully to the spiritual improvement of the parish clergy, he founded his own order dedicated to the Sacred Hearts of Jesus and Mary, and established numerous seminaries in the dioceses of France. His spiritual writings express the emphases typical of the French School of the seventeenth century.

O my well-beloved Jesus, I give myself to Thee to derive the benefits of these words of thy apostle: "You are dead: and your life is hid with Christ in God" (Col. 3:3). Hide me utterly with Thee in God. Bury my mind, my heart, my will and my being, so that I may no longer have any thoughts, desires, or affections, any sentiments and dispositions other than Thine own.

THE FRENCH SCHOOL OF SPIRITUALITY

During the first half of the seventeenth century, a group of French spiritual authors formulated an approach to the spiritual life that became normative for much of the Catholic world during the three centuries that followed. In many ways, they (together with the Jesuits) set the tone for what most modern Catholics think of as "traditional spirituality."

Chief among these authors and founder of the "French School" was Pierre de Bérulle (1575–1629), founder of the French Oratory, later known as the "Sulpicians." His successor as superior-general of the Sulpicians, Charles de Condren (1588–1641), developed the ideas of the school further, as did Jean-Jacques Olier (1608–1657), the founder of the seminary of St. Sulpice in Paris.

The following section contains quotations from the works of these three authors. Other important members of the French School included St. Vincent de Paul (a brief quotation from a contemporary life of this saint is included here) and St. John Eudes, promoter of the devotion to the hearts of Jesus and Mary. A later key author of the French School was St. Louis Grignion de Montfort (1673– 1716), author of True Devotion to the Blessed Virgin Mary, *with its emphasis on the devotion of "holy slavery."*

Except for De Montfort, few of the works of these authors have been translated into English. In order to familiarize readers with them, it has seemed advisable to present here a collection of relatively brief quotations from various works, grouped thematically.

Even though there are significant differences among the authors of the French School, most themes are common to all of them, with differences only of nuance. All stress a radical christocentrism, an emphasis on the "virtue of religion" leading to an attitude of honor and respect rather than intimacy in prayer, an insistence on identification of the individual Christian with the interior "states" (attitudes, feelings, outlooks) of Christ, and a strong devotion to Mary and the Eucharist. The French School was permeated with a pessimistic Augustinian view of man and sin, which gave rise to a great stress on abnegation and "annihilation."

Because of their pervasive influence even down to our own century, the authors of the French School are of considerable importance for an understanding of spirituality today.

I. The "Vow of Servitude"

"With this desire, I make to thee, O Jesus my Lord, and to thy deified humanity, a humanity truly thine in its deification, and truly mine in its humiliation, in its sorrows, in its sufferings: to thee and to it I make an oblation and entire gift absolute and irrevocable, of all that I am through thee in being, by nature and in the order of grace . . . I leave myself then wholly to thee, O Jesus, and to thy sacred humanity, in the most humble and binding condition which I know, the condition and relation of servitude; which I acknowledge to be due to thy humanity as much on account of the greatness of the state to which it is raised through the hypostatic union, as on account of the excess of voluntary abasement to which it became reduced and humbled for my salvation and glory, in its life, its cross, and in its death. . . . To this end and this homage I set and place my soul, my state, and my life, both now and for ever in a state of subjection and in relations of dependence and servitude in regard to thee and to thy humanity thus deified and thus humiliated together." —Bérulle, *Grandeurs de Jesus*, Discourse II (*Oeuvres complètes*, ed. Migne, Paris, 1856, pp. 181ff.).

"I vow and dedicate myself to Jesus Christ, my Lord and Saviour, in the state of perpetual servitude to his most holy Mother the Blessed Virgin Mary. In perpetual honour of the Mother and the Son, I desire to be in a state and condition of servitude as regards her office of being the Mother of my God, in order to honour more humbly, more holily, so high and divine a rank; and I give myself to her as a slave in honour of the gift which the eternal Word has made of himself as Son, through the mystery of the Incarnation that he deigned to bring about in her and through her." —Bérulle, *Oeuvres complètes,* p. 527.

II. Christocentric Spirituality

"A surpassing mind of this century is ready to maintain that the sun is the centre of the world and not the earth; that it is motionless and that the earth, in accordance with its circular shape, moves as regards the sun, by this contrary opinion satisfying every appearance which compels our senses to believe that the sun is in continual movement round the earth. This new opinion, little known in the science of the stars, is useful and ought to be followed in the science of salvation. For Jesus is the sun, motionless in his greatness, moving all things. Jesus is like unto his Father and, being seated on his right hand, is as immovable as he and gives motion to all. Jesus is the true centre of the world, and the world ought to be in continual motion towards him. Jesus is the sun of our souls whence they receive all grace, light, and influence. And the earth of our hearts should be in continual movement towards him in order to receive in all its parts and powers the favourable aspects and benign influences of this great luminary."—Bérulle, *Grandeurs de Jesus,* Discourse II (*Oeuvres complètes,* p. 161).

III. The Virtue of Religion

"There is nothing in him (Jesus) which does not deserve homage, honour, deep reverence and submission from all creatures in heaven, on earth, and in hell: *ut in nomine Jesu omne genu flectatur coelestium, terrestrium et infernorum* (Phil. ii, 10). It is the most essential act and exercise of religion, the first obligation of the creature towards God, the chief duty of the Christian towards Jesus Christ our Saviour." —Bourgoing, *Préface aux Oeuvres du Card. de Bérulle*, in *Oeuvres complètes*, p. 86.

IV. Augustinianism and Abnegation

"As the humanity of Jesus has no other being, life, and subsistence than in the divinity, we also must have no other life and subsistence than in his humanity and in his divinity—that is to say, than in him as God and man, the life, the salvation, and the glory of men. This state, considered well from every point of view, forces us very straitly, very strictly, and very continually to die to ourselves, to renounce ourselves." —Bérulle, *Oeuvres complètes*, p. 1161.

"Jesus is all, and ought to be all in us, and we ought to be nothing, to treat ourselves as nothing, to be nothing in ourselves and have our being only in him. As we are by him and not by ourselves so also we should be for him and not for ourselves. This is what we should begin on earth that it may be finished in heaven, where Jesus Christ will be all in all. This is the perfection to which it becomes us to aspire." —Bérulle, *Oeuvres complètes*, p. 1179.

"The life and form of grace which God now gives to man is a kind of grace of annihilation and of the cross; and grace, either earthly or heavenly, is a way of grace which draws the soul out of itself by means of a kind of annihilation and transports it, fixes it, and grafts it into Jesus Christ, as, in him, our humanity is grafted into his divinity . . . And, as in the Incarnation, there is a kind of annihilation of human nature, which is stripped of its own proper subsistence or human person in order to become one with the divine Person of the Word; so also in the grace which flows from this adorable Incarnation, as from a living source, there is a kind of annihilation in ourselves and permanent fixing in Jesus. Annihilation both of power and of subsistence, but with this difference, that the power in us which precedes the grace of Jesus Christ, being only a power which leads to our undoing, is truly set aside, and we are drawn into his own power in order to accomplish our work. But our subsistence is not taken from us in the same way; it is only annihilated as regards our use of it in morality, and in its authority and not in its existence." —Bérulle, *Oeuvres complètes*, p. 1166.

"The Christian, in fact, possesses two lives—the life of Adam and that of our Lord; the life of the flesh and that of the Spirit. These two lives are opposed to each other; it is needful for one to be wholly annihilated in order that the other become absolutely perfect. Now, so long as we are here below, the life of the flesh is never wholly destroyed. By a special privilege, however, and in reward for heroic mortifications or for great faithfulness to the Holy Spirit, it happens to the soul to feel itself occasionally dead to this imperfect life; but this is never other than for a time and in part. Moreover, the life of Jesus Christ within us is never in this world so peaceful or wholly perfect. We must always have the sword in hand in order to overcome our enemies and those of God; it is always necessary for us to labour in order to mortify and destroy the old man." —Olier, unpublished texts presented by G. Letourneau, *Pensées choisies* (Paris, 1916), p. 48. "The Christian man, according to the teaching of St. Paul, comprises two things, one is called the flesh, the other the spirit. It is thus that man is divided in Scripture." *Catéchisme Chrétien*, I, xiv in *Oeuvres complètes de M. Olier* (Paris: Migne, 1856).

"It is by these two exercises that we must begin the interior and divine life. We must first of all labour for the mortification of self; and then, being dead to the flesh, we must endeavour to live by the Spirit. Without this, we shall never do anything, and all other exercises will only serve to our loss. All the rest is like a salve which encloses our evil without removing it, which hides it and in no way heals it." —*Introduction à la vie Chrétienne*, Chap. VIII in *Oeuvres complètes de M. Olier*.

"It is necessary for the soul to be in fear and distrust of self; it must testify to this distrust by avoiding occasions and encounters in which it may satisfy the heart by love and delight in some creature. It should make its pleasure and joy depend on sacrificing to Jesus all joy and pleasure which it may have apart from himself. And when taking part in those things in which by Providence it is obliged to be occupied, such as eating, drinking, and conversation with creatures, it must be sparing in all, must discard what is superfluous, and must renounce, in the use of them, the joy and pleasure to be found therein, uniting and giving itself to Jesus as often as it feels itself tempted to enjoy something apart from him and not himself." —*Journée chrétienne* Part I, in *Oeuvres complètes de M. Olier.*

"What else have we in ourselves but nothingness and sin? Let us, then hold it as certain that in all things and everywhere we deserve to be repulsed and always despised, because of our natural opposition to the sanctity and perfections of God, to the life of Jesus Christ, and to the operations of grace; and that which convinces us of this truth the more is our natural and continual inclination to evil and our impotence for good." —*Vie de Saint Vincent de Paul*, by Abelly, Book III, Chap XXX, quoted in J. D. Icard, *Doctrine de M. Olier* (Paris, 1891), p. 64.

V. Adherence to the States of Christ

"The mysteries of Jesus Christ are in some circumstances past, and in another way they remain and are present and perpetual. They are past as regards their performance but they are present as regards their virtue, and their virtue never passes, nor will the love with which they have been accomplished ever pass. The spirit, then, the state, the virtue, the merit of the mystery is always present. The spirit of God, by whom this mystery was wrought, the interior state of the external mystery, the efficacy, and the virtue which render this mystery living and operative within us, this state and virtuous disposition, the merit by which he has gained us for his Father and merited heaven, life, and himself; even the actual taste, the living disposition, through which Jesus has brought about this mystery, is always alive, actual, and present to Jesus. So much so that if it were necessary for us, or if it were pleasing to God the Father, he would be quite ready to depart and to accomplish this work, this action, this mystery, afresh." —Bérulle, *Oeuvres complètes*, pp. 1052–53.

"At the moment of the Incarnation, our Lord consecrated himself entirely to the Father, himself and all his members. . . . He continues ever to live with the same dispositions that he had during his whole life; he never interrupts them and ever offers himself, in himself and in all his members, to God in all those circumstances in which they ought to serve him, honour him and glorify him . . . Our Lord, in order to extend his holy religion in God's direction and to

increase it in our souls, comes into us and leaves himself on earth
in the hands of his priests, as a sacrifice of praise, to join us with
this state of sacrifice, to adapt us to his praise, to communicate to us
inwardly the sentiments of his religion. He spreads himself in us,
he instills himself in us, he embalms our soul and fills it with the
inward dispositions of his religious spirit; so that he makes our soul
and his but one, which he animates with the same spirit of respect,
love, praise, and the inward and outward sacrifice of all things to
the glory of God his Father; and thus he places our soul in fellowship with his religion, in order to make us in himself true religious
of his Father." —Olier, *Catéchisme chrétien*, I, xx, and *Introduction
à la vie chrétienne*, Chap. i, in *Oeuvres complètes de M. Olier.*

The state of imitation of Christ crucified "is a state in which the
heart cannot be moved in its depths; and although the world shows
it its beauties, its honours, its riches, it is the same as though these
were offered to a dead man who is motionless and without any
desires, insensible to all that is offered him. The Christian, in this
state of inward death, is inwardly undisturbed by all that the
senses show him, all that the wickedness of the world arouses;
outwardly he may be agitated in this life, but inwardly he is ever at
peace; he remains insensible to all and esteems it as nothing,
because he is dead in our Lord: *Mortui enim estis* (Col. iii, 3) . . .
(and) because of the divine life which absorbs all that is mortal in
(his soul)." —Olier, *Catéchisme chrétien*, I, xxii, in *Oeuvres complètes de M. Olier.*

VI. Devotion to Mary

"What our Lord is to his Church, he is *par excellence* to his holy
Mother. Thus he is her inward and divine plenitude; and as he
sacrificed himself more particularly for her than for the whole
Church, he gives her the life of God more abundantly than to the
whole Church. . . .

"We must then consider Jesus Christ, our all, living in the most
holy Virgin in the fulness of the life of God, as much in that life
which he received from his Father as that which he obtained and
merited for men through the ministry of the life of his Mother . . .

"There is nothing more wonderful than this life of Jesus in Mary,
the holy life that he pours continuously into her, the divine life

with which he animates her, loving and praising and adoring God his Father in her, giving a worthy supplement to her heart wherein he abounds with pleasure. All the life of Jesus and all his love in the remainder of the Church even in his apostles and his dear disciples, is nothing in comparison with that which he has in the heart of Mary. He dwells there in plenitude; he works there to the full extent of his divine Spirit, he is but one heart, one soul, one life with Mary." —Olier, *Journée chrétienne*, Part II, end, in *Oeuvres complètes de M. Olier.*

VII. The Eucharist and the States of Christ

"Since our Lord deigned to make me a participator in his state of the Host in the most holy Sacrament, speaking truly, it is no longer I that live; it is he himself who lives in me. Each day after Holy Communion I feel him diffused all through me, as though I felt his presence in all my members, although in Holy Communion he is not wedded to the body, which will only be purified in the day of judgement. He leads me, he animates me, as though he were my soul and my life. He performs in a measure in my regard, what he did to (his) sacred humanity, leading me, stopping me, opening my lips, closing them, directing and regulating my sight—in a word, doing all for me. Willing that I should represent him in his adorable sacrament, he is not content thus to come into my heart to consume it in himself, but he dwells in me in order to produce in souls the effects of divine communions and diffuses himself thence in them as through a Host and a sacrament." —Faillon, *Vie de M. Olier* (Paris, 1873), II, 228.

BRO. LAWRENCE OF THE RESURRECTION

Practice of the Presence of God

A native of Lorraine, Brother Lawrence (born Nicolas Herman, 1611–1691) joined the Discalced Carmelites in Paris and spent most of his life as a cook. Despite his humble station, he was known and revered by many leading figures of the Church in France in an age which thrived on the study and practice of mystical prayer. He carried on significant correspondence as a spiritual director.

Many souls get stuck among systems and particular devotions and neglect that love which is their real end. This can be seen at once in their works, and is the reason why we see so little solid virtue. . . .

Bro. Lawrence said that he gave thought neither to death nor to his sins, neither to Heaven nor to Hell, but only to the doing of small things for the love of God—small things because he was incapable of big ones. He need trouble no further, for whatever came after would be according to God's will.

ST. FRANCIS DE SALES
Treatise on the Love of God

The bishop of Geneva and its surroundings, Francis de Sales (1567–1622) devoted his life to developing new approaches to religion that might inspire a rebirth of Catholic devotion and thus win back converts from the teachings of the Calvinist reformers. Ordained in 1593 after studying in Paris and Padua, Francis devoted his energies above all to writing and spiritual direction and to the foundation and direction (together with St. Jane Frances de Chantal) of the Order of the Visitation.

St. Francis de Sales is famous for two works on the spiritual life: The Introduction to the Devout Life *(1608), a treatise written above all for lay persons beginning a serious spiritual life; and the* Treatise on the Love of God *(1616), which develops a teaching on all stages of spirituality. The following selection is taken from Book IX of the* Treatise.

FROM CHAPTER IV

. . . The indifferent heart is as a ball of wax in the hands of its God, receiving with equal readiness all the impressions of the Divine pleasure; it is a heart without choice, equally disposed for everything, having no other object of its will than the will of its God, and placing its affection not upon the things that God wills, but upon the will of God who wills them. Wherefore, when God's will is in various things, it chooses, at any cost, that in which it appears most. God's will is found in marriage and in virginity, but because it is more in virginity, the indifferent heart makes choice of virginity though this cost it its life, as with S. Paul's dear spiritual daughter S. Thecla, with S. Cecily, S. Agatha, and a thousand others. God's will is found in the service of the poor and of the rich, but yet somewhat more in serving the poor; the indifferent heart will choose that side. God's will lies in moderation amid consolations, and in patience amid tribulations: the indifferent heart prefers the latter, as having more of God's will in it. To conclude, God's will is the sovereign object of the indifferent soul; wheresoever she sees it she runs after the odour of its perfumes, directing her course ever thither where it most appears, without considering anything else. She is conducted by the Divine will, as by a beloved chain; which way soever it goes, she follows it: she would prize hell more with God's will than heaven without it; nay she would even prefer hell before heaven if she perceived only a little more of God's good-pleasure in that than in this, so that if by supposition of an impossible thing she should know that her damnation would be more agreeable to God than salvation, she would quit her salvation and run to her damnation.

CHAPTER V

THAT HOLY INDIFFERENCE EXTENDS TO ALL THINGS

Indifference is to be practised in things belonging to the natural life, as in health, sickness, beauty, deformity, weakness, strength: in the affairs of the spiritual life, as in dryness, consolations, relish, aridity; in actions, in sufferings,—briefly, in all sorts of events. Job, in his natural life was struck with the most horrible sores that ever eye beheld, in his civil life he was scorned, reviled, contemned, and that by his nearest friends; in his spiritual life he was oppressed with languors, oppression, convulsions, anguish, darkness, and with all kinds of intolerable interior griefs, as his complaints and lamentations bear witness. The great Apostle proclaims to us a general Indifference; to show ourselves the true servants of God, *in much patience, in tribulation, in necessities, in distresses, in stripes, in prisons, in seditions, in labours, in watchings, in fastings, in chastity; in knowledge, in long-suffering, in sweetness, in the Holy Ghost, in charity unfeigned, in the word of truth, in the power of God; by the armour of justice on the right hand and on the left, through honour and dishonour, by evil report and good report: as deceivers, and yet true; as unknown and yet known; as dying, and behold we live; as chastised and not killed; as sorrow-*

ful, yet always rejoicing: as needy, yet enriching many; as having nothing, and possessing all things.[1]

Take notice, I pray you, Theotimus,[2] how the life of the Apostles was filled with afflictions: in the body by wounds, in the heart by anguish, according to the world by infamy and prisons, and in all these,—O God! what Indifference they had! Their sorrow is joyous, their poverty rich, their death life-giving, their dishonour honourable, that is, they are joyful for being sad, content to be poor, strengthened with life amid the dangers of death, and glorious in being made vile, because—such was the will of God. And whereas the will of God was more recognized in sufferings than in the actions of virtues, he ranks the exercise of patience first, saying: *But in all things let us exhibit ourselves as the ministers of God, in much patience, in tribulation, in necessities, in distresses:* and then, towards the end, *in chastity, in knowledge, in long-suffering.*

In like manner our divine Saviour was incomparably afflicted in his civil life, being condemned as guilty of treason against God and man; beaten, scourged, reviled, and tormented with extraordinary ignominy; in his natural life, dying in the most cruel and sensible torments that heart could conceive; in his spiritual life enduring sorrows, fears, terrors, anguish, abandonment, interior oppressions, such as never had, nor shall have, their like. For though the supreme portion of his soul did sovereignly enjoy eternal glory, yet love hindered this glory from spreading its delicious influence into the feelings, or the imagination, or the inferior reason, leaving thus his whole heart at the mercy of sorrow and distress.

Ezechiel saw the likeness of a hand, which took him by a single lock of the hairs of his head, lifting him up between heaven and earth;[3] in like manner our Saviour, lifted up on the cross between heaven and earth, seemed to be held in his Father's hand only by the very extremity of the spirit, and, as it were, by one hair of his head, which, touching the sweet hand of his eternal Father, received a sovereign affluence of felicity, all the rest being swallowed up in sorrow and grief: whereupon he cries out: *My God, why hast thou forsaken me?*

They say that the fish termed lantern-of-the-sea in the midst of the tempest thrusts out of the water her tongue, which is so luminous, resplendent and clear, that it serves as a light or beacon for mariners. So in the sea of passions by which Our Lord was overwhelmed, all the faculties of his soul were, so to say, swallowed up and buried in the whirlpool of so many pains, excepting only the

point of his spirit, which, exempt from all trouble, remained bright
and resplendent with glory and felicity. Oh how blessed is the love
which reigns in the heights of the spirit of faithful souls, while they
are tossed upon the billows and waves of interior tribulations!

CHAPTER VI

OF THE PRACTICE OF LOVING INDIFFERENCE, IN THINGS BELONGING TO THE SERVICE OF GOD.

The divine good-pleasure is scarcely known otherwise than by
events, and as long as it is unknown to us, we must keep as close as
possible to the will of God which is already declared or signified to
us: but as soon as the Divine Majesty's pleasure appears, we must
at once lovingly yield ourselves to its obedience.

My mother (or it would be the same of myself) is ill in bed: how
do I know whether God intends death to follow or not? Of course I
cannot know; but I know well that while awaiting the event from
his good-pleasure, he wills, by his declared will, that I use remedies
proper to effect a cure. But if it be the Divine pleasure that the
disease, victorious over the remedies, should at last bring death—
as soon as ever I am certain of this by the actual event, I will
amorously acquiesce, in the point of my spirit, in spite of all the
opposition of the inferior powers of my soul. Yes, Lord, I will say, it
is my will because thy good-pleasure is such; thus it has pleased
thee, and so it shall please me, who am the most humble servant of
thy will.

But if the Divine pleasure were declared to me before the event
took place, as was to the great S. Peter the manner of his death, to
the great S. Paul his chains and prisons, to Jeremias the destruction of his dear Jerusalem, to David the death of his son,—then we
should have at the same instant to unite our will to God's in
imitation of the great Abraham, and, like him, if we had such a
command, we should have to undertake the execution of the eternal decree even in the slaying of our children: Oh admirable union
of this patriarch's will to the will of God, when, believing that it
was the Divine pleasure that he should sacrifice his child, he willed
and undertook it so courageously! admirable that of the child, who
so meekly submitted himself to his father's sword, to have God's
good-pleasure performed at the price of his own death!

But note here, Theotimus, a mark of the perfect union of an
indifferent heart with the Divine pleasure. Behold Abraham with
the sword in his hand, his arm extended ready to give the death-

blow to his dear only son: he is doing this to please the Divine will; and see at the same time an angel, who, on the part of this same will, suddenly stops him, and immediately he holds his stroke, equally ready to sacrifice or not to sacrifice his son; whose life and whose death are indifferent to him in the presence of God's will. When God gives him an order to sacrifice his son he does not grow sad, when God dispenses with the order given he does not rejoice, all is one to this great heart, so that God's will be fulfilled.

Yes, Theotimus, for God ofentimes to exercise us in this holy Indifference, inspires us with very high designs, which yet he will not have accomplished, and as then we are boldly, courageously and constantly to commence and to pursue the work as far as we can, so are we sweetly and quietly to acquiesce in such result of our enterprise as it pleases God to send us. S. Louis by inspiration passed the sea to conquer the Holy Land; the event answered not his expectation, he sweetly acquiesces. I more esteeem the tranquillity of this submission than the magnanimity of his enterprise. S. Francis went into Egypt to convert the infidels, or amongst the infidels to die a martyr; such was the will of God: yet he returned without performing either, and that was also God's will. It was equally the will of God that S. Anthony of Padua desired martyrdom and that he obtained it not. Blessed (S.) Ignatius of Loyola having with such pains put on foot the Company of the name of Jesus, from which he saw so many fair fruits and foresaw many more in the time to come, had yet the nobility of soul to promise himself that though he should see it dissolved (which would be the bitterest pain that could befal him), within half an hour afterwards he would be stayed and tranquil in the will of God. John of Avila, that holy and learned preacher of Andalusia, having a design to form a company of reformed priests for the advancement of God's glory, and having already made good progress in the matter, as soon as he saw the Jesuits in the field, thinking they were enough for that time, immediately stopped his own undertaking, with an incomparable meekness and humility. Oh how blessed are such souls, bold and strong in the undertakings God proposes to them, and withal tractable and facile in giving them over when God so disposes! These are marks of a most perfect Indifference, to leave off doing a good when God pleases, and to return from half way when God's will, which is our guide, ordains it. Jonas was much to blame in being angry because God, as he considered, did not fulfil his prophecy upon Ninive. Jonas did God's will in announcing the destruction of Ninive; but he mingled his own interest and will

with that of God; whence, seeing that God did not fulfil his predic-
tion according to the rigour of the words he had used in announcing
it, he was offended and shamefully murmured. Whereas if God's
will had been the only motive of his actions, he would have been as
well content to have seen it accomplished in remission of the
penalty which Ninive had merited, as in punishment of the fault
which Ninive had committed. We desire that what we undertake or
manage should succeed, but it is not reasonable that God should do
all after our liking. If God wills Ninive to be threatened, and yet
not overthrown (since the threat is sufficient to correct it), why
should Jonas think himself aggrieved?

But if this be so, we are then to care for nothing, but abandon
our affairs to the mercy of events? Pardon me, Theotimus, we are to
omit nothing which is requisite to bring the work which God has
put into our hands to a happy issue, yet upon condition that, if the
event be contrary, we should lovingly and peaceably embrace it.
For we are commanded to have great care in what appertains to
God's glory and to our charge, but we are not bound to, or responsible for, the event, because it is not in our power. *Take care of him*,
was it said to the innkeeper, in the parable of the poor man who lay
half-dead between Jerusalem and Jericho. It is not said, as St.
Bernard remarks, cure him, but, *take care of him*. So the Apostles
with most earnest affection preached first to the Jews, though they
foresaw that in the end they would be forced to leave them as an
unfruitful soil, and betake themselves to the Gentiles. It is our part
to plant and water carefully, but to give increase—that belongs
only to God.

The great Psalmist makes this prayer to our Saviour as by an
exclamation of joy and with presage of victory: *O Lord in thy
comeliness and thy beauty, bend thy bow, proceed prosperously and
mount thy horse.*[4] As though he would say that by the arrows of his
heavenly love shot into human hearts, he made himself master of
men, and then handled them at his pleasure, not unlike to a horse
well trained. O Lord thou art the royal rider, who turnest the
hearts of thy faithful lovers every way about: sometimes thou
givest them the rein, and they run at full speed in the courses to
which thou impellest them: and then, when it seems good to thee,
thou makest them stop in the midst of their career and at the
height of their speed.

But further, if the enterprise begun by inspiration fail by the
fault of those to whom it was committed, how can it then be said
that a man is to acquiesce in God's will? For, some one will say to

me, it is not God's will that hinders the success, but my fault. This is not caused by God's will, for God is not author of sin; but yet for all that, it is God's will that your fault should be followed by the overthrow and failure of your design, in punishment of your fault; for though his goodness cannot permit him to will your fault, yet does his justice make him will the punishment you suffer for it. So God was not the cause that David offended, yet it was God that inflicted upon him the pain due to his sin. He was not the cause of Saul's sin, but he was the cause that in punishment of it the victory fell from his hands.

When therefore it happens that in punishment of our fault our holy designs have not good success, we must equally detest the fault by a solid repentance, and accept its punishment; for as the sin is against the will of God, so the punishment is according to his will.

CHAPTER VII

OF THE INDIFFERENCE WHICH WE ARE TO HAVE AS TO OUR ADVANCEMENT IN VIRTUES.

God has ordained that we should employ our whole endeavours to obtain holy virtues, let us then forget nothing which might help our good success in this pious enterprise. But after we have planted and watered, let us then know for certain that it is God who must give increase to the trees of our good inclinations and habits, and therefore from his Divine Providence we are to expect the fruits of our desires and labours, and if we find the progress and advancement of our hearts in devotion not such as we would desire, let us not be troubled, let us live in peace, let tranquillity always reign in our hearts. It belongs to us diligently to cultivate our heart, and therefore we must faithfully attend to it, but as for the plenty of the crop or harvest, let us leave the care thereof to our Lord and Master. The husbandman will never be reprehended for not having a good harvest, but only if he did not carefully till and sow his ground. Let us not be troubled at finding ourselves always novices in the exercise of virtues, for in the monastery of a devout life every one considers himself always a novice, and there the whole of life is meant as a probation; the most evident argument, not only that we are novices, but also that we are worthy of expulsion and reprobation, being, to esteem and hold ourselves professed. For according to the rule of this Order not the solemnity but the accomplishment of the vows makes the novices professed, nor are the vows ever fulfilled while there remains yet something to be done for their observance, and the obligation of serving God and making progress in his love lasts always until death. But after all, will some one say, if I know that it is by my own fault my progress in virtue is so slow, how can I help being grieved and disquieted? I have said this in the *Introduction to a Devout Life*, but I willingly say it again, because it can never be said sufficiently. We must be sorry for faults with a repentance which is strong, settled, constant, tranquil, but not troubled, unquiet or fainthearted. Are you sure that your backwardness in virtue has come from your fault? Well then, humble yourself before God, implore his mercy, fall prostrate before the face of his goodness and demand pardon, confess your fault, cry him mercy in the very ear of your confessor, so as to obtain absolution; but this being done remain in peace, and having detested the offence, embrace lovingly the abjection which you feel in yourself by reason of delaying your advancement in good.

Ah! my Theotimus, the souls in Purgatory are there doubtless for their sins, and for sins which they have detested and do supremely detest, but as for the abjection and pain which remain from being detained in that place, and from being deprived for a space of the enjoyment of the blessed love which is in Paradise, they endure this lovingly, and they devoutly pronounce the canticle of the Divine justice: *Thou art just, O Lord, and thy judgment is right.* [5] Let us therefore await our advancement with patience, and instead of disquieting ourselves because we have so little profited in the time past, let us diligently endeavour to do better in the time to come.

Behold, I beseech you, this good soul. She has greatly desired and endeavoured to throw off the slavery of anger; and God has assisted her, for he has quite delivered her from all the sins which proceed from anger. She would die rather than utter a single injurious word, or let any sign of hatred escape her, and yet she is subject to the assaults and first motions of this passion, that is, to certain startings, strong movements and sallies of an angry heart, which the Chaldaic paraphrase calls stirrings, saying: Be stirred and sin not;—where our sacred version says: *Be angry and sin not.* [6] In effect it is the same thing, for the prophet would only say that if anger surprise us, exciting in our hearts the first stirrings of sin, we should be careful not to let ourselves be carried further into this passion, for so we should offend. Now, although these first movements and stirrings be no sin, yet the poor soul that is often attacked by them, troubles, afflicts and disquiets herself, and thinks she does well in being sad, as if it were the love of God that provoked her to this sadness. And yet, Theotimus, it is not heavenly love that causes this trouble, for that is never offended except by sin; it is our self-love that desires to be exempt from the pains and toils which the assaults of anger draw on us. It is not the offence that displeases us in these stirrings of anger, there being none at all committed, it is the pain we are put to in resisting which disquiets us.

These rebellions of the sensual appetite, as well in anger as in concupiscence, are left in us for our exercise, to the end that we may practise spiritual valour in resisting them. This is that Philistine, whom the true Israelites are ever to fight against but never to put down; they may weaken him, but never annihilate him. He only dies with us, and always lives with us. He is truly accursed, and detestable, as springing from sin, and tending towards sin: wherefore, as we are termed earth, because we are formed of earth and shall return to earth, so this rebellion is named sin by the great Apostle, as having sprung from sin and tending to sin, though it never makes us guilty unless we second and obey it. Whereupon he exhorts us *that we permit it not to reign in our mortal body to obey the concupiscence thereof*.[7] He prohibits not the sentiment of sin, but the consenting to it. He does not order us to hinder sin from coming into us and being in us, but he commands that it should not reign in us. It is in us when we feel the rebellion of the sensual appetite, but it does not reign in us unless we give consent unto it. The physician will never order his feverish patient not to be athirst, for that would be too great a folly; but he will tell him that though he be thirsty he must abstain from drinking. No one will tell a woman with child not to have a longing for extravagant things, for this is not under her control, but she may well be told to discover her longings, to the end that if she longs for hurtful things one may divert her imagination, and not let such a fancy get a hold on her brain.

The *sting of the flesh, an angel of Satan*, roughly attacked the great S. Paul, in order to make him fall into sin. The poor Apostle endured this as a shameful and infamous wrong, and on this account called it a buffeting and ignominious treatment, and petitioned God to deliver him from it, but God answered him: *Paul, my grace is sufficient for thee, for virtue is made perfect in infirmity*.[8] Thereupon this great holy man said in acquiescence:—*Gladly will I glory in my infirmities that the power of Christ may dwell in me*.

But take notice, I beseech you, that there is sensual rebellion even in this admirable vessel of election, who in running to the remedy of prayer teaches us that we are to use the same arms against the temptations we feel. Note further that Our Lord does not always permit these terrible revolts in man for the punishment of sin, but to manifest the strength and virtue of the Divine assistance and grace. Finally, note that we are not only not to be disquieted in our temptations and infirmities, but we are even *to glory in our infirmity that thereby God's virtue may appear in us*, sustaining our weakness against the force of the suggestion and temptation: for the glorious Apostle calls the stings and attacks of impurity which he endured his *infirmities*, and says that he glories in them, because, though he had the sense of them by his misery, yet through God's mercy he did not give consent to them.

Indeed, as I have said above, the church condemned the error of certain solitaries, who held that we might be perfectly delivered even in this world from the passions of anger, concupiscence, fear, and the like. God wills us to have enemies, and it is also his will that we should repulse them. Let us then behave ourselves courageously between the one and the other will of God, enduring with patience to be assaulted, and endeavouring with courage by resistance to make head against and resist our assailants.

ANGELUS SILESIUS

The Cherubic Wanderer

A native of Breslau, Johann Scheffler (1624–1677) published his poems under the pen name of "Angelus Silesius" ("The Silesian Angel"). After studying medicine and philosophy at Strasbourg, Leyden and Padua, Scheffler served as a court physician and fell under the influence of the great contemporary Lutheran mystic, Jakob Boehme. After an intense period of theological study, Scheffler converted to Catholicism in 1653 and was ordained a priest in 1661.

Scheffler published volumes of controversial theology in an attempt to vindicate Roman Catholicism against German Protestants, but much of the piety of his early Lutheran education shows through in his poetry. His poems on the spiritual life reveal a range

*of intense mystical experience similar in many ways to the spiritu-
ality described by the fourteenth-century Rhineland mystics. He
shares with them a love for paradox and a sometimes audacious,
questionably orthodox sense of oneness with God. The following
selections are taken from* Der cherubinische Wandersmann *("The
Cherubic Wanderer," 1674), a collection of rhyming epigrams. The
translation attempts to convey the startling turns of Scheffler's
thought and something of his poetic style.*

God blooms in his branches
If thou art born of God, then God doth bloom in thee;
Thy sap and foliage fine is his divinity.

Godhead a-greening
The Godhead is my sap: what greens and blooms of me,
That is his Holy Ghost, who moves my energy.

A Sign Unto God
A mighty stream is God, he swallows mind and sense;
Ah, that I were—not yet—drowned in his flood immense!

The Brook becomes the sea
Here still I flow to God, a brook in time's abyss;
There I will be the sea of everlasting bliss.

God does not live without me
I know that without me God cannot live a moment:
If I return to naught, he too gives up the ghost!

God can do nothing without me
Without me God can't make a single, paltry worm;
If I preserve it not with him, it must straightway dissolve!

I have it from God and God from me
I am as great as God, He is as small as I;
He can't be over me, beneath him I can't be.

A Christian is God's son
I too am God's own Son, I sit at his right hand;
He knows in me his soul, his very flesh and blood.

God works like fire
As fire doth melt and join, so if you find your source,
Your spirit must with God be melted into one.

Spiritual alchemy
Lead will turn into gold, the marvel then performed—
When with God and through God to God I am transformed.

God has no will
We pray: Thy Will be done, my Master and my God—
But look: he has no will—he is eternal silence!

The wandering tent of God
The soul in whom God dwells—it is (O blest delight!)
A wandering, flowing tent of glory's endless light.

We know God through the sun
The sun is but a ray, and all its light a beam;
A thunderbolt—how bright!—my God and Sun must gleam!

You yourself must be the sun
I must become the sun, and with my rays portray
The pallid, darkling sea of Godhead's blinding day.

To be born of God is to be wholly God
God begets but God; if he makes thee his Son,
Then thou art God in God, Lord on the Lord's own throne.

God becomes me, for I was before him
Becoming what I am, God takes humanity;
I was before he was; and so, he follows me!

The Spiritual birth
The Spirit of the Lord comes touching you himself,
So there is born in you eternity's own child.

Only you are lacking
Ah, if my heart could be naught but a crib for him,
Our God would come anew, a child on earth again!

Through Manhood to Godhead
Would you catch for yourself the pearly dew divine?
Then must you, calm and still, hold to his manhood fine.

What is manhood?
Ask you what manhood is? I'll tell you right away:
In a word, it is a more-than-angelhood!

Love draws to the beloved
My love, it draws me on. 'Tis true that we love God?
Then we are pulled by love, all forward into God!

God is our target
What God does to himself! He is my heart's true aim—
I shoot always at him; I hit him if I will!

What the saint does, God does in him
God himself does all that we in saints behold—
Walks, stands, lies, sleeps, wakes, eats, drinks, is bold.

To God all works are the same
To God all works are one: when saints but take a drink,
It pleases God as well as when they pray and sing.

God's lute
A heart that in its depths is silent unto God
Follows his touch and will—it is his well-loved lute.

God's echo
My love and every thing is but God's echoing
When he hears me cry out: My Lord, my God, my all!

All is imaged after God
God is from days of old the imager of all:
He is the form itself, so nothing is too small.

Everything is perfect
Naught is imperfect, man; the pebble's good as pearls;
A frog is quite as fair as Angel Seraphim!

The Rose
The rose which here below thy outer eye doth see
Hath bloomed full fresh in God from all eternity.

No reason why
A rose is but a rose, it blooms because it blooms;
It thinks not on itself, nor asks if it is seen.

Little is needed for blessedness
But little do you need for endless blessedness—
Only a whisp will help: it's called Abandonment.

The Most Mysterious abandonment
Abandon all, and then you will dwell close to God.
But then, abandon God—few men can grasp this step!

Contemplation
Be pure, still, learn to yield, and climb to darkest heights:
Then you will come o'er all to contemplate your God.

You must be what God is
If I would find my End, and see my earliest Source,
Then must I ground myself in God and God in me,
Become what he is: Light from Light must I then be,
A Word in Word, A God in God, that must I also be!

To be united with God is good for endless pain
He who is joined to God can never be condemned—
For God himself would jump with him to death and flames.

God denies himself to no one
Take, drink as much as you want and can, to you 'tis free—
The whole Divinity is your own hostelry!

Body, soul, and Godhead
A crystal is the soul, divinity its gleam:
The body where you dwell is cupboard for them both.

Conclusion
Friend, now you've heard enough; in case you more would read,
Go and become yourself the Book, yourself the Deed.

JEAN-PIERRE DE CAUSSADE

Abandonment to Divine Providence

A French Jesuit (1675–1751), Caussade spent his life as teacher, preacher, confessor, and spiritual director in many parts of France. His work on Abandonment to Divine Providence *is a compilation of spiritual advice written to the nuns of the Visitation Convent in Nancy from 1729 until his death.*

What God arranges for us to experience at each moment is the best and holiest thing that could happen to us.

Part VI Notes

St. Teresa of Avila

Life

Chapter XI
1. [*Honra.* This is an example of the use of the word to denote something reprehensible in nuns: elsewhere she adjures her sisters to think (in another sense) of their own *honra*, or reputation.]
2. [*Lit.:* "hardly have they touched us in a point of honour." Cf. the use of "punto de honra" or "pundonor" in Spanish drama.]
3. "P. Pedro Ibáñez", observes a manuscript note to a copy of the first edition of St. Teresa's works.
4. The reference is to the twenty-second epistle of St. Jerome "Ad Eustochium", which describes how vividly there would come to him in the desert pictures of the pomps and vanities of pagan Rome.
5. [The metaphors here follow the Spanish exactly.]
6. [*Lit.:* "is growing fat and taking strength." Fatness is often spoken of in Spain as synonymous with robustness and made a subject of congratulation.]

Chapter XXIX
1. The most probable date of Teresa's first imaginary vision is January 25, 1560; we may therefore date the writing of this chapter about the summer of 1565.
2. *Dar higas*—i.e., make a sign of contempt.
3. This phrase would seem to indicate that the first vision was on June 29 (or possibly on June 30: the Commemoration of St. Paul) and not on January 25. If this deduction and my dating of the year as 1560 are both correct, this part of the book was not written until the very end of 1565.

4. This cross was later given by St. Teresa's sister Juana to Doña María Enríquez de Toledo, Duchess of Alba. After the Duchess's death the Carmelites claimed possession of it and until the end of the eighteenth century it was preserved in their Valladolid convent. It was lost during the religious persecution of 1835.

5. Psalm 42:1: "As the hart panteth after the fountains of water, so my soul panteth after thee, O God."

6. [*Lit.:* "too low for so high an ill."]

7. St. Teresa wrote "Cherubims", but P. Báñez added the marginal note: "it seems more like those which are called Seraphims", and Fray Luis de León, in his edition, adopted this form.

8. Carmelite tradition has it that St. Teresa received the same favour again while Prioress of the Incarnation, between 1571 and 1574. On May 25, 1726, Pope Benedict XIII appointed a festival and office for the Transverberation, which is observed on August 27. First instituted for the Discalced Carmelites, it was extended to Spain as a whole by Clement XII on December 11, 1733.

Interior Castle (First Mansion)
Chapter I

1. [*Aposentos*—a rather more pretentious word than the English "room": dwelling-place, abode, apartment.]

2. [*Moradas:* derived from *morar*, to dwell, and not, therefore, absolutely identical in sense with "mansions". The reference, however, is to St. John xiv, 2.]

3. Proverbs viii, 31.

4. Genesis i, 26.

5. Here the Saint erased several words and inserted others, leaving the phrase as it is in the text.

6. *Moradas* (see note 2).

7. St. John ix, 2.

8. Genesis xix, 26.

9. *Lit.*, "into such bestiality".

10. P. Gracián, one of Teresa's editors, corrects this to "thirty-eight years." St. John v, 5.

11. St. Matthew vi, 21.

Chapter II

1. "Mustard-seeds," writes Gracián, an editor, interlineally, deleting the bracketed sentence which follows and adding the words: "It is so, for I have seen it."

2. Colossians iii, 3. Gracián deletes "for that . . . my purpose" and supplies text and source in the margin.

3. [*Lit.:* "Whether this be so or not." But the meaning is clear from the context.]

4. The words "I meant . . . at all" are omitted from the *editio princeps.*

5. A characteristically emphatic phrase—*en fin, fin.*

6. The reference here is clearly to Canticles ii, 4.

7. St. Luke xxii, 15.

8. St. Teresa herself.

St. Francis de Sales

    1. 2 Cor. vi. 4–10.

    2. "God-fearing One" (St. Francis' name for the fervent person to whom the treatise is addressed).

    3. Ezech. viii. 3.

    4. Ps. xliv. 6.

    5. Ps. cxviii. 137.

    6. Ps. iv. 5.

    7. Rom. vi. 12.

    8. 2 Cor. xii. 9.

Part VII

SPIRITUALITY OF THE PAST HUNDRED YEARS

Our Lord repeated a teaching which He had traced for me in outline yesterday. It is this: that although, in order to adore God, I make use of that knowledge which He gives me of Himself in prayer, I ought to adore the unknown in Him more than the known, and consider the lights He gives me concerning Himself as so many perceptions of, and glances into, the Divinity. "Beyond what thou knowest," Jesus said to me interiorly, "there is the *Unknown* which is infinite."
Lucie Christine, 1844–1908

CHARLES DE FOUCAULD

Writings from Nazareth (1897—1900)

Most spiritual writers from the seventeenth to the nineteenth centuries were quite derivative, drawing their doctrines almost entirely from Counter-Reformation currents. Jesuit spirituality, the Carmelite tradition, and the ideas of the French School were combined in various ways by all the major figures of this period.

A new note is sounded by Charles de Foucauld (1858–1916), a French army officer who became a convert to Catholicism in 1886 and devoted the rest of his life to as literal as possible an imitation of Christ, particularly the Christ of the "hidden life" of Nazareth. De Foucauld combines the qualities of contemplative and apostle, individualist and "universal brother," founder and eccentric, poor man and world traveler. Although he longed all his life to found a new form of religious life characterized by contemplation, extreme poverty, and an apostolate of "witness" among non-Christian peoples, he never succeeded in attracting any followers. It was only after his death and the publication of his life that new groups (the Little Brothers and Little Sisters of Jesus) sprung up in imitation of him.

The key themes of De Foucauld's spirituality are quite traditional: abandonment, christocentrism, repentance, devotion to the Eucharist, and asceticism. What is new is the radical way in which he attempted to live out all these Christian realities among the Moslem nomads of the Sahara.

The following writings are drawn from de Foucauld's notes taken during retreats and meditations.

Your vocation: Preach the Gospel silently as I did in my hidden life, and as also did Mary and Joseph.

Your rule: Follow me. Do what I did. In every situation ask yourself: What would our Lord have done? Then do that. That is your only rule, but it is absolutely binding on you.

Your mind: It should be full of love of God, forgetful of yourself. It should be full of the contemplation and joy of my beatitude, of compassion and sorrow for my sufferings, and of joy at my joys. It should be full of suffering for the sins committed against me and an ardent longing to glorify me. It should be a mind full of love for your neighbor for my sake, for I love all men as a father loves his children. It should be full of longing for the spiritual and material good of all men for my sake. It should be a mind free, tranquil, at peace. Everything in it should be there for God's sake alone; nothing for your own sake, or for the sake of any creature.

Your interior prayer: First method: 1. What do you want to say to me, O God? 2. For my own part, this is what I want to tell you—3. Saying nothing else, gaze on the Beloved.—Second Method: *Quis? Quid? Ubi? Quibus auxiliis? Cur? Quomodo? Quando?* [Who? What? Where? With what help? Why? How? When?]

Attendance at Mass: Divide it into three parts: 1. Up to the consecration: offer me and offer yourself to my Father and bring your intentions before him. Give thanks to me for my cross, asking my forgiveness for having made it necessary. 2. From the consecration to the Communion: adore me on the altar. 3. After the Communion: adore me in your heart, give thanks to me, love me, rejoice, be silent.

Thinking about death: Remember that you ought to die as a martyr, stripped of everything, stretched naked on the ground, unrecognizable, covered with wounds and blood, killed violently and painfully—and desire that it be today. That I may grant you this infinite grace, watch loyally, carry your cross faithfully. Remember that your death must inevitably flow out of your life—and on that account, realize the insignificance of a great many things. Think often of death, so as to prepare for it and appraise things at their true value. . . .

THE SUFFERINGS OF JESUS

You want me to meditate on your passion, my God. Inspire my thoughts yourself, for such images always leave me powerless.

The passion—what memories! The knocks and blows from the high priests' servants: "Prophesy . . . who is he that struck thee?"

Silence before Herod and Pilate; the scourging; crowning with thorns; the way of the cross; the crucifying; the cross. "Father, into thy hands I commend my spirit." What visions, O God, what images! And if I love you, then *what tears!* What *remorse* when I remember it was to make fitting expiation for my sins that you suffered so. How deeply I am moved when I remember that you faced these torments, even willed them, to prove your love for me, to proclaim it down the centuries. O the remorse I feel for having loved you so little! The remorse of having done so little penance for the sins for which you performed such a penance as this. How greatly I long to love you at last, in my turn, and prove my love to you in every possible way.

What ways are there, O God, how I can love you? How can I tell you I love you? "He who loves me is he who keeps my commandments . . . Greater love than this no man hath, that a man lay down his life for his friends." To fulfill your commandments (*mandata*) is to fulfill not only your orders but also your counsels, to follow your least piece of advice, follow your example in the smallest things. One of your most important counsels was that we should imitate you: "Follow me . . . they that follow me walk no longer in darkness . . . I have given you an example that as I have done to you, so you do also . . . It is enough for the disciple that he be as his master." While we live, we must follow as accurately as possible all the instructions and examples you gave; then we must die for your Name: that is how we can love you and prove to you that we love you—it is the way you yourself described for us in the Gospel, O God.

Love, O God, asks yet one more thing, and the Gospel also tells me of it, not by words, but by the example of the Blessed Virgin and St. Mary Magdalene at the foot of the cross: *Stabat Mater.* Compassion, weeping for your sufferings, is indeed also a grace: faced with the spectacle of your cross, I cannot by my own power draw cries of grief from my stony heart, for, alas, it has become terribly hard! But at least I can ask you for compassion: I owe it to you, but if I am to be able to give it to you, I must first ask you for it. I have to ask you for everything I owe you.

My God, from the depths of your mercy, from the treasury of your mystical and infinite goodness, you have given me the great grace of living under that sky and in that land where you lived, of walking over the very ground you walked over—and, alas, watered with your tears, sweat and blood. Do not leave me tearless as I visit the places that witnessed your sufferings; do not leave me tearless when I kiss the path your footsteps trod in Gethsemane, along the Way of Sorrows, to the pretorium and Cavalry. Give me a heart of flesh in place of my heart of stone, and because you have given me this inexpressible grace, let me kiss this most holy soil, let me kiss it with my heart and my soul, and with the tears you want me to have, the tears I ought to have, O my Lord, my King, my Master, my Beloved, my Saviour, my God!

I resolve: To ask for martyrdom, long for it, and if it pleases God, suffer it in order to love Jesus with a greater love;

To have zeal for souls, a burning love for the salvation of souls—which have all been ransomed at so unique a price;

To despise no one, but to desire the greatest good for everyone, because everyone is covered by the blood of Jesus as though by a cloak;

To do what I can for the salvation of souls, in whatever way my situation allows, because they all cost Jesus so much and were all—and still are—so greatly loved by him;

To be perfect, to be holy myself, for Jesus held me so dear that he gave his love for me;

To have a great longing for perfection, to believe that when my confessor orders me to do some particular thing, I can do anything, for everything is possible to God's glory. How could God refuse me just one grace when he has already given all his blood for me?

To have an infinite horror of sin and the imperfection that leads to it, because it has already cost Jesus so dear;

To suffer when I see others sin and God offended, because sin is so horrible to him that he chose to expiate it by such torments;

To have absolute trust in the love of God, an inextinguishable faith in his love, because he has proved it to me by being willing to suffer such pains for me;

To be humble at the thought of all he has done for me, and the little I have done for him;

To long for sufferings to give him love for love, and imitate him, and not be crowned with roses whereas he was crowned with thorns, to expiate the sins of mine he has already expiated with such suffering, to share in his work, offering myself with him in sacrifice—though I am nothing—as a victim for the sanctification of men.

"Stay you here and watch with me."
Matt. 26:38

Was our Lord saying these words only to his apostles? No, he was speaking to us all, all those he loves, all those he was thinking about during his agony—all of us whose loyal and loving company is consolation to him in these painful moments. Let us then be loyal to the practice of "watching" with him every Thursday evening, keeping him company, supporting him, consoling him, being with him wholeheartedly in his agony. The Thursday evening vigil with our Lord in agony should be one of the practices to which we are faithful throughout our lives. For love of our Lord's Heart we should never fail to be there. He is asking it of us formally in these words addressed to his apostles. Can we fail him?

"And being in an agony,
he prayed the longer."
Luke 22:43

O God, I beseech you, let us follow your example. The more we suffer and the more we are tempted, the more we should pray. In prayer is our only help, our only strength, our only consolation. We pray that the pain and power of temptation will not paralyze our prayer. The devil puts forth all his strength to stop it at such times. But far from yielding to this temptation, far from yielding to the natural weakness that would like to see the soul absorbed in its pain and conscious of nothing else, we must look for our Saviour who is there, close to us, and we must talk with him. He is before us, looking lovingly upon us, straining to hear us, telling us to speak to him, telling us that he is there, that he loves us. And we have no word for him, not a glance to give him. How unworthy! Let us gaze on him, talk to him constantly, as one does when one is in love, as our Lord is doing now to his Father. The deeper into agony we fall, the more necessary it is for us to throw ourselves into the embrace of our Beloved, pressing ourselves against him in uninterrupted prayer. O God, give me this grace—the grace to follow your example by fulfilling so compelling and sweet a duty.

"Father, into thy hands
I commend my spirit."
Luke 23:46

This was the last prayer of our Master, our Beloved. May it also be ours. And may it be not only that of our last moment, but also of our every moment. "Father, I put myself in your hands; Father, I abandon myself to you, I entrust myself to you. Father, do with me as it pleases you. Whatever you do with me, I will thank you for it. Giving thanks for anything, I am ready for anything, I accept anything, give thanks for anything. As long as your will, my God, is done in me, as long as your will is done in all your creatures, in all your children, in all those your heart loves, I ask for nothing else, O God. I put my soul into your hands. I give it to you, O God, with all the love of my heart, because I love you, and because my love requires me to give myself. I put myself unreservedly in your hands. I put myself in your hands with infinite confidence, because you are my Father."

> *"It is consummated."*
> John 19:30

These are our Lord's last words to his Father cited in St. John. "I have done all you gave me to do." My God, may these words also be ours at our last hour—though they will not then have the same meaning and the same perfection. We are only worthless human beings; but granted our wretchedness, may they at least be ours as far as they can be.

What must I do if they are to be, O God? I must ask you what it is you have given me to do, and I must ask you—from whom alone strength comes—to do it. I beseech you, my Lord and my God, to let me see clearly what your will for me is. Then give me the strength to do it, fulfilling it loyally till the end, in thanksgiving and love.

THE RESURRECTION AND ASCENSION

You are rising from the dead and going up into heaven. You are there, in your glory. You are suffering no longer, you will never suffer again. You are in bliss, and will be eternally. O God, loving you, how happy I ought to be! If what I care about above all things is your good, how I ought to rejoice, how pleased and delighted I ought to be! You, my God, are in bliss for all eternity: you lack nothing; you are infinitely and eternally happy.

But I too am happy, my God, for I love you above all things. Because you are in bliss, I too can say I lack nothing, I am in heaven, I am blessed whatever happens, whatever may befall me.

A resolve: When we are unhappy, in despair over ourselves, or other people, or things, we must remember that Jesus is in glory, sitting at the right hand of the Father, blessed forever. And we must remember, too, that if we love him as we ought, the beatitude of the infinite being will be acting continually in our souls on the unhappiness there—unhappiness originating in a finite being. Therefore our souls ought to be full of joy at the beatitude of our God, and the troubles that oppress them should vanish like clouds before the sun: for our God is in bliss. We should rejoice unceasingly, for the evils suffered by creatures are minute beside the Creator's bliss.

There will always be unhappiness in our lives, and it is right that there should be: unhappiness for the sake of the love we bear—and rightly bear—ourselves and all men, and for the sake, too, of the love we bear Jesus, and in memory of his sufferings. Then there will be the unhappiness caused by the longing we cannot but have for justice—that is, for the glory of God—and the pain we are bound to undergo when we see injustice, and God being insulted.

But right as these sufferings are, they should not last long in our souls. They should be transitory. What should endure and be *our normal state—the state to which we should constantly return— is joy in the glory of God*, joy at seeing that Jesus is suffering no longer, and will suffer no more, but is in bliss forever at the right hand of God.

JESUS IN THE HOLY EUCHARIST

Lord Jesus, you are in the Holy Eucharist. You are there, a yard away in the tabernacle. Your body, your soul, your human nature, your divinity, your whole being is there, in its twofold nature. How close you are, my God, my Saviour, my Jesus, my Brother, my Spouse, my Beloved!

You were not nearer to the Blessed Virgin during the nine months she carried you in her womb than you are to me when you rest on my tongue at Holy Communion. You were no closer to the Blessed Virgin and St. Joseph in the caves at Bethlehem or the house at Nazareth or during the flight into Egypt, or at any moment of that divine family life than you are to me at this moment—and so many others—in the tabernacle. St. Mary Magdalene was no closer to you when she sat at your feet at Bethany than I am here at the foot of this altar. You were no nearer to your apostles when you were sitting in the midst of them than you are to me now, my God. How blessed I am!

It is wonderful, my Lord, to be alone in my cell and converse there with you in the silence of the night—and you are there as God, and by your grace. But to stay in my cell when I could be before the Blessed Sacrament—why, it would be as though St. Mary Magdalene had left you on your own when you were at Bethany to go and think about you alone in her room! It is a precious and devout thing, O God, to go and kiss the places you made holy during your life on earth—the stones of Gethsemane and Calvary, the ground along the Way of Sorrows, the waves of the sea of Galilee—but to prefer it to your tabernacle would be to desert the Jesus living beside me, to leave him alone, going away alone to venerate the dead stones in places where he is no longer. It would be to leave the room he is in—and with it his divine companionship—to go to kiss the floor of a room he was in, but is in no longer. To leave the tabernacle to go and venerate statues would be to leave the Jesus living at my side to go into another room to greet his portrait.

Is it not true that someone in love feels that he has made perfect use of all the time he spends in the presence of his beloved? Apart from then, is not that time used best which is employed in doing the will or furthering the welfare of his beloved in some other place?

Wherever the sacred Host is to be found, there is the living God, there is your Saviour, as really as when he was living and talking in Galilee and Judea, as really as he now is in heaven. Never deliberately miss Holy Communion. Communion is more than life, more than all the good things of this world, more than the whole universe: it is God himself, it is I, Jesus. Could you prefer anything to me? Could you, if you love me at all, however little, voluntarily lose the grace I give you in this way? Love me in all the breadth and simplicity of your heart.

A LETTER FROM THE SAHARA

On June 9, 1908, Father de Foucauld wrote to the Abbé Caron, one of his friends:

The corner of the Sahara where I am digging alone extends 1250 miles from north to south, and 625 miles from east to west. There are 100,000 Moslems in the area, and not a single Christian, apart from French soldiers of all ranks. And there are not many of these: eighty or a hundred scattered over the whole expanse, for in the Saharan squadrons only the officers are French, the soldiers being natives. In the seven years I have been here I have not made a single real conversion. Two baptisms—but God knows what the souls baptized are now and will be in the future. One was a small child who is being brought up by the White Fathers—and God knows how he will turn out. The other is a poor, blind old woman; what goes on in her poor head and how far is her conversion real? Its value in serious terms is nothing. And I can add something sadder still: the longer I go on, the more I come to believe that it is no use at the moment to try to make individual converts (except in special cases), for the level of the mass of the people is too low, their attachment to the faith of Islam is too strong, and the intellectual state of the inhabitants makes it very difficult at the moment for them to recognize the falseness of their religion and the truth of ours.

Except in exceptional cases anyone seeking to bring about individual conversions today would have that worst of all things: conversions that are self-interested and assumed. These Moslems, who are semi-barbarians, must be approached in a different way from the idolators and fetishists, a completely savage people, barbarians whose religion is wholly inferior. Then again, one needs another approach to the civilized inhabitants. It is possible to set the Catholic faith before the civilized inhabitants directly: they are equipped to understand grounds of credibility and to recognize their truth. One can do the same with the completely barbaric, because their superstitions are so inferior that they are easily made to realize the superiority of the religion of the one God. It seems that with the Moslems the right way would be to civilize them first, to educate them, making them into people like us; when that has been done, their conversion will almost have been accomplished too, for Mohammedanism cannot stand up in the face of education—history and philosophy expose its errors, and it falls like night before day.

Thus the work to be done here, as among all Moslems, is one of moral uplift: raising them morally and intellectually by all possible means, coming close to them, having contact with them, tying the bonds of friendship with them, breaking down their prejudices against us through daily friendly relations, and changing their ideas by the manner and example of our lives. Then we must concern ourselves with this real education—in a word, we must educate them completely. By means of schools and colleges, we must teach them the things taught in schools and colleges, and through daily and close contact with them we must instruct them in the things one learns through one's family—we must become their family.

When this objective has been gained, their ideas will be completely changed, and at the same time their customs will have improved. It will then be easy to bring them to the Gospel. God could, of course, do all this. If it were his will, he could convert the Moslems by his grace in a moment; but up till now it has not been his will. It would even seem that it is not in accordance with his designs to convert them through holiness alone, for if holiness alone were needed, how was it that it was not granted to St. Francis of Assisi to convert them?

All that remains therefore is to make use of what seem to be the most reasonable means, while making oneself as holy as one can and remembering that one does good insofar as one *is* good. The slow and unrewarding means at our disposal for use among a people who reject us, calling us "savages" and "heathen" and who are so far from us in language and customs and so many other ways—our slow and unrewarding means are education through contact and instruction. Above all, we must not be discouraged by difficulties, but must remind ourselves that the more difficult a work is, the slower and more unrewarding it is, the more necessary it is to set to work with great dispatch and make great efforts. We should always keep in mind that saying of St. John of the Cross: "We should not measure our labors by our weakness, but our efforts by our tasks."

But faced with this task, what should one person alone do?

By vocation, I ought to be living a hidden life in solitude, not talking and traveling. On the other hand, some traveling is required of me by the needs of the souls in these lands where I am alone—so long as there are no other workers here. I am trying to reconcile these two things. I have two hermitages a thousand miles apart. Every year I spend three months in the northern one, six months in the southern one and three months coming and going. When I am at one of the hermitages, I live there as an enclosed monk, trying to build for myself a life of work and prayer—the life of Nazareth. On my journeys, I think of the flight into Egypt and the annual journeys of the holy family to Jerusalem. Both at my hermitages and when traveling, I try to make contact as much as possible with the native peoples.

GERARD MANLEY HOPKINS
"God's Grandeur"

Famed as an English poet, Gerard Manley Hopkins (1844-1889) was converted to Catholicism at the age of twenty-two, and baptized by John Henry Newman. In 1868 he entered the Society of Jesus and was ordained in 1877. Although his poetic output was small it enabled him to attain and express an unmatched, universal, and all encompassing vision of God and creation which more prolific poets cannot.

And for all this, nature is never spent;
   There lives the dearest freshness deep down things;
And though the last flights off the black West went
   Oh, morning, at the brown brink eastward, springs—
Because the Holy Ghost over the bent
   World broods with warm breast and with ah! bright wings.

ST. THÉRÈSE OF LISIEUX
Story of a Soul

Thérèse Martin (1873–1897) was born of an intensely pious bourgeois French family and grew up in the small provincial cities of Alençon and Lisieux.

Remarkable from her early childhood for the intensity of her imagination and the power of her relationship with God, Thérèse was admitted to the Carmel of Lisieux at the age of fifteen, after a long series of petitions for admission that eventually reached even Pope Leo XIII. Within the Carmelite convent, Thérèse led a simple but very intense spiritual life recorded in the reminiscences, man-

*ifestations of conscience, and letters that were later gathered to-
gether to form a complete picture of her spirituality. It was only after
her death from tuberculosis at the age of twenty-four that she became known throughout the Christian world. Her "little way" of
purity of heart, abandonment, and love has exerted an enormous
influence, particularly during the first half of the twentieth century.*

Jesus†   J.M.J.T.   January 1895

SPRINGTIME STORY
OF A LITTLE WHITE FLOWER
WRITTEN BY HERSELF AND DEDICATED
TO THE REVEREND MOTHER AGNES OF JESUS

It is to you, dear Mother, to you who are doubly my Mother,
that I come to confide the story of my soul. The day you asked me to
do this, it seemed to me it would distract my heart by too much
concentration on myself, but since then Jesus has made me feel
that in obeying simply, I would be pleasing Him; besides, I'm going
to be doing only one thing: I shall begin to sing what I must sing
eternally: *"The Mercies of the Lord."*[1]

Before taking up my pen, I knelt before the statue of Mary[2]
(the one which has given so many proofs of the maternal preferences of heaven's Queen for our family), and I begged her to guide
my hand that it trace no line displeasing to her. Then opening the
Holy Gospels my eyes fell upon these words: "And going up a
mountain, he called to him men of his own choosing, and they came
to him." (St. Mark, chap. III, v. 13) This is the mystery of my
vocation, my whole life, and especially the mystery of the
privileges Jesus showered upon my soul. He does not call those who
are worthy but those whom He pleases or as St. Paul says: "God
will have mercy on whom he will have mercy, and he will show pity
to whom he will show pity. So then there is question not of him who
wills nor of him who runs, but of God showing mercy." (Ep. to the
Rom., chap. IX, v. 15 and 16)

I wondered for a long time why God has preferences, why all
souls don't receive an equal amount of graces. I was surprised when
I saw Him shower His extraordinary favors on saints who had
offended Him, for instance, St. Paul and St. Augustine, and whom
He forced, so to speak, to accept His graces. When reading the lives
of the saints, I was puzzled at seeing how Our Lord was pleased to
caress certain ones from the cradle to the grave, allowing no obsta-

cle in their way when coming to Him, helping them with such favors that they were unable to soil the immaculate beauty of their baptismal robe. I wondered why poor savages died in great numbers without even having heard the name of God pronounced.

Jesus deigned to teach me this mystery. He set before me the book of nature; I understood how all the flowers He has created are beautiful, how the splendor of the rose and the whiteness of the Lily do not take away the perfume of the little violet or the delightful simplicity of the daisy. I understood that if all flowers wanted to be roses, nature would lose her springtime beauty, and the fields would no longer be decked out with little wild flowers.

And so it is in the world of souls, Jesus' garden. He willed to create great souls comparable to Lilies and roses, but He has created smaller ones and these must be content to be daisies or violets destined to give joy to God's glances when He looks down at His feet. Perfection consists in doing His will, in being what He wills us to be.

I understood, too, that Our Lord's love is revealed as perfectly in the most simple soul that resists His grace in nothing as in the most excellent soul; in fact, since the nature of love is to humble oneself, if all souls resembled those of the holy Doctors who illumined the Church with the clarity of their teachings, it seems God would not descend so low when coming to their heart. But He created the child who knows only how to make his feeble cries heard; He has created the poor savage who has nothing but the natural law to guide him. It is to their hearts that God deigns to lower Himself. These are the wild flowers whose simplicity attracts Him. When coming down in this way, God manifests His infinite grandeur. Just as the sun shines simultaneously on the tall cedars and on each little flower as though it were alone on the earth, so Our Lord is occupied particularly with each soul as though there were no others like it. And just as in nature all the seasons are arranged in such a way as to make the humblest daisy bloom on a set day, in the same way, everything works out for the good of each soul.

Perhaps you are wondering, dear Mother, with some astonishment where I am going from here, for up until now I've said nothing that resembles the story of my life. But you asked me to write under no constraint whatever would come into my mind. It is not, then, my life properly so called that I am going to write; it is my *thoughts* on the graces God deigned to grant me. I find myself at a period in my life when I can cast a glance upon the past; my soul has matured in the crucible of exterior and interior trials. And now, like a flower strengthened by the storm, I can raise my head and see the words of Psalm 22 realized in me: "The Lord is my Shepherd, I shall not want; he makes me lie down in green pastures. He leads me beside still waters; he restores my soul. Even though I walk through the valley of the shadow of death, I fear no evil; for thou art with me . . ."[3] To me the Lord has always been "merciful and good, slow to anger and abounding in steadfast love." (Psalm 102:v. 8)

It is with great happiness, then, that I come to sing the mercies of the Lord with you, dear Mother. It is for *you alone* I am writing the story of the *little flower* gathered by Jesus. I will talk freely and without any worries as to the numerous digressions I will make. A mother's heart understands her child even when it can but stammer, and so I'm sure of being understood by you, who formed my heart, offering it up to Jesus!

It seems to me that if a little flower could speak, it would tell simply what God has done for it without trying to hide its blessings. It would not say, under the pretext of a false humility, it is not beautiful or without perfume, that the sun has taken away its splendor and the storm has broken its stem when it knows that all this is untrue. The flower about to tell her story rejoices at having to publish the totally gratuitous gifts of Jesus. She knows that nothing in herself was capable of attracting the divine glances, and His mercy alone brought about everything that is good in her.

It was He who had her born in a holy soil, impregnated with a *virginal perfume*. It was He, too, who had her preceded by eight Lilies of dazzling whiteness. In His love He wished to preserve His little flower from the world's empoisoned breath. Hardly had her petals begun to unfold when this divine Savior transplanted her to Mount Carmel where already two Lilies, who had taken care of her in the springtime of her life, spread their sweet perfume. Seven years have passed by since the little flower took root in the garden of the Spouse of Virgins, and now *three* Lilies bloom in her presence. A little farther off another lily expands under the eyes of Jesus. The two stems who brought these flowers into existence are now reunited for all eternity in the heavenly Fatherland. There they have found once again the four Lilies the earth had not seen develop. Oh! may Jesus deign not to allow a long time to pass on these strange shores for the flowers left in exile. May the Lily-plant be soon complete in Heaven![4]

J.M.J.T.

September 8, 1896

(To my dear Sister Marie of the Sacred Heart)

O Jesus, my Beloved, who could express the tenderness and sweetness with which You are guiding my soul! It pleases You to cause the rays of Your grace to shine through even in the midst of the darkest storm! Jesus, the storm was raging very strongly in my soul ever since the beautiful feast of Your victory, the radiant feast of Easter; one Saturday in the month of May,[1] thinking of the mysterious dreams which are granted at times to certain souls, I said to myself that these dreams must be a very sweet consolation, and yet I wasn't asking for such a consolation. In the evening, considering the clouds which were covering her heaven, my little soul said again within herself that these beautiful dreams were not for her. And then she fell asleep in the midst of the storm. The next day was May 10, the second SUNDAY of Mary's month, and perhaps the anniversary of the day when the Blessed Virgin deigned to smile upon her little flower.[2]

At the first glimmerings of dawn I was (in a dream) in a kind of gallery and there were several other persons, but they were at a distance. Our Mother was alone near me. Suddenly, without seeing how they had entered, I saw three Carmelites dressed in their mantles and long veils. It appeared to me they were coming for our Mother, but what I did understand clearly was that they came from heaven. In the depths of my heart I cried out: "Oh! how happy I would be if I could see the face of one of these Carmelites!" Then, as though my prayer were heard by her, the tallest of the saints advanced towards me; immediately I fell to my knees. Oh! what happiness! the Carmelite *raised her veil or rather she raised it and covered me with it*. Without the least hesitation, I recognized *Venerable Anne of Jesus*,[3] Foundress of Carmel in France. Her face was beautiful but with an immaterial beauty. No ray escaped from it and still, in spite of the veil which covered us both, I saw this heavenly face suffused with an unspeakably gentle light, a light it didn't receive from without but was produced from within.

I cannot express the joy of my soul since these things are experienced but cannot be put into words. Several months have passed since this sweet dream, and yet the memory it has left in my soul has lost nothing of its freshness and heavenly charms. I still

see Venerable Mother's glance and smile which was FILLED
WITH LOVE. I believe I can still feel the caresses she gave me at
this time.

Seeing myself so tenderly loved, I dared to pronounce these
words: "O Mother! I beg you, tell me whether God will leave me for
a long time on earth. Will He come soon to get me?" Smiling
tenderly, the saint whispered: *"Yes, soon, soon, I promise you."* I
added: "Mother, tell me further if God is not asking something
more of me than my poor little actions and desires. Is He content
with me?" The saint's face took on an expression *incomparably
more tender* than the first time she spoke to me. Her look and her
caresses were the sweetest of answers. However, she said to me:
"God asks no other thing from you. He is content, very content!"
After again embracing me with more love than the tenderest of
mothers has ever given to her child, I saw her leave. My heart was
filled with joy, and then I remembered my Sisters, and I wanted to
ask her some favors for them, but alas, I awoke!

O Jesus, the storm was no longer raging, heaven was calm and
serene. I *believed*, I *felt* there was a *heaven* and that this *heaven* is
peopled with souls who actually love me, who consider me their
child. This impression remains in my heart, and this all the more
because I was, up until then, *absolutely indifferent* to *Venerable
Mother Anne of Jesus*. I never invoked her in prayer and the
thought of her never came to my mind except when I heard others
speak of her which was seldom. And when I understood to what a
degree *she loved me*, how *indifferent* I had been towards her, my
heart was filled with love and gratitude, not only for the Saint who
had visited me but for all the blessed inhabitants of heaven.

O my Beloved! this grace was only the prelude to the greatest
graces You wished to bestow upon me. Allow me, my only Love, to
recall them to You today, *today* which is the sixth anniversary of
our union. Ah! my Jesus, pardon me if I am unreasonable in
wishing to express my desires and longings which reach even unto
infinity. Pardon me and heal my soul by giving her what she longs
for so much!

To be Your *Spouse*, to be a *Carmelite*, and by my union with
You to be the *Mother* of souls, should not this suffice me? And yet it
is not so. No doubt, these three privileges sum up my true *vocation:
Carmelite, Spouse, Mother*, and yet I feel within me other *vocations*. I feel the *vocation* of the WARRIOR, THE PRIEST, THE
APOSTLE, THE DOCTOR, THE MARTYR. Finally, I feel the
need and the desire of carrying out the most heroic deeds for *You, O*

Jesus. I feel within my soul the courage of the *Crusader*, the *Papal Guard*, and I would want to die on the field of battle in defense of the Church.

I feel in me the *vocation of* the PRIEST. With what love, O Jesus, I would carry You in my hands when, at my voice, You would come down from heaven. And with what love would I give You to souls! But alas! while desiring to be a *Priest*, I admire and envy the humility of St. Francis of Assisi and I feel the *vocation* of imitating him in refusing the sublime dignity of the *Priesthood*.

O Jesus, my Love, my Life, how can I combine these contrasts? How can I realize the desires of my poor *little soul*?

Ah! in spite of my littleness, I would like to enlighten souls as did the *Prophets* and the *Doctors*. I have the *vocation of the Apostle*. I would like to travel over the whole earth to preach Your Name and to plant Your glorious Cross on infidel soil. But *O my Beloved*, one mission alone would not be sufficient for me, I would want to preach the Gospel on all the five continents simultaneously and even to the most remote isles. I would be a missionary, not for a few years only but from the beginning of creation until the consummation of the ages. But above all, O my Beloved Savior, I would shed my blood for You even to the very last drop.

Martyrdom was the dream of my youth and this dream has grown with me within Carmel's cloisters. But here again, I feel that my dream is a folly, for I cannot confine myself to desiring *one kind* of martyrdom. To satisfy me I need *all*. Like You, my Adorable Spouse, I would be scourged and crucified. I would die flayed like St. Bartholomew. I would be plunged into boiling oil like St. John; I would undergo all the tortures inflicted upon the martyrs. With St. Agnes and St. Cecilia, I would present my neck to the sword, and like Joan of Arc, my dear sister, I would whisper at the stake Your Name, O JESUS. When thinking of the torments which will be the lot of Christians at the time of Anti-Christ, I feel my heart leap with joy and I would that these torments be reserved for me. Jesus, Jesus, if I wanted to write all my desires, I would have to borrow Your *Book of Life*,[4] for in it are reported all the actions of all the saints, and I would accomplish all of them for You.

O my Jesus! what is your answer to all my follies? Is there a soul more *little*, more powerless than mine? Nevertheless even because of my weakness, it has pleased You, O Lord, to grant my *little childish desires* and You desire, today, to grant other desires that are *greater* than the universe.

During my meditation, my desires caused me a veritable martyrdom, and I opened the Epistles of St. Paul to find some kind of answer. Chapters 12 and 13 of the First Epistle to the Corinthians fell under my eyes. I read there, in the first of these chapters, that *all* cannot be apostles, prophets, doctors, etc., that the Church is composed of different members, and that the eye cannot be the hand *at one and the same time.*[5] The answer was clear, but it did not fulfill my desires and gave me no peace. But just as Mary Magdalene found what she was seeking by always stooping down and looking into the empty tomb, so I, abasing myself to the very depths of my nothingness, raised myself so high that I was able to attain my end.[6] Without becoming discouraged, I continued my reading, and this sentence consoled me: *"Yet strive after THE BETTER GIFTS, and I point out to you* a yet more excellent way."[7] And the Apostle explains how all *the most PERFECT gifts* are nothing without *LOVE.* That *Charity is the EXCELLENT WAY* that leads most surely to God.

    I finally had rest. Considering the mystical body of the Church, I had not recognized myself in any of the members described by St. Paul, or rather I desired to see myself in them *all. Charity* gave me the key to my *vocation.* I understood that if the Church had a body composed of different members, the most necessary and most noble of all could not be lacking to it, and so I understood that the Church *had a Heart and that this Heart* was *BURNING WITH LOVE. I understood it was Love alone* that made the Church's members act, that if *Love* ever became extinct, apostles would not preach the Gospel and martyrs would not shed their blood. I understood that LOVE COMPRISED ALL VOCATIONS, THAT LOVE WAS EVERYTHING, THAT IT EMBRACED ALL TIMES AND PLACES. . . . IN A WORD, THAT IT WAS ETERNAL!

    Then, in the excess of my delirious joy, I cried out: O Jesus, my Love. . . . my *vocation*, at last I have found it. . . . MY VOCATION IS LOVE!

    Yes, I have found my place in the Church and it is You, O my God, who have given me this place; in the heart of the Church, my Mother, I shall be *Love.* Thus I shall be everything, and thus my dream will be realized.

    Why spreak of a delirious joy? No, this expression is not exact, for it was rather the calm and serene peace of the navigator perceiving the beacon which must lead him to the port . . . O luminous Beacon of love, I know how to reach You, I have found the secret of possessing Your flame.

I am only a child, powerless and weak, and yet it is my weakness that gives me the boldness of offering myself as *VICTIM of Your Love, O Jesus!* In times past, victims, pure and spotless, were the only ones accepted by the Strong and Powerful God. To satisfy Divine *Justice*, perfect victims were necessary, but the *law of Love* has succeeded to the law of fear, and *Love* has chosen me as a holocaust, me, a weak and imperfect creature. Is not this choice worthy of *Love?* Yes, in order that Love be fully satisfied, it is necessary that It lower Itself, and that It lower Itself to nothingness and transform this nothingness into *fire*.

O Jesus, I know it, love is repaid by love alone,[8] and so I searched and I found the way to solace my heart by giving you Love for Love. "Make use of the riches which render one unjust in order to make friends who will receive you into everlasting dwellings."[9] Behold, Lord, the counsel You give Your disciples after having told them that "The children of this world, in relation to their own generation, are more prudent than are the children of the light."[10] A child of light, I understood that *my desires of being everything*, of embracing all vocations, were the riches that would be able to render me unjust, so I made use of them *to make friends*. Remembering the prayer of Eliseus to his Father Elias when he dared to ask him for HIS DOUBLE SPIRIT,[11] I presented myself before the angels and saints and I said to them: "I am the smallest of creatures; I know my misery and my feebleness, but I know also how much noble and generous hearts love to do good. I beg you then, O Blessed Inhabitants of heaven, I beg you to ADOPT ME AS YOUR CHILD. *To you alone will be the glory* which you will make me merit, but deign to answer my prayer. It is bold, I know; however, I dare to ask you to obtain for me YOUR TWOFOLD SPIRIT."

Jesus, I cannot fathom the depths of my request; I would be afraid to find myself overwhelmed under the weight of my bold desires. My excuse is that I am a *child*, and children do not reflect on the meaning of their words; however, their parents, once they are placed upon a throne and possess immense treasures, do not hesitate to satisfy the desires of the *little ones* whom they love as much as they love themselves. To please them they do foolish things, even going to the extent of *becoming weak* for them. Well, I am the *Child of the Church* and the Church is a Queen since she is Your Spouse, O divine King of kings. The heart of a child does not seek riches and glory (even the glory of heaven). She understands that this glory belongs by right to her brothers, the angels and saints. Her own glory will be the reflected glory which shines on her Mother's forehead. What this child asks for is Love. She knows only one thing: to love You, O Jesus. Astounding works are forbidden to her; she cannot preach the Gospel, shed her blood; but what does it matter since her brothers work in her stead and she, *a little child*, stays very close to the *throne* of the King and Queen. She *loves* in her brothers' place while they do the fighting. But how will she prove her *love* since *love* is proved by works? Well, the little child *will strew flowers*, she will perfume the royal throne with their *sweet scents*, and she will sing in her silvery tones the canticle of *Love*.

Yes, my Beloved, this is how my life will be consumed. I have no other means of proving my love for you other than that of strewing flowers, that is, not allowing one little sacrifice to escape, not one look, one word, profiting by all the smallest things and doing them through love. I desire to suffer for love and even to rejoice through love; and in this way I shall strew flowers before Your throne. I shall not come upon one without *unpetalling* it for You. While I am strewing my flowers, I shall sing, for could one cry while doing such a joyous action? I shall sing even when I must gather my flowers in the midst of thorns, and my song will be all the more melodious in proportion to the length and sharpness of the thorns.

O Jesus, of what use will my flowers be to You? Ah! I know very well that this fragrant shower, these fragile, worthless petals, these songs of love from the littlest of hearts will charm You. Yes, these nothings will please You. They will bring a smile to the Church Triumphant. She will gather up my flowers unpetalled *through love* and have them pass through Your own divine hands, O Jesus. And this Church in heaven, desirous of playing with her little child, will cast these flowers, which are now infinitely valuable because of Your divine touch, upon the Church Suffering in order to extinguish its flames and upon the Church Militant in order to gain the victory for it!

O my Jesus! I love You! I love the Church, my Mother! I recall that *"the smallest act of PURE LOVE is of more value to her than all other works together."* [12] But is PURE LOVE in my heart? Are my measureless desires only but a dream, a folly? Ah! if this be so, Jesus, then enlighten me, for You know I am seeking only the truth. If my desires are rash, then make them disappear, for these desires are the greatest martyrdom to me. However, I feel, O Jesus, that after having aspired to the most lofty heights of Love, if one day I am not to attain them, I feel that I shall have tasted *more sweetness in my martyrdom and my folly* than I shall taste in the bosom of the *joy of the Fatherland,* unless You take away the memory of these earthly hopes through a miracle. Allow me, then, during my exile, the delights of love. Allow me to taste the sweet bitterness of my martyrdom.

Jesus, O Jesus, if the *desire of loving You* is so delightful, what will it be to possess and enjoy this Love?

How can a soul as imperfect as mine aspire to the possession of the plenitude of *Love*? O Jesus, *my first and only Friend,* You whom I *love* UNIQUELY, explain this mystery to me! Why do You not reserve these great aspirations for great souls, for the *Eagles* that soar in the heights?

I look upon myself as a *weak little bird,* with only a light down as covering. I am not an *eagle,* but I have only an eagle's EYES AND HEART. In spite of my extreme littleness I still dare to gaze upon the Divine Sun, the Sun of Love, and my heart feels within it all the aspirations of an *Eagle.*

The little bird wills *to fly* towards the bright Sun which attracts its eye, imitating its brothers, the eagles, whom it sees climbing up towards the Divine Furnace of the Holy Trinity. But alas! the only thing it can do is *raise its little wings;* to fly is not within its *little* power!

What then will become of it? Will it die of sorrow at seeing itself so weak? Oh no! the little bird will not even be troubled. With bold surrender, it wishes to remain gazing upon its Divine Sun. Nothing will frighten it, neither wind nor rain, and if dark clouds come and hide the Star of Love, the little bird will not change its place because it knows that beyond the clouds its bright Sun still shines on and that its brightness is not eclipsed for a single instant.

At times the little bird's heart is assailed by the storm, and it seems it should believe in the existence of no other thing except the clouds surrounding it; this is the moment of *perfect joy* for the *poor little weak creature.* And what joy it experiences when remaining there just the same! and gazing at the Invisible Light which remains hidden from its faith!

O Jesus, up until the present moment I can understand Your love for the little bird because it has not strayed far from You. But I know and so do You that very often the imperfect little creature, while remaining in its place (that is, under the Sun's rays), allows itself to be somewhat distracted from its sole occupation. It picks up a piece of grain on the right or on the left; it chases after a little worm; then coming upon a little pool of water, it wets its feathers still hardly formed. It sees an attractive flower and its little mind is occupied with this flower. In a word, being unable to soar like the eagles, the poor little bird is taken up with the trifles of earth.

And yet after all these misdeeds, instead of going and hiding away in a corner, to weep over its misery and to die of sorrow, the little bird turns towards its beloved Sun, presenting its wet wings to its beneficent rays. It cries like a swallow and in its sweet song it recounts in detail all its infidelities, thinking in the boldness of its full trust that it will acquire in even greater fullness the love of *Him* who came to call not the just but sinners.[13] And even if the Adorable Star remains deaf to the plaintive chirping of the little creature, even if it remains hidden, well, the little one will remain *wet*, accepting its numbness from the cold and rejoicing in its suffering which it knows it deserves.

O Jesus, Your *little bird* is happy to be *weak and little*. What would become of it if it were big? Never would it have the boldness to appear in Your presence, *to fall asleep* in front of You. Yes, this is still one of the weaknesses of the little bird: when it wants to fix its gaze upon the Divine Sun, and when the clouds prevent it from seeing a single ray of that Sun, in spite of itself, its little eyes close, its little head is hidden beneath its wing, and the poor little thing falls asleep, believing all the time that it is fixing its gaze upon its Dear Star. When it awakens, it doesn't feel desolate; its little heart is at peace and it begins once again its work of *love*. It calls upon the angels and saints who rise like eagles before the consuming Fire, and since this is the object of the little bird's desire the eagles take pity on it, protecting and defending it, and putting to flight at the same time the vultures who want to devour it. These vultures are the demons whom the little bird doesn't fear, for it is not destined to be their *prey* but the prey of the *Eagle* whom it contemplates in the center of the Sun of Love.

O Divine Word! You are the Adored Eagle whom I love and who alone *attracts me*! Coming into this land of exile, You willed to suffer and to die in order *to draw* souls to the bosom of the Eternal Fire of the Blessed Trinity. Ascending once again to the Inaccessible Light, henceforth Your abode, You remain still in this "valley of tears," hidden beneath the appearances of a white host. Eternal Eagle, You desire to nourish me with Your divine substance and yet I am but a poor little thing who would return to nothingness if Your divine glance did not give me life from one moment to the next.

O Jesus, allow me in my boundless gratitude to say to You that

Your *love reaches unto folly.* In the presence of this folly, how can
You not desire that my heart leap towards You? How can my
confidence, then, have any limits? Ah! the saints have committed
their *follies* for You, and they have done great things because they
are eagles.

Jesus, I am too little to perform great actions, and my own *folly*
is this: to trust that Your Love will accept me as a victim. My *folly*
consists in begging the eagles, my brothers, to obtain for me the
favor of flying towards the Sun of Love with the *Divine Eagle's own
wings!* [14]

As long as You desire it, O my Beloved, Your little bird will
remain without strength and without wings and will always stay
with its gaze fixed upon You. It wants to be *fascinated* by Your
divine glance. It wants to become the *prey* of Your Love. One day I
hope that You, the Adorable Eagle, will come to fetch me, Your
little bird; and ascending with it to the Furnace of Love, You will
plunge it for all eternity into the burning Abyss of this Love to
which it has offered itself as victim.

O Jesus! why can't I tell all *little souls* how unspeakable is
Your condescension? I feel that if You found a soul weaker and
littler than mine, which is impossible, You would be pleased to
grant it still greater favors, provided it abandoned itself with total
confidence to Your Infinite Mercy. But why do I desire to communicate Your secrets of Love, O Jesus, for was it not You alone who
taught them to me, and can You not reveal them to others? Yes, I
know it, and I beg You to do it. I beg You to cast Your Divine Glance
upon a great number of *little* souls. I beg You to choose a legion of
little Victims worthy of Your LOVE!

> *The very little Sister Therese of the Child Jesus*
> *and the Holy Face, unworthy religious of Carmel*

SIMONE WEIL

Waiting On God

*The French Jewish writer Simone Weil (1909-1943), radical in
her political and social thought, was deeply drawn to Catholicism
although never formally converting. Pursuing the careers of*

teacher, worker, and social activist, she died of exhaustion while working in England for the Free French forces during World War II. Her best known work is Waiting On God.

We live in a world of unreality and dreams. To give up our imaginary position as the centre, to renounce it, not only intellectually but in the imaginative part of our soul, that means to awaken to what is real and eternal, to see the true light and hear the true silence. A transformation then takes place at the very roots of our sensibility, in our immediate reception of sense impressions and psychological impressions. It is a transformation analogous to that which takes place in the dusk of evening on a road, where we suddenly discern as a tree what we had at first seen as a stooping man; or where we suddenly recognise as a rustling of leaves what we thought at first was whispering voices. We see the same colours, we share the same sounds, but not in the same way.

THE WAY OF THE PILGRIM

The nineteenth century saw a revival of Eastern Orthodox spirituality, particularly within Russia. The continuity of this movement with the hesychast writers–and indeed with the fourth-century Fathers of the Desert–is striking. A typical example of this spirituality lived in great intensity is given in an anonymous spiritual narrative first published in 1884 entitled The Way of the Pilgrim. *Purporting to be an account of a peasant who wandered on foot across Russia in the mid-nineteenth century, this work is one of the best sources of teaching on the "Jesus Prayer" and a powerful witness to the renewed vitality of Orthodox spirituality. The first chapter is reproduced here.*

By the grace of God I am a Christian man, by my actions a great sinner, and by calling a homeless wanderer of the humblest birth who roams from place to place. My wordly goods are a knap-

sack with some dried bread in it on my back, and in my breast-
pocket a Bible. And that is all.

On the 24th Sunday after Pentecost I went to church to say my
prayers there during the Liturgy. The first Epistle of St. Paul to the
Thessalonians was being read, and among other words I heard
these—*"Pray without ceasing."* It was this text, more than any
other, which forced itself upon my mind, and I began to think how
it was possible to pray without ceasing, since a man has to concern
himself with other things also in order to make a living. I looked at
my Bible, and with my own eyes read the words which I had heard,
i.e., that we ought always, at all times and in all places, to pray
with uplifted hands. I thought and thought, but knew not what to
make of it. "What ought I to do?" I thought. "Where shall I find
someone to explain it to me? I will go to the churches where famous
preachers are to be heard; perhaps there I shall hear something
which will throw light on it for me." I did so. I heard a number of
very fine sermons on prayer; what prayer is, how much we need it,
and what its fruits are; but no one said how one could succeed in
prayer. I heard a sermon on spiritual prayer, and unceasing
prayer, but how it was to be done was not pointed out.

Thus listening to sermons failed to give me what I wanted, and
having had my fill of them without gaining understanding, I gave
up going to hear public sermons. I settled on another plan—by
God's help to look for some experienced and skilled person who
would give me in conversation that teaching about unceasing
prayer which drew me so urgently.

For a long time I wandered through many places. I read my
Bible always, and everywhere I asked whether there was not in the
neighbourhood a spiritual teacher, a devout and experienced
guide, to be found. One day I was told that in a certain village a
gentleman had long been living and seeking the salvation of his
soul. He had a chapel in his house. He never left his estate, and he
spent his time in prayer and reading devotional books. Hearing
this, I ran rather than walked to the village named. I got there and
found him.

"What do you want of me?" he asked.

"I have heard that you are a devout and clever person", said I.
"In God's name please explain to me the meaning of the Apostle's
words, *'Pray without ceasing.'* How is it possible to pray without
ceasing? I want to know so much, but I cannot understand it at all."

He was silent for a while and looked at me closely. Then he

said: "Ceaseless interior prayer is a continual yearning of the human spirit towards God. To succeed in this consoling exercise we must pray more often to God to teach us to pray without ceasing. Pray more, and pray more fervently. It is prayer itself which will reveal to you how it can be achieved unceasingly; but it will take some time."

So saying, he had food brought to me, gave me money for my journey, and let me go.

He did not explain the matter.

Again I set off. I thought and thought, I read and read, I dwelt over and over again upon what this man had said to me, but I could not get to the bottom of it. Yet so greatly did I wish to understand that I could not sleep at night.

I walked at least a hundred and twenty-five miles, and then I came to a large town, a provincial capital, where I saw a monastery. At the inn where I stopped I heard it said that the Abbot was a man of great kindness, devout and hospitable. I went to see him. He met me in a very friendly manner, asked me to sit down, and offered me refreshment.

"I do not need refreshment, holy Father," I said, "but I beg you to give me some spiritual teaching. How can I save my soul?"

"What? Save your soul? Well, live according to the commandments, say your prayers, and you will be saved."

"But I hear it said that we should pray without ceasing, and I don't know how to pray without ceasing. I cannot even understand what unceasing prayer means. I beg you, Father, explain this to me."

"I don't know how to explain further, dear brother. But, stop a moment, I have a little book, and it is explained there." And he handed me St. Dmitri's book on *The Spiritual Education of the Inner Man*, saying, "Look, read this page."

I began to read as follows: "The words of the Apostle '*Pray without ceasing*' should be understood as referring to the creative prayer of the understanding. The understanding can always be reaching out towards God, and pray to Him unceasingly."

"But", I asked, "what is the method by which the understanding can always be turned towards God, never be disturbed, and pray without ceasing?"

"It is very difficult, even for one to whom God Himself gives such a gift", replied the Abbot.

He did not give me the explanation.

I spent the night at his house, and in the morning, thanking him for his kindly hospitality, I went on my way; where to, I did not know myself. My failure to understand made me sad, and by way of comforting myself I read my Bible. In this way I followed the main road for five days.

At last towards evening I was overtaken by an old man who looked like a cleric of some sort. In answer to my question he told me that he was a monk belonging to a monastery some six miles off the main road. He asked me to go there with him. "We take in pilgrims," said he, "and give them rest and food with devout persons in the guest house." I did not feel like going. So in reply I said that my peace of mind in no way depended upon my finding a resting-place, but upon finding spiritual teaching. Neither was I running after food, for I had plenty of dried bread in my knapsack.

"What sort of spiritual teaching are you wanting to get?" he asked me. "What is it puzzling you? Come now! Do come to our house, dear brother. We have *startsi*[1] of ripe experience well able to give guidance to your soul and to set it upon the true path, in the light of the word of God and the writings of the holy Fathers."

"Well, it's like this, Father", said I. "About a year ago, while I was at the Liturgy, I heard a passage from the Epistles which bade men pray without ceasing. Failing to understand, I began to read my Bible, and there also in many places I found the divine command that we ought to pray at all times, in all places; not only while about our business, not only while awake, but even during sleep, '*I sleep, but my heart waketh.*' This surprised me very much, and I was at a loss to understand how it could be carried out and in what way it was to be done. A burning desire and thirst for knowledge awoke in me. Day and night the matter was never out of my mind. So I began to go to churches and to listen to sermons. But however many I heard, from not one of them did I get any teaching about how to pray without ceasing. They always talked about getting ready for prayer, or about its fruits and the like, without teaching one *how* to pray without ceasing, or what such prayer means. I have often read the Bible and there made sure of what I have heard. But meanwhile I have not reached the understanding that I long for, and so to this hour I am still uneasy and in doubt."

Then the old man crossed himself and spoke. "Thank God, my dear brother, for having revealed to you this unappeasable desire for unceasing interior prayer. Recognise in it the call of God, and calm yourself. Rest assured that what has hitherto been accomplished in you is the testing of the harmony of your own will with the voice of God. It has been granted to you to understand that the

heavenly light of unceasing interior prayer is attained neither by
the wisdom of this world, nor by the mere outward desire for
knowledge, but that on the contrary it is found in poverty of spirit
and in active experience in simplicity of heart. That is why it is not
surprising that you have been unable to hear anything about the
essential work of prayer, and to acquire the knowledge by which
ceaseless activity in it is attained. Doubtless a great deal has been
preached about prayer, and there is much about it in the teaching
of various writers. But since for the most part all their reasonings
are based upon speculation and the working of natural wisdom,
and not upon active experience, they sermonise about the qualities
of prayer, rather than about the nature of the thing itself. One
argues beautifully about the necessity of prayer, another about its
power and the blessings which attend it, a third again about the
things which lead to perfection in prayer, *i.e.*, about the absolute
necessity of zeal, an attentive mind, warmth of heart, purity of
thought, reconciliation with one's enemies, humility, contrition,
and so on. But what is prayer? And how does one learn to pray?
Upon these questions, primary and essential as they are, one very
rarely gets any precise enlightenment from present-day preachers.
For these questions are more difficult to understand than all their
arguments that I have just spoken of, and require mystical knowledge, not simply the learning of the schools. And the most deplor-
able thing of all is that the vain wisdom of the world compels them
to apply the human standard to the divine. Many people reason
quite the wrong way round about prayer, thinking that good actions and all sorts of preliminary measures render us capable of
prayer. But quite the reverse is the case, it is prayer which bears
fruit in good works and all the virtues. Those who reason so, take,
incorrectly, the fruits and the results of prayer for the means of
attaining it, and this is to depreciate the power of prayer. And it is
quite contrary to Holy Scripture, for the Apostle Paul says, *'I exhort
therefore that first of all supplications be made'* (1 Tim., ii, 1). The
first thing laid down in the Apostle's words about prayer is that the
work of prayer comes before everything else: *'I exhort therefore that
the first of all . . .'* The Christian is bound to perform many good
works, but before all else what he ought to do is to pray, for without
prayer no other good work whatever can be accomplished. Without
prayer he cannot find the way to the Lord, he cannot understand
the truth, he cannot crucify the flesh with its passions and lusts, his
heart cannot be enlightened with the light of Christ, he cannot be
savingly united to God. None of those things can be effected unless

they are preceded by constant prayer. I say 'constant,' for the perfection of prayer does not lie within our power; as the Apostle Paul says, 'For we know not what we should pray for as we ought' (Rom. viii, 26). Consequently it is just to pray often, to pray always, which falls within our power as the means of attaining purity of prayer, which is the mother of all spiritual blessings. 'Capture the Mother, and she will bring you the children,' said St. Isaac the Syrian. Learn first to acquire the power of prayer and you will easily practise all the other virtues. But those who know little of this from practical experience and the profoundest teaching of the holy Fathers, have no clear knowledge of it and speak of it but little."

During this talk, we had almost reached the monastery. And so as not to lose touch with this wise old man, and to get what I wanted more quickly, I hastened to say, "Be so kind, Reverend Father, as to show me what prayer without ceasing means and how it is learnt. I see you know all about these things."

He took my request kindly and asked me into his cell. "Come in," said he; "I will give you a volume of the holy Fathers from which with God's help you can learn about prayer clearly and in detail."

We went into his cell and he began to speak as follows. "The continuous interior Prayer of Jesus is a constant uninterrupted calling upon the divine Name of Jesus with the lips, in the spirit, in the heart; while forming a mental picture of His constant presence, and imploring His grace, during every occupation, at all times, in all places, even during sleep. The appeal is couched in these terms, 'Lord Jesus Christ, have mercy on me.' One who accustoms himself to this appeal experiences as a result so deep a consolation and so great a need to offer the prayer always, that he can no longer live without it, and it will continue to voice itself within him of its own accord. Now do you understand what prayer without ceasing is?"

"Yes indeed, Father, and in God's name teach me how to gain the habit of it," I cried, filled with joy.

"Read this book," he said. "It is called *The Philokalia*,[2] and it contains the full and detailed science of constant interior prayer, set forth by twenty-five holy Fathers. The book is marked by a lofty wisdom and is so profitable to use that it is considered the foremost and best manual of the contemplative spiritual life. As the revered Nicephorus said, 'It leads one to salvation without labour and sweat.'"

"Is it then more sublime and holy than the Bible?" I asked.

"No, it is not that. But it contains clear explanations of what the Bible holds in secret and which cannot be easily grasped by our short-sighted understanding. I will give you an illustration. The sun is the greatest, the most resplendent and the most wonderful of heavenly luminaries, but you cannot contemplate and examine it simply with unprotected eyes. You have to use a piece of artificial glass which is many millions of times smaller and darker than the sun. But through this little piece of glass you can examine the magnificent monarch of stars, delight in it, and endure its fiery rays. Holy Scripture also is a dazzling sun, and this book, *The Philokalia*, is the piece of glass which we use to enable us to contemplate the sun in its imperial splendour. Listen now, I am going to read you the sort of instruction it gives on unceasing interior prayer."

He opened the book, found the instruction by St. Simeon the New Theologian, and read: "Sit down alone and in silence. Lower your head, shut your eyes, breathe out gently and imagine yourself looking into your own heart. Carry your mind, *i.e.*, your thoughts, from your head to your heart. As you breathe out, say 'Lord Jesus Christ, have mercy on me.' Say it moving your lips gently, or simply say it in your mind. Try to put all other thoughts aside. Be calm, be patient, and repeat the process very frequently."

The old man explained all this to me and illustrated its meaning. We went on reading from *The Philokalia* passages of St. Gregory of Sinai, St. Callistus and St. Ignatius, and what we read from the book the *starets* explained in his own words. I listened closely and with great delight, fixed it in my memory, and tried as far as possible to remember every detail. In this way we spent the whole night together and went to Matins without having slept at all.

The *starets* sent me away with his blessing and told me that while learning the Prayer I must always come back to him and tell him everything, making a very frank confession and report; for the inward process could not go on properly and successfully without the guidance of a teacher.

In church I felt a glowing eagerness to take all the pains I could to learn unceasing interior prayer, and I prayed to God to come to my help. Then I began to wonder how I should manage to see my *starets* again for counsel or confession, since leave was not given to remain for more than three days in the monastery guesthouse, and there were no houses near.

However, I learned that there was a village between two and

three miles from the monastery. I went there to look for a place to live, and to my great happiness God showed me the thing I needed. A peasant hired me for the whole summer to look after his kitchen garden, and what is more gave me the use of a little thatched hut in it where I could live alone. God be praised! I had found a quiet place. And in this manner I took up my abode and began to learn interior prayer in the way I had been shown, and to go to see my *starets* from time to time.

For a week, alone in my garden, I steadily set myself to learn to pray without ceasing exactly as the *starets* had explained. At first things seemed to go very well. But then it tired me very much. I felt lazy and bored and overwhelmingly sleepy, and a cloud of all sorts of other thoughts closed round me. I went in distress to my *starets* and told him the state I was in.

He greeted me in a friendly way and said, "My dear brother, it is the attack of the world of darkness upon you. To that world, nothing is worse than heartfelt prayer on our part. And it is trying by every means to hinder you and to turn you aside from learning the Prayer. But all the same the enemy only does what God sees fit to allow, and no more than is necessary for us. It would appear that you need a further testing of your humility, and that it is too soon, therefore, for your unmeasured zeal to approach the loftiest entrance to the heart. You might fall into spiritual covetousness. I will read you a little instruction from *The Philokalia* upon such cases."

He turned to the teaching of Nicephorus and read, " 'If after a few attempts you do not succeed in reaching the realm of your heart in the way you have been taught, do what I am about to say, and by God's help you will find what you seek. The faculty of pronouncing words lies in the throat. Reject all other thoughts (you can do this if you will) and allow that faculty to repeat only the following words constantly, "Lord Jesus Christ, have mercy on me." Compel yourself to do it always. If you succeed for a time, then without a doubt your heart also will open to prayer. We know it from experience.'

"There you have the teaching of the holy Fathers on such cases," said my *starets*, "and therefore you ought from to-day onwards to carry out my directions with confidence, and repeat the Prayer of Jesus as often as possible. Here is a rosary. Take it, and to start with saying the Prayer three thousand times a day. Whether you are standing or sitting, walking or lying down, continually repeat 'Lord Jesus Christ, have mercy on me.' Say it quietly and without hurry, but without fail exactly three thousand times a day without deliberately increasing or diminishing the number. God will help you and by this means you will reach also the unceasing activity of the heart."

I gladly accepted this guidance and went home and began to carry out faithfully and exactly what my *starets* had bidden. For two days I found it rather difficult, but after that it became so easy and likeable, that as soon as I stopped, I felt a sort of need to go on saying the Prayer of Jesus, and I did it freely and willingly, not forcing myself to it as before.

I reported to my *starets*, and he bade me say the Prayer six thousand times a day, saying, "Be calm, just try as faithfully as possible to carry out the set number of prayers. God will vouchsafe you His grace."

In my lonely hut I said the Prayer of Jesus six thousand times a day for a whole week. I felt no anxiety. Taking no notice of any other thoughts however much they assailed me, I had but one object, *i.e.*, to carry out my *starets*' bidding exactly. And what happened? I grew so used to my Prayer that when I stopped for a single moment, I felt, so to speak, as though something were missing, as though I had lost something. The very moment I started the Prayer again, it went on easily and joyously. If I met anyone I had no wish to talk to him. All I wanted was to be alone and to say my Prayer, so used to it had I become in a week.

My *starets* had not seen me for ten days. On the eleventh day he came to see me himself, and I told him how things were going. He listened and said, "Now you have got used to the Prayer. See that you preserve the habit and strengthen it. Waste no time, therefore, but make up your mind by God's help from to-day to say the Prayer of Jesus twelve thousand times a day. Remain in your solitude, get up early, go to bed late, and come and ask advice of me every fortnight."

I did as he bade me. The first day I scarcely succeeded in finishing my task of saying twelve thousand prayers by late evening. The second day I did it easily and contentedly. To begin with, this ceaseless saying of the Prayer brought a certain amount of weariness, my tongue felt numbed, I had a stiff sort of feeling in my jaws, I had a feeling at first pleasant but afterwards slightly painful in the roof of my mouth. The thumb of my left hand, with which I counted my beads, hurt a little. I felt a slight inflammation in the whole of that wrist, and even up to the elbow, which was not unpleasant. Moreover, all this aroused me, as it were, and urged

me on to frequent saying of the Prayer. For five days I did my set
number of twelve thousand prayers, and as I formed the habit I
found at the same time pleasure and satisfaction in it.

Early one morning the Prayer woke me up as it were. I started
to say my usual morning prayers, but my tongue refused to say
them easily or exactly. My whole desire was fixed upon one thing
only—to say the Prayer of Jesus, and as soon as I went on with it I
was filled with joy and relief. It was as though my lips and my
tongue pronounced the words entirely of themselves without any
urging from me. I spent the whole day in a state of the greatest
contentment, I felt as though I was cut off from everything else. I
lived as though in another world, and I easily finished my twelve
thousand prayers by the early evening. I felt very much like still
going on with them, but I did not dare to go beyond the number my
starets had set me. Every day following I went on in the same way
with my calling on the Name of Jesus Christ, and that with great
readiness and liking. Then I went to see my *starets* and told him
everything frankly and in detail.

He heard me out and then said, "Be thankful to God that this
desire for the Prayer and this facility in it have been manifested in
you. It is a natural consequence which follows constant effort and
spiritual achievement. So a machine to the principal wheel of
which one gives a drive, works for a long while afterwards by itself;
but if it is to go on working still longer, one must oil it and give it
another drive. Now you see with what admirable gifts God in His
love for mankind has endowed even the bodily nature of man. You
see what feelings can be produced even outside a state of grace in a
soul which is sinful and with passions unsubdued, as you yourself
have experienced. But how wonderful, how delightful and how
consoling a thing it is when God is pleased to grant the gift of
self-acting spiritual prayer, and to cleanse the soul from all sensuality! It is a condition which is impossible to describe, and the
discovery of this mystery of prayer is a foretaste on earth of the
bliss of Heaven. Such happiness is reserved for those who seek
after God in the simplicity of a loving heart. Now I give you my
permission to say your Prayer as often as you wish and as often as
you can. Try to devote every moment you are awake to the Prayer,
call on the Name of Jesus Christ without counting the number of
times, and submit yourself humbly to the will of God, looking to
Him for help. I am sure He will not forsake you, and that He will
lead you into the right path."

Under this guidance I spent the whole summer in ceaseless

oral prayer to Jesus Christ, and I felt absolute peace in my soul. During sleep I often dreamed that I was saying the Prayer. And during the day if I happened to meet anyone, all men without exception were as dear to me as if they had been my nearest relations. But I did not concern myself with them much. All my ideas were quite calmed of their own accord. I thought of nothing whatever but my Prayer, my mind tended to listen to it, and my heart began of itself to feel at times a certain warmth and pleasure. If I happened to go to church the lengthy service of the monastery seemed short to me, and no longer wearied me as it had in time past. My lonely hut seemed like a splendid palace, and I knew not how to thank God for having sent to me, a lost sinner, so wholesome a guide and master.

But I was not long to enjoy the teaching of my dear *starets*, who was so full of divine wisdom. He died at the end of the summer. Weeping freely I bade him farewell, and thanked him for the fatherly teaching he had given my wretched self, and as a blessing and a keepsake I begged for the rosary with which he said his prayers.

And so I was left alone. Summer came to an end and the kitchen garden was cleared. I had no longer anywhere to live. My peasant sent me away, giving me by way of wages two roubles, and filling up my bag with dried bread for my journey. Again I started off on my wanderings. But now I did not walk along as before, filled with care. The calling upon the Name of Jesus Christ gladdened my way. Everybody was kind to me, it was as though everyone loved me.

Then it occurred to me to wonder what I was to do with the money I had earned by my care of the kitchen garden. What good was it to me? Yet stay! I no longer had a *starets*, there was no one to go on teaching me. Why not buy *The Philokalia* and continue to learn from it more about interior prayer?

I crossed myself and set off with my Prayer. I came to a large town, where I asked for the book in all the shops. In the end I found it, but they asked me three roubles for it, and I had only two. I bargained for a long time, but the shopkeeper would not budge an inch. Finally he said, "Go to this church near by, and speak to the churchwarden. He has a book like that, but it's a very old copy. Perhaps he will let you have it for two roubles." I went, and sure enough I found and bought for my two roubles a worn and old copy of *The Philokalia*. I was delighted with it. I mended my book as much as I could, I made a cover for it with a piece of cloth, and put it into my breast pocket with my Bible.

And that is how I go about now, and ceaselessly repeat the Prayer of Jesus, which is more precious and sweet to me than anything in the world. At times I do as much as forty-three or four miles a day, and do not feel that I am walking at all. I am aware only of the fact that I am saying my Prayer. When the bitter cold pierces me, I begin to say my Prayer more earnestly and I quickly get warm all over. When hunger begins to overcome me, I call more often on the Name of Jesus, and I forget my wish for food. When I fall ill and get rheumatism in my back and legs, I fix my thoughts on the Prayer and do not notice the pain. If anyone harms me I have only to think, "How sweet is the Prayer of Jesus!" and the injury and the anger alike pass away and I forget it all. I have become a sort of half-conscious person. I have no cares and no interests. The fussy business of the world I would not give a glance to. The one thing I wish for is to be alone, and all by myself to pray, to pray without ceasing; and doing this, I am filled with joy. God knows what is happening to me! Of course, all this is sensuous, or as my departed *starets* said, an artificial state which follows naturally upon routine. But because of my unworthiness and stupidity I dare not venture yet to go on further, and learn and make my own, spiritual prayer within the depths of my heart. I await God's time. And in the meanwhile I rest my hope on the prayers of my departed *starets*. Thus, although I have not yet reached that ceaseless spiritual prayer which is self-acting in the heart, yet I thank God I do now understand the meaning of those words I heard in the Epistle—*"Pray without ceasing."*

JOHN HENRY NEWMAN (1801-1890)

Prayers

Brilliant patristic scholar and leader of the Oxford Movement within the Anglican Church, John Henry Newman (1801–1890) converted to Roman Catholicism at the age of 44. Despite great misunderstanding from both the Anglican and the Catholic sides, Newman became the most profound spokesman for Catholicism in nineteenth-century England. He was created a Cardinal by Pope Leo XIII in 1879. Newman's numerous writings on spirituality betray an Augustinian sense of intuitive immediacy in the experience of God.

Thou alone canst fill the soul of man, and Thou has promised to do so. Thou art the living flame, and ever burnest with love of men; enter into me and set me on fire after Thy pattern and likeness.

TEILHARD DE CHARDIN

Pierre Theilhard de Chardin (1881–1956), French Jesuit and specialist in paleontology, struggled throughout his life to integrate traditional Catholic spirituality with the evolutionary theories dominant in modern physical science. Teilhard developed a form of discipleship, redolent of a deeply authentic personal mysticism, that attempted to overcome the traditional Neoplatonic distrust of the senses and the physical world. Instead of stressing detachment and rising above matter, he sought to present a spirituality of passionate involvement, of plunging into the realities of the physical and social world in order to build up the pleroma *of Christ.*

Judged dangerous and unorthodox during his life, Teilhard's writings on spirituality appeared fully only after his death. They have exerted a very powerful impact on Christians during the past twenty years. The following excerpts are taken from The Divine Milieu, *his most important treatise on spirituality, and from* Hymn of the Universe, *a collection of some of his earliest and most poetic writings.*

The Divine Milieu

PART ONE

THE DIVINISATION OF OUR ACTIVITIES

Note. .... We use the word 'activity' in the ordinary, everyday sense, without in any way denying—far from it—all that occurs between *grace* and the *will* in the infra-experimental spheres of the soul. To repeat: what is most divine in God is that, in an absolute sense, we are nothing apart from him. The least admixture of what may be called Pelagianism would suffice to ruin immediately the beauties of the divine *milieu* in the eyes of the 'seer'.

Of the two halves or components into which our lives may be divided, the most important, judging by appearances and by the price we set upon it, is the sphere of activity, endeavour and development. There can, of course, be no action without reaction. And, of course, there is nothing in us which in origin and at its deepest is not, as St. Augustine said, *'in nobis, sine nobis'*.[1] When we act, as it seems, with the greatest spontaneity and vigour, we are to some extent led by the things we imagine we are controlling. Moreover, the very expansion of our energy (which reveals the core of our autonomous personality) is, ultimately, only our obedience to a will to be and to grow, of which we can master neither the varying intensity nor the countless modes. We shall return, at the beginning of Part Two, to these essentially passive elements, some of which form part of the very marrow of our being, while others are diffused among the inter-play of universal causes which we call our 'character', our 'nature' or our 'good and bad luck'. For the moment let us consider our life in terms of the categories and definitions which are the most immediate and universal. Everyone can distinguish quite clearly between the moments in which he is acting and those in which he is acted upon. Let us look at ourselves in one of those phases of dominant activity and try to see how, with the help of our activity and by developing it to the full, the divine presses in upon us and seeks to enter our lives.

1. THE UNDOUBTED EXISTENCE OF THE FACT AND THE DIFFICULTY OF EXPLAINING IT: THE CHRISTIAN PROBLEM OF THE SANCTIFICATION OF ACTION

Nothing is more certain, dogmatically, than that human action can be sanctified. 'Whatever you do,' says St. Paul, 'do it in the name of our Lord Jesus Christ.' And the dearest of christian traditions has always been to interpret those words to mean: in intimate union with our Lord Jesus Christ. St. Paul himself, after calling upon us to 'put on Christ', goes on to forge the famous series of words *collaborare, compali, commori, con-ressuscitare*,[2] giving them the fullest possible meaning, a literal meaning even, and expressing the conviction that every human life must—in some sort—become a life in common with the life of Christ. The actions of life, of which Paul is speaking here, should not, as everyone knows, be understood solely in the sense of religious and devotional 'works' (prayers, fastings, almsgivings). It is the whole of human life, down to its most 'natural' zones, which, the Church teaches, can be sanctified. 'Whether you eat or whether you drink', St. Paul says. The whole history of the Church is there to attest it. Taken as a whole, then, from the most solemn declarations or examples of the pontiffs and doctors of the Church to the advice humbly given by the priest in confession, the general influence and practice of the Church has always been to dignify, ennoble and transfigure in God the duties inherent in one's station in life, the search for natural truth, and the development of human action.

The fact cannot be denied. But its legitimacy, that is its logical coherence with the whole basis of the christian temper, is not immediately evident. How is it that the perspectives opened up by the kingdom of God do not, by their very presence, shatter the distribution and balance of our activities? How can the man who believes in heaven and the Cross continue to believe seriously in the value of worldly occupations? How can the believer, in the name of everything that is most christian in him, carry out his duty as man to the fullest extent and as whole-heartedly and freely as if he were on the direct road to God? That is what is not altogether clear at first sight; and in fact disturbs more minds than one thinks.

The question might be put in this way:

According to the most sacred articles of his *Credo*, the Christian believes that life here below is continued in a life of which the joys, the sufferings, the reality, are quite incommensurable with the present conditions in our universe. This contrast and disproportion are enough, by themselves, to rob us of our taste for the world and our interest in it; but to them must be added a positive doctrine of judgment upon, even disdain for, a fallen and vitiated world. 'Perfection consists in detachment; the world around us is vanity and ashes.' The believer is constantly reading or hearing these austere words. How can he reconcile them with that other counsel, usually coming from the same master and in any case written in his heart by nature, that he must be an example unto the Gentiles in devotion to duty, in energy, and even in leadership in all the spheres opened up by man's activity? There is no need for us to consider the wayward or the lazy who cannot be bothered to acquire an understanding of their world, or seek with care to advance their fellow' welfare—from which they will benefit a hundredfold after their last breath—and only contribute to the human task 'with the tips of their fingers'. But there is a kind of human spirit (known to every spiritual director) for whom this difficulty assumes the shape and importance of a besetting and numbing uncertainty. Such spirits, set upon interior unity, become the victims of a veritable spiritual dualism. On the one hand a very sure instinct, mingled with their love for that which is, and their taste for life, draws them to the joy of creating and of knowing. On the other hand a higher will to love God above all else makes them afraid of the least division or deflection in their allegiances. In the most spiritual layers of their being they experience a tension between the opposing ebb and flow caused by the drawing power of the two rival stars we spoke of at the beginning: God and the world. Which of the two is to make itself more nobly adored?

Depending on the greater or less vitality of the nature of the individual, this conflict is in danger of finding its solution in one of the three following ways: either the Christian will repress his taste for the tangible and force himself to confine his concern to purely religious objects, and he will try to live in a world that he has divinised by banishing the largest possible number of earthly objects; or else, harassed by that inward conflict which hampers him, he will dismiss the evangelical counsels and decide to lead what seems to him a complete and human life; or else, again, and this is the most usual case, he will give up any attempt to make sense of his situation; he will never belong wholly to God, nor ever wholly to things; incomplete in his own eyes, and insincere in the eyes of his fellows, he will gradually acquiesce in a double life. I am speaking, it should not be forgotten, from experience.

For various reasons, all three of these solutions are to be feared. Whether we become distorted, disgusted, or divided, the result is equally bad, and certainly contrary to that which Christianity should rightly produce in us. There is, without possible doubt, a fourth way out of the problem: it consists in seeing how, without making the smallest concession to 'nature' but with a thirst for greater perfection, we can reconcile, and provide mutual nourishment for, the love of God and the healthy love of the world, a striving towards detachment and a striving towards the enrichment of our human lives. . . .

Let us look at the two solutions that can be brought to the christian problem of 'the divinisation of human activity', the first partial, the second complete.

2. AN INCOMPLETE SOLUTION: HUMAN ACTION HAS NO VALUE OTHER THAN THE INTENTION WHICH DIRECTS IT

If we try somewhat crudely to reduce to its barest bones the immediate answer given by spiritual directors to those who ask them how a Christian, who is determined to disdain the world and jealously to keep his heart for God, can love what he is doing (his work)—in conformity with the Church's teaching that the faithful should take *not a lesser* but a *fuller* part than the pagan—it will run along these lines:

You are anxious, my friend, to restore its value to your human endeavour; to you the characteristic viewpoints of christian asceticism seem to set for too little store by such activity. Very well then, you must let the clear spring water of purity of intention flow into your work, as if it were its very substance. Cleanse your intention, and the least of your actions will be filled with God. Certainly the material side of your actions has no definitive value. Whether men discover one truth or one fact more or less, whether or not they make beautiful music or beautiful pictures, whether their organisation of the world is more or less successful—all that has no direct importance for heaven. None of these discoveries or creations will become one of the stones of which is built the New Jerusalem. But what *will* count, up there, what *will* always endure, is this: that you have acted in all things *conformably* to the will of God.

God obviously has no need of the products of your busy activity, since he could give himself everything without you. The only thing that concerns him, the only thing he desires intensely, is your faithful use of your freedom, and the preference you accord him over the things around you.

Try to grasp this: the things which are given to you on earth are given you purely as an exercise, a 'blank sheet' on which you make your own mind and heart. You are on a testing-ground where God can judge whether you are capable of being translated to heaven and into his presence. You are on trial. So that it matters very little what becomes of the fruits of

the earth, or what they are worth. The whole question is
whether you have used them in order to learn how to obey and
how to love.

You should not, therefore, set store by the coarse outer-
covering of your human actions: this can be burnt like straw or
smashed like china. Think, rather, that into each of these
humble vessels you can pour, like a sap or a precious liquor,
the spirit of obedience and of union with God. If worldly aims
have no value in themselves, you can love them for the opportunity they give you of proving your faithfulness to God.

We are not suggesting that the foregoing words have ever been
actually used; but we believe they convey a nuance which is often
discernible in spiritual direction, and we are sure that they give a
rough idea of what a good number of the 'directed' have understood
and retained of the exhortations given them.

On this assumption let us examine the attitude which they
recommend.

In the first place this attitude contains an enormous part of
truth. It is perfectly right to exalt the role of a good intention as the
necessary start and foundation of all else; indeed—a point which
we shall have to make again—it is the golden key which unlocks
our inward personal world to God's presence. It expresses vigor-
ously the primary worth of the divine will which, by virtue of this
attitude, becomes for the Christian (as it was for his divine model)
the fortifying marrow of all earthly nourishment. It reveals a sort
of unique *milieu*, unchanging beneath the diversity and number of
the tasks which, as men and women, we have to do, in which we can
place ourselves without ever having to withdraw.

These various features convey a first and essential approxima-
tion to the solution we are looking for; and we shall certainly retain
them in their entirety in the more satisfactory plan of the interior
life which will soon be suggested. But they seem to us to lack the
achievement which our spiritual peace and joy so imperiously
demand. The divinisation of our endeavour by the value of the
intention put into it, pours a priceless *soul* into all our actions; but
it does not confer the hope of resurrection upon their bodies. Yet that
hope is what we need if our joy is to be complete. It is certainly a
very great thing to be able to think that, if we love God, something
of our inner activity, of our *operatio*, will never be lost. But will not
the work itself of our minds, of our hearts, and of our hands—that is
to say, our achievements, what we bring into being, our *opus*—will

not this, too, in some sense be 'eternalised' and saved?

Indeed, Lord, it will be—by virtue of a claim which you yourself have implanted at the very centre of my will! I desire and need that it should be.

I desire it because I love irresistibly all that your continuous help enables me to bring each day to reality. A thought, a material improvement, a harmony, a unique nuance of human love, the enchanting complexity of a smile or a glance, all these new beauties that appear for the first time, in me or around me, on the human face of the earth—I cherish them like children and cannot believe that they will die entirely in their flesh. If I believed that these things were to perish for ever, should I have given them life? The more I examine myself, the more I discover this psychological truth: that no one lifts his little finger to do the smallest task unless moved, however obscurely, by the conviction that he is contributing infinitesimally (at least indirectly) to the building of something definitive—that is to say, to your work, my God. This may well sound strange or exaggerated to those who act without thoroughly scrutinising themselves. And yet it is a fundamental law of their action. It requires no less than the pull of what men call the Absolute, no less than you yourself, to set in motion the frail liberty which you have given us. And that being so, everything which diminishes my explicit faith in the heavenly value of the results of my endeavour, diminishes irremediably my power to act.

*Show all your faithful, Lord, in what a full and true sense 'their work follows them' into your kingdom—*opera sequuntur illos. *Otherwise they will become like those idle workmen who are not spurred by their task. And even if a sound human instinct prevails over their hesitancies or the sophisms of an incompletely enlightened religious practice, they will remain fundamentally divided and frustrated; and it will be said that the sons of heaven cannot compete on the human level, in conviction and hence on equal terms, with the children of the world.*

3. THE FINAL SOLUTION: ALL ENDEAVOUR COOPERATES TO COMPLETE THE WORLD IN CHRISTO JESU

The general ordering of the salvation (which is to say the divinisation) of what we do can be expressed briefly in the following syllogism.

At the heart of our universe, each soul exists for God, in our Lord.

But all reality, even material reality, around each one of us, exists for our souls.

Hence, all sensible reality, around each one of us, exists, through our souls, for God in our Lord.

Let us examine each proposition of the syllogism in turn and separately. Its terms and the link between them are easy to grasp. But we must beware: it is one thing to have understood its words, and another to have penetrated the astonishing world whose inexhaustible riches are revealed by its calm and formal exactitude.

A. *At the heart of our universe, each soul exists for God in our Lord*

The major of the syllogism does no more than express the fundamental Catholic dogma which all other dogmas merely explain or define. It therefore requires no proof here; but it does need to be strictly understood by the intelligence. Each soul exists for God in our Lord. We should not be content to give this destination of our being in Christ a meaning too obviously modelled on the legal relationships which in our world link an object to its owner. Its nature is altogether more physical and deeper. Because the consummation of the world (what Paul calls the Pleroma) is a communion of persons (the communion of saints), our minds require that we should express the links within that communion by analogies drawn from society. Moreover, in order to avoid the perverse pantheism and materialism which lie in wait for our thought whenever it applies to its mystical concepts the powerful but dangerous resources of analogies drawn from organic life, the majority of theologians (more cautious on this point than St. Paul) do not favour too realist an interpretation of the links which bind the limbs to the head in the Mystical Body. But there is no reason why caution should become timidity. If we want a full and vivid understanding of the teachings of the Church (which alone makes them beautiful and acceptable) on the value of human life and the promises or threats of the future life—then, without rejecting anything of the forces of freedom and of consciousness which form the natural endowment proper to the human soul, we must perceive the existence of links between us and the Incarnate Word no less precise than those which control, in the world, the affinities of the elements in the building up of 'natural' wholes.

There is no point, here, in seeking a new name by which to

designate the super-eminent nature of that dependence, where all
that is most flexible in human combinations and all that is most
intransigent in organic structures, merge harmoniously in a moment of final incandescence. We will continue to call it by the name
that has always been used: *mystical* union. Far from implying
some idea of diminution, we use the term to mean the strengthen-
ing and purification of the reality and urgency contained in the
most powerful interconnections revealed to us in every order of the
physical and human world. On that path we can advance without
fear of over-stepping the truth; for everyone in the Church of God is
agreed upon the fact itself, if not upon its systematic statement: by
virtue of the powerful incarnation of the Word, our soul is wholly
dedicated to Christ and centred upon him.

B. *'In our universe,' we went on to say, 'in which each soul exists for
God, in our Lord, all that is sensible, in its turn, exists for the soul.'*

In the form in which we have given it, the minor of our syllogism is
tinged with a certain 'finalist' doctrine which may shock those with
a positivist cast of mind. Nevertheless it does no more than express
an incontrovertible natural fact—which is that our spiritual being
is continually nourished by the countless energies of the perceptible world. Here, again, proof is unnecessary. But it is essential to
see—to see things as they are and to see them really and intensely.
We live at the centre of the network of cosmic influences as we live
at the heart of the human crowd or among the myriads of stars,
without, alas, being aware of their immensity. If we wish to live
our humanity and our Christianity to the full, we must overcome
that insensitivity which tends to conceal things from us in proportion as they are too close to us or too vast. It is worthwhile
performing the salutary exercise which consists in starting with
those elements of our conscious life in which our awareness of
ourselves as persons is most fully developed, and moving out from
these to consider the spread of our being. We shall be astonished at
the extent and the intimacy of our relationship with the universe.

Where are the roots of our being? In the first place they plunge
back and down into the unfathomable past. How great is the
mystery of the first cells which were one day animated by the
breath of our souls! How impossible to decipher the welding of
successive influences in which we are for ever incorporated! In each
one of us, through matter, the whole history of the world is in part
reflected. And however autonomous our soul, it is indebted to an
inheritance worked upon from all sides—before ever it came into

being—by the totality of the energies of the earth: it meets and rejoins life at a determined level. Then, hardly has it entered actively into the universe at that particular point than it feels, in its turn, besieged and penetrated by the flow of cosmic influences which have to be ordered and assimilated. Let us look around us: the waves come from all sides and from the farthest horizon. Through every cleft the world we perceive floods us with its riches—food for the body, nourishment for the eyes, harmony of sounds and fullness of the heart, unknown phenomena and new truths, all these treasures, all these stimuli, all these calls, coming to us from the four corners of the world, cross our consciousness at every moment. What is their role within us? What will their effect be, even if we welcome them passively or indistinctly, like bad workmen? They will merge into the most intimate life of our soul and either develop it or poison it. We only have to look at ourselves for one moment to realise this, and either feel delight or anxiety. If even the most humble and most material of our foods is capable of deeply influencing our most spiritual faculties, what can be said of the infinitely more penetrating energies conveyed to us by the music of tones, of notes, of words, of ideas? We have not, in us, a body which takes its nourishment independently of our soul. Everything that the body has admitted and has begun to transform must be transfigured by the soul in its turn. The soul does this, no doubt, in its own way and with its own dignity. But it cannot escape from this universal contact nor from that unremitting labour. And that is how the characteristic power of understanding and loving, which will form its immaterial individuality, is gradually perfected in it for its own good and at its own risk. We hardly know in what proportions and under what guise our natural faculties will pass over into the final act of the vision of God. But it can hardly be doubted that, with God's help, it is here below that we give ourselves the eyes and the heart which a final transfiguration will make the organs of a power of adoration, and of a capacity for beatification, particular to each individual man and woman among us.

The masters of the spiritual life incessantly repeat that God wants only souls. To give those words their true value, we must not forget that the human soul, however independently created our philosophy represents it as being, is inseparable, in its birth and in its growth, from the universe into which it is born. In each soul, God loves and partly saves the whole world which that soul sums up in an incommunicable and particular way. But this summing-up, this welding, are not given to us ready-made and complete with the first awakening of consciousness. It is we who, through our own activity, must industriously assemble the widely scattered elements. The labour of seaweed as it concentrates in its tissues the substances scattered, in infinitesimal quantities, throughout the vast layers of the ocean; the industry of bees as they make honey from the juices broadcast in so many flowers—these are but pale images of the ceaseless working-over that all the forces of the universe undergo in us in order to reach the level of spirit.

Thus every man, in the course of his life, must not only show himself obedient and docile. By his fidelity he must *build*— starting with the most natural territory of his own self—a work, an *opus*, into which something enters from all the elements of the earth. *He makes his own soul* throughout all his earthly days; and at the same time he collaborates in another work, in another *opus*, which infinitely transcends, while at the same time it narrowly determines, the perspectives of his individual achievement: the completing of the world. For in presenting the christian doctrine of salvation, it must not be forgotten that the world, taken as a whole, that is to say in so far as it consists in a hierarchy of souls—which appear only successively, develop only collectively and will be completed only in union—the world, too, undergoes a sort of vast 'ontogenesis' (a vast becoming what it is) in which the development of each soul, assisted by the perceptible realities on which it depends, is but a diminished harmonic. Beneath our efforts to put spiritual form into our own lives, the world slowly accumulates, starting with the whole of matter, that which will make of it the Heavenly Jerusalem or the New Earth.

C. *We can now bring together the major and minor of our syllogism so as to grasp the link between them and the conclusion*

If it is true, as we know from the Creed, that souls enter so intimately into Christ and God, and if it is true, as we know from the most general conclusions of psycho-analysis, that the perceptible enters vitally into the most spiritual zones of our souls—then we must also recognise that in the whole process which from first to last activates and directs the elements of the universe, *everything forms a single whole.* And we begin to see more distinctly the great sun of Christ the King, of Christ *amictus mundo*,[3] of the universal Christ, rising over our interior world. Little by little, stage by stage, everything is finally linked to the supreme centre *in quo*

omnia constant.[4] The streams which flow from this centre operate
not only within the higher reaches of the world, where human
activities take place in a distinctively supernatural and meritorious form. In order to save and establish these sublime forces, the
power of the Word Incarnate penetrates matter itself; it goes down
into the deepest depths of the lower forces. And the Incarnation
will be complete only when the part of chosen substance contained
in every object—given spiritual import once in our souls and a
second time with our souls in Jesus—shall have rejoined the final
centre of its completion. *Quid est quod ascendit, nisi quod prius
descendit, ut repleret omnia?*[5]

It is through the collaboration which he stimulates in us that
Christ, starting from *all* created things, is consummated and attains his plenitude. St. Paul himself tells us so. We may, perhaps,
imagine that the creation was finished long ago. But that would be
quite wrong. It continues still more magnificently, and at the
highest levels of the world. *Omnis creatura adhuc ingemiscit et
parturit.*[6] And we serve to complete it, even by the humblest work
of our hands. That is, ultimately, the meaning and value of our
acts. Owing to the interrelation between matter, soul and Christ,
we bring part of the being which he desires back to God *in whatever
we do.* With each one of our *works*, we labour—in individual separation, but no less really—to build the Pleroma; that is to say, we
bring to Christ a little fulfilment.

4. COMMUNION THROUGH ACTION

Each one of our works, by its more or less remote or direct effect
upon the spiritual world, helps to make perfect Christ in his mystical totality. That is the fullest possible answer to the question: How
can we, following the call of St. Paul, see God in all the active half of
our lives? In fact, through the unceasing operation of the Incarnation, the divine so thoroughly permeates all our creaturely energies that, in order to meet it and lay hold on it, we could not find a
more fitting setting than that of our action.

To begin with, in action I adhere to the creative power of God; I
coincide with it; I become not only its instrument but its living
extension. And as there is nothing more personal in a being than
his will, I merge myself, in a sense, through my heart, with the
very heart of God. This commerce is continuous because I am
always acting; and at the same time, since I can never set a

boundary to the perfection of my fidelity nor to the fervour of my intention, this commerce enables me to liken myself, ever more strictly and indefinitely, to God.

The soul does not pause to relish this communion, nor does it lose sight of the material end of its action; for it is wedded to a *creative* effort. The will to succeed, a certain passionate delight in the work to be done, form an integral part of our creaturely fidelity. It follows that the very sincerity with which we desire and pursue success for God's sake reveals itself as a new factor—also without limits—in our being knit together with him who animates us. Originally we had fellowship with God in the simple common exercise of wills; but now we unite ourselves with him in the shared love of the end for which we are working; and the crowning marvel is that, with the possession of this end, we have the utter joy of discovering his presence once again.

All this follows directly from what was said a moment back on the relationship between natural and supernatural actions in the world. Any increase that I can bring upon myself or upon things is translated into some increase in my power to love and some progress in Christ's blessed hold upon the universe. Our work appears to us, in the main, as a way of earning our daily bread. But its essential virtue is on a higher level: through it we complete in ourselves the subject of the divine union; and through it again we somehow make to grow in stature the divine term of the one with whom we are united, our Lord Jesus Christ. Hence whatever our role as men may be, whether we are artists, working-men or scholars, we can, if we are Christians, speed towards the object of our work as though towards an opening on to the supreme fulfilment of our beings. Indeed, without exaggeration or excess in thought or expression—but simply by confronting the most fundamental truths of our faith and of experience—we are led to the following observation: God is inexhaustibly attainable in the *totality* of our action. And this prodigy of divinisation has nothing with which we dare to compare it except the subtle, gentle sweetness with which this actual change of shape is wrought; for it is achieved without disturbing at all (*non minuit, sed sacravit* . . .)[7] the completeness and unity of man's endeavour.

Hymn of the Universe

CHRIST IN THE WORLD OF MATTER

Three stories in the style of Benson[1]

My friend[2] is dead, he who drank of life everywhere as at a sacred spring. His heart burned within him. His body lies hidden in the earth in front of Verdun. Now therefore I can repeat some of those words with which he initiated me one evening into that intense vision which gave light and peace to his life.

'You want to know,' he said, 'how the universe, in all its power and multiplicity, came to assume for me the lineaments of the face of Christ? This came about gradually; and it is difficult to find words in which to analyze life-renewing intuitions such as these; still, I can tell you about some of the experiences through which the light of this awareness gradually entered into my soul as though at the gradual, jerky raising of a curtain . . .'

THE PICTURE

'At that time,' he began, 'my mind was preoccupied with a problem partly philosophical, partly aesthetic. I was thinking: Suppose Christ should deign to appear here before me, what would he look like? How would he be dressed? Above all, in what manner would he take his place visibly in the realm of matter, and how would he stand out against the objects surrounding him? . . . And confusedly I found myself saddened and shocked at the idea that the body of Christ could stand in the midst of a crowd of inferior bodies on the world's stage without their sensing and recognizing, through some perceptible change, this Intensity so close beside them.

'Meanwhile my gaze had come to rest without conscious intention on a picture representing Christ offering his heart to men. The picture was hanging in front of me on the wall of a church into which I had gone to pray. So, pursuing my train of thought, I began to ask myself how an artist could contrive to represent the holy humanity of Jesus without imposing on his body a fixity, a too precise definition, which would seem to isolate him from all other men, and without giving to his face a too individual expression so that, while being beautiful, its beauty would be of a particular kind, excluding all other kinds.

'It was, then, as I was keenly pondering over these things and looking at the picture, that my vision began. To tell the truth, I cannot say at what precise moment it began, for it had already reached a certain degree of intensity when I became conscious of it. The fact remains that as I allowed my gaze to wander over the figure's outlines I suddenly became aware that these were *melting away:* they were dissolving, but in a special manner, hard to describe in words. When I tried to hold in my gaze the outline of the figure of Christ it seemed to me to be clearly defined; but then, if I let this effort relax, at once these contours, and the folds of Christ's garment, the lustre of his hair and the bloom of his flesh, all seemed to merge as it were (though without vanishing away) into the rest of the picture. It was as though the planes which marked off the figure of Christ from the world surrounding it were melting into a single vibrant surface whereon all demarcations vanished.

'It seems to me that this transformation began at one particular point on the outer edge of the figure; and that it flowed on thence until it had affected its entire outline. This at least is how the process appeared to me to be taking place. From this initial moment, moreover, the metamorphosis spread rapidly until it had affected everything.

'First of all I perceived that the vibrant atmosphere which surrounded Christ like an aureole was no longer confined to a narrow space about him, but radiated outwards to infinity. Through this there passed from time to time what seemed like trails of phosphorescence, indicating a continuous gushing-forth to the outermost spheres of the realm of matter and delineating a sort of blood stream or nervous system running through the totality of life.

'*The entire universe was vibrant!* And yet, when I directed my gaze to particular objects, one by one, I found them still as clearly defined as ever in their undiminished individuality.

'All this movement seemed to emanate from Christ, and above all from his heart. And it was while I was attempting to trace the emanation to its source and to capture its rhythm that, as my attention returned to the portrait itself, I saw the vision mount rapidly to its climax.

'I notice I have forgotten to tell you about Christ's garments. They had that luminosity we read of in the account of the Transfiguration; but what struck me most of all was the fact that no weaver's hand had fashioned them—unless the hands of angels are those of Nature. No coarsely spun threads composed their weft; rather it was matter, a bloom of matter, which had spontaneously woven a marvellous stuff out of the inmost depths of its substance;

and it seemed as though I could see the stitches running on and on indefinitely, and harmoniously blending together in to a natural design which profoundly affected them in their own nature.

'But, as you will understand, I could spare only a passing glance for this garment so marvellously woven by the continuous co-operation of all the energies and the whole order of matter: it was the transfigured face of the Master that drew and held captive my entire attention.

'You have often at night-time seen how certain stars change their colour from the gleam of blood-red pearls to the lustre of violet velvet. You have seen, too, the play of colours on a transparent bubble. So it was that on the unchanging face of Jesus there shone, in an indescribable shimmer or iridescence, all the radiant hues of all our modes of beauty. I cannot say whether this took place in answer to my desires or in obedience to the good pleasure of him who knew and directed my desires; what is certain is that these innumerable gradations of majesty, of sweetness, of irresistible appeal, following one another or becoming transformed and melting into one another, together made up a harmony which brought me complete satiety.

'And always, beneath this moving surface, upholding it and at the same time gathering it into a higher unity, there hovered the incommunicable beauty of Christ himself. Yet that beauty was something I divined rather than perceived; for whenever I tried to pierce through the covering of inferior beauties which hid it from me, at once other individual and fragmentary beauties rose up before me and formed another veil over the true Beauty even while kindling my desire for it and giving me a foretaste of it.

'It was the whole face that shone in this way. But the centre of the radiance and the iridescence was hidden in the transfigured portrait's eyes.

'Over the glorious depths of those eyes there passed in rainbow hues the reflection—unless indeed it were the creative prototype, the Idea—of everything that has power to charm us, everything that has life ... And the luminous simplicity of the fire which flashed from them changed, as I struggled to master it, into an inexhaustible complexity wherein were gathered all the glances that have ever warmed and mirrored back a human heart. Thus, for example, these eyes which at first were so gentle and filled with pity that I thought my mother stood before me, became an instant later, like those of a woman, passionate and filled with the power to subdue, yet at the same time so imperiously pure that under their domination it would have been physically impossible for the emotions to go astray. And then they changed again, and became filled with a noble, virile majesty, similar to that which one sees in the eyes of men of great courage or refinement or strength, but incomparably more lofty to behold and more delightful to submit to.

'This scintillation of diverse beauties was so complete, so captivating, and also so swift that I felt it touch and penetrate all my powers simultaneously, so that the very core of my being vibrated in response to it, sounding a unique note of expansion and happiness.

'Now while I was ardently gazing deep into the pupils of Christ's eyes, which had become abysses of fiery, fascinating life, suddenly I beheld rising up from the depths of those same eyes what seemed like a cloud, blurring and blending all that variety I have been describing to you. Little by little an extraordinary expression, of great intensity, spread over the diverse shades of meaning which the divine eyes revealed, first of all permeating them and then finally absorbing them all . . .

'And I stood dumbfounded.

'For this final expression, which had dominated and gathered up into itself all the others, was *indecipherable*. I simply could not tell whether it denoted an indescribable agony or a superabundance of triumphant joy. I only know that since that moment I thought I caught a glimpse of it once again—in the glance of a dying soldier.

'In an instant my eyes were bedimmed with tears. And then, when I was once again able to look at it, the painting of Christ on the church wall had assumed once again its too precise definition and its fixity of feature.'

THE MONSTRANCE

When he had reached the end of his narrative my friend remained for some time silent and lost in thought, his clasped hands resting in a characteristic attitude on his crossed knees. The light was fading. I pressed a switch, and the lamp on my desk lit up. It was a very pretty lamp; its pedestal and shade were made of diaphanous sea-green glass, and the bulbs were so ingeniously placed that the entire mass of crystal and the designs which decorated it were illumined from within.

My friend gave a start; and I noticed that his gaze remained fixed on the lamp, as though to draw from it his memories of the past, as he began again to confide in me.

'On another occasion,' he said, 'I was again in a church and had just knelt down before the Blessed Sacrament exposed in a monstrance when I experienced a very strange impression.

'You must, I feel sure, have observed that optical illusion which makes a bright spot against a dark background seem to expand and grow bigger? It was something of this sort that I experienced as I gazed at the host, its white shape standing out sharply, despite the candles on the altar, against the darkness of the choir. At least, that is what happened to begin with; later on, as you shall hear, my experience assumed proportions which no physical analogy could express.

'I had then the impression as I gazed at the host that its surface was gradually spreading out like a spot of oil but of course much more swiftly and luminously. At the beginning it seemed to me that I alone had noticed any change, and that it was taking place without awakening any desire or encountering any obstacle. But little by little, as the white orb grew and grew in space till it seemed to be drawing quite close to me, I heard a subdued sound, an immeasurable murmur, as when the rising tide extends its silver waves over the world of the algae which tremble and dilate at its approach, or when the burning heather crackles as fire spreads over the heath.

'Thus in the midst of a great sigh suggestive both of an awakening and of a plaint the flow of whiteness enveloped me, passed beyond me, overran everything. At the same time everything, though drowned in this whiteness, preserved its own proper shape, its own autonomous movement; for the whiteness did not efface the features or change the nature of anything, but penetrated objects at the core of their being, at a level more profound even than their own life. It was as though a milky brightness were illuminating the universe from within, and everything were fashioned of the same kind of translucent flesh.

'You see, when you switched on the lamp just now and the glass which had been dark became bright and fluorescent, I recalled how the world had appeared to me then; and indeed it was this association of images which prompted me to tell you this story.

'So, through the mysterious expansion of the host the whole world had become incandescent, had itself become like a single giant host. One would have said that, under the influence of this inner light which penetrated it, its fibres were stretched to breaking-point and all the energies within them were strained to the utmost. And I was thinking that already in this opening-out of its activity the cosmos had attained its plenitude when I became aware that a much more fundamental process was going on within it.

'From moment to moment sparkling drops of pure metal were forming on the inner surface of things and then falling into the heart of this profound light, in which they vanished; and at the same time a certain amount of dross was being volatilized: a transformation was taking place in the domain of love, dilating, purifying and gathering together every power-to-love which the universe contains.

'This I could realize the more easily inasmuch as its influence was operative in me myself as well as in other things: *the white glow was active;* the whiteness was consuming all things from within themselves. It had penetrated, through the channels of matter, into the inmost depths of all hearts and then had dilated them to breaking-point, only in order to take back into itself the substance of their affections and passions. And now that it had established its hold on them it was irresistibly pulling back towards its centre all the waves that had spread outwards from it, laden now with the purest honey of all loves.

'And in actual fact the immense host, having given life to everything and purified everything, *was now slowly contracting;* and the treasures it was drawing into itself were joyously pressed close together within its living light.

'When a wave recedes or a flame dies down, the area which has been cov.ered for a moment by sea or fire is marked by the shining pools, the glowing embers, which remain. In the same way, as the host closed in on itself like a flower closing its petals, certain refractory elements in the universe remained behind, outside it, in the exterior darkness. There was indeed still something which lit them, but it was a heart of perverted light, corrosive, poisonous; these rebellious elements burned like torches or glowed red like embers.

'I heard then the *Ave verum* being sung.

'The white host was enclosed once again in the golden monstrance; around it candles were burning, stabbing the darkness, and here and there the sanctuary lamps threw out their crimson glow.'

THE PYX

As I listened to my friend my heart began to burn within me and my mind awoke to a new and higher vision of things. I began to realize vaguely that the multiplicity of evolutions into which the world-process seems to us to be split up is in fact fundamentally the working out of one single great mystery; and this first glimpse of light caused me, I know not why, to tremble in the depths of my soul. But I was so accustomed to separating reality into different planes and categories of thought that I soon found myself lost in this spectacle, still new and strange to my tyro mind, of a cosmos in which the dimensions of divine reality, of spirit, and of matter were also intimately mingled.

Seeing that I was waiting anxiously for further enlightenment, my friend went on:

'The last story I would like to tell you concerns an experience which happened to me just recently. This time, as you'll see, it was not a question of vision properly so called: it was a more general impression which affected, and still affects, my whole being.

'This is what happened.

'At that time my regiment was in line on the Avocourt plateau. The German attack on Verdun was still going on, and fighting was heavy on this side of the Meuse. So, like many priests during battle, I was carrying on me the eucharistic Species in a little pyx shaped like a watch.

'One morning, when there was an almost complete lull in the trenches, I went down into my dug-out and there, as I withdrew into a sort of meditation, my thoughts very naturally turned to the treasure I was carrying on me, with nothing but the thin gilt of the pyx between it and my breast. Many times already I had derived joy and sustenance from the fact of this divine presence. But this time a new idea dawned on me, which soon drove out all other preoccupations whether of recollection or of adoration: I suddenly realized just how extraordinary and how disappointing it was to be thus *holding so close to oneself* the wealth of the world and the very source of life *without being able to possess it* inwardly, *without being able either to penetrate it* or to assimilate it. How could Christ be at once so close to my heart and so far from it, so closely united to my body and so remote from my soul?

'I had the feeling that an intangible but invincible barrier separated me from him with whom nevertheless I could hardly be in closer contact since I was holding him in my hands. I fretted at the thought of holding Happiness in a sealed receptacle. I was reminded of a bee buzzing round a pot filled with nectar but tightly closed. And impatiently I pressed the pyx against me, as though this instinctive action could cause Christ to enter more deeply into me. Finally, feeling I could not continue thus any longer, and it being now the hour when I usually said Mass when things were quiet, I opened the pyx and gave myself Holy Communion.

'But now it seemed to me that in the depths of my being, though the Bread I had just eaten had become flesh of my flesh, nevertheless *it remained outside of me.*

'I then summoned to my aid all my powers of recollection. I concentrated on the divine particle, the deepening silence and mounting love of my mind and heart. I made myself limitlessly humble, as docile and tractable as a child, so as not to run counter in any way to the least desires of my heavenly guest but to make myself indistinguishable from him, and through my submission to him, to become one with the members of the physical organism which his soul so completely directed. I went on and on without respite trying to purify my heart so as to make my inmost being ever more transparent to the light which I was sheltering within me.

'Vain yet blessed attempt!

'Still the host seemed to be always ahead of me, always further on in a more complete concentration and opening out of my desires, further on in a greater permeability of my being to the divine influences, further on in a more absolute limpidity of my affective powers. By my withdrawal into myself and my continual purification of my being I was penetrating ever more deeply into it: but I was like a stone that rolls down a precipice without ever reaching the bottom. Tiny though the host was, I was losing myself in it without ever being able to grasp it or to coincide with it: its centre was *receding from me as it drew me on.*

'Since I could never reach the inmost depths of the host, it struck me that I might at least manage to grasp it by its whole surface. For that surface was very smooth and very small. I tried therefore to coincide with it externally, to correspond exactly to its contours.

'But there a new infinity awaited me; which dashed my hopes.

'When I tried to envelope the sacred particle in my love, so jealously that I clung to it without losing an atom's breadth of precious content with it, what happened was, in effect, that each touch produced a new differentiation, a new complexity, so that each time I thought to have encompassed it I found that what I was holding was not the host at all but one or other of the thousand entities which make up our lives: a suffering, a joy, a task, a friend to love or to console . . .

'Thus, in the depths of my heart, through a marvellous substitution, the host was eluding me by means of its own surface, and leaving me at grips with the entire universe which had reconstituted itself and drawn itself forth from its sensible appearances.

'I will not dwell on the feeling of rapture produced in me by this revelation of the universe placed between Christ and myself like a magnificent prey. I will only say, returning to that special impression of "exteriority" which had initiated the vision, that I now understood the nature of the invisible barrier which stood between the pyx and myself. From the host which I held in my fingers I was separated *by the full extent and the density of the years* which still remained to me, to be lived and to be divinized.'

Here my friend hesitated a moment. Then he added:

'I don't know why it is, but for some time now I have had the impression, as I hold the host in my hands, that between it and me there remains only a thin, barely-formed film . . .

'I had always,' he went on, 'been by temperament a "pantheist".[3] I had always felt the pantheist's yearnings to be native to me and unarguable; but had never dared give full reign to them because I could not see how to reconcile them with my faith. Now, since these various experiences (and others as well) I can affirm that I have found my interest in my existence inexhaustible, and my peace indestructible.

'I live at the heart of a single, unique Element, the Centre of the universe and present in each part of it: personal Love and cosmic Power.

'To attain to him and become merged into his life I have before me the entire universe with its noble struggles, its impassioned quests, its myriads of souls to be healed and made perfect. I can and I must throw myself into the thick of human endeavour, and with no stopping for breath. For the more fully I play my part and the more I bring my efforts to bear on the whole surface of reality, the more also will I attain to Christ and cling close to him.

'God, who is eternal Being-in-itself, is, one might say, everywhere in process of formation *for us*.

'And God is also the heart of everything; so much so that the vast setting of the universe might be engulfed or wither away or be taken from me by death without my joy being diminished. Were creation's dust, which is vitalized by a halo of energy and glory, to be swept away, the substantial Reality wherein every perfection is incorruptibly contained and possessed would remain intact: the rays would be drawn back into their Source, and there I should still hold them all in a close embrace.

'This is why even war does not disconcert me. In a few days'

time we shall be thrown into battle for the recapture of Douaumont: a grandiose, almost a fantastic exploit which will mark and
symbolize a definitive advance of the world in the liberation of
souls. And I tell you this: I shall go into this engagement in a
religious spirit, with all my soul, borne on by a single great impetus in which I am unable to distinguish where human emotions
end and adoration begins.

'And if I am destined not to return from those heights I would
like my body to remain there, moulded into the clay of the fortifica-
tions, like a living cement thrown by God into the stone-work of the
New City.

Thus my dear friend spoke to me, one October evening: he
whose soul was instinctively in communion with the life, the one
life, of all reality and whose body rests now, as he wished, somewhere in the wild countryside around Thiaumont.

*Written before the Douaumont engagement (Nant-le-Grand, 14 Oc-
tober 1916)*

FRANCIS THOMPSON

"The Hound of Heaven"

*English poet and critic Francis Thompson (1859-1907) was
marked by failure to achieve a career as priest, physician, salesman,
or soldier. Despair led him into drug addiction and a derelict life in
the London streets and alleys. Rescued by Wilfred Meynell, and
successfully rehabilitated, the last twenty years of his life were
marked by a successful literary career. His best known poem is "The
Hound of Heaven" (1890).*

I fled Him, down the nights and down the days;
I fled Him, down the arches of the years;
I fled Him, down the labyrinthine ways
Of my own mind; and in the mist of tears
I hid from Him, and under running laughter.

THOMAS MERTON

Contemplative Prayer

Thomas Merton (1915–1968), a Trappist monk of Gethsemane Abbey in Kentucky, has been the most influential proponent of traditional monastic spirituality in American history. In a series of writings dating from the mid-1940's until his death, Merton popularized traditional Western spirituality and gradually expanded his interests and those of his readers to other forms of spirituality, notably those of the Far East. He is a powerful witness to the continuing vitality of Christian spirituality in the modern world. The following excerpts are taken from Contemplative Prayer, *one of Merton's last published works.*

CHAPTER XI

What is the purpose of meditation in the sense of "the prayer of the heart"?

In the "prayer of the heart" we seek first of all the deepest ground of our identity in God. We do not reason about dogmas of faith, or "the mysteries." We seek rather to gain a direct existential grasp, a personal experience of the deepest truths of life and faith, *finding ourselves in God's truth.* Inner certainty depends on *purification.* The dark night rectifies our deepest intentions. In the silence of this "night of faith" we return to simplicity and sincerity of heart. We learn *recollection* which consists in listening for God's will, in direct and simple attention to *reality.* Recollection is awareness of the unconditional. *Prayer* then means yearning for the simple presence of God, for a personal understanding of his word, for knowledge of his will and for capacity to hear and obey him. It is thus something much more than uttering petitions for good things external to our own deepest concerns.

Our desire and our prayer should be summed up in St. Augustine's words: *Noverim te, noverim me.*[1] We wish to gain a true evaluation of ourselves and of the world so as to understand the meaning of our life as children of God redeemed from sin and death. We wish to gain a true loving knowledge of God, our Father and Redeemer. We wish to lose ourselves in his love and rest in him. We wish to hear his word and respond to it with our whole being. We wish to know his merciful will and submit to it in its totality. These are the aims and goals of *meditatio* and *oratio*. This preparation for prayer can be prolonged by the slow, "sapiential" and loving recitation of a favorite psalm, dwelling on the deep sense of the words for us here and now.

In the language of the monastic fathers, all prayer, reading, meditation and all the activities of the monastic life are aimed at *purity of heart*, an unconditional and totally humble surrender to God, a total acceptance of ourselves and of our situation as willed by him. It means the renunciation of all deluded images of ourselves, all exaggerated estimates of our own capacities, in order to obey God's will as it comes to us in the difficult demands of life in its exacting truth. *Purity of heart* is then correlative to a new spiritual identity—the "self" as recognized in the context of realities willed by God—Purity of heart is the enlightened awareness of the new man, as opposed to the complex and perhaps rather disreputable fantasies of the "old man."

Meditation is then ordered to this new insight, this direct knowledge of the self in its higher aspect.

What am I? I am myself a word spoken by God. Can God speak a word that does not have any meaning?

Yet am I sure that the meaning of my life is the meaning God intends for it? Does God impose a meaning on my life from the *outside*, through event, custom, routine, law, system, impact with others in society ? Or am I called to *create from within*, with him, with his grace, a meaning which reflects his truth and makes me his "word" spoken freely in my personal situation? My true identity lies hidden in God's call to my freedom and my response to him. This means I must use my freedom in order to *love*, with full responsibility and authenticity, not merely receiving a form imposed on me by external forces, or forming my own life according to an approved social pattern, but directing my love to the personal reality of my brother, and embracing God's will in its naked, often unpenetrable mystery.[2] I cannot discover my "meaning" if I try to evade the dread which comes from first experiencing my meaninglessness!

By meditation I penetrate the inmost ground of my life, seek the full understanding of God's will for me, of God's mercy to me, of my absolute dependence upon him. But this penetration must be authentic. It must be something genuinely *lived* by me. This in turn depends on the authenticity of my whole concept of my life, and of my purposes. But my life and aims tend to be artificial, inauthentic, as long as I am simply trying to adjust my actions to certain exterior norms of conduct that will enable me to play an approved part in the society in which I live. After all, this amounts to little more than learning a *role*. Sometimes methods and programs of meditation are aimed simply at this: learning to play a religious role. The idea of the "imitation" of Christ and of the saints can degenerate into mere *impersonation*, if it remains only exterior.

It is not enough for meditation to investigate the *cosmic order* and situate me in this order. Meditation is something more than gaining command of a *Weltanschauung* (a philosophical view of the cosmos and of life). Even though such a meditation seems to bring about resignation to God's will as manifested in the cosmic order or in history, it is not deeply Christian. In fact, such a meditation may be out of contact with the deepest truths of Christianity. It consists in learning a few rational formulas, explanations, which enable one to remain resigned and indifferent in the great crises of life, and thus, unfortunately, it may make evasion possible where a direct confrontation of our nothingness is demanded. Instead of a stoical acceptance of "providential" decrees and events, and other manifestations of "law" in the cosmos, we should let ourselves be brought naked and defenceless into the center of that dread where we stand alone before God in our nothingness, without explanation, without theories, completely dependent upon his providential care, in dire need of the gift of his grace, his mercy and the light of faith.

We must approach our meditation realizing that "grace," "mercy" and "faith" are not permanent inalienable possessions which we gain by our efforts and retain as though by right, provided that we behave ourselves. They are *constantly renewed gifts*. The life of grace in our hearts is renewed from moment to moment, directly and personally by God in his love for us. Hence the "grace of meditation" (in the sense of "prayer of the heart") is also a special gift. It should never be taken for granted. Though we can say it is a "habit" which is in some sense permanently present to us, when we have received it, yet it is never something which we can claim as though by right and use in a completely autonomous and self-determining manner according to our own good pleasure, without regard for God's will—though we can make an autonomous use of our *natural* gifts. The gift of prayer is inseparable from another grace: that of humility, which makes us realize that the very depths of our being and life are meaningful and real only in so far as they are oriented toward God as their source and their end.

When we seem to possess and use our being and natural faculties in a completely autonomous manner, as if our individual ego were the pure source and end of our own acts, then we are in illusion and our acts, however spontaneous they may seem to be, lack spiritual meaning and authenticity.

Consequently: first of all our meditation should begin with the realization of our nothingness and helplessness in the presence of God. This need not be a mournful or discouraging experience. On the contrary, it can be deeply tranquil and joyful since it brings us in direct contact with the source of all joy and all life. But one reason why our meditation never gets started is perhaps that we never make this real, serious return to the center of our own nothingness before God. Hence we never enter into the deepest reality of our relationship with him.

In other words we meditate merely "in the mind," in the imagination, or at best in the desires, considering religious truths from a detached objective viewpoint. We do not begin by seeking to "find our heart," that is to sink into a deep awareness of the ground of our identity before God and in God. "Finding our heart" and recovering this awareness of our inmost identity implies the recognition that our external, everyday self is to a great extent a mask and a fabrication. It is not our true self. And indeed our true self is not easy to find. It is hidden in obscurity and "nothingness," at the center where we are in direct dependence on God. But since the reality of all Christian meditation depends on this recognition, our attempt to meditate without it is in fact self-contradictory. It is like trying to walk without feet.

Another consequence: even the capacity to recognize our condition before God is itself a grace. We cannot always attain it at will. To learn meditation does not, therefore, mean learning an artificial technique for infallibly producing "compunction" and the "sense of our nothingness" whenever we please. On the contrary, this would be the result of violence and would be inauthentic. Meditation implies the capacity to *receive* this grace whenever God wishes to grant it to us, and therefore a permanent disposition to humility, attention to reality, receptivity, pliability. To learn to meditate then means to gradually get free from habitual hardness of heart, torpor and grossness of mind, due to arrogance and non-acceptance of simple reality, or resistance to the concrete demands of God's will.

If in fact our hearts remain apparently indifferent and cold, and we find it morally impossible to "begin" meditating in this way, then we should at least realize that this coldness is itself a sign of our need and of our helplessness. We should take it accordingly as a motive for prayer. We might also reflect that perhaps without meaning to we have fallen into a spirit of routine, and are not able to see how to recover our spontaneity without God's grace, for which we must wait patiently, but with earnest desire. This waiting itself will be for us a school of humility.

CHAPTER XIV

Meditation is not merely the intellectual effort to master certain *ideas about God* or even to impress upon our minds the mysteries of our Catholic faith. Conceptual knowledge of religious truth has a definite place in our life, and that place is an important one. Study plays an essential part in the life of prayer. The spiritual life needs strong intellectual foundations. The study of theology is a necessary accompaniment to a life of meditation. But meditation itself is not "study" and is not a purely intellectual activity. The purpose of meditation is not merely to acquire or to deepen objective and speculative knowledge of God and of the truth revealed by him.

In meditation we do not seek to know *about* God as though he were an object like other objects which submit to our scrutiny and can be expressed in clear scientific ideas. We seek to know God himself, beyond the level of all the objects which he has made and which confront us as "things" isolated from one another, "defined," "delimited," with clear boundaries. The infinite God has no boundaries and our minds cannot set limits to him or to his love. His presence is then "grasped" in the general awareness of loving faith, it is "realized" without being scientifically and precisely known, as we know a specimen under a microscope. His presence cannot be verified as we would verify a laboratory experiment. Yet it can be spiritually realized as long as we do not insist on verifying it. As soon as we try to verify the spiritual presence as an object of exact knowledge, God eludes us.

Returning to the classical passages of St. John of the Cross on the "dark night" of contemplation, we see that his doctrine about faith is often misrepresented. To some readers, he seems to be saying no more than that if you turn away from sensible and visible objects, you will come to see invisible objects. This is Neoplatonism, not the doctrine of St. John of the Cross. On the contrary, he teaches that the soul

> ... must not only be in darkness with respect to that part that concerns the creatures and temporal things ... *but likewise it must be blinded and darkened according to the part which has respect to God and spiritual things*, which is the rational and higher part. ... It must be like to a blind man leaning upon dark faith, taking it for guide and light, and leaning upon none of the things that he understands, experiences, feels and imagines. For all these are darkness and will cause him to stray; and faith is above all that he understands, experiences, feels and imagines. And if he be not blinded as to this, and remain not in total darkness, he attains not to that which is greater—namely, that which is taught by faith.[1]

Once again, however, this darkness is not merely negative. It brings with it an enlightenment which escapes the investigation and control of the understanding. "For who shall prevent God from doing that which he wills in the soul that is resigned, annihilated and detached?"[2]

This teaching of St. John of the Cross is not to be set aside merely as a peculiar form of "Carmelite spirituality." It is in the direct line of ancient monastic and patristic tradition, from Evagrius Ponticus, Cassian and Gregory of Nyssa on down through Gregory the Great and the followers of Pseudo-Dionysius in the West.

St. John Chrysostom writes of the "incomprehensibility of God":

> Let us invoke him as the inexpressible God, incomprehensible, invisible and unknowable; let us avow that he surpasses all power of human speech, that he eludes the grasp of every mortal intelligence, that the angels cannot penetrate him nor the seraphim see him in full clarity, nor the cherubim fully understand him, for he is invisible to the principalities and powers, the virtues and all creatures without exception; *only the Son and the Holy Spirit know him*.[3]

St. Gregory of Nyssa describes the "mystical night":

Night designates the contemplation (*theoria*) of invisible things after the manner of Moses who entered into the darkness where God was, this God who makes of darkness his hiding place.[4] Surrounded by the divine night the soul seeks him who is hidden in darkness. *She possesses indeed the love of him* whom she seeks, but the Beloved escapes the grasp of her thoughts. . . . *Therefore abandoning the search* she recognizes him whom she desires by the very fact that his knowledge is beyond understanding. Thus she says, "Having left behind all created things and abandoned the aid of the understanding, by faith alone I have found my Beloved. And I will not let him go, holding him with the grip of faith, until he enters into my bedchamber." The chamber is the *heart, which is capable* of the indwelling when it is restored to its primitive state.[5]

And Evagrius says (in the *Treatise on Prayer*, long attributed to St. Nilus): "Just as the light that shows us all has no need of another light in order to be seen, so God, who shows us all things, has no need of a light in which we may see him, for he is himself light by essence,"[6] and "See no diversity in yourself when you pray, and let your intelligence take on the impression of no form; but go immaterially to the immaterial and you will understand. . . . Aspiring to see the face of the Father who is in heaven, seek for nothing in the world to see a form or figure at the time of prayer."[7]

Returning to the mystics of the Rhineland we find John Tauler saying typically: "All that a man rests in with joy, all that he retains as a good belonging to himself is all worm-eaten except for absolute and simple vanishing in the pure, unknowable, ineffable and mysterious good which is God, by renunciation of ourselves and of all that can appear in him."

And Ruysbroeck:

The interior man enters into himself in a simple manner, above all activity and all values, to apply himself to a simple gaze in fruitive love. There he encounters God without intermediary. And from the unity of God there shines into him a simple light. This simple light shows itself to be darkness, nakedness and nothingness. In this darkness, the man is enveloped and he plunges in a state without modes, in which he is lost. In nakedness, all consideration and distraction of things escape him, and he

is informed and penetrated by a simple light. In nothingness he sees all his works come to nothing, for he is
overwhelmed by the activity of God's immense love, and
by the fruitive inclination of his Spirit he . . . becomes one
spirit with God.[8]

The doctrine of purity of heart and "imageless" contemplation
is summed up in the *Philokalia:* "That heart is pure which, always
presenting to God a formless and imageless memory, is ready to
receive nothing but impressions which come from him and by
which he is wont to desire to become manifest to it."[9]

In a word, God is invisibly present to the ground of our being:
our belief and love attain to him, but he remains hidden from the
arrogant gaze of our investigating mind which seeks to capture
him and secure permanent possession of him in an act of knowledge that gives *power over him.* It is in fact absurd and impossible
to try to grasp God as an object which can be seized and comprehended by our minds.

The knowledge of which we are capable is simply knowledge
about him. It points to him in analogies which we must transcend
in order to reach him. But we must transcend ourselves as well as
our analogies, and in seeking to know him we must forget the
familiar subject-object relationship which characterizes our ordinary acts of knowing. Instead we know him in so far as we become
aware of ourselves as known through and through by him. We
"possess" him in proportion as we realize ourselves to be possessed
by him in the inmost depths of our being. Meditation or "prayer of
the heart" is the active effort we make to keep our hearts open so
that we may be enlightened by him and filled with this realization
of our true relation to him. Therefore the classic form of "meditation" is repetitive invocation of the name of Jesus in the heart
emptied of images and cares.

Hence the aim of meditation, in the context of Christian faith,
is not to arrive at an objective and apparently "scientific" knowledge about God, but to come to know him through the realization
that our very being is penetrated with his knowledge and love for
us. Our knowledge of God is paradoxically a knowledge not of him
as the object of our scrutiny, but of ourselves as utterly dependent
on his saving and merciful knowledge of us. It is in proportion as we
are known to him that we find our real being and identity in Christ.
We know him in and through ourselves in so far as his truth is the
source of our being and his merciful love is the very heart of our life

and existence. We have no other reason for being, except to be loved by him as our Creator and Redeemer, and to love him in return. There is no true knowledge of God that does not imply a profound grasp and an intimate personal acceptance of this profound relationship.

The whole purpose of meditation is to deepen the consciousness of this basic relationship of the creature to the Creator, and of the sinner to his Redeemer.

It has been said above that the doctrine of mystical "unknowing," by which we ascend to the knowledge of God "as unseen" without "form or figure" beyond all images and indeed all concepts, must not be misunderstood as a mere turning away from the ideas of material things to ideas of the immaterial. The mystical knowledge of God, which already begins in a certain inchoative manner in living faith, is not a knowledge of immaterial and invisible essences as distinct from the visible and material. If in a certain sense *nothing* that we can see or understand can give us a fully adequate idea of God (except by remote analogy), then we can say that images and symbols and even the material which enters into sacramental signs and works of art regain a certain dignity in their own right, since they are no longer rejected in favor of other "immaterial" objects which are considered to be superior, as if they were capable of making us "see" God more perfectly. On the contrary, since we are well aware that images, symbols and works of art are only material, we tend to use them with greater freedom and less risk of error precisely because we realize the limitations of their nature. We know that they can only be means to an end, and we do not make "idols" out of them. On the contrary, today the more dangerous temptation is to raise ideas and ideologies to the status of "idols," worshipping them for their own sakes.

So we can say here, if only in passing, that image, symbol, art, rite and of course the sacraments above all, rightly and properly bring material things into the life of prayer and meditation, using them as means to enter more deeply into prayer. Denis de Rougemont has called art "a calculated trap for meditation." The aesthetic aspect of the life of worship must not be neglected, especially today when we are barely recovering from an era of abomination and desolation in sacred art, due in part to a kind of manichaean attitude toward natural beauty on the one hand, and a rationalistic neglect of sensible things on the other. So, all that has been said above in quotations from St. John of the Cross and other doctors of Christian mysticism about "dark contemplation" and "the night of sense" must not be misinterpreted to mean that the normal culture of the senses, of artistic taste, of imagination, and of intelligence should be formally renounced by anyone interested in a life of meditation and prayer. On the contrary, such culture is *presupposed*. One cannot go beyond what one has not yet attained, and normally the realization that God is "beyond images, symbols and ideas" dawns only on one who has previously made a good use of all these things, who has a thorough and mature "monastic culture,"[10] and having reached the limit of symbol and idea goes on to a further stage in which he does without them, at least temporarily. For even if these human and symbolic helps to prayer lose their usefulness in the higher forms of contemplative union with God, they still have their place in the ordinary everyday life even of the contemplative. They form part of the environment and cultural atmosphere in which he usually lives.

The function of image, symbol, poetry, music, chant, and of ritual (remotely related to sacred dance) is to open up the inner self of the contemplative, to incorporate the senses and the body in the totality of the self-orientation to God that is necessary for worship and for meditation. Simply to neglect the senses and body altogether, and merely to let the imagination go its own way, while attempting to plunge into a deeply abstracted interior prayer, will end in no result even for one who is proficient in meditation.

All religious traditions have ways of integrating the senses, on their own level, into higher forms of prayer. The greatest mystical literature speaks not only of "darkness" and "unknowing" but also, and almost in the same breath, of an extraordinary flowering of "spiritual senses" and aesthetic awareness underlying and interpreting the higher and more direct union with God "beyond experience." In fact, what is beyond experience has to be mediated, in some way, and interpreted in the ordinary language of human thought before it can be deeply reflected upon by the subject himself, and before it can be communicated to others. Of course, there is no denying that one may enter into deep contemplative prayer without being able to reflect on it, still less communicate anything whatever of the experience to others. But in mystical literature, which obviously implies communication through images, symbols and ideas, we find that contemplation in "unknowing" is generally accompanied by unusual poetic and theological gifts, whenever the fruit of contemplation is to be shared with others.

We find St. John of the Cross, for instance, describing the "Living Flame of Love" in very concrete and beautiful language which obviously reflects an even more concrete and beautiful experience which is here translated into symbolic terms. But he says without any ambiguity that what he is describing is "the savor of eternal life" and "an experience of the life of God" and the activity of the Holy Spirit. He says:

> How can we say that this flame wounds the soul, when there is nothing in the soul to be wounded, since it is wholly consumed by the fire of love? It is a marvelous thing: for, as love is never idle, but is continually in motion, it is continually throwing out sparks, like a flame, in every direction; and, as the office of love is the wound, that it may enkindle with love and cause delight, so, when it is as it were a living flame, within the soul, it is ever sending forth its arrow-wounds, like most tender sparks of delicate love, joyfully and happily exercising the arts and wiles of love. Even so, in his palace, at his marriage, did Ahasuerus show forth his graces to Esther his bride, revealing to her there his riches and the glory of his greatness. Thus that which the Wise Man said in Proverbs is now fulfilled in this soul, namely: I was delighted every day as I played before him always, playing over the whole earth, and my delight is to be with the sons of men, namely, by giving myself to them. Wherefore these wounds, which are the playing of God, are the sparks of these tender touches of flame which touch the soul intermittently and proceed from the fire of love, which is not idle, but whose flames, says the stanza, strike and wound

> My soul in its deepest center.

For this feast of the Holy Spirit takes place in the substance of the soul, where neither the devil nor the world nor sense can enter; and therefore the more interior it is, the more it is secure, substantial and delectable; for the more interior it is the purer is it, and the more of purity there is in it, the more abundantly and frequently and widely does God communicate himself. And thus the delight and rejoicing of the soul and the spirit is the greater herein because it is God that works all this and the soul of its own power does naught therein; for the soul can do naught of itself, save through the bodily senses and by their help, from which in this case the soul is very free and very far removed; its only work is to receive God in the depths of the soul, who alone, without the aid of the senses, can move the soul in that which it does.[11]

When St. John of the Cross himself says that we must not attempt to attain to union with God by trying to conjure up images of such experiences in our hearts, he is obviously not invalidating what he has said in an attempt to communicate an experience of God *after* the fact. He is on the contrary trying to protect his reader against an egocentric and spiritually blind manipulation of images and concepts in order to attain to a supposed knowledge of God as an object which the mind of man can understand and enjoy on intellectual and aesthetic terms. There is indeed a certain kind of knowledge of God attained by images and reasoning but this is not at all the kind of experiential knowledge that St. John of the Cross describes. Indeed, the use of image and concept can become very dangerous in a climate of egocentricity and false mysticism.

The dangerous abuse of image and symbol is seen, for example, in the case of someone who tries to conjure up the "living flame" by an exercise of will, imagination and desire, and then persuades himself that he has "experienced God." In such a case, this obvious fabrication would be paid for dearly, because there is all the difference in the world between the *fruits* of genuine religious experience, a pure gift of God, and the results of mere imagination. As Jakob Boehme bluntly said: "Where does it stand in Scripture that a harlot can become a virgin by issuing a decree?"

The living experience of divine love and the Holy Spirit in the "flame" of which St. John of the Cross is speaking is a true awareness that one has died and risen in Christ. It is an experience of mystical renewal, an inner transformation brought about entirely by the power of God's merciful love, implying the "death" of the self-centered and self-sufficient ego and the appearance of a new and liberated self who lives and acts "in the Spirit." But if the old self, the calculating and autonomous ego, merely seeks to imitate the effects of such regeneration, for its own satisfaction and advantage, the effect is exactly the opposite—the ego seeks to confirm itself in its own selfish existence. The grain of wheat has not fallen into the ground and died. It remains hard, isolated and dry and there is no fruit at all, only a lying and blasphemous boast—a ridiculous pretense! If lying and fabrication are psychologically harmful even in ordinary relations with other men (a sphere where a certain amount of falsification is not uncommon) all falsity is

disastrous in any relation with the ground of our own being and
with God himself, who communicates with us through our own
inner truth. To falsify our inner truth under pretext of entering
into union with God would be a most tragic infidelity to ourselves
first of all, to life, to reality itself, and of course to God. Such
fabrications end in the dislocation of one's entire moral and intellectual existence.

CHAPTER XIX

Is the Christian life of prayer simply an evasion of the prob-
lems and anxieties of contemporary existence? If what we have
said has been properly understood, the answer to this question
should be quite obvious. If we pray "in the Spirit" we are certainly
not running away from life, negating visible reality in order to "see
God." For "the Spirit of the Lord has filled the whole earth." Prayer
does not blind us to the world, but it transforms our vision of the
world, and makes us see it, all men, and all the history of mankind,
in the light of God. To pray "in spirit and in truth" enables us to
enter into contact with that infinite love, that inscrutable freedom
which is at work behind the complexities and the intricacies of
human existence. This does not mean fabricating for ourselves
pious rationalizations to explain everything that happens. It in-
volves no surreptitious manipulation of the hard truths of life.

Meditation does not necessarily give us a privileged insight
into the meaning of isolated historical events. These can remain
for the Christian as much of an agonizing mystery as they do for
anyone else. But for us the mystery contains, within its own darkness and its own silences, a presence and a meaning which we
apprehend without fully understanding them. And by this spiritual contact, this act of faith, we are ourselves properly situated in
the events around us, even though we may not quite see where they
are going.

One thing is certain: the humility of faith, if it is followed by
the proper consequences—by the acceptance of the work and sacrifice demanded by our providential task—will do far more to
launch us into the full current of historical reality than the pomp-
ous rationalizations of politicians who think they are somehow the
directors and manipulators of history. Politicians may indeed
make history, but the meaning of what they are making turns out,
inexorably, to have been something in a language they will never
understand, which contradicts their own programs and turns all

their achievements into an absurd parody of their promises and
ideals.

Of course, it is true that religion on a superficial level, religion
that is untrue to itself and to God, easily comes to serve as the
"opium of the people." And this takes place whenever religion and
prayer invoke the name of God for reasons and ends that have
nothing to do with him. When religion becomes a mere artificial
facade to justify a social or economic system—when religion hands
over its rites and language completely to the political propagan-
dist, and when prayer becomes the vehicle for a purely secular
ideological program, then religion does tend to become an opiate. It
deadens the spirit enough to permit the substitution of a superficial fiction and mythology for this truth of life. And this brings
about the alienation of the believer, so that his religious zeal
becomes political fanaticism. His faith in God, while preserving its
traditional formulas, becomes in fact faith in his own nation, class
or race. His ethic ceases to be the law of God and of love, and
becomes the law that might-makes-right: established privilege
justifies everything. God is the *status quo*.

In the last book to come to us from the hand of Raïssa Maritain,
her commentary on the Lord's Prayer, we read the following passage, concerning those who barely obtain their daily bread, and are
deprived of most of the advantages of a decent life on earth by the
injustice and thoughtlessness of the privileged:

> If there were fewer wars, less thirst to dominate and to
> exploit others, less national egoism, less egoism of class
> and caste, if man were more concerned for his brother, and
> really wanted to collect together, for the good of the
> human race, all the resources which science places at his
> disposal especially today, there would be on earth fewer
> populations deprived of their necessary sustenance, there
> would be fewer children who die or are incurably
> weakened by undernourishment.[1]

She goes on to ask what obstacles man has placed in the way of
the Gospel that this should be so. It is unfortunately true that those
who have complacently imagined themselves blessed by God have
in fact done more than others to frustrate his will. But Raïssa
Maritain says that perhaps the poor, who have never been able to
seek the kingdom of God, may be found by it "when they leave the
world which has not recognized in them the image of God."[2]

Religion always tends to lose its inner consistency and its supernatural truth when it lacks the fervor of contemplation. It is the contemplative, silent, "empty" and apparently useless element in the life of prayer which makes it truly a *life*. Without contemplation, liturgy tends to be a mere pious show and paraliturgical prayer is plain babbling. Without contemplation, mental prayer is nothing but a sterile exercise of the mind. And yet not everyone can be a "contemplative." That is not the point. What matters is the *contemplative orientation* of the whole life of prayer.

If the contemplative orientation of prayer is its emptiness, its "uselessness," its purity, then we can say that prayer tends to lose its true character in so far as it becomes busy, full of ulterior purposes, and committed to programs that are beneath its own level. Now this does not mean that we can never "pray for" particular goods. We can and must use the prayer of petition, and this is even compatible, in a very simple and pure form, with the spirit of contemplation.

One can pass from the prayer of petition directly into contemplation when one has a very profound faith and a great simplicity of theological hope.[3] *But when prayer allows itself to be exploited* for purposes which are beneath itself and have nothing directly to do with our life in God, or our life on earth oriented to God, then it becomes strictly impure.

Prayer must penetrate and enliven every department of our life, including that which is most temporal and transient. Prayer does not despise even the seemingly lowliest aspects of man's temporal existence. It spiritualizes all of them and gives them a divine orientation. But prayer is defiled when it is turned away from God and from the spirit, and manipulated in the interests of group fanaticism.

In such cases, religion is understood to be at least implicitly misdirected, and therefore the "God" whom it invokes becomes, or tends to become, a mere figment of the imagination. Such religion is insincere. It is merely a front for greed, injustice, sensuality, selfishness, violence. The cure for this corruption is to restore the purity of faith and the genuineness of Christian love: and this means a restoration of the contemplative orientation of prayer.

Real contemplatives will always be rare and few. But that is not a matter of importance, as long as the whole Church is predominantly contemplative in all her teaching, all her activity and all her prayer. There is no contradiction between action and contemplation when Christian apostolic activity is raised to the level of pure charity. On that level, action and contemplation are fused into one entity by the love of God and of our brother in Christ. But the trouble is that if prayer is not itself deep, powerful and pure and filled at all times with the spirit of contemplation, Christian action can never really reach this high level.

Without the spirit of contemplation in all our worship—that is to say without the adoration and love of God above all, for his own sake, because he is God—the liturgy will not nourish a really Christian apostolate based on Christ's love and carried out in the power of the *Pneuma*.

The most important need in the Christian world today is this inner truth nourished by this Spirit of contemplation: the praise and love of God, the longing for the coming of Christ, the thirst for the manifestation of God's glory, his truth, his justice, his Kingdom in the world. These are all characteristically "contemplative" and eschatological aspirations of the Christian heart, and they are the very essence of monastic prayer. Without them our apostolate is more for our own glory than for the glory of God.

Without this contemplative orientation we are building churches not to praise him but to establish more firmly the social structures, values and benefits that we presently enjoy. Without this contemplative basis to our preaching, our apostolate is no apostolate at all, but mere proselytizing to insure universal conformity with our own national way of life.

Without contemplation and interior prayer the Church cannot fulfill her mission to transform and save mankind. Without contemplation, she will be reduced to being the servant of cynical and worldly powers, no matter how hard her faithful may protest that they are fighting for the Kingdom of God.

Without true, deep contemplative aspirations, without a total love for God and an uncompromising thirst for his truth, religion tends in the end to become an opiate.

Part VII Notes

St. Thèrése of Lisieux

January 1895
    1. Psalm 88:2.
    2. "Virgin of the Smile" which is in the present shrine of St. Therese. The Martin Family held it in special veneration. In January, 1895, it was in the room outside her cell.

3. Psalm 22:1-4.

4. In this figurative language Therese describes her family. When she was writing, there were "three Lilies" with her in Carmel, viz., Marie, Pauline, and Celine; another was in the Visitation convent at Caen, Leonie. Therese describes her two parents by "the two stems reunited for all eternity."

September 8, 1896

1. May 9, 1896.

2. It was on the second Sunday in May that the Virgin smiled on Therese in 1883. But that year the second Sunday was May 13.

3. Anne de Lobera (1545-1621) was born in Spain. She entered in 1570 St. Joseph's Convent at Avila, the first monastery of the reformed Carmel. She became counsellor and companion of St. Teresa of Avila. She obtained the *Spiritual Canticle* from St. John of the Cross, and she founded the Teresian Carmel in France and Holland.

4. Apocalypse 20:12.

5. I Corinthians 12:29, 21.

6. Allusion to the poem of St. John of the Cross: "I went out seeking love."

7. I Corinthians 12:31; 13:1.

8. St. John of the Cross, *Spiritual Canticle,* stanza 9, no. 7. St. Therese inscribed these words on her coat of arms, January, 1896.

9. Luke 16:9.

10. Luke 16:8.

11. 2 Kings 2:9.

12. St. John of the Cross, *Spiritual Canticle,* stanza 29, no. 2.

13. Matthew 9:11.

14. Deuteronomy 32:11.

The Way of the Pilgrim

1. Plural of *starets*. A *starets* is a monk distinguished by piety, experience, and the gift of guiding souls.

2. A collection of mystical and ascetic writings by the Fathers of the Eastern Orthodox Church.

Teilhard de Chardin

1. "In us, but without us."

2. "To work with, to suffer with, to die with, to rise with."

3. "Clothed with the world."

4. "In whom all things have their consistency."

5. "What does his ascending mean, unless he first descended, in order to fill all things?"

6. "All creation still groans and is in labor."

7. "He did not lessen, but consecrated . . ."

Hymn of the Universe

1. Père Teilhard sometimes called these stories *histoires*, sometimes *contes*, written in the manner of Benson; a story about mysticism by R. H. Benson had made a lasting impression on him.

2. In these stories, too intimate in character for the author not to feel the need to disguise his identity, the 'friend' is clearly himself.

3. Taking 'pantheism' in a very real sense, indeed in the etymological sense of the word (*En pasi panta Theos*, i.e., in St Paul's phrase, God 'all in all') but at the same time in an absolutely legitimate sense: for if in the last resort christians become 'one with God' this unity is achieved not by way of identification, God *becoming* all things, but by the action—at once differentiating and unifying—of love, God being all *in* all, which latter concept is strictly in accord with christian orthodoxy.

Thomas Merton

Chapter XI

1. "May I know you, may I know myself!" (All notes to the selections from Merton were written by the author himself.)

2. Romans 11:33–36.

Chapter XIV

1. *Ascent of Mount Carmel*, II, iv, 2.

2. *Ibid.*

3. *Incomprehensibility of God*, III, p. 166.

4. Psalm 17:12.

5. P.G. 44:892–893.

6. See Hausherr, *Les Leçons d'un Contemplatif* (Paris, 1960), p. 145.

7. *Ibid.*

8. *The Adornment of the Spiritual Marriage*, II.

9. Kadloubovsky and Palmer, *Writings from the Philokalia* (London, 1957), p. 23.

10. The term "monastic culture" is beginning to be seriously discussed today. It implies the development of a set of tastes and skills, of openness to certain specifically monastic values in all the arts and disciplines that have relation to the monastic life in all its fullness. One could say for example that for a twentieth-century Christian monk, "monastic culture" would imply not only an education in all that is living and relevant in monastic theology, tradition, and literature, as well as art, architecture, poetry, etc., but also in other religious cultures. Hence a certain knowledge of Zen, of Sufism, of Hinduism can rightly claim a place in the monastic culture of the modern monk of the West.

11. *Living Flame of Love*, I, 8–9.

Chapter XIX

1. *Notes sur le Pater* (Paris, 1962), p. 98.

2. *Ibid.*, p. 100.

3. St. John of the Cross identifies this hope with the night, or emptiness, of the memory.